Hermann Carl George Brandt

A First Book in German

Containing the Accidence and Syntax of the Author's German Grammar, New

Indices, and Lodeman's Exercises

Hermann Carl George Brandt

A First Book in German
Containing the Accidence and Syntax of the Author's German Grammar, New Indices, and Lodeman's Exercises

ISBN/EAN: 9783337280734

Printed in Europe, USA, Canada, Australia, Japan

Cover: Foto ©Paul-Georg Meister /pixelio.de

More available books at **www.hansebooks.com**

A

FIRST BOOK IN GERMAN

CONTAINING

THE ACCIDENCE AND SYNTAX OF THE AUTHOR'S
GERMAN GRAMMAR, NEW INDICES, AND
LODEMAN'S EXERCISES

BY H. C. G. BRANDT
HAMILTON COLLEGE, CLINTON, N.Y.

Boston
ALLYN AND BACON
1888

PREFACE.

AT the suggestion made by several teachers, Part I. of the Grammar and Lodeman's Exercises with the complete English-German Vocabulary have been here bound together for use in secondary schools, whose younger pupils had been first put into one of the many short grammars. I should have liked to include the chapters on Accent and on Word-Formation from Part II.; but there are practical objections to this. The indices of the Grammar are added to this unchanged.

PREFACE TO THE FOURTH EDITION OF THE GRAMMAR.

THIS is the first thoroughly revised edition. Of the criticisms of this work, I have been able to accept and embody especially those of Prof. A. L. Ripley, of Yale College, and of Prof. George O. Curme, of Cornell College (Iowa), to both of whom I express my sincere thanks. The strictures made upon my classification of nouns and upon the standard of pronunciation I do not think well founded. The classification of nouns is historical and scientific. If the standard pronunciation should finally settle upon *kh*, *jh* (§ **375**) for g and not upon *k* (surd stop), nothing would please me better. "Hard" g, except after n, is a bitter pill for a North German. To the objection that the work is too concise, let me say that I have worked hard to make it concise. The Accidence and Part II. were once as large again as they are now. The first contained too much syntax, until, following the excellent method of the French grammarians, I resolved to separate entirely inflection and syntax. I have in this edition transferred several paragraphs from Part I. to Part II. Part II. is a historical foundation broad enough for Part I. to rest upon. It is not intended to be a minute historical reference-grammar for teachers and specialists only.

The word-index has been very much enlarged. With the demand for the traditional list of irregular verbs, "which no grammar should be without," I have complied so far as to include all the irregular verbs in the word-index (see introductory remarks on page 271). I wanted to make the German-English vocabulary cover all the sentences and words, but found that it would swell the book too much. It is complete only for Part I. (see page 271).

The list of reference-books has been omitted at the suggestion of Professor Ripley.

It may not be out of place to enumerate the distinguishing features of the grammar: (1) the complete separation of inflection and syntax; (2) the historical treatment of the latter, which should make it a welcome aid in the reading of 16th, 17th, and 18th century Literature; (3) the attempt to treat German grammar with regard to the present stage of Germanic philology; (4) the scientific analysis of German sounds and accent.

THE AUTHOR.

TABLE OF CONTENTS.

PART I. SECTION 1.

	PAGE
ACCIDENCE	1–47
Pronunciation with Alphabets	1–5
The Articles	6–7
Declension of Nouns	7–17
Declension and Comparison of the Adjective	17–21
Numerals	21–23
Pronouns	23–30
Conjugation	30–47
Weak Verbs	35–37
Strong Verbs	37–43
Anomalous Verbs	44–47

SECTION 2.

SYNTAX.

SPECIAL SYNTAX	51–130
Articles	51–55
Nouns	56–74
Gender	56–62
Singular and Plural	62–64
Cases	64–74
Adjectives	74–80
Numerals	80–82
Pronouns	82–96
Personal Pronouns	82–85
Reflexive and Reciprocal Pronouns	86

TABLE OF CONTENTS.

	PAGE
Possessive Pronouns	86–88
Demonstrative Pronouns	88–91
Interrogative Pronouns	91–93
Relative Pronouns	93–95
Indefinite Pronouns	95–96
VERBS	97–118
Classification of Verbs	97
Auxiliary Verbs	97–99
Modal Auxiliaries	99–102
Voice	102–104
Tenses	104–110
Moods	110–112
Infinitive	113–116
Participles	116–118
Gerundive	118
ADVERB	119
PREPOSITION	119–130
CONJUNCTION	130
GENERAL SYNTAX	131–154
THE SIMPLE SENTENCE	131–135
THE COMPOUND SENTENCE	135–147
Coordinate Sentences	135–137
Subordinate Sentences	137–147
Substantive Clauses	137–138
Adjective Clauses	139
Adverbial Clauses	140–147
WORD-ORDER	147–154
ABBREVIATIONS AND SYMBOLS	265
SUBJECT-INDEX	266–270
WORD-INDEX AND GERMAN-ENGLISH VOCABULARY	271–286
EXERCISES FOR TRANSLATING INTO GERMAN, PREPARED AND ARRANGED TO ACCOMPANY THE GRAMMAR BY A. LODEMAN	1–87

FIRST PART.

FIRST SECTION.

ACCIDENCE.

THE GERMAN ALPHABET.

1—2.

German type.	German script.	Name.	German type.	German script.	Name.
U a		ah	N n		en
B b		bay	O o		oh
C c		tsay	P p		pay
D d		day	Q q		koo
E e		(b)ay	R r		air
F f		ef	S ſ s ß		es
G g		gay	T t		tay
H h		hah	U u		(t)oo
I i		e	V v		fou(l)
J j		yot	W w		vay
K k		kah	X x		ix
L l		el	Y y		ipsilon
M m		em	Z z		tset

Ae ä Ä		ah-umlaut (h)ai(r)	tsay-hah
Oe ö Ö		oh-umlaut	tsay-kah
Ue ü Ü		oo-umlaut	es-tsay-hah (= sh)
Äu		au-umlaut (= oi)	

PRONUNCIATION.

The German sounds are here only very inaccurately represented by English words and letters. A full analysis is found in the second part, p. 160. The following description, with a few key-words, will suffice for the beginner; but it is meant to be only a popular description. As soon as the student begins to read, he ought to study Part II., p. 160–174.

3. ā as in Eng. *rather*: Vater, Aal, Zahl. ă, not in Eng., but similar to Scotch *a* as in Sc. *hand, land*: Mann, Land, Hand.

4. b = Eng. *b*, but surd (= *p*) at the end of words: Bube, Haube, Dieb, Laub.

5. c, ď = Eng. *k*: Carl, Backe, Bäcker.

6. ch, not in Eng., but in Scotch as in *loch*. A single guttural sound. Two kinds: 1. Palatal (forward) after palatal vowels, viz.: e, i, ö, ü, ä, ei, eu, and in the suffix =chen, e.g., ich, Wächter, Blech, möchte, euch, Gerücht, weich, Mädchen, Mamachen. 2. Back-guttural after the other vowels, a, o, u, au, e.g., ach, Dach, Loch, Buch, Bauch (betrog in N. G.). In Charfrei'tag and in foreign words = *k*: Chara'kter, Chor; also like sch in foreign words: Champa'gner, changie'ren, Chance.

7. d = Eng. *d*, but surd (= *t*) finally: du, doch, Bad, lud.

8. e, long, similar to Eng. *a, ay*, as in *pay, pate, rate*; short, like Eng. *ĕ*, as in *met*, ē: gehn, Beet, wert; ĕ: recht, Wette.

9. f = Eng. *f*: hoffen, Hafen, führen, Flagge.

10. g = Eng. *g*, but surd (= *k*) finally: glauben, plagen, graben; but Tag, Zug, fragte, trug, Balg.

11. h = Eng. *h* if it stands initially: Hund, Hose, Hase. After a vowel and after a t it is silent: stehn, seh(e)n, sah, thun, That, Thal. See the dropping of h, p. 159.

12. ĭ similar to Eng. *i*: bin, finde, bringe.

ī or ie = Eng. *ee* in *feet*: vier, fliegen, mir, dir, Igel, Biber.

13. j similar to Eng. *y*: jung, jagen, Jagd.

14. f, ct = Eng. *k*: Katze, Zacke, Haken.

15. l similar to Eng. *l*: Lage, lachen, wohl, Saal, bald.

16. m = Eng. *m*: Molch, Saum, schwimmen.

17. n = Eng. *n*. 1. Initially, finally, and before a dental: Nagel, nun, fein, senden, Sant, Fund. 2. In the stem-syllable before f, and combined with g like Eng. *ng* in *sing, singer*: Anfang, Sänger, Finger, Bank, senken, blinken; but an=gekommen, un=geheuer.

18. ō = Eng. *o, oa*, in *hold, foal*: Bote, Boot, tot, rot, Loos, los, Thon (clay). ŏ not in Eng., but short Sc. *o*; e. g.: Woche, Loch, Stock, Rock (not at all like Eng. *stock, rock*, but see p. 164).

19. p = like Eng. *p*: plagen, Kappe, Trapper, Galo'pp.

pf = *p + f*: Pfund, Napf, Sumpf, tapfer. In Eng. only in accidental juxtaposition, e. g., "a cap for him," "stop for me."

ph in foreign words only = *f*: Philologie', Telegra'ph.

20. q always followed by u, similar to Eng. *qu*: quer, Quast, Quart, bequem.

21. r unlike Eng. *r*. 1. Trilled: Regen, Rache, fern, Furt, treu. This is the standard *r*. 2. Uvular or guttural in N. G., very much like the guttural ch, but sonant.

22. f, ff, s, ß = Eng. surd *s*: Haus, Mäuse, Wasser, Fluß, Muße, sein; but initially and after a vowel it begins surd and ends sonant, as in N. and M. G. Standard unsettled. But see p. 175.

23. sch = Eng. *sh* (surd): schicken, schenken, haschen, Schlange.

24. st, sp = scht, schp initially in the standard pronunciation and in S. and M. G. But in the middle and at the end of words, in N. G. also at the beginning of words = Eng. *st, sp*; scht, schp: Stein, Straße, Stuhl, Spaß, sprießen; *st, sp*: hast, wüste, bersten, Wurst, Wespe, haspeln. N. G.: Spieß, Stock.

25. t, tһ = Eng. *t*: hat, hatte, That, Naht.

26. u = Eng. *oo* in *too*: Hut, Wut, Blume, Buch, Buhle.
ŭ = Eng. *u* in *put*: Butter, stutzen, Gulden.

27. v = Eng. *f* in German words: Vater, Frevel, viel. v = German w in foreign words: Vika'r, vindizie'ren, Vaka'nz.

28. w like Eng. *v* dento-labial: Wetter, Wasser, warnen. After sch labio-labial like u after q, but not quite like Eng. *w*: Schwester, Schweiß, Schwelle. But see p. 170.

29. x in foreign words and chs, chs = Eng. *x*: Alexander, Wachs, Fuchs, Füchsin, sechs.

y = ü, which see.

30. z, tz = Eng. *ts*, as in *cats, rats*: Zunge, Zeug, Warze, Mütze, Pfütze.

c in foreign words before e, i, y, ä = *ts*: cerebral, Cäsu'r, Cika'be, Cyklo'p; but the spelling is unsettled: Ziga'rre, Zentner, Zensu'r.

31. Modified Vowels (Umlauts).

ä long = Eng. *ai* in *fair*: Väter, Räder, stählern.

ä short = Eng. and Ger. ĕ: Hände, Wände, fällen.

ö not in Eng. It has the lip-position of o, the tongue-position of e: long in böse, lösen, Herzöge; short in Böller, Zölle, Geröll.

ü not in Eng. It has the lip-position of u, the tongue-position of i: long in Mühle, Bücher, Küchlein; short in Müller, Sünde, Büttel.

y = ü, as in Cya'n, Cypre'sse, only in foreign words.

32. Diphthongs.

ai (rare) and ei = Eng. *i* in *find*: Kaiser, Mai, leise, weiß, bleiben. au = Eng. *ou* in *house*: blau, Haus, Maus.

äu and eu similar to Eng. *oi* in *exploit*: Mäuse, läuten, Beute, heute.

Quantity of Vowels.

33. Vowels are long in an open syllable, *e. g.*, Ta=ges, ſo=gen, Bü=cher. They are also indicated: 1. By doubling, but only in the case of a, e, o: Saal, Seele, Moos. 2. By h after the vowel and after t: Hahn, Ohm, ihn, Thran, Thor. 3. By e after i: lieb, Tier, viel. 4. a and e are generally long before r, rt, rd : war, rar, der, wert, werden, zart, Pferd. Short in fertig (< Fahrt), Warte, Scharte, Herz, Schmerz.

34. The vowels are short before more than one consonant: handeln, bergen, Nacht, Gelübde, haſſen.

35. ß counts as a single consonant; it becomes ſſ medially (see "Rules," § 12), *e. g.*, Fluß — Fluſſes, Flüſſe; fließen — floß, gefloſſen. The vowel remains long before inflectional endings, *e. g.*, loben, lobſt, gelobt (but gehabt, gemocht); also in a closed syllable, when the stem-vowel stands in an open syllable under inflection, *e. g.*, Tag, Ta=ges; Zug, Zu=ges. But see p. 175.

Since ch cannot be doubled, there is no telling the quantity of the preceding vowel from the mere looks of the word : *e. g.*, long in Buch — Buches; Tuch — Tuches; brach — brachen; but short in Bach — Baches; lachen, wachen. As a rule, shortness may be expected.

36. The division into syllables differs somewhat from the English custom. The "Rules" § 26 show how words are divided at the end of a line. The following examples will illustrate sufficiently: ha-ben, ſuch=te, be-ehren, Bee-re, ver=irren, ge=irrt, Waſ=ſer, Stra=ße, lö=ſchen, ro-ter, Fin=ger (but see 17), He-xe, Wei=zen, Hit=ze, Kar-pfen, be=ob=achten, nach=ſa=gen, be=glau=bi=gen.

37. German orthography is now regulated by the government, and the student who is to write German should provide himself with the official, Regeln und Wörterverzeichnis für die deutſche Rechtſchreibung in den preußiſchen Schulen. Berlin. It is a small convenient guide of 46 pages, with a quite full word-list. See 361, 2.

THE ARTICLES.

38. The definite article is der, die, das + *the;* the indefinite, ein, eine, ein + *one, an, a.*

The definite article declines:

		masc.	fem.	neuter.	common gender.
Sing.	N.	der	die	das	*Plu.* die
	G.	des	der	des	der
	D.	dem	der	dem	den
	A.	den	die	das	die

The indefinite article declines:

Sing.	N.	ein	eine	ein
	G.	eines	einer	eines
	D.	einem	einer	einem
	A.	einen	eine	ein

39. The articles are unaccented.

The definite article is the weakened demonstrative pronoun, which has chief stress. It retains the short original forms of the same. The indefinite article is the weakened numeral ein, which also has chief stress. To mark the demonstrative pronoun and the numeral, they are sometimes printed spaced or with a capital letter: Nur Einen Schritt, so bist du frei, F. 4563; but Es war einmal ein König, F. 2212. Der Mohr kann gehn (Sch.). Es thut mir lang' schon weh, daß ich dich in d e r Gesellschaft seh', F. 3470-1.

40. Owing to their lack of accent both articles suffer aphæresis and apocope, and contraction with the preceding word, most frequently with a preposition: dem and das are, according to good usage, combined with the following prepositions: an, auf, bei, durch, für, hinter, in, über, um, unter, von, vor, and zu; *e. g.*, am, ans, aufs, ins, ums, vom, etc. In general, contractions with dissyllabic prepositions are rarer in the classics, common in the spoken language, which allows the contraction of den whether dative plural or accusative singular masculine with the above and also with other prepositions. Some such are even in the classics: in = in'n, F. 2429, „in Sessel," Lessing's Nathan, „in Sack," „in Kopf," „an Tag." In, um contain long (see 389, 5) consonants and the article is not absent, as is generally explained. In conversation is heard: um Arm, von Bäumen, auf'n Feldern, mit'n Händen, durch'n Wald. The apostrophe in auf's, über's, etc., is not at all indispensable. Der, dative singular feminine, combines properly only with zu into zur.

41. Attractions of the definite article, especially of the neuter, to preceding words other than prepositions are common in the spoken language, e.g., „ich will's Buch holen," „er hat sich's Bein gebrochen." „Bind't's Pferd hauß an" (G.). „Und hast's Küssen verlernt" (F. 4485).

1. The aphæresis of „ein" common in the spoken language is also found in the written, e.g., „Warf auf 'nen Stuhl die Handschuh'"(Uh.). Bold abbreviations are these in Chamisso's, „'s war mal 'ne Katzenkönigin." The dropping of ein before mal is not unusual: „Es war mal ein Kaiser;" „Auch war mal ein Abt" (Bü.). Notice so'ne for so eine. The early N. H. G. (16th century) eim for einem (comp. M. H. G. *eime* for *eineme*), einn or ein for einen occur still in some South German dialects. In M. H. G. the aphæresis of "*ein*" is unheard of, while the definite article is much more pliant than in the present classical language. Apocope of the same is still allowable in certain S. G. dialects.

DECLENSION OF NOUNS.

42. *There are three systems of Declension, the Strong (Vowel, Old), the Weak (Consonant, n-Declension or New), and the Mixed.*

The strong declension (see **43**, 1) *has* (e)s *in the genitive singular; the weak has* (e)n *in all cases, singular and plural, except in the nominative singular; the mixed has* (e)s *in the genitive singular,* (e)n *in the whole plural.*

General Rules.

43. 1. Feminine nouns never vary in the singular.

2. The only case-endings are (e)s for the genitive singular and (e)n for the dative plural.

3. e in the case-suffix ought to stand in nouns ending in f, ß, sch, z, d, t, st.

e is always dropped after el, en, em, er, chen, lein. In other cases it is optional. If the genitive singular has es, then the dative singular has e as a rule: Hauses, zu Hause.

a. Distribution of nouns among these declensions according to gender:

1. The bulk of feminine nouns belong to the n-declension. No neuters at all.
2. To the strong declension belong mainly masculine and neuter nouns, and a few feminines.
3. The mixed declension includes a few masculine and neuter nouns.

Strong Declension.

44. We distinguish for practical reasons four classes, according to the formation of the plural:

1. No sign unless it be umlaut: das Wunder, die Wunder; der Vater, die Väter.
2. –e without umlaut: der Tag, die Tage; das Los, die Lose.
3. –e with umlaut: der Sohn, die Söhne; die Kraft, die Kräfte.
4. –er always with umlaut: das Bad, die Bäder; das Haus, die Häuser.

45. First Class.—*a.* No sign:

Sing. N.	der Spaten	das Gewerbe	der Engel
G.	des Spatens	des Gewerbes	des Engels
Plu. D.	den Spaten	den Gewerben	den Engeln

All other cases singular and plural like nominative singular.

b. With umlaut:

Sing. N., D., A.	der Faden	der Bruder
G.	des Fadens	des Bruders
Plu. N., G., A.	die Fäden	die Brüder
D.	den Fäden	den Brüdern

46. To this class, which never take e in the G. and D. sing., belong:

1. Masculine and neuter nouns in –el, –er, –en, –chen, –lein, –sel, e. g., der Hebel, der Ritter, der Boden, der Hopfen, das Hündchen, das Kindlein, das Rätsel.

2. Neuters of the form Ge–e, e. g., das Getreide, Geschmeide.

3. The names of kindred in –er: Vater, Bruder, Tochter, Mutter, Schwager, all with umlaut. Also der Käse.

4. Certain nouns, if they take –n in the nominative singular, as they may according to usage: der Felsen, der Brunnen, der Tropfen, der Schrecken (these so generally). The following not so frequently in the written language: der Funke(n), Balke(n), Friede(n), Gedanke(n), Gefalle(n), Glaube(n), Haufe(n), Name(n), Same(n), Schade(n).

47. 1. Atem (Odem), Brodem, Eidam, Brosam stand isolated. The plural, if it occurs, is the –e of the next class. Brosamen, f., is more common than Brosame. See 501.

2. All nouns sub 4, except Friede, Gefalle, and Gedanke, were weak in M. H. G., and are not yet fully established in the strong declension. Since usage is unsettled, they might all be put under the mixed or weak declension.

48. 1. The nouns of this class that take umlaut, besides the names of kindred in –er, are : der Apfel + apple, Acker + acre, Boden + bottom, soil ; Faden, thread (die Faden + fathoms), Garten + garden, Hafen, harbor, + haven ; Hammer + hammer, Laden (?), shutter, shop (store) ; Mangel, want, Nagel + nail, Ofen + oven, stove ; Sattel + saddle, Schaben, harm (but es ist Schade, it is too bad); Schnabel beak, Schwager brother-in-law, Vogel, bird, + fowl. Two neuters take umlaut: Kloster + cloister < L. *claustrum*, and Lager (?), camp.

2. In none of these is there any cause that could produce umlaut as in *i* and *jo* stems or before –*ir*. Umlaut has arisen from analogy with these. Väter, Mütter, Brüder, Töchter had umlaut already in M. H. G. This way of forming the plural is on the increase, because it is so convenient and some way of indicating the plural seems necessary. Wägen, Läger, etc., still sound objectionable, but have no worse and no better claim to correctness than the above.

49. SECOND CLASS.—Plural -e, no umlaut.

Sing. N., A.	Hund	die Drangsal	das Jahr
G.	des Hundes	der Drangsal	des Jahres
D.	dem Hunde	der Drangsal	dem Jahre
Plu. N., G., A.	Hunde	Drangsale	Jahre
D.	Hunden	Drangsalen	Jahren

50. To this class belong:

1. A small number of feminines in –nis and -sal, *e. g.*, die Drangsal, Trübsal; die Finsternis, Betrübnis, pl. -nisse.

2. Many masculines; some capable of umlaut, but without it. These may be considered exceptions to the third class: der Aal + eel, Aar eagle, Arm + arm, Besuch visit, Amboß + anvil, Dachs badger, Docht wick, Grad + degree, Halm, blade, + haulm, Huf + hoof, Hund dog, + hound; Lachs salmon, Laut sound, Luchs + lynx, Pfad + path, Punkt + point, Schuh + shoe, Tag + day, Stoff material, + stuff; Thron + throne, Versuch, attempt, and a very few others.

3. Masculines in -ig, -(i)ch, -ing, -ling, -(e)nd, -at, -is, -icht, *e. g.*, der Freund + friend, Gänserich + gander, Habicht + hawk, Hering + herring, Iltis (pl. Iltisse) pole-cat, Jüngling + youth, König + king, Molch salamander, Monat + month.

4. Many neuters, among which monosyllabics; those with the prefix Ge–; in –nis, –sal: das Jahr + year, Geschenk present, Gefängnis (pl. -sse) prison, Schicksal fate.

51. The group sub 2 is on the decrease, because we cannot tell on the surface whether a noun has umlaut or not. To avoid the difficulty, several nouns form very anomalous plurals: der Bau, die Bauten instead of Baue. Of Mord, pl. Morde is rare, rather Mordthaten; of Schmuck, pl. Schmucke is rare, rather Schmucksachen; Schluck, pl. Schlucke is seldom used, since it stands in the singular after a number, *e. g.*, drei Schluck Branntwein. See **173**.

52. Third Class.—Plural -e, with umlaut.

Sing. N., A.	der Stamm	die Kuh	die Braut
G.	des Stammes	der Kuh	der Braut
D.	dem Stamme	der Kuh	der Braut
Plu. N., A., G.	Stämme	Kühe	Bräute
D.	Stämmen	Kühen	Bräuten

53. To this class belong:

1. The majority of strong masculine nouns, mostly monosyllabics: der Gesang + song, Gebrauch use, Ball + ball, Gast + guest, Sohn + son, etc.

2. A number of feminine nouns: die Angst + anxiety, Axt + axe, Bank + bench + bank, Brunst, heat, lust; Brust + breast, Faust + fist, Frucht + fruit, Gans + goose, Gruft vault, Hand + hand, Haut + hide, Kluft + cleft, -kunft in compounds as in Einkunft + income; Laus + louse, Luft air, Lust desire, Macht + might, Magd + maid, servant; Maus + mouse, Nacht + night, Naht seam, Nuß + nut, Sau + sow Schnur string, Stadt city, Wand wall (of a room), Wurst sausage, Zunft guild; Ausflucht evasion, Armbrust cross-bow, Geschwulst + swelling.

54. Only two modern neuter nouns belong here, the last of which is of doubtful gender, viz.: Das Floß raft (**429,** 1); der or das Chor + choir, chorus.

55. No neuters belong here really except O. H. G. *meri*, das Meer, die Meere, now according to 2d Class. Der and das Chor, borrowed from church Latin "chorus," has joined the group sub 2. Das Boot, die Böte because it was also der Boot, a modern borrowed word < D. Die Boote is more elegant. Das Rohr, die Röhre is not good. Besides there is die Röhre, feminine singular, the pipe, tube.

56. Fourth Class.—Plural *-er*, always with umlaut:

Sing. N., A.	das Rad	Irrtum
G.	des Rades	des Irrtums
D.	dem Rade	dem Irrtume
Plu. N., G., A.	Räder	Irrtümer
D.	den Rädern	den Irrtümern

57. To this class belong:

1. About sixty neuter monosyllabics: das Aas (Äser), Blatt, Dach, Fach, etc.
2. All in *-tum*, whether masculine or neuter: das Herzogtum, der Reichtum.
3. Some masculines, viz.: der Bösewicht*, Dorn*, Geist, Gott, Leib, Mann, Ort*, Rand, Strauch*, Vormund, Wald, Wurm.
4. A few neuters, with the prefix Ge-: das Gemach, Gemüt, Geschlecht*, Gesicht*, Gespenst, Gewand*.

58. Only neuters had this plural *-er* at first. Of the sixty sub 1, some twenty form a different plural, and usage is unsettled; so do those sub 3 and 4 marked with a *. In the following a distinction is made in meaning between the different forms of the plural:

Sub 1, 2, 4,—

das Band,	Bande, ties,	Bänder, ribbons.
Denkmal,	-male, monuments,	-mäler, figurative sense.
Ding,	Dinge, things,	Dinger, coll., *e. g.*, girls.
Gesicht,	Gesichte, visions,	Gesichter, faces.
Gewand,	Gewande (poetic),	Gewänder (commonly).
Land,	Lande (poetic),	Länder (commonly).
Licht,	Lichte, candles (only),	Lichter, lights.
Schild,	masc. Schilde, shields,	Schilder (sign-board).
Stift,	masc. Stifte, pencils,	Stifter, institutions.
Tuch,	Tuche, kinds of cloth,	Tücher, cloths, shawls.
Wort,	Worte, words (their meaning),	Wörter, parts of speech.

DECLENSION OF NOUNS.

Sub 3,—

der Mann,	Mannen, retinue,	Männer, men.
Ort,	Orten, D. pl. only,	Oerter, places, towns.

59. Trümmer occurs in the plural only. But a weak plural Trümmern occurs in the classics. Singular Trumm + thrum. „Häupten," as dative plural, is isolated in „zu den Häupten." Mann was originally a *cons*-stem, *mann*- (see Kluge's Dict.). The form Mann in fünfzig Mann is the real nominative plural of the *cons*-stem. Mensch was originally neuter, being an adjective O. H. G. *mennisco*. Das Mensch, die Menscher, now implies a slur, speaking of woman = strumpet (see Kluge's Dict.). Wicht in Bösewicht was also once a neuter, + wight. See **431**.

60. In early N. H. G. many of the neuters still occur without -er. Kindes Kind werden deine Werk preisen (B.). Kinder und Kindes Kind (erzählen) von dem Holz noch und seinen Scharen (Sch.).

The plural in -s is not elegant. Säbels, Jungens, Frauens, Fräuleins are more than colloquial, though found in the classics. This -s is strictly Low German, and identical with English *s*. The parts of speech are used with s: die Achs, die Abers, die Wenns.

Weak or n-Declension.

61. Characteristics: (e)n in the plural and also in the singular of masculine, except the nominative.

Masc.	Fem.
Sing. N. der Bote	Whole *sing.* Zunge
G. des Boten	
All through *sing.* and *plu.*	Whole *plu.* Zungen

Only feminine and masculine nouns belong to this declension.

Like Zunge decline all feminines, except: 1. Mutter and Tochter. 2. The few in -nis and -sal (see **50.** 1). 3. The strong of the 3d class (see **53,** 2).

62. Of the masculines belong here:

1. All of two or more syllables ending in e, except Käse and the doubtful strong ones sub 4, 1st class (see **46**).

2. The following which generally do not show the e, which belongs to them: der Bär, Bauer, Bursch, Fürst, Fink, Geck, Gesell(e), Graf, Hagestolz, Held, Herr, Hirte, Insasse, Mensch, Mohr, Narr, Ochse, Prinz, Pfau, Spatz, Spross, Steinmetz, Thor (fool), Vorfahr.

3. Many nouns of foreign origin, which are difficult to tell from strong nouns, many of them names of persons and animals. They generally end in –t, –nt, –st, with the suffix –graph, –arch, –krat, –log(e), –nom, e. g., Poe't, Bandi't, Jsraeli't, Patrio't, Archite'kt, Kome't, Plane't, Konsona'nt, Stude'nt, Phanta'st, Telegra'ph, Geogra'ph, Patria'rch, Mona'rch, Autokra't, Demokra't, Astrolo'g(e), Philolo'ge, Astrono'm, Ökono'm (polite for "farmer"); also Tyra'nn.

4. Some names of nationalities in –ar, and –er, e. g., der U'ngar, Bulga'r(e), Tata'r, Baier, Pommer, Kaffer.

5. The adjective used as a noun when preceded by the article (see **220**).

REMARK.—An isolated form is now „auf Erben." Erbe was either weak or strong. But „in Ehren," „mit Freuden" are old datives plural (see **434, 1**). Notice the spelling Königin, pl. Königinnen.

Mixed Declension.

63. Characteristics : G. sing. (e), the whole plu. (e)n.

Only masculine and neuter nouns belong to this declension, and very few have not double forms for genitive singular and for the plural. The following generally belong here:

1. Auge, Bett, Ende, Gevatter, Hemd, Lorbeer, Mast, Muskel, Ohr, Panto'ffel, Schmerz, See, Stachel, Staat. Nachbar, Unterthan, Vetter sometimes retain in genitive singular the (e)n of their former declension. Bauer, peasant sub **62, 2** is sometimes classed here.

Das Herz inflects G. des Herzens, D. dem Herzen, A. das Herz; allowing for its being a neuter, which always has nominative and accusative singular alike, it really comes under 1st Class, strong, sub 4 (see **46**). Schmerz rarely has Schmerzens. Der Sporn, des Sporns, has taken an -n in the singular, but the old weak plural Sporen is still the rule, though Spornen occurs. Thronen, borrowed in M. H. G. < Gr.-L. *thronos*, is very rare. The plural of Dorn is either Dorne (old) or generally Dornen; also Dörner.

The mixed declension is quite modern, and does not exist in M. H. G.

2. Foreign nouns in -or (o long and accented in the plural, short and unaccented in the singular), *e. g.*, der Do'ktor, die Dokto'ren, der Profe'ssor, die Professo'ren. Also Inse'kt, Intere'sse, Juwe'l, Statu't, and others.

Colloquially one hears sometimes -n after nouns in -el and -er: die Hummern, lobsters; Stiefeln, boots; but they are not to be imitated.

Declension of Foreign Nouns.

64. Those which are fully naturalized come under the declensions already treated of. It remains to speak of those not at all or partly naturalized, and their inflection is very irregular and complicated.

1. Those that retain their foreign inflection, *e. g.*, Jesus Christus, Jesu Christi; Mari'a, Mariae; Modus, pl. Modi; Casus, pl. Casus; Cherub, pl. Cherubim; Conto, pl. Conti; Saekulum, pl. Saekula; Lord, pl. Lords; Tempus, pl. Tempora. Their number is decreasing.

2. Those which take a German plural ending, -en for instance, and do not inflect in the singular, *e. g.*: das Drama, pl. Dramen; Thema, pl. Themen; Individ'uum, pl. Individuen. Globus, Rythmus. But these are also found with -s in genitive singular, and then come under the mixed declension.

3. Nouns whose foreign plural ended in *-ia* take *-ien*: Studium, pl. Studien; Gymnasium, pl. Gymnasien. The ending of the singular may have been lost, and they have -s in genitive singular, as Adve'rb, Partici'p, Semina'r, Minera'l, Fossi'l, pl.

Adverbien, Fossilien, etc. Notice Pri′mas, Prima′ten; A′tlas, Atla′nten; Krisis, Krisen. On the whole, there is a great deal of irregularity, and therefore freedom, in the inflection of foreign words.

Declension of Proper Nouns.

65. 1. The names of nations and peoples are inflected both in the singular and plural. Those in –er (except Baier and Pommer, where –er is not suffix, denoting origin) go according to 1st Class (strong). All the others go according to the n-declension: der Hamburger, des Hamburgers, etc., D. pl. den Hamburgern. But der Sachse, des Sachsen; der Preuße, des Preußen, etc.

2. Certain geographical names (see **147**), which always have the definite article, are treated like any common noun, *e. g.*, der Rhein, des Rheins, das Fichtelgebirge des –es; das Elsaß, des Elsasses; die Schweiz, der Schweiz, etc.

3. Names of persons are uninflected if preceded by the article (an adjective or title between article and name makes no difference), *e. g.*, des Karl, des Kaisers Karl, dem großen Friedrich. If the title follows the name, or if the name in the genitive, modified by an adjective, stands before the noun upon which it depends, then the name takes –s, *e. g.*, das Reich Ludwigs des Frommen, des großen Friedrichs Generäle.

4. Names of persons, places, and countries without an article take a genitive in –es: Goethe, Goethes; England, Englands; Anna, Annas. But names of males ending in a sibilant, if inflected at all and an apostrophe is not preferred, and feminine names in –e, form a genitive in –ens, *e. g.*, Marens, Franzens, Mariens, Sophiens. Surnames in a sibilant certainly prefer an apostrophe, *e. g.*, Musäus' Volksmärchen, Opitz' Werke, Gauß' Tod. Names of places in a sibilant are constructed with von: die Reichsfreiheit von Ko′nstanz, die Befestigungen von Pari′s.

66. A dative and an accusative in –en of names of persons are hardly in use now, as *e. g.*, Schillern, Goethen, Klopstocken. Christian feminine names retain them more easily than masculine, *e. g.*, Hast du Marien gesprochen? See **68, 3**. Such genitives as Mutters Tob, Tantens Geburtstag are hardly proper.

67. Plurals of names of persons are formed in various ways. The general rule is: –e for masculine and –e(n) for feminine names, *e. g.*, Heinriche, Marien; but also Brunhilde, Elisabete. –s forms the plural of masculines ending in a vowel and of feminines in –a: Annas, Hugos.

68. 1. Here also belongs the plural of surnames denoting the members of the family, formed by –s if ending in a consonant not a sibilant; by –(e)n if ending in a vowel or a sibilant (occurs only in familiar language however), *e. g.*, Steinbrüggen, the Steinbrügges; Suhlings, the Suhling family; Kücks. Other endings for the plural, generally of foreign names however, are –ne, –nen: Cato, Catone; Scipionen, Ottone, and Ottonen; but the first n belongs to the stem of course. Compare L. *Scipio, Scipionis*. This s was perhaps originally a G. sing.

2. Biblical names retain foreign inflection: Evangelium Matthaei, in Jesu Christo, Mariae Heimsuchung.

3. It should be borne in mind that the rule in the classical writers before Goethe's death is not the rule now. Lessing wrote des Luthers, des Melanchthons; Goethe, Leiden des jungen Werthers. The dative and accusative in –en are the rule in them, the exception now, haben Sie Karlen geschrieben, Wilhelmen gesucht?

DECLENSION OF THE ADJECTIVE.

69. *The adjective is inflected according to two systems of declension, the Strong and the Weak. It is inflected strong when there is no limiting word before it; weak, when there is an article or demonstrative pronoun. It is uninflected in the predicate.*

DECLENSION OF ADJECTIVES.

1. Strong:

	masc.	fem.	neuter.		common gender.
Sing. N.	guter	gute	gutes	Plu. N.	gute
G.	gutes	guter	gutes	G.	guter
D.	gutem	guter	gutem	D.	guten
A.	guten	gute	gutes	A.	gute

2. Weak:

	masc.	fem.	neuter.
Sing. N.	der gute	die gute	das gute
A.	den guten	die gute	das gute

All other cases, *sing.* and *plu.*, guten.

Notice that the nominative and accusative singular of the feminine and neuter forms are alike.

70. After ein, kein, and the possessive pronouns the adjective is strong in the nominative singular of all genders and in the accusative singular of feminine and neuter, since it is like the nominative. The whole pl. is weak.

Sg. N. ein großer Dichter, eine rote Kirsche, ein herrliches Gedicht
G. eines großen Dichters, einer roten Kirsche, eines herrlichen Gedichtes
D. einem großen Dichter, einer roten Kirsche, einem herrlichen Gedichte
A. einen großen Dichter, eine rote Kirsche, ein herrliches Gedicht.

71. Adjectives ending in –el, –er, –en as a rule drop the e of these suffixes when inflected, sometimes however the e of the case-ending –en, *e.g.*, ebel, ebler, eble, ebles; mager, magrer, magre, magres; eigen, eigner, eigne, eignes; but heitern and heitren, eblen and ebeln. Those in –er like to retain both e's: heiterer, heitere, heiteres. Note therefore: Ein magrer Ochse, eines magern or magren Ochsen, etc.; der heitere or heitre Himmel, des heiteren, heitren, or heitern Himmels, etc.; mein eignes Haus, meines eigenen or eignen Hauses, etc. For hoch, hoher, hohe, hohes see **490**, 3, *b*.

72. The genitive singular masculine and neuter, –es, is now so regularly replaced by –en, that this should perhaps appear in the paradigm. Though strictly according to rule, –es has become the exception; –en has prevailed since the 17th century. Voss, Klopstock, and Grimm opposed it. Goethe favors it. Ein, kein, the possessive and the demonstrative pronouns never allow –en for –es; never keinen Mannes, diesen Buches.

COMPARISON OF THE ADJECTIVE.

73. Adjectives are compared by means of the inflectional suffixes –er and –(e)ſt, *e. g.*:

positive.	comparative.	superlative.
jung	jünger	jüngſt
ſchön	ſchöner	ſchönſt
reich	reicher	reichſt

Those in –el, –en, –er lose this e before the comparative –er; but retain it and lose the e of –eſt in the superlative, *e. g.*, mager, magrer, magerſt; dunkel, dunkler, dunkelſt. e in –eſt is as a rule retained after d, t, ꞩ, ſe, z, rch, ß, and ſt, but not necessarily, *e. g.*, lauteſte, gewiſſeſte, ſüßeſte. Größte alone is classical, but in the spoken language ſüßte, heißte, kürzte, etc., are heard. „Hoch" retains the former h in the comparative höher, and h in nahe becomes ch: nächſt. See **490, 3,** *b.*

74. The umlaut generally takes place, but it is very difficult to tell when it does not. A not small number are doubtful, *e. g.*, blaß, geſund, fromm, etc. No umlaut in: 1. Those with the stem-vowel au, *e. g.*, lau, blau, etc. 2. Foreign ones: brav, nobel, etc. 3. Participles: beſucht, gewandt, etc. 4. Derivatives: ſtrafbar, ſchalthaft, langſam, unglaublich, etc. 5. Bunt, blank, dumpf, falſch, flach, froh, hohl, hold, kahl, klar, lahm, laß, los, matt, morſch, platt, plump, raſch, roh, rund, ſanft, ſatt, ſchlaff, ſchlank, ſchroff, ſtarr, ſtolz, ſtraff, toll, voll, wahr, zahm, zart.

75. The comparative and superlative forms are declined just like the positive. Examples:

Größerer Spaß, größeres or größeren Spaßes, etc.; der größere Spaß, des größeren Spaßes, etc.; ein größerer Spaß

Klarſtes Waſſer, das klarſte Waſſer, ein klarſtes Waſſer.

Edlerer Mann, der edlere Mann, ein edlerer Mann; eitelſter Burſch, der eitelſte Burſch, ein eitelſter Burſch.

Heiſrer Sänger, der heiſrere Sänger, ein heiſrerer Sänger, G. eines heiſreren Sängers, etc.; der heiſerſte Sänger.

76. 1. Irregular Comparison.

By the use of different stems:

Positive.	Comparative.	Superlative.
gut + good	beſſer, adv. baß + better	beſt + best
viel	mehr + more	meiſt + most
	mehrer	mehrſt
gering or wenig	minder	mindeſt

Gut and viel are never compared regularly. Mehrer and mehrſt are due to double comparison. „Mehrſt," though occurring in Goethe and Schiller, is not classical. Mehr and minder are really not adjectives, but are used adverbially and substantively. „Baß" (mehr, very, much) is now archaic. „Doch baß hetzt ihn der linke Mann" (Bü.). Fürbaß (onward); „baß" also means ſehr, ſtark: „Das macht, er thät ſich baß hervor" (Sch.). „Und ward nicht mehr geſehn" (G.). Morgen ein mehreres = to-morrow (I will write) more.

2. Defective and Redundant Comparison.

a. There is a class of adjectives derived from adverbs and prepositions:

Adv. or prep.	Comparative.	Superlative.
(außer)	äußer	äußerſt
(hinter)	hinter	hinterſt
(inner)	inner	innerſt
(nieder)	nieder (rare)	niederſt
(ob[er])	ober	oberſt
(unter)	unter	unterſt
(vor, fort)	vorder	vorderſt

For the derivation of these adverbs, see **551**, 3. The superlative suffix –ſt is added to the comparative. This is due to their former full comparison, as for instance, O. H. G. pos. *hintaro*, comp. *hintaróro*, superl. *hintaróst*. The present comparatives hintere, obere are not even now felt as real comparatives; äußer has a spurious umlaut; „öberste" and „förderste" are colloquial; „vorder" comes from „fort," O. H. G. *fordar;* compare Eng. *further*, which has nothing to do with *far*.

Positive.	Comparative.	Superlative.
b. (mittel) + middle	mittler	mittelst
(ehe, conj.)	(eher, adv.) + ere	erst + erst
(laß + late)		letzt + last
(für)	(fürder, adv.)	Fürst (subst.) + first

The first compares regularly like an adjective in -el. The positive occurs only in compounds now, and the comparative has the force of the positive.

NUMERALS.

77. Cardinals.

eins, + one
zwei, + two
drei, + three
vier, + four
fünf, + five
sechs, + six
sieben, + seven
acht, + eight
neun, + nine
zehn, + ten
elf, eilf, ölf, + eleven
zwelf, zwölf, + twelve
dreizehn, + thirteen
vierzehn, + fourteen
fünfzehn, + fifteen
sech(s)zehn, + sixteen
zwanzig, + twenty
ein und zwanzig, + twenty-one
zwei und zwanzig, + twenty-two
drei und zwanzig, + twenty-three
dreißig, + thirty
ein und dreißig, + thirty-one
vierzig, + forty
fünfzig, funfzig, + fifty
sechszig, sechzig, + sixty
sieb(en)zig, + seventy
achtzig, + eighty
neunzig, + ninety
hundert (das Hundert), + a hundred
(ein) hundert und ein(s), + a hundred and one
(ein) hundert und zwei, + a hundred and two
(ein) hundert (und) zehn, + a hundred and ten

(ein) hundert und zwanzig, + a hundred and twenty
(ein) hundert ein und zwanzig, + a hundred and twenty-one
(ein) hundert acht und achtzig, + a hundred and eighty-eight
zweihundert, + two hundred
dreihundert sechs und siebzig, + three hundred and seventy-six
tausend (das Tausend), + a thousand
(ein) tausend und ein(s), + a thousand and one
(ein) tausend drei und vierzig, + a thousand and forty-three
(ein) tausend einhundert or elfhundert, + a thousand and one hundred
ein tausend achthundert drei und achtzig or achtzehn hundert drei und achtzig, + one thousand eight hundred and eighty-three
drei(mal) hundert tausend, + three hundred thousand
eine Millio′n, + a million
eine Millia′rde, a thousand millions
eine Billio′n, + a billion

78. Inflection.

Fully inflected are only eins, zwei, drei, as follows:

	Masc.	Fem.	Neuter.
N.	einer	eine	ein(e)s
G.	eines	einer	eines, when used substantively.
N.	ein	eine	ein, like the indefinite article when used attributively.

„'s war einer dem's zu Herzen ging" (Ch.); „eins von beiden," one of two things.

| N. zwei | G. zweier | D. zweien | A. zwei |
| N. drei | G. dreier | D. dreien | A. drei |

79. Older inflections were masc. zween, fem. zwo. Zwei, the neuter, has crowded out the masculine and feminine forms, which may still be found in the older modern classics, and still in use in the S. G. dialects. Was zweien recht ist, ist dreien zu enge. Durch zweier Zeugen Mund wird allerwärts die Wahrheit kund (F., I. 3013). Zween, die mit mir überfuhren

.... (Uh.). Zwo Hosen eines Tuchs, cut from the same cloth. „Zwo Jungfern in den besten Jahren" (Gellert). The plurals zwei and drei are in analogy with the strong noun and adjective declensions From 4–12 the e in the plural represents O. H. G. *i* when they were *i*-stems, fünfe < *fimfi*. The only other case in which these numbers are inflected is the dative plural (in -en): auf allen Vieren kriechen, alle Viere von sich strecken; mit Sechsen fahren; zu Dreien. Zweier, zweien are according to the adjective inflection.

80. Ordinals.

The ordinals are formed from the cardinals by adding -te to the numbers from 2–19, and -ste from 20 on.

(der) erste,	+ first	sechste,	+ sixth
zweite,	+ second	sechzehnte,	+ sixteenth
dritte,	+ third	zwanzigste,	+ twentieth
vierte,	+ fourth	hundertste,	+ hundredth
fünfte,	+ fifth	tausendste,	+ thousandth

Their inflection is that of adjectives; zweiter, der zweite, ein zweiter; G. eines zweiten. See **438**, 1.

PRONOUNS

81. Personal Pronouns.

		Common gender.		Special forms for gender in the singular.		
	I.	II.	III.	III.		
				Masc.	Fem.	Neuter.
Sing. N.	ich	du		er	sie	es
G.	meiner	deiner	seiner	seiner	ihrer	seiner
	(mein)	(dein)	(sein)	(sein)		(sein, es)
D.	mir	dir	sich	ihm	ihr	ihm
A.	mich	dich	sich	ihn	sie	es
Plu. N.	wir	ihr	—		sie	
G.	unser	euer	—		ihrer	
	(unsrer)	(eurer)				
D.	uns	euch	sich		ihnen	
A.	uns	euch	sich		sie	

The first and second persons and the plural of the third person are of common gender. The singular of the third person has a form for each gender.

82. In the genitive singular the longer forms in –er are common; the others are now archaic and poetic, *e. g.*, „Vergiß=meinnicht" (the flower). „Ich denke Dein," etc. (G.). The lengthened forms eurer, unsrer are not yet sanctioned, though common in the spoken language, and, especially eurer, not very rare in the classics, *e. g.*, „(Wie er) bei Tafel Eurer selbst nicht achtet" (Sch.). „Dann bedarf es unserer nicht„ (Sch.). The genitive singular neuter „es" occurs still in certain constructions, generally called an accusative: „Er hat es keinen Hehl daß . . . ." (Sch.). Ich bin es müde. Es nimmt mich Wunder. (See **183, 199,** 2.)

83. Reflexive Pronouns.

For the first and second persons the personal pronouns serve as such, *e. g.*, ich fürchte mich, wir freuen uns, ihr scheut euch. For the third person the forms are made up of the personal and the old reflexive pronouns:

	Masc. and neuter.	Fem.		Common gender.
Sing. G.	seiner	(ihrer, pers. pron.)	*Plu.*	(ihrer, pers. pron.)
D., A.	sich	sich		sich

84. The reciprocal pronoun has no special form; as such are used uns, euch, sich, einander, meaning "each other," "one another." Ex.: Ihr schlagt euch. Wir schelten einander nicht.

The Possessive Pronouns.

85. The possessive pronouns are: mein + my; dein + thy; sein, his, its; ihr, her; unser + our; euer + your; ihr, their; Ihr, your; der meine + mine ; der deine + thine, etc.; der meinige + mine; der deinige + thine, etc.

They are inflected like adjectives (see **69**); but the first group, mein, dein, sein, etc., like the indefinite article (see **38**), in which the nominative singular masculine and the nominative and accusative singular neuter are uninflected. *e.g.*:

		Neuter.	Feminine.
Sing. N., A.		mein Tuch	deine Nichte
	G.	meines Tuches	deiner Nichte
	D.	meinem Tuche	deiner Nichte
Plu. N., A.		meine Tücher	deine Nichten
	G.	meiner Tücher	deiner Nichten
	D.	meinen Tüchern	deinen Nichten

For the declension of der meine, der meinige, see the weak adjective, **69**, 2. The rest stand uninflected used predicatively and when they follow the noun (now archaic), *e. g.*, Was mein ist, das ist dein und was dein ist, das ist mein (B.). Du hast das Herze mein so ganz genommen ein (Song).

86. Euer, Eure, Seiner, Seine are often abbreviated into Ew., Sr., Se.: Se. Majestät, Ew. Wohlgeboren. Jhro is archaic, *e. g.*, Jhro Gnaden. It is an imitation of the old G. bero (see **89**). It does not occur before the seventeenth century. It stands for masculine and feminine singular and plural: Jhro Gnaden, Eminenz, Durchlaucht.

87. The possessive pronouns form certain compounds with wegen, halben, willen, and gleichen. Ex.: meinetwegen, ihretwegen, meinethalben, ihresgleichen, euresgleichen. The compounds with wegen and halben are really D. plu. meinen wegen, deinen halben. After n sprang up the excrescent t = meinentwegen, deinenthalben, current in the sixteenth century. These became the now classical meinetwegen, deinethalben, though the longest forms are still heard; also meinthalben, even meintshalben, occur, but they are not good. Meinetwillen < meinentwillen < meinenwillen are original accusatives, *e. g.*, um meinen willen = for my sake.

The origin of ihresgleichen, etc., is not so clear. Gleichen is without doubt the adjective used as a noun and governing a preceding genitive, which was at first the genitive of the personal pronoun and became later the possessive pronoun agreeing with gleichen (M. H. G. *sîne gelîchen*). But whence s? Is it the genitive sign –es in compound nouns, Liebesbrief, Mittagsstunde, which was looked upon as a mere connective? (See **518**, 2.) In M. H. G. was a Gen. *mînes, dînes*, which with *mîner*, stood for *mîn*, almost exclusively before *selbes*. But beinesgleichen is not old enough to connect with M. H. G. *dines selbes*.

Other compounds with the possessive, like meinesteils, meinerseits (see 552), are clearly genitives.

Demonstrative Pronouns.

88. These are: 1. der, die, das + the, that; 2. dieser, diese, dieses + this; jener, jene, jenes, that, + yon. The first, when used with the noun, differs only in accent and not in declension from the article (see **39**). When used substantively (without the noun) it declines:

	Masc.	Fem.	Neuter.	Common gender.
Sing. N.	der	die	das	*Plu.* die
G.	dessen	deren	dessen	deren
	des	der	des	derer (der)
D.	dem	der	dem	denen
A.	den	die	das	die

89. The spelling of „deß" for „des" is unwarranted. It implies that it is an abbreviation of „dessen," which it is not.

„Dero" is the O. H. G. form retained in certain phrases, as in dero Gnaden. Derentwegen, -halben, etc., are forms like meinetwegen, etc., but rarely lose the n before t. For their explanation see **87**.

	Masc.	Fem.	Neuter.	
90.	dieser	diese	dieses and dies	+ this
	jener	jene	jenes	+ yon, that

These are declined like strong adjectives, and stand adjectively and substantively: diese Feder, dieses Tintenfaß, jener Baum. Jenes dort ist mein Buch.

91. Another group of demonstrative pronouns, sometimes called "determinative," consists of:

Masc.	Fem.	Neuter.
derjenige	diejenige	dasjenige, the, that
derselbe	dieselbe	dasselbe, the same
derselbige	dieselbige	dasselbige, the same
selber, selbst (uninflected), selbiger	selbige	selbiges, the same
solch(er)	solch(e)	solch(es), + such

1. The inflection of the first three is that of „der" and a weak adjective, *e. g.*, derjenige, desjenigen, demjenigen, etc. Their composition is apparent. –ig is the usual adjective suffix (see **525**, 1).

In the 16th century der is still separated from selb–, jen–, and earlier the latter were even declined strong, der jener, dem selbem, but they soon followed the n-declension. „Der jene," from which „derjenige" developed, becomes obsolete in the 17th century. „Derselbige" < „derselbe.". Accent: be'rjenige, but derse'lbe.

2. Selber is a stereotyped form like voller, and selbst is a genitive singular of selb, M. H. G. *selbes*. The excrescent t appears first in the 16th century.

3. Solch is inflected like any adjective, even with –en in the genitive singular, *e. g.*, solchenfalls, solchen Glaubens. It may be uninflected, always if followed by ein and generally if followed by another adjective. An apostrophe after solch is uncalled for. Solch ein Mann, solch schöne Blumen. Eine solche Beleidigung kann ich nicht vergessen. Als er solches sah . . . . (B.).

92. Interrogative Pronouns.

Wer + who; was + what; welcher + which; was für ein, what sort of.

1. Wer declines:

	Masc. and fem.	Neuter.
N.	wer	was
G.	wessen, wes	wessen, wes
D.	wem	—
A.	wen	was

Weß or weſs: wes as dessen: des. See **89**. The genitive lengthened by –en like des > dessen was not yet established in the 16th century. Wes is now archaic, except in compounds, *e. g.*, weshalb, weswegen. For wessenthalben, see dessent–, derenthalben, **87, 89**.

2. Welch + which, what, declines strong. Before „ein" it is

always, and before an adjective it is often left uninflected, also in poetry when used adjectively: Welch Getümmel Straßen auf! (Sch.). Welch ein Gefühl (F. 1011). Welcher Mann war es?

3. Was für, was für ein, what, what kind of. „Ein" alone is inflected like the indefinite article if used adjectively; like a strong adjective if used substantively: „Was für Berge, was für Wüsten . . . . trennen uns denn noch?" (Le.). Was für ein Baum ist das? Was für Dinte ist dies?

93. Relative Pronouns.

1. Der, die, das, which, + that, who, declines like the demonstrative, but the genitive plural is never derer : Keiner siegte noch, der nicht gestritten hat (Bo.).

2. Welcher, welche, welches, + which, who, that, always declines strong: Das Buch, welches ich gelesen habe.

3. Wer, + who, whoever. The inflection is the same as that of the interrogative: Wer es (auch) sei, whoever it be.

4. Was, + what, whatsoever. The inflection is the same as that of the interrogative: Was er (auch) sagen mag, no matter what he says.

Indefinite Pronouns and Indefinite Numerals.

94. Anderer, andere, anderes, + other, different : der andere, die andere, das andere, die anderen. Declined like any adjective, used substantively and adjectively.

95. Einer, eine, eines, + one, the numeral with its derivatives kein, none, and einige, generally only plural " some."

Ein- is always strongly inflected and stands only substantively. Standing adjectively it is declined like the indefinite article (see **39**). With def. art.: der eine, die einen.

Kein is inflected like the indefinite article, but standing substantively is declined keiner, keine, kein(e)s : Keiner wird als Meister geboren (Prov.).

96. Etlich–, some; etwas, anything; wer, anybody; was, anything, something; welch–, some, any.

Etlich– and welch– are always inflected strong. The singular of etlich is rare, having the force of "tolerable," "some": mit etlichem Erfolge, with some success.

97. Compounds with je: jeder, every, each; jeglich, jedweder (= jeder) stand adjectively and substantively; jedermann, everybody; jemand, anybody; niemand, nobody.

Jeder, jeglich–, jedweder, each, every, are declined like strong adjectives. Jeglich and jedweder are not common now; they have the same meaning. Jedermann has only a genitive singular in –s. Jemand and niemand decline:

    N. jemand
    G. jemand(e)s
    D. jemandem, –den
    A. jemanden

The accusative and dative are N. H. G., taken from the adjective inflection. Though the classics are full of these cases, the best usage for the spoken language favors no case-ending for accusative and dative.

98. Man, one, any one. It is only nominative. The other cases are made up from ein– or wir. Man is old spelling for Mann, from which in M. H. G. it was not distinguished. Its corresponding possessive is sein: Man glaubt ihm nicht. Man kann seinen eigenen Kopf nicht essen (Prov.).

99. Nichts, nothing, allows of no further inflection. It is itself the genitive of M. H. G. *niht = ni-wiht* and *nio-wiht*. Compare Eng. naught = na-wiht. Nichts, the genitive, stands for the emphatic combination *nihtes niht*, "not a thing" = gar nichts.

Zu nichte, mit nichten, "not at all," show still that nicht was once a noun fully inflected: Besser etwas denn nichts (Prov.).

100. As indefinite numerals it is customary to classify all + all; beide + both; beides + each or either; ganz, whole; lauter, "nothing but;" manch + many; mehr + more; mehrere, several; die meisten + most, the majority; die mehrsten (= die meisten); ein paar, a few, lit. "a pair;" sämtliche, all, altogether; das übrige, die übrigen, the rest; viel, much, many; wenig, little, few; ein wenig, a little.

Of these, all, ganz, manch, viel, wenig may stand uninflected. Otherwise they are inflected like adjectives: Viel Steine gab's und wenig Brot (Uh.). Ganz Deutschland lag in Schmach und Schmerz (Mosen). Das ganze Deutschland soll es sein (Arndt).

Lauter, mehr, ein paar, ein wenig are indeclinable.

CONJUGATION.

101. The verb varies for person and number; for tense (present and preterit) and mood (indicative and subjunctive). From the present stem are formed the imperative and the noun-forms of the verb, viz., the infinitive, present participle with the gerundive, and the past participle in –(e)t. According to the formation of the preterit we distinguish two great systems of conjugations, the "*strong*' and the "*weak.*" The strong verbs form the preterit by substituting a different stem-vowel from that of the present, e. g., geben — gab, tragen — trug; the weak, by adding –(e)te to the stem, e. g., loben — lobte, glauben — glaubte.

102. The infinitive, the preterit, and the past participle are generally given as the "principal parts" of a verb. The infinitive represents the forms with the present stem. Knowing the preterit or the past participle, one can tell whether a verb is weak or strong. If the preterit ends in –(e)te the past participle ends in –(e)t; if the preterit is strong, the past participle ends in –en, e. g., sagen, sagte, gesagt; saugen, sog, gesogen.

The infinitive and the past participle help form the compound tenses.

103. The following paradigms show the various inflections:

WEAK.			STRONG.			
PRESENT.		**PRETERIT.**	**PRESENT.**		**PRETERIT.**	
Ind.	*Subj.*	*Ind. and subj.*	*Ind.*	*Subj.*	*Ind.*	*Subj.*
ich lobe	lobe	lobte	singe	singe	sang	sänge
du lobst	lobest	lobtest	singst	singest	sangst	sängest
er lobt	lobe	lobte	singt	singe	sang	sänge
wir loben	loben	lobten	singen	singen	sangen	sängen
ihr lobt	lobet	lobtet	singt	singet	sangt	sänget
sie loben	loben	lobten	singen	singen	sangen	sängen

	Imp.	*Inf.*		*Imp.*	*Inf.*
2. *sg.*	lobe (du)	loben	2. *sg.*	sing(e) (du)	singen.
1. *pl.*	loben wir	*Pres. part., Gerundive.*	1. *pl.*	singen wir	*Pres. part., Gerundive.*
2. *pl.*	{ lob(e)t (ihr) / loben Sie	lobend	2. *pl.*	{ sing(e)t (ihr) / singen Sie	singend
		Past part. gelobt			*Past part.* gesungen

104. The personal **suffixes** are:

Sg. 1. p. –e, except for strong preterit.
    2. p. –(e)st for both tenses and moods.
    3. p. –(e)t for the present indicative. In the pres. subj. and in the pret. ind. and subj. the 3. p. is like the first.

Pl. 1. p. –(e)n for both tenses and moods.
    2. p. –(e)t for both tenses and moods; also for the imperative.
    3. p. –(e)n for both tenses and moods.

The retention or rejection of the thematic or connecting vowel –e- is treated later. See 118.

105. Imperative. The 2. p. sg. ends in –e in all verbs excepting those strong ones that have the interchange of e—i or e—ie in the 2. and 3. p. sg. pres. ind., e. g., Traue, schaue, bete, bitte, grabe, hebe, but sprich, friß, nimm.

106. Infinitive. It always ends in –en except in those weak verbs in which it is preceded by –el, –er: wandeln, wandern; also in sein, thun, which are non-thematic verbs. See **449**, 2.

107. Participles. The present part. and the gerundive always end in –end: hoffend, helfend, ein Liebender, ein zu beweisender Satz, a proposition to be demonstrated. They are declined like adjectives.

The past participle is formed by the prefix ge–, and the suffix –(e)t for weak verbs, the suffix –en for strong ones: lieben — geliebt, blättern — geblättert, tragen — getragen, singen — gesungen.

108. Ge– does not stand:

1. Before heißen, lassen, sehen, helfen, lernen (?), lehren (?), hören, when an infinitive depends upon them in a compound tense: Ich habe ihn gehen heißen, kommen lassen, sagen hören. For lernen and lehren, gelernt and gelehrt are better usage.

2. In the preterit-present verbs (= modal auxiliaries, see **134**) which form similar past participles, viz., können, dürfen, mögen, müssen, sollen, wollen. Man hat das wilde Tier nicht fangen können. See **113**.

3. In the past participles of verbs having inseparable prefixes, e. g., verlassen, entsagt, bedeckt, gedacht, except fressen < ver + essen and verbs in which b and g are no longer felt to be the prefixes be and ge (see **543**), e. g., gefressen, geblieben < bleiben; geglaubt; geglichen < gleichen. See gegessen, **128**.

4. In verbs with the foreign ending –i'eren, e. g., marschieren — marschiert; probieren — probiert. Even when these are compounded with separable Germanic prefixes, they take no ge–: ausmarschiert, einstudiert.

5. Worden < werden never takes ge–, when it is an auxiliary in the passive voice, e. g., Er ist gelobt worden.

Compound Tenses.

109. These are formed by means of the auxiliary verbs haben, sein, werden; the last in the future active and the whole passive; haben and sein in the active voice. As a matter of convenience the simple tenses of these auxiliaries are given here.

110.

	PRESENT.		PRETERIT.		PRESENT.		PRETERIT.	
	Ind.	*Subj.*	*Ind.*	*Subj.*	*Ind.*	*Subj.*	*Ind.*	*Subj.*
	ich habe	habe	hatte	hätte	bin	sei	war	wäre
	du hast	habest	hattest	hättest	bist	seiest	warst	wärest
	er hat	habe	hatte	hätte	ist	sei	war	wäre
	wir haben	haben	hatten	hätten	sind	seien	waren	wären
	ihr habt	habet	hattet	hättet	seid	seiet	waret	wäret
	sie haben	haben	hatten	hätten	sind	seien	waren	wären

	Imperative.	*Inf.*		*Imperative.*	*Inf.*
2. sg.	habe (du)	haben	2. sg.	sei (du)	sein
1. pl.	haben wir	*Pres. part., gerund.* habend	1. pl.	seien wir	*Pres. part.* seiend
2. pl.	{ habet (ihr) / haben Sie }		2. pl.	{ seid (ihr) / seien Sie }	*Past part.* gewesen
		Past part. gehabt			

	PRESENT.		PRETERIT.			*Imperative.*
	Ind.	*Subj.*	*Ind.*	*Subj.*		
	ich werde	werde	ward, wurde	würde	2. sg.	werde (du)
	du wirst	werdest	wardst, wurdest	würdest	1. pl.	werden wir
	er wird	werde	ward, wurde	würde	2. pl.	{ werdet (ihr) / werden Sie }
	wir werden	werden	wurden	würden		
	ihr werdet	werdet	wurdet	würdet		*Inf.* werden
	sie werden	werden	wurden	würden		*Pres. part.* / *Gerund.* } werdend
						Past part. worden

111. 1. Haben has contracted forms for the 2. and 3. pers. sing.: hast < *hâst* < *habest*; hat < *hât* < *habet*. The pret. has undergone the same contractions: hatte < *hâte* < *habete*, etc. The pret. subj. has umlaut due to the influence of strong and pret.-pres. verbs. In dialect the old contracted forms with *â*, prevailing through the whole present, are still heard. In M. H. G. *haben* as auxiliary has the contracted forms; as an independent verb, the uncontracted.

2. Werben is a regular strong verb of the 3. class. It is the only verb that has retained the two pret. vowels, generally the vowel of the sing. prevailing over that of the plural. Warb is more common as independent verb; wurbe, as auxiliary. In elevated style warb is preferable.

112. The **Perfect** is formed with the present of haben or sein and the past participle, *e. g.*, ich habe getragen, I have borne; ich bin gefahren, subj. ich sei gefahren, I have ridden. Perfect Infinitive: getragen haben, gefahren sein, to have carried, ridden.

The **Pluperfect** is formed with the preterit of haben or sein: ich hatte getragen, subj. ich hätte getragen, I had borne; ich war gefahren, subj. ich wäre gefahren, I had ridden.

113. The past participles without ge- accompanied by an infinitive (see **108,** 1, 2), the modal auxiliaries and weak verbs which followed their analogy, form such tenses as these: Ich habe ihn gehen heißen, I have ordered him to leave. Sie haben einen Rock machen lassen, you have had a coat made or ordered a coat to be made. Der Knabe hat die Lektion nicht lernen können, the boy has not been able to learn the lesson. Er hat es nur sagen hören, he has only heard it said. Der Nachbar hat den Bettler arretieren lassen wollen (or wollen arretieren lassen), my neighbor wanted to have the beggar arrested.

114. The **Future** ind. and subj. is formed with the present of werden and the infinitive, *e. g.*, ich werde tragen, ich werde fahren, I shall carry, ride.

The **Future Perfect** is formed with the present of werden and the perfect infinitive, *e. g.*, ich werde getragen haben, ich werde gefahren sein, I shall have carried, ridden.

115. The first **Conditional** is formed with the preterit subj. of werden and the infinitive, *e. g.*, ich würde tragen or fahren, I should carry or ride.

The second or perfect **Conditional** is formed with the preterit subj. of werden and the perfect infinitive: ich würde getragen haben or gefahren sein, I should have carried or ridden.

Passive Voice.

116. The passive voice is formed by werden and the past participle. The tense of the auxiliary with the past participle of the verb forms the corresponding passive tense. Werden forms its compound tenses with sein and werden.

PRESENT : ich werde gelobt, I am praised, am being praised.
PRETERIT : ich ward or wurde gelobt, I was praised.
PERFECT : ich bin gelobt worden, I have been praised.
PLUPERFECT : ich war gelobt worden, I had been praised.
FUTURE : ich werde gelobt werden, I shall be praised.
FUTURE PERFECT : ich werde gelobt worden sein, I shall have been praised.
1. CONDITIONAL : ich würde gelobt werden, I should be praised.
2. or CONDITIONAL PERFECT : ich würde gelobt worden sein, I should have been praised.
IMPERATIVE : sei (du) gelobt, be (thou) praised.
seid (ihr) gelobt } be (you) praised.
seien Sie gelobt }
INFINITIVE : gelobt werden, to be praised.
gelobt worden sein, to have been praised.

Weak Conjugation.

117. The weak conjugation forms the principal parts by suffixing –te or –ete in the preterit: loben, lobte, retten, rettete; by prefixing ge– and suffixing –t or –et in the past participle: gelobt, gerettet. For the simple tenses see **103**, for the compound, **112–115**.

<small>1. Verbs of this conjugation are with few exceptions derivative verbs, and most of them can be recognized as such by certain marks of derivation, such as suffixes (-eln, -ern, -igen, -ieren, -sen, -schen) or umlaut. (But there are a few strong verbs with umlaut: lügen, trügen, gebären, etc.).</small>

118. 1. The connecting vowel always stands before t, whether personal suffix (3. p. sg. and 2. p. pl.) or in the participle and preterit, if the stem ends in d or t (th); if the stem ends in m and n, preceded by another consonant which is not m or n, *e. g.*, er rebet, ihr melbet, wir walteten, getröstet, er atmete, ich zeichnete.

Those in m and n have lost an e before these consonants. Compare them with their nouns: Atem, Zeichen. Those in n are often treated like those in el, er, to which they really belong (see sub 3): zeichente, regente. But these forms are not elegant.

2. The connecting vowel stands in the 2. p. sg. present ind. also after stems in s, sch, ß, ss, z, tz, besides the stem-endings sub 1, *e. g.*, du rebest, waltest, schmachtest, rechnest, reisest, fischest, spaßest, saffest, widmest, beizest, stutzest.

3. Verbs in –eln and –ern rarely show the connecting vowel e, *e. g.*, ich handelte, er handelt, gelächelt, wir wanderten. In the 1. p. sg. present ind. and subj., in the imperative 2. p. sg. they generally lose their own e, *e. g.*, ich wandle, wandre, schmeichle (du).

4. In solemn diction and in poetry any verb may retain the connecting vowel. On the other hand, the poet and the people take many liberties in the omission of it (sub 1 and 2). For instance, Das neue Haus ist aufgerichtʼt (Uh.). Seib mir gegrüßt, befreundʼte Scharen! (Sch.). Redʼst du von einem der da lebet? (id.). Gegrüßet seid mir, edle Herren! Gegrüßt ihr, schöne Damen (G.). See F. 3217, 3557. In fact though such full forms as du fischest, rasest, saffest, putzest, etc., are written, one generally hears du fischt, rast, faßt, putzt, etc. This applies also to strong verbs, *e. g.*, du wäschst, stößt, reißt.

5. The present subj. nearly always shows full forms, but the preterit ind. and subj. have coincided: daß du liebest, ihr liebet; daß ich liebte, rebete.

Irregular Weak Verbs.

119. There are two groups of these verbs. One has a difference of vowel which looks like ablaut, the other has besides different vowels also a change in consonants.

1. The stems show nn or nd:

Inf.	Pret. ind.	Subj.	Past participle.
brennen	brannte	brennte	gebrannt
senden	sandte	sendete	gesandt

Here belong brennen, + burn; kennen, to be acquainted with, + ken; nennen, + name; rennen, + run; senden, + send; wenden, to turn, + wend, went. The last two have also a preterit ind. sendete, wendete.

2. The stems show nf, ng. Here belong:

Inf.	Pret. ind.	Subj.	Past participle.
denken	dachte	dächte	gedacht
dünken	{ deuchte (däuchte)	deuchte	gedeucht
	{ dünkte	dünkte	gedünkt
bringen	brachte	brächte	gebracht

Strong Conjugation.

120. Strong verbs must have different stem-vowels in the preterit and present, since in this way difference of tense is expressed. But the vowel of the past participle may coincide with that of the present, as in geben, gab, gegeben v, fahren, fuhr, gefahren vi, halten, hielt, gehalten vii; or with that of the preterit, as in beißen, biß, gebissen I, biegen, bog, gebogen II, glimmen, glomm, geglommen viii. The past participle ends in –en, and has the prefix ge-, e. g., gestohlen, gerufen. For simple tenses see **103**.

121. The personal suffixes are the same as in weak verbs. Compare liebte, liebtest, liebte, etc.; sah, sahst, sah, etc. The imperative 2. p. sg. has no ending when the present ind. has interchange of e–i, ie, e. g., ich berge, du birgst, er birgt; imp. birg; brechen —brich; essen—iß. This interchange of e–i, ie occurs in III 3, IV, V; in verbs which do not have it there is no difference of stem-vowel in the imperative and the present, e. g., halten—halt; schwimmen—schwimm. But often e is added in analogy with weak verbs, always when the verb is either strong or weak, e. g., rufen—rufe VII; schlagen—schlage VI; always webe, bewege, erwäge VIII. In the last group there is of course no interchange of e–i, e. g., du bewegst, er bewegt. When the stem ends in t, -tet in the 3. p. sg. is contracted to single t, if the stem-vowel changes. M. H. G. *giltet* > *gilt't* > *gilt*. *E. g.*, gelten — er gilt; fechten — er ficht; raten, rät; but reitet, schneidet. Special mention is made of these peculiarities under each class and verb. The preterit subj. always has umlaut and the 1. and 3. p. sg. end in e, e. g., ich ſah, du ſahſt, er ſah, etc.; but ich ſähe, du ſäheſt, er ſähe.

The verbs are best classified according to the ablaut-series. (See **393**.)

122. I. Class. Ablaut: ei   i, ie   i, ie.

1. Division: ei   i   i.

The stem ends in ß (ff), f, ch, t, d—t.

Examples: beißen, biß, gebiſſen; ſchleifen, ſchliff, geſchliffen; ſchreiten, ſchritt, geſchritten; weichen, wich, gewichen; leiden, litt, gelitten.

The following verbs belong here: beißen, + bite; bleichen (intrans.), + bleach, but also weak, always when trans.; ſich befleißen, to apply one's self; gleichen, to be + like, strong since the 17th century, in the sense of + liken it is still weak, a N. H. G. distinction, M. H. G. only weak; gleißen, + glitter, nothing to do with the rare gleiſen < gelîhsen, to deceive, or entgleiſen, to run off the track < Geleiſe, track; gleiten, + glide; greifen, to seize, + gripe; greinen, + grin, rare and generally weak, grinſen, its derivative, has taken its place; keifen, to quarrel, is strong or weak, < L. G.; kneifen, to pinch, L. G. > N. H. G.; kreiſchen and kreißen, to scream, are related, both weak and strong, not H. G.; leiden, to suffer, + loathe; pfeifen, to whistle, + pipe < L. pipare; reißen, to tear, + write, draw; reiten, + ride on horseback; ſchleichen, to sneak (+ slick and sleek); ſchleifen, to grind, + slip, weak in the sense of "to drag, raze"; ſchleißen, + slit, split; ſchmeißen, + smite, throw; ſchneiden, to cut; ſchreiten, to stride; ſpleißen, + split, L. and M. G.; ſtreichen, to wipe, cross, +strike, etc., with very varying meanings; ſtreiten, to strive; weichen, to yield; compare weich, + weak, wicker; weak, it means to soak, soften.

2. Division: ei   ie   ie.

Examples: gedeihen, gedieh, gediehen; reiben, rieb, gerieben.

Here belong: bleiben, to remain (+ leave); gedeihen, to thrive, the part. has a doublet, gediehen, thriven, gediegen, solid, pure; leihen, to borrow, + lend; meiden, to avoid; preiſen, + to praise, strong only since the 15th century, < Preis < M. H. G. prîs < O. Fr. pris < L. prĕtium, analogous to Fr. priser; reiben, to rub (+ rive); ſcheiden, to separate; ſcheinen, + shine; ſchreiben, to write (+ shrive); ſchreien, to scream (?); ſchweigen, to be silent, weak in the sense of "to still a child"; ſpeien, to spit, + spew; ſteigen, to climb; treiben, + to drive; weiſen, to point out, in the 16th century still weak; zeihen, to accuse (+ indict).

123. Notice the interchange of b–t in the first division, *e. g.*, ſchneiden, ſchnitt, geſchnitten; but not in the second, viz., meiden, mied, gemieden; ſcheiden, ſchied, geſchieden. (See 416.) When the stem ends in ß or ſ, the 2. p. sg. present ind. is heard merely as ending in ſt, whether spelt so or not. The full form ‑eſt stands only in elevated diction, *e. g.*, bu ſchmeißt, beißt, befleißt bich; bu weiſeſt and weiſt, bu preiſeſt and preiſt. (See 118, 4.) Notice also the doubling of t and f in ſchreiten, ſchritt; ſtreiten, ſtritt; ſchleifen, ſchliff, etc.

124. II. Class. Ablaut: ie (ü, au)   ŏ, ō   ŏ, ō.

1. Division: ie (au)   ŏ   ŏ.

The stem ends in ß (ſſ), ch, ſ.

Examples: ſließen, ſloß, geſloſſen; triefen, troff, getroffen.

Here belong: verdrießen, to disgust, vex; ſließen, + flow (+ fleet); gießen, to pour; kriechen, + to crouch, creep (?); genießen, to enjoy; riechen, to smell, + reek; ſchießen, + to shoot; ſchliefen, to slip, rare, supplanted by its derivative ſchlüpfen; ſchließen, to close, lock; ſprießen, + to sprout; triefen, + to drip; ſaufen, to drink (of animals); ſieben, see index.

2. Division: ie, ü, au   ō   ō.

Examples: ſliegen, ſlog, geſlogen; trügen, trog, getrogen; ſaugen, ſog, geſogen.

Here belong: 1. In ie: biegen, to bend; bieten, to offer, + to bid; ſliegen, + to fly; ſliehen, + to flee; frieren, + to freeze; ſlieben, + to cleave, split; ſchieben, + to shove; ſtieben, to scatter; verlieren, + to lose; ziehen (zog, gezogen)), to draw.

2. In ü: küren (kieſen), + to choose; lügen, + lie; trügen, to deceive.

3. In au: ſaugen, + to suck; ſchnauben (ſchnieben), to snort, L. and M. G.; ſchrauben, to screw (+ ?), L. G. > late M. H. G.

2., 3. pers. sg. pres. show archaic forms sometimes in eu: fleußt, kreucht, fleugt. (See 406.) Of those in au only ſaufen has umlaut, viz., ſäufſt, ſäuft. The stem ending in ß, the 2. p. sg. may be bu ſchießt, genießt. Notice the interchange of h–g in ziehen, zog, gezogen, but h is silent. (See 416.) Notice also the doubling of f: ſaufen, ſoff, etc.

125. III. Class. Ablaut: ĕ, i   ă   ŭ, ŏ.

1. Division: i   ă   ŭ.

The stem ends in n + cons. (b, g, k).

Examples: binden, band, gebunden; ſpringen, ſprang, geſprungen.

Here belong : binden, + to bind ; dingen, to hire, originally and still at times weak, the isolated weak past part. bedingt is a regular adjective ; bringen, to penetrate ; finden, + to find ; gelingen, to be successful ; klingen, to be heard, resound ; ringen, to struggle, + wring ; ſchinden, + to skin, pret. ſchund ; ſchlingen, to twine, + sling, it also has the force of the now lost ſchlinden, to swallow ; ſchwinden, to disappear ; ſchwingen, + to swing, ſingen, + to sing ; ſinken, + to sink ; ſpringen, + to spring ; ſtinken, + to stink ; trinken, + to drink ; winden, + to wind ; zwingen, to force.

2. Division :   ĭ   ă   ŏ.

The stem ends in mm and nn.

Examples : ſpinnen, ſpann, subj. ſpänne and ſpönne, geſponnen ; ſchwimmen, ſchwamm, ſchwämme and ſchwömme, geſchwommen.

Here belong : beginnen, + to begin ; rinnen, to flow, + run ; ſinnen, to think ; ſchwimmen, + to swim ; ſpinnen, + to spin ; gewinnen, + to win.

3. Division :   e–i   ă   ŏ.

The stem ends in l, r + cons. except dreſchen.

Examples : helfen (hilfſt), half (hülfe, hälfe), geholfen ; werfen (wirfſt), warf (würfe), geworfen.

Here belong : bergen, to hide, + bury, burrow ; berſten, + to burst ; dreſchen, + to thrash ; gelten, to be worth, pass for ; helfen, + to help ; ſchelten, + to scold ; ſterben, to die (+ starve) ; verderben, to spoil (intrans.) ; verderben (weak), to corrupt ; werben, to enlist, woo ; werden, to become, + worth (see 110) ; werfen, to throw (+ warp).

126. Notice the double preterite subj. (See 464, 3.) Sub 2, rinnen never has „ränne." The 3. division has generally and better ü, because you cannot tell „hülfe" from „helfe" by ear. Dreſchen and berſten, once belonging to the next class, have bröſche — bräſche, bärſte — börſte.

The 2. and 3. p. sg. present ind. have i instead of e. (See 403.) As to the suffix, berſten has du birſt, birſteſt, er birſt ; gelten, du giltſt (pronounced gilſt), er gilt ; werden, du wirſt, er wird ; ſchelten like gelten.

127. IV. Class.   Ablaut :   ă,ĕ,ĭ — i, ie   ā   ō, ŏ.

The stem contains l, r, m after or before the root-vowel.

Examples : brechen (brichſt), brach (bräche), gebrochen ; ſtehlen (ſtiehlſt), ſtahl (ſtähle, ſtöhle), geſtohlen.

Here belong : brechen, + to break ; gebären, + to bear, bring forth ; befehlen, to command ; empfehlen, to recommend ; erschrecken (erschrak), to be frightened; nehmen, to take, + nim ; sprechen, to speak ; stechen, + to stick, stab ; stehlen, + to steal ; treffen (traf), to hit ; kommen, kam, gekommen, + to come. (See 489, 1.)

Befehlen and empfehlen belonged to the III. Class, and have double subjunctives, beföhle — befähle, etc. So has stehlen, stöhle — stähle. The umlaut in gebären is only graphic for ē < ě. Those in -hl and gebären have ie in 2. and 3. p. sg. present ind. : empfiehlt, gebiert. The rest have i : triffst, sprichst ; du kömmst, er kömmt are quite common, but not elegant.

128. V. Class. Ablaut: i, ĕ, ē — i, ie   ā   ĕ, ē.

The stem ends in any sound but a liquid.

1. Division: e, ē — i, ie   ā   ĕ, ē.

Example : geben (giebst, gibst), gab (gäbe), gegeben.

Here belong: essen, + eat ; fressen, + eat (said of animals) ; geben, + give ; genesen, to recover ; geschehen, to happen ; lesen, to read ; messen, + to measure, + mete ; sehen, + to see ; treten, + to tread ; vergessen, + to forget ; (wesen) war, gewesen, to be, + was.

2. Division : i, ie   ā   ĕ, ē.

Here belong: bitten, bat, gebeten, to ask, + bid ; liegen, lag, gelegen, + to lie ; sitzen, saß, gesessen, + to sit.

The form of the 2. and 3. persons sg. of the present ind. of verbs ending in ss is -st ; of those in s is st for both persons : du, er ißt, vergißt, frißt ; du, er liest. But genesen, du, er genest, has no ie, probably because genetest would have coincided with genießt < genießen, genoß, II. ; du sitzest may be contracted > sitzst, pronounced merely „sitzt." The participle of essen, viz., gegessen, has ge- twice, because geessen was contracted into gessen very early. This is now colloquial. (See F. 2838, 4415.) Notice du trittst, er tritt ; du bittest, er bittet.

129. VI. Class. Ablaut : ă, ā-ä   u   ă, ā.

The stem-vowel is short before more than one consonant ; also in buk.

Example: backen, (bäckst), buk (büke), gebacken.

Here belong : backen, + to bake, in N. G. generally weak ; fahren, to ride, + fare ; graben, to dig; laben, to invite, and laben, + load ; laben (strong),

\+ to load, and laben (weak), to invite, have been confounded since early N. H. G.; they are of different origin; ſchaffen (ſchuf), to create (weak, "to work"); ſchlagen, to strike, + slay; tragen, to carry; wachſen, to grow, + wax; waſchen, + to wash; (ſtehen), ſtund, ſtand (ſtünde, ſtände), geſtanden, + to stand, ſtund is still common in S. G.

Here belonged also formerly: heben (hebſt), hub, gehoben, to raise, + heave; ſchwören (ſchwörſt), ſchwur—ſchwor, geſchworen, + to swear. Fragen (frägſt), frug (but never gefragen), "to ask," are frequently heard; also jagen (jägſt), jug, "to chase." The forms are still frowned upon by grammarians because they are "wrong," but the people use them just the same.

<small>In the 2. and 3. p. present ind. ä is the rule excepting ſchaffen, ſchafft, which is under the influence of the weak verb. Notice bu and er wächſt, bu wäſchſt (pronounced wäſcht). Isolated participles: gemahlen, ground; mahlen is now weak, mahlen, mahlte, gemahlt, to grind; erhaben, lofty, < erheben, erhoben.</small>

130. **VII. Class.** Characteristic is te in the preterit, which is no ablaut, while the past participle always has the vowel of the infinitive.

For convenience we make two groups.

1. Division. The seeming ablaut is: ă, ā   ie   ă, ā.

a before more than one consonant, ie = short i before –ng.

Examples: fangen (fängſt), fieng, gefangen; braten (brätſt, brät), briet, gebraten.

Here belong: blaſen, + blow, + blare (?); braten, to roast, fry; fallen (fiel), + to fall; fangen (rarer fahen),, to catch; (gehen), gieng, gegangen, + go, went, gone; halten, + to hold; hangen, + to hang; laſſen, + to let, cause; raten, to advise; ſchlafen, + to sleep.

<small>Umlaut is the rule in the 2. and 3. p. present ind. Notice bu rätſt, er rät; bu, er bläſt; bu hältſt (pronounced „hälſt"), er hält; bu läſſeſt or bu, er läßt. The umlaut in this whole class is late; in later M. H. G. they have it rarely. The "Rules" prefer the spelling i to ie, viz., hing, fing, ging.</small>

131. 2. Division: au, ei, ō, ū   ie   au, ei, ō, ū.

Here belong: hauen, hieb (b < w), gehauen, + to hew; laufen, lief, gelaufen, to run, + leap; heißen, hieß, geheißen, to call, command, + hight; ſtoßen (ſtieß), to kick, thrust; rufen (rief), to call.

Only ſtoßen and generally laufen take the umlaut: bu, er ſtößt; bu läufſt.

Scheiben, once of this class, has gone into I; „gehießen," according to I, is sometimes heard, but must still be rejected as incorrect. Of this class there are a great many isolated participles of verbs that have changed conjugation, *e. g.*, beſchetben, modest (but beſchieben, "ordered"); geſchroten, rough-ground; geſalzen, + salt; geſpalten, "split"; gewalzen, rolled, etc. Rufen, rufte, geruft is not correct.

132. VIII. Class. Characteristic is o in the preterit and past participle, long or short according to the following consonants.

The verbs belonging here are stragglers from all the other ablaut-series. There must be therefore a number that are still afloat; that is, according to the usage of the period in which they are taken, they belong to their regular class or to this. Present usage in the spoken language always favors o — o, *e. g.*, ſchwören, ſchwor, geſchworen, VI; breſchen, broſch, gebroſchen, III; heben, hob, gehoben, VI, which have been assigned by us, however, to their proper classes. Lügen, II, and trügen, II, have sprung from liegen and triegen under the influence of the nouns Lüge, Trug. They might be classed here; as also füren, II, for fieſen; compare the noun Kur(-fürſt), elector.

133. The vowels of the present may be e, i, a, ä, ö.

The ablaut is most frequently   e   o   o.

We count here: bellen (bellt, billt), to bark, III; fechten (fichtſt, ficht), + to fight, IV, III; flechten (flichtſt, pronounced flichſt, flicht), to braid, IV, III; pflegen, to carry on, undertake, V, IV, in the sense of "to be accustomed," "to care for," always weak; melten (melkt and milkt), + to milk III; quellen (quillt), to swell, gush, III; ſchellen (ſchillt archaic), generally ſchallen the weak verb, "to resound," weak = to cause to resound, ring, III; ſchmelzen (ſchmilzſt, ſchmilzt), + to melt, III; ſchwellen (ſchwillt), + to swell, III; weben (webſt), strong and weak, + to weave, V; bewegen (bewegſt), to induce, weak = to move, V; glimmen, to glow, III, 2; klimmen, + to climb, III, 2; gären (gärt), to ferment, also weak, IV; erwägen (erwägſt), to consider; wägen or wiegen (if it, II), wägſt, wiegſt, + to weigh (-wägen, wiegen, -wegen are in M. H. G. the same word, V); rächen (rächt), + to wreak, sometimes has roch, gerochen, but is generally weak, IV; erlöſchen, intrans., to die out (of a flame), (erliſcheſt, erliſcht), but trans. löſchen, to extinguish, III; verwirren, to confuse, III, is generally weak, but has an isolated participle, verworren = intricate, complicated; ſcheren (ſchierſt, ſchiert) + shear, IV, is sometimes weak.

ANOMALOUS VERBS.

I. The Preterit-Present Verbs.

134. To this group belong the modal auxiliaries and wiſſen. They are originally strong verbs, whose preterits are used as presents. New preterits, past participles, and infinitives were formed weak. The infinitives, the present plural, and the new strong participle have the same vowel, sometimes with an irregular umlaut: können (inf.), wir können, können (past part.). The different vowels of the present in the sg. and pl. weiß, wiſſen; the subjunct., with umlaut, mag, möge; the lack of t in the 3. p. sg., er mag, are still traces of their strong conjugation. The weak preterit was formed without connecting vowel, and has umlaut in the subjunctive: mögen, mochte, möchte, gemocht. (See **119**, 2, and **454**, 3.) The strong participle in –en stands in the compound tenses, when an infinitive depends upon the auxiliary: ich habe ſchreiben müſſen, but ich habe gemußt. An imperative, the meaning permitting, is made up from the subjunctive, *e. g.*, wolle, möge.

135. 1. Wiſſen, I, to know, + to wit (wot, he wist).

Inf.	Pret. ind.	Subj.	Participles.
wiſſen	wußte	wüßte	{ wiſſend { gewußt

The pres. ind. inflects: ich weiß, du weißt, er weiß, wir wiſſen, ihr wiſſ(e)t, ſie wiſſen. Subj.: ich wiſſe, wiſſeſt, wiſſe, etc. Imp.: wiſſe, wiſſet, wiſſen Sie.

2. Dürfen, III, to be permitted.

Inf.	Pres. sg.	Pret. ind.	Subj.	Past part.
dürfen	darf	durfte	dürfte	{ gedurft { dürfen

Pres. ind.: darf, darfſt, darf, dürfen, dürft, dürfen. Subj.: dürfe, dürfeſt, dürfe, etc.

3. Können, III, to be able, + can.

Inf.	Pres. sg.	Pret. ind.	Subj.	Past part.
können	kann	konnte	könnte	{ gekonnt { können

Pres. ind.: kann, kannst, kann, können, etc. Subj.: könne, könnest, könne, etc. Imp.: könne, könnt, können Sie.

4. Mögen, V, IV, to be able, + may.

Inf.	Pres. sg.	Pret. ind.	Subj.	Past part.
mögen	mag	mochte	möchte	{ gemocht { mögen

Just like können.

5. Sollen, IV, + shall.

Inf.	Pres. sg.	Pret. ind. and subj.	Past part.
sollen	soll	sollte	{ gesollt { sollen

Pres. ind.: soll, sollst, soll, sollen, etc.

This is almost entirely weak now. The vowel-difference in the pres. has been levelled away. Comp. Eng. shall, should.

6. Müssen, VI, + must.

Inf.	Pres. sg.	Pret. ind.	Subj.	Past part.
müssen	muß	mußte	müßte	{ gemußt { müssen

Pres. ind.: muß, mußt, muß. Subj.: müsse, etc.

This too is almost entirely weak.

7. Wollen, I, + will.

Inf.	Pres. sg.	Subj.	Ind. and subj. Pret.	Past part.
wollen	will	wolle	wollte	{ gewollt { wollen

Pres. ind.: will, willst, will, wollen, wollt, wollen. (See **472**, 2.)

II. The verbs gehn, + to go, stehn, + to stand, thun, + to do.

136. 1. **Geh(e)n**.

Pres. ind.: ich gehe, du gehst, er geht, wir gehn, ihr geht, sie gehn.
Subj.: ich gehe, du gehest, er gehe, etc.
Imp. sg.: geh; pl., geht, gehen Sie. Part.: gehend.
Pret. ind.: ich gieng. Subj.: ich gienge.
Part.: gegangen. According to VII; from a stem "*gang.*"

2. **Steh(e)n**.

Pres. ind.: ich stehe, du stehst, er steht, wir stehn, ihr steht, sie stehn.
Subj.: ich stehe, du stehest, er stehe, etc.
Imp. sg.: steh; pl., steht, stehen Sie. Part.: stehend.
Pret. ind.: ich stand (stund). Subj.: stände (stünde).
Part.: gestanden. According to VI; from a stem "*stand.*"

3. **Thun**.

Pres. ind.: ich thue, du thust, er thut, wir thun, ihr thut, sie thun.
Subj.: ich thue, du thuest, er thue, wir thun, ihr thut, sie thuen.
Imp. sg.: thu; pl., thut, thun Sie. Part.: thuend.
Pret. ind.: ich that, du thatst, er that, wir thaten, ihr thatet, sie thaten. Subj.: ich thäte, du thätest, er thäte, etc.
Part.: gethan.

The full forms with e of these three verbs are not used in the indicative. The h is merely graphic, and is not pronounced, *e. g.*, ich gehe is not ge-he, but gē or gē'e.

137. The **compound verbs** are not inflected differently from the simple verbs. Notice the position of the separable prefix, and ge– in separable compound verbs: ich schreibe an, schrieb an; imp. schreibe (du) an, ich habe angeschrieben, ich werde anschreiben. The separable prefix stands apart from the verb in the simple tenses (pres. and pret.), but only in main clauses; ge–, zu– stand between prefix and verb, angeschrieben, anzuschreiben. Ex.: Ich schreibe, schrieb den Brief ab, but während ich den Brief abschrieb (dependent clause). In inseparable compounds notice the participle has no ge : ich verstehe, verstand, habe verstanden, werde verstehn. (See **108**, 3.)

1. Notice a class of inseparable compounds derived from compound nouns. These have ge. They can be easily recognized by the chief stress falling on the first element: das Frü′hſtück, verb frü′hſtücken, frühſtückte, gefrühſtückt, to breakfast; der Ra′tſchlag, verb ra′tſchlagen, ratſchlagte, geratſchlagt, to take council.

138. Example of a **reflexive** verb, *e. g.*, ſich freuen, to rejoice:
Pres. ich freue mich, du freuſt dich, er freut ſich, wir freuen uns, ihr freut euch, ſie freuen ſich; ich freute mich, habe mich gefreut, werde mich freuen, werde mich gefreut haben.

FIRST PART.

SECOND SECTION.

SYNTAX.

SYNTAX.

139. For practical reasons we divide the Syntax into Special and General Syntax.

The **Special** treats of the function of the word, inflected or uninflected, in a sentence.

The **General** treats of the combination of words into a sentence, of the word-order, and of the combination of clauses into a compound sentence.

> It is of course difficult to keep these two divisions separate, as in fact all the different branches of grammar. Thus the separation of inflection and function, of phonology and inflection, of word-formation and syntax is a violent one. The division into special and general syntax is the custom of French grammarians, who have succeeded best in freeing their grammatical system from the strait-jacket of Latin and Greek grammars.

SPECIAL SYNTAX.

The parts of speech are treated here in the same order as they are in the Accidence.

Syntax of the Article.

140. The use of the demonstrative pronoun as definite article is much older than that of the numeral „ein" as indefinite article. „Ein" was used where the definite article could not stand; hence the plural of ein Mann is still Männer. In O. H. G. the article is still lacking; its use spread in M. H. G., so that now it is almost a necessity.

Some General Cases of Absence of the Article.

141. Proper names, names of materials always when preceded by nouns expressing quantity and measure, have no article. Ex.: Goethe erreichte ein hohes Alter. Schiller starb verhältnismäßig jung. Blei ist weicher als Gold. Ein Pfund Zucker.

142. No noun preceded by a genitive can take an article: Des Denkens Faden ist zerrissen (F. 1748). Der alten Götter bunt Gewimmel (G.).

143. There is no article before nouns (connected by und, weder, noch or unconnected) in certain set and adverbial phrases; in an enumeration of objects belonging to the same class or genus. Ex.: Geld und Gut. Haus und Hof. Mit Gott für König und Vaterland. In Saus und Braus. Sinn und Verstand verlier' ich schier (F. 2504). Nicht irdisch ist des Thoren Trank noch Speise (F. 301). Soll ich mit Griffel, Meißel, Feder schreiben? (F. 1732). Urahne, Großmutter, Mutter und Kind in dumpfer Stube beisammen sind (Schwab). Zu Tisch, zu Bette. Haus an Haus, Stein auf Stein, nach Osten, gen Süden, von Norden (but notice im Osten, im Süden, etc.

144. All pronouns exclude the article, except solch, manch, welch, was für, which allow an indefinite article after them, and all(e), which allows the definite article after it; *e. g.*: Was soll all der Schmerz und Lust (G.). Welch ein geschäftig Volk eilt ein und aus (id.). Was für ein Landsmann bist du, Jäger? (Sch.).

145. An abstract noun, and any noun denoting profession, rank, position have no article in the predicate after neuter verbs; *e. g.*: Philokte't, der ganz Natur ist, bringt auch den Neoptole'm zu seiner Natur wieder zurück (Le.). Heiße Magister; heiße Doctor gar (F. 360). (Ich) bin Soldat, komme niemals wieder (Sch.), Eng., I am *a* soldier.

146. 1. In technical phrases some nouns and adjectives used as such take no article: Schreiber dieses, the writer of this; Kläger, plaintiff; Besagter; Gedachter; Obiges; Folgendes, etc. In headings: Ueber Anmut und Würde (Sch.). Casuslehre, Flexionslehre.

2. In folk-lore and folk-songs: Rotkäppchen, Little Red Riding-hood; Schneewittchen. Knabe sprach: ich breche dich. Röslein sprach: ich steche dich (G.). Thürchen knarrt. Mäuslein pfeift.

Article with Proper Nouns.

147. The rule is: no article before proper nouns just as in English.

1. Names of persons may take an article when the bearer is

well known and his name has become a common noun; to express familiarity and intimacy, also contempt; to mark gender and case more clearly (this applies also to names of places and countries); when the author's or artist's name is used for his work; before names of planets, of ships, of the characters of a play, of titles of books taken from a person. Ex.: Ein Washington, der Welfe, die Ottonen. Schiller's Tell and Wallenstein, Goethe's Götz and Lessing's M. von Barnhelm are full of examples of the second use (familiarity, etc.). Die Büste des Sokrates. Wär' ich dem Ferdinand gewesen, was Octavio mir war . . . (Sch.). Läßt sich nennen den Wallenstein (Sch.) (contempt). Devrient spielte den Nathan. Mein Freund hat den Corot verkauft (painting by Corot). Der Herkules ist beschädigt.

2. Names of countries and provinces which are not neuter take the definite article. Most of these are feminine and a few masculine, viz., compounds: der Breisgau, Rheingau, der Sundgau; also der Haag (+the Hague); der, das Elsaß. Feminines in -ei: die Türkei', Wallachei'; in -au: die Moldau, die Wetterau; in -mark: die Neumark, die Ostmark; die Lausitz, die Schweiz, die Krimm, die Levante, die Pfalz. Some neuters in -land: das Vogtland, das Wendtland, die Niederlande, pl.

3. Names of oceans, lakes, straits, rivers, mountains, and forests always have the definite article, e. g., das Mittelmeer, die Ostsee, der Bodensee, der Belt, der Sund, der Rhein, die Donau, der Harz, der Spessart, die Alpen, der Schwarzwald.

4. Names of the seasons, months, days of the week, of the streets of a city: „Der Winter ist ein Ehrenmann" (Claudius). Im Januar, des Sonntags, auf or in der Kaiserstraße, im Frühling.

148. Appellatives have an article as in English: die Thräne quillt, die Erde hat mich wieder (F. 784). For exceptions see **141-146**.

149. Abstract nouns have no article when they denote a characteristic or state of mind: Mut zeiget auch der Mameluck;

Gehorsam ist des Christen Schmuck (Sch.). Freude war in Troja's Hallen (id.) Krieg ist ewig zwischen List und Argwohn (id.). But when they denote an act or motion they are treated as appellatives. They may also take the article that has generalizing force, e. g., Der Tod ist der Sünden Sold (B.). Die Wahl steht dir noch frei (Sch.). Die Kunst ist lang und kurz ist unser Leben (F. 558-9). Die Botschaft hör' ich wohl, allein mir fehlt der Glaube (F. 765). Das war ein Schuß! (Sch.).

150. Names of materials have the generalizing article, which denotes the whole kind or substance, or an article that singles out a certain kind or quantity, e. g., Der Wein erfreut des Menschen Herz (B.). Das Gold ist kostbar. Die Steinkohle ist schwarz oder braun. Without article: Silber und Gold habe ich nicht (B.). Blut ist geflossen (Sch.). Laß mir den besten Becher Weins in purem Golde reichen (G.).

151. Collective nouns take an article except when taken in a partitive sense: Was rennt das Volk? (Sch.). Weit dahinten war noch das Fußvolk (id.). Wir haben Fußvolk und Reiterei (id.).

152. All classes of nouns qualified by an adjective, by a genitive, by a relative clause, etc., take an article in the singular, excepting names of materials and nouns in the vocative, in the predicate or in certain adverbial phrases. The plural has the definite article or none. Ex.: Der kleine Gott der Welt bleibt stets von gleichem Schlag (F. 281). Der Gott, der Eisen wachsen ließ ... (Arndt). Die Hauptstadt von Frankreich. But (Sie) sprachen laut voll hohen Sinns und Gefühles (G.). Nach alter Weise. Es gab schönre Zeiten als die unsern (Sch.). Der alte Barbarossa (Uh.).

153. The genitive preceding a noun always has the article except a proper name: In des Marmors kalte Wangen (Sch.). In des Waldes Mitte (id.). Schiller's „an Ufer's Rand" Goethe would have made a compound, „Ufersrand." Comp. „Bergeshöhle" and other compounds of Goethe.

154. The definite article stands for an Eng. possessive pronoun, when the possessor cannot be mistaken. There may or may not be a personal pronoun as object in the sentence. Ex.: Der Kopf thut mir so weh (Song). Habt ihr mir den Finger blos genommen? (Sch.). (Sie) rührt ihm leise die Schulter (H. and D. 4, 63). See **243**, 3.

155. 1. In S. G. the definite article is always applied to members of the family instead of the possessive pronouns. In N. G., as in Eng., no article is necessary: Grüß' den Vater und Vaters Brüder! (Sch.).

2. As with proper names so names of materials and abstract nouns often have the definite article in the genitive and dative merely to show the case: der Milch Wasser vorziehen.

156. The definite article is used in German for the indefinite in English in a distributive sense: Butter kostet anderthalb Mark das Pfund, a pound; dieses Tuch kostet 90 Pfennig(e) die Elle; fünfmal das Jahr or im Jahre. This "a" in Eng. represents the preposition "on," and is not the indefinite article.

157. Ein can stand in German before certain indefinite pronouns and neuter adj. where it does not stand in Eng.: ein jeder, ein jeglicher, ein solcher, ein mancher (better manch einer); ein festes, = a fixed sum; ein mehreres, = more; ein weniges, = little. Ich schreibe nächstens ein mehreres.

Repetition of the Article.

158. Before each of several nouns of different gender the article must be repeated if it stand at all: Der Vater, die Mutter die gingen vor des Hauptmanns Haus (Song). If two nouns, connected by und, denote different persons the article should be repeated: Der Onkel und Pathe des Kindes war bei der Taufe zugegen (one person). But der Onkel und der Pathe . . . (two persons).

Both rules are often offended against by Luther, Goethe, and Lessing, and frequently in the spoken language: Wenn man den Maler und Dichter mit einander vergleichen will . . . (Le.).

The article before an apposition is treated as in English.

SYNTAX OF THE GENDER.

159. The grammatical gender of nouns is threefold, masculine, feminine, neuter. As to living beings, the nouns denoting males are masculine, and those denoting females feminine. Ex.: der Fuchs, Löwe, der gute Mann, Neffe, Knecht, Ochs, Bock; die Kuh, Ziege, Base, schöne Magd, die Sau, Stute.

1. Exceptions: nouns denoting the young of animals, diminutives, and das Weib, das Mensch (see **59**), das Frauenzimmer are neuter. Ex.: das Ferkel, Füllen, Kalb, Mädchen, Fräulein.

2. Any grammatical gender is ascribed to the names of the species without regard to sex. Neuter: das Pferd, das Schwein, das Schaf, das Reh. Fem.: die Nachtigall, Ameise, Biene, Maus, Ratte. Masc.: der Fisch, Hase, Dachs, Luchs.

160. Where the grammatical gender does not coincide with the natural, the following rules may be of service, based on the meanings of nouns and on their derivation. See **159**, 1.

GENDER ACCORDING TO MEANING.

1. Masculine are:

The names of the points of compass, of the winds, seasons, months, days of the week; of mammals (a few small ones like die Maus, die Ratte excepted), most of the larger birds, most fish, and stones.

Ex.: der Nord or Norden; Sommer; Februar, Augu'st; Montag, Sonnabend; der Esel, Löwe, Elefant; der Strauß, Adler, Storch; der Hai, Aal, Karpfen (all compounds with –fisch, of course, as der Walfisch, Klippenfisch); der Kiesel, Diama'nt, Feldspat.

2. Feminine are:

The names of most rivers, trees, plants, and flowers (in –e), insects, small singing birds, and nearly all derivative abstract nouns.

Ex.: die Weser, Oder, Elbe ; die Eiche, Tanne, Buche ; die Nelke, Rose, Rübe, Nessel, Kartoffel; die Ameise, Wanze, Biene; die Nachtigall, Schwalbe, Lerche; also die Krähe, Eule. Die Liebe, Tugend, Jugend, Demut, Freundlichkeit, etc.

3. Neuter are :

The names of places and countries except those always having the article (see **147, 2**), collective nouns (particularly those with Ge-); most names of materials including metals, of the letters of the alphabet; other parts of speech used as nouns, particularly adjectives not denoting persons (see **169**).

Ex.: „das schöne Spanien," „ein klein Paris," das Volk, Heer, Gebirge, Geschütz; das Holz, Heu, Schmalz, Obst; das Eisen, Blei, Kupfer, Zinn; das W, Y; das Bummeln, „Das Wenn und das Aber," das Gute, das Wahre, das Schöne.

REMARK.—So many rivers are feminine because they are compounded with -aha (+ Lat. aqua): Weser and Werra < Weserâ(h), Werraha; die Salza(ch). But notice der Rhein, Main. Die Schweiz, Türkei have the article really on account of their exceptional gender. American rivers are masculine: der Hudson, der Mohawk.

161. GENDER ACCORDING TO DERIVATION AND ENDINGS.

1. Masculine are :

Most monosyllabics by ablaut, *e. g.*, der Spruch, Sproß, Stich, Schirm; those in –er, –ler, –ner (denoting agents); in –el (denoting instrument); all in –ling; many in –en; dissyllabics in –z according to the n-declension (denoting living beings); in –ich.

Ex.: der Schreiber, Künstler, Pförtner; der Deckel, Hebel, der Fremdling, Günstling, Säugling; der Segen, Degen; corresponding to Eng. –om, Busen, Besen; der Knabe, Löwe, Bote; Gänserich, Wüterich, Fittich.

2. Feminine are:

Many dissyllabics (by ablaut, see **496**) in –e; abstract nouns in –e, mainly from adjectives ; in –ie, mostly foreign; many in

–t; all in –ei, –in, –ung, –heit, –keit, –schaft; some in –nis and –sal; foreign ones in –age (see **163**, 5).

Ex.: die Größe, Höhe; die Sprache, Gabe: die Philosophie, Galanterie; die Haft, Macht, Kraft; die Jägerei, Juristerei, Melodei; die Freundin, Lehrerin; die Duldung, Widmung; die Freiheit, Frömmigkeit; Freundschaft; die Wildnis, Fäulnis; die Blamage, Courage.

3. Neuter are:

All in –chen, –lein; most in –sel, –sal, –nis, –tum; nearly all of the form Ge–e or Ge– without e; some in –el.

Ex.: das Hündchen, Knäblein; das Rätsel, Überbleibsel; das Schicksal, Labsal; das Gedächtnis, Vermächtnis; das Königtum, Christentum (only two masc., der Reichtum and Irrtum); das Gefilde, Gemälde; das Gebild, Geschick; das Bündel, Gesindel, and the S. G. diminutives das Rindel, Bübel, etc.

<small>On the whole the gender of nouns has changed very little in the history of the language. Ex. of changes are: die Sitte < O. H. G. *der situ*, already M. H. G. sometimes *diu site*. Die Blume was O. H. G. both masc. and fem. Die Fahne was O. H. G. *der fano*.</small>

162. The following groups of nouns have varying genders, though some are of the same origin and have the same meaning. They should be fully treated in the dictionary, to which the student is referred. Only a few examples are given in each group.

1st group. The same form and meaning, but double gender (m. and n.); der and das Meter, Thermome′ter, Barome′ter, Bereich, Schrecken, Zeug, etc.

2d group. Double gender (m. and f.) with varying forms, but the same meaning and origin: der Schurz — die Schürze; der Trupp — die Truppe; der Quell — die Quelle; der Spalt — die Spalte.

3d group. Double gender, the same form in sg. and pl. if the plural be formed of both genders, but of different meaning and sometimes of different origin (the latter with *).

All adjectives: der Gute, + the good man; die Gute, + the good woman; pl. die Guten.

der Heide, heathen	die Heide, heath	pl. die Heiden
*der Bulle, bull	die Bulle (document)	die Bullen
der Erbe, heir	das Erbe, inheritance	die Erben
der Verdienst, earnings	das Verdienst, desert, merit	die Verdienste
*der Geisel, hostage	die Geißel, scourge	die Geißeln –feln
*der Messer, measurer	das Messer, knife	die Messer

There are perhaps forty in all.

4th group. Double gender, double plural, but different meaning and sometimes different origin (the latter marked *). Perhaps a dozen or more.

der Band, volume	pl. Bände	das Band, ribbon	pl. Bänder
*der Marsch, march	Märsche	die Marsch, marsh	Marschen
der Schild, shield	Schilde	das Schild, sign-board	Schilder
*der Thor, fool	Thoren	das Thor, gate	Thore

GENDER OF FOREIGN WORDS.

163. Foreign words retain generally the original gender: die Pein < L. *poena,* later *pēna;* das Kloster < L. *claustrum;* der Kerker < L. *carcer(em).*

Many have changed gender for various reasons. They were fully Germanized and followed German models according to ending or meaning, or they followed French (Romance) rules. Some changes are difficult to account for.

1. Examples of neuter nouns that became masculine, masculines that became neuter, and feminines that became neuter: der Palaſt, < *palatium;* der Balſam, < *balsamum;* der Mantel, < *mantellum;* der Preis, < *prĕtium;* der Punkt, < *punctum.* Neuter nouns in –at: das Konſulat, < *consulatus;* das Format, *formatum* or *–us;* das Ries, < V. L. *risma* (f.); das Kreuz, < *cruc(em)* (f.).

2. Examples of nouns that have changed gender in analogy with German words similar in meaning and ending: der Ziegel, < *tegula;* der

Marmor, *marmor*, n., on account of der Stein (see **160**, 1); der Körper, < *corpus*, n.; der Kada'ver, < *cadaver*, n., on account of der Leib, der Leichnam, and the many masculines in –er; die Nummer, < *numerus*, since die Zahl. Europa, Sparta, Athen, Troja, now all neuter (sec **160**, 3).

3. Nouns in *–arium, –orium, –erium, –are*, became all masculine in analogy with H. G. words in –er, < *œre* < *ari*: der Alta'r, < *altare*; der Keller, < *cellarium*; der Psalter, < *psalterium*; der Weiher, < O. H. G. *wiwâri* < *vivarium*; der Piaster, < It. *piastra*, f., < V. L. *plastrum*.

4. Neuter nouns, whose plural ended in *–a* in Gr. or L., became feminine in German from analogy with feminines in *–e*, < *â*, and also through Romance influence: die Bibel, < *biblion*, V. L. *biblia*; die Orgel, < *organum, –a*; die Pfründe, < V. L. *provenda* (pl.); die Stube, < *studium*; die Prämie, < *præmium*.

5. Words in *–a'ge*, masculine and feminine in French, are all feminine in G., e. g., die Baga'ge, die Blama'ge, die Coura'ge, etc. Die Schrift, < *scriptum*, die Pacht, < *pactum*, are due to analogy with G. nouns in –t, viz., die Fracht, Sicht, Schicht, Macht, etc.

GENDER OF COMPOUND NOUNS.

164. Compound nouns have the gender of the last noun: der Birnbaum, die Hausthür, das Schilderhaus, das Frauenzimmer (lady).

EXCEPTIONS: *a*. Many compounds with –mut: die Demut, die Wehmut, die Sanftmut; but der Hochmut, der Freimut, etc. They are, however, only seeming exceptions, -mut going back to compounds with O. H. G. and M H. G. *–muot*, m., and *–muoti*, f. This has given rise to the double gender of the same noun: O. H. G. *hôhmuoti*, f. only, but M. H. G. *hochmüete, hochmuot*, f., and *hochmuot*, m.; die Demut, < M. H. G. *diemüete, diemuot*, always feminine: der Kleinmut, die Anmut, die Großmut; also der Großmut; always der Hochmut. For Armut, which is no compound with –mut, see **511**, 2, *a*.

b. Der Abscheu seems an exception, because die Scheu is old and more common than der Scheu.

c. Names of cities and places are neuter even if ending in nouns of different gender: das schöne Hamburg, Lüneburg, Annaberg, etc.; but die Wartburg, Herrenburg, because these are castles, = Burgen, f., and not towns.

d. Der Mittwoch (Woche, f.) appears by the side of the legitimate die Mittwoch, already in M. H. G. It has followed the other days of the week, which are all masculine. (See 160, 1).

e. Die Antwort had double gender in O. H. G., but the neuter was more common. Luther has still die and das Antwort.

Concord of Genders.

165. This subject can be best treated under the head of concords as between noun and adjective, noun and pronoun, subject and predicate. The general rule that adjectives and pronouns take the grammatical gender of the noun to which they refer is only set aside when the grammatical gender does not coincide with the sex. In that case the pronoun or adjective can take the natural gender.

166. Mädchen, Mägdlein, Weib, Fräulein admit of this construction according to the sense, most commonly; not so, Kind, Frauenzimmer, Männlein, Söhnlein, and the other diminutives: Und schnell war ihre Spur verloren, sobald das Mädchen Abschied nahm (Sch.). Jenes Mädchen ist's, das vertriebene, die du gewählt hast (H. and D., IV. 210). Du gebenedeiete unter den Weibern (B.). Sie unglücklicher, Sie unglückliche, you unhappy man, woman. The adjective therefore also agrees with the sex.

Fräulein and the diminutives of names of females have „die" sometimes in colloquial language: die Fräulein, die Sophie'chen, die Dortchen (Dorothy). But „Ihre Fräulein Tochter" is quite common and correct: Ihre Fräulein Tochter . . . war ausgelassen (unrestrained) (G.).

167. Names in the predicate, not capable of forming a feminine from a masculine, like Lehrerin < Lehrer, Vorsteherin < Vorsteher, of course retain the grammatical gender, no matter what the sex of the subject: Sie ward . . . gleich mit besonderer Achtung als Gast behandelt (G.). But even predicate nouns capable of forming a feminine by suffix if used in the abstract sense, and not the personal, form an exception, *e. g.*, Herr, Meister sein or werden, "to be or become master of." Denn ich bin euer König (Sch.). Sie war der Verbrecher (id.).

168. The neuter pronouns (es, jedes, das, alles, etc.) may refer to a masc. or fem. noun, even to the plural and to a masc. and fem. noun together: Sie kommen hervor ein Weib da, ein Mann . . . das recht nun, es will sich ergetzen sogleich, die Knöchel zur Runde, = they stretch their bones for the dance, eager to enjoy themselves (in Goethe's „Totentanz"). Alles rennet, rettet, flüchtet (Sch.). Da mag denn Schmerz und Genuß, Gelingen und Verdruß mit einander wechseln wie es kann (F. 1756-8). Stillschweigend hörten sie (three persons) zu, indem jedes in sich selbst zurückkehrte (G.).

169. When adjectives are used substantively, the masculine and feminine denote sex, the neuter an abstract noun or thing: der Gute, die Gute, the good man, woman; das Gute, the good (abstract). Komm' herab, o holde Schöne, und verlaß dein stolzes Schloß (Sch.). Du hast Herrliches vollbracht (id.). Das Böse, das ich nicht will, das thue ich (B.).

SYNTAX OF SINGULAR AND PLURAL.

170. Names of persons and materials can take a plural only when they denote several persons, species, or kinds, viz., die Heinriche, die Berthas, die Öle (the various kinds of oil), die Gräser, die Fette, die Salze.

171. Abstract nouns do not as a rule admit of a plural, but as in English the plurals of such nouns were once quite common, viz., Minne, Gnade, Wonne, Huld, Ehre. Some of these plurals are left in certain phrases: in Ehren, zu Ehren; von Gottes Gnaden; zu Schulden kommen lassen, to be guilty of; Ew. Gnaden; die Herrschaften. Compare Eng. thanks, loves (in Shakspere), favors, regards.

172. To the sg. -mann in composition corresponds often -leute, pl. only, which in sense really corresponds to Mensch, Menschen, without regard to sex. Examples: Edelmann — Edelleute, gentry; Landmann, peasant, — Landleute, country folk: Ehemann, married man, — Eheleute, married people; but the pl Ehemänner means "married men"; Fuhrmann — Fuhrleute, drivers, carters; Kaufmann — Kaufleute, merchants, etc. But Biedermann, honest man; Ehrenmann, man of honor; Staatsmann, and a few more, form only the regular plural in -er.

173. For certain nouns which form no plural, plural compounds are used, some of which have also a singular.—*E. g.*:

das Feuer	die Feuersbrünste
der Tod	die Todesfälle
der Rat	die Ratschläge
der Dank	die Danksagungen

174. Nouns only used in the plural are:

a. Diseases: Blattern, Masern, Röteln.

b. Certain dates: Ostern, Pfingsten, Weihnachten, Ferien, Fasten, in Wochen = in childbed.

c. Names of relationship: Eltern; Gebrüder, brothers, as Gebrüder Grimm, the brothers Grimm, but generally only in the names of firms; Geschwister, brothers and sisters, rarely in the sg. = brother and sister; other nouns as Gefilde, Zinsen, Briefschaften, Einkünfte, etc.

175. Masc. and neuter nouns denoting quantity, weight, extent, preceded by numerals, stand in the singular, but fem. nouns (except Mark) in the plural as in Eng., *e. g.*, 6 Glas Bier, 10 Faß Wein; „an die dreimal hunderttausend Mann" (Song of Prince Eugene), 5 Fuß tief, 3 Mark 70 Pfennig(e), 70 × 7 = siebenzig mal sieben mal (B.). Feminines: 3 Meilen breit, 10 Flaschen Portwein, 12 Stunden. The coins, das Jahr, der Monat, Schritt generally stand in the plural, *e. g.*, 50 Pfennige machen 5 Groschen, 3 Dukaten, 20 Schritte lang; yet also sing., „90 Jahr—gebückt zum Tode"; 7 Monat(e) alt; but zehn Mark.

176. In older German the plural was used in all genders just as in Eng. That the singular was ever used came from the analogy of masc. nouns and "*diu marc*" with the neuter nouns, in all of which sing. and pl. would not be distinguished. See **431**, 2. The fem. of the n-declension never followed this analogy. For Mann see **59**. Compare the Eng. "a ten-year-old boy," now colloquial. "Year" is an old plural just like Jahr. In the D. pl. the coins, etc., in **175** almost always have en.

177. Notice the use of the singular in German for English plural in such phrases as: unter dem vierten und fünften Grade nördlicher Breite (Hu.); der erste und der fünfte Vers wurde(n) gesungen; die drei Schüler müssen zur Strafe die Hand auf den Mund legen; viele haben das Leben verloren, many lives were lost or many lost their lives.

SYNTAX OF THE CASES.

Nominative.

178. The nominative is the case of the subject and of direct address: Mein Freund, die Zeiten der Vergangenheit sind uns ein Buch mit sieben Siegeln (F. 575-6). Mit euch, Herr Doctor, zu spazieren ist ehrenvoll und ist Gewinn (F. 941). Absolute N. **297**.

179. Neuter verbs and verbs in the passive voice which govern two accusatives in the active, are construed with a predicate nominative. See **270**.

Such are: 1. Sein, werden, bleiben, dünken, scheinen, heißen (to be called); gelten, wachsen, sterben, etc.: Des Himmels Fügungen sind immer die besten (Le.). Aller Tod wird neues Leben (He.). Er wird ein großer Prinz bis an sein Ende scheinen (Sch.). Das allein macht schon den Weisen, der sich jeder dünkt zu sein (Le.). These verbs denote a state or transition. Preceded by als the construction may be called an apposition: Allein er starb als Christ (F. 2953). Ich komme als Gesandter des Gerichts (Sch.). Er gilt als ein reicher Mann, = He passes for . . .

2. Verbs of calling, thinking, making, choosing. scolding, viz., genannt, gedacht, angesehen, gemacht, betrachtet, gewählt, gescholten werden, and others: Wilhelm von Oranien wird der Schweiger genannt, Wilhelm von der Normandie, der Eroberer. Er ward ein Dieb gescholten, als ein Taugenichts betrachtet. Ich darf mich nicht des Glückes Liebling schelten (Körner).

Genitive.

180. The genitive is used chiefly as the complement of nouns and adjectives, but also of the verb (object). The genitive with nouns expresses the most varied relations. The principal ones are briefly given and illustrated below. German does not differ from other languages.

1. *G. of origin*, cause, authorship, relationship: Das Wunder ist des Glaubens liebstes Kind (F. 766). Goethes Faust. Die Früchte des Baumes.

2. *Subjective G.*: Die Liebe Gottes, welche höher ist denn alle Vernunft (B.). Der Gesang der Vögel. Das ist der Kampf der Pferde und Fische (Hu.).

3. *Objective G.*: Der Anblick dieser Gegend (Hu.). Die Erfindung der Buchdruckerkunst.
The personal pronoun is rarely found in this construction. Instead of „die Liebe seiner" stands die Liebe zu ihm, gegen ihn.

4. *Possessive G.*: Des Fatums unsichtbare Hand (Sch.). Der Garten des Königs. Doch besser ist's, ihr fallt in Gottes Hand als in (die) der Menschen (Sch.). Sometimes the possessive pronoun is put after the G. in colloquial language. Lessing has it several times: Das schien der alten Artisten ihr Geschmack nicht zu sein (Le.). See **242**, 2.

5. *G. of quality* or *characteristic*: Der Jüngling edlen Gefühles (H. and D., IV. 66).
This G. and the preceding stand also in the predicate after neuter verbs: Selig sind, die reines Herzens sind (B.). Einer Meinung sein; des Todes sein. Ein solcher Wasserstand war also e i n e s Alters mit den rohen Denkmälern menschlichen Kunstfleißes (Hu.).

6. *Appositive* or *specifying G.*: Der Fehler des Argwohns; das Laster der Trunksucht; die Sünde der Undankbarkeit. Karl erhielt den Beinamen des Großen.
This G. and that of characteristic are frequently supplanted by von + Dative: Eine Eiche von hohem Alter wurde vom Blitze getroffen. Dieb von (einem) Bedienten; Teufel von Weibe (Le.). See Prepositions, **303**, 15.

7. *Partitive G.*, dependent upon nouns of quantity, weight, measure; with numerals, various pronouns; comparative and superlative. Ex.: Thut nichts (= no matter). Er (der Mantel) hat der Tropfen mehr (Le.). Nun der Bescheidenheit genug (id.). Dem reichte sie der Gaben beste, der Blumen allerschönste dar (Sch.). Fünf unsers Ordens waren schon . . . des kühnen Mutes Opfer worden (id.). Laßt mir den besten Becher Weins in purem Golde reichen (G.). Du schlugst dich durch mit hundert achtzig Mann durch ihrer Tausend (Sch.). Unser einer kann sich das nicht leisten, = "One like (of) us cannot afford that."

181. In the spoken language and also in the classics (excepting poetry) this partitive G. has passed into mere apposition; especially after nouns of weight, measure; after numerals; after nichts, nicht, and the indefinite pronouns. Ex.: Ein Pfund Thee; drei Scheffel Korn. Etwas Schönes, nichts Böses, viel Gutes are no longer felt as genitives. The adjective used as noun is governed independently of the pronoun or numeral. Ex.: Zeigt das verfälschte Blatt nicht, man wolle zu nichts Gutem uns verbinden? (Sch.). Das könnte zu etwas Schrecklichem führen (id.). From Luther to Lessing this G. is still quite frequent, and it still remains in certain phrases, *e. g.*, Hier ist meines Bleibens nicht, "I cannot stay here." Viel Aufhebens machen, "to make much ado." Wenn ich mit Menschen- und mit Engelzungen redete und hätte der Liebe nicht . . . (B.), literally "and had nought of charity." It is supplanted by von, aus, unter + D. See Prepositions, 303. Wer von uns, unter uns?

Genitive Dependent upon Adjectives.

182. It stands after adjectives denoting possession and interest or lack and want; fulness or emptiness; knowledge or ignorance; desire or disgust; guilt or innocence; *e. g.*, fähig, *habhaft, sicher, teilhaftig, unfähig; bar, *los; *voll, *satt, leer, quitt, verlustig; kundig, *gewahr, unkundig; *müde, begierig; schuldig, ledig, etc. Ex.: Des langen Haders müde (Bü.). Des Leibes bist du ledig (id.). Des Gerichts schuldig (B.). (Hengste) begierig des Stalles (H. and D., VI. 313). Sie sind voll süßen Weins (B.). Du bist es doch zufrieden, Ritter? (Le.).

183. The adjectives marked * and others not given admit also of the accusative. In the last illustration „es" was felt as A., and therefore „das" is much more common. See Pronouns, **199,** 2. *E. g.*, Ich bin das satt, müde, "I have enough of it," "am tired of it."

The prepositions nach, von, etc., + D. frequently supplant the genitive, *e. g.*, „begierig nach dem Stalle" would be commoner; voll, rein sein von etwas.

Genitive after Verbs.

184. It may stand as nearer object, as remoter object, and adverbially.

As direct object after verbs with meanings similar to the adjectives in **182**; also achten, warten, harren, spotten, lachen, schonen genießen, sterben, pflegen, denken, vergessen, lohnen, verfehlen, brauchen, and others.

Ex.: Das Vergißmeinnicht. Ich benke bein (G.). Hungers sterben. Das lohnt sich der Mühe nicht, = It is not worth the trouble. Es sind nicht alle frei die ihrer Ketten spotten (Le.). Gebraucht der Zeit, sie geht so schnell von hinnen (F. 1908).

185. After verbs governing an A. of the person the G. of the thing stands as remoter object, such as judicial verbs, those with privative meaning, verbs of emotion; after many reflexive verbs with meanings similar to the adjectives in **182**, *e.g.*, zeihen, verklagen, freisprechen, beschuldigen, berauben, entladen, entlassen, entbinden, überheben, versichern, belehren, mahnen, and others; sich freuen, bedienen, erinnern, schämen, befleißen, erfrechen, sich wehren.

Ex.: Entlaßt mich meiner Ahnenprobe, ich will euch eurer wiederum entlassen (Le.). Wer kann mich einer Sünde zeihen? (B.). Jemand des Landes verweisen; eines Verbrechens anklagen, überführen, etc. Entschlage dich aller schwarzen Gedanken (Le.). Du darfst dich deiner Wahl nicht schämen (Sch.). But many of these genitives are supplanted by auf, über + A., and by A. alone.

186. Certain impersonal verbs expressing feelings, which are construed with the A. of the person feeling and with the G. of the cause and object of the feeling.

Ex.: Es ekelt mich, es reut, erbarmt, jammert, verdrießt mich; es lohnt sich. Darob erbarmt den Hirten des alten hohen Herrn (Uh.). Und da er das Volk sahe, jammerte ihn desselbigen (B.). But the nominative supplants here the A. of the person, and the A. the G. in the spoken language as a rule; „es" was again felt as A. See **183**. Ex.: Das gereut mich, dauert mich. Der Gerechte erbarmt sich seines Viehes (B.).

Adverbial Genitive.

187. It expresses place, time, manner, and other adverbial relations.

Ex.: Place: linker Hand, rechter Hand, aller Orten, "everywhere." Ich möchte (it is not likely that . . .) dieses Weges sobald nicht wieder kommen (Le.).
Time: dieser Tage, des Abends, „des Morgens in der Frühe."
Manner: trocknen Fußes, dry-shod; stehenden Fußes, immediately; vernünftiger Weise, reasonably. Sie kamen unverrichteter Sache zurück, they returned without having accomplished their object.

A large number of these genitives have passed into adverbs, *e. g.*, flugs, rechts, morgens, abends, nachmittags.

For genitive after Prepositions, see **302**.

Genitive in Exclamations.

188. Interjections are followed by a genitive only when it denotes the cause or occasion of the exclamation. Wohl and weh(e) have often a dative of the person and a genitive of cause or origin: O des Franzosen, der keinen Verstand, dieses zu überlegen, kein Herz dieses zu fühlen gehabt hat (Le.). O des Glücklichen, dem es vergönnt ist, e i n e Luft mit euch zu atmen (Sch.).

DATIVE.

189. It is the case of the indirect object, less remote than the genitive. The nearer object can also stand in the dative, but is more remote than the nearer object (the direct one) in the accusative.

190. The dative stands as nearer object after intransitive verbs denoting: 1, approach and removal, similarity and dissimilarity; 2, pleasure and displeasure; 3, advantage and disadvantage; 4, command and obedience; 5, yielding and resistance; 6, belonging to, agreement, trust, etc. A large number of these verbs are compounds, viz., those with ent-, ver-, ab-, an-, auf-, bei-, ein-, mis-, nach-, vor-, voran-, wider-, zu-, and those with noun, adjective, or adverb: leid thun, wohlwollen, sauer werden, zustatten kommen, weis machen, zu teil werden, das Wort reden, "to defend," etc. 1, nahen, nachgehen, begegnen, gleichen, ähneln, zusehen, entsprechen, fehlen, entgehen, nachstehen; 2, gefallen, danken, genügen, behagen, huldigen, mißfallen, schmeicheln, lassen (to look), drohen, grollen, fluchen; 3, helfen, nützen, dienen, beistehen, frommen, wehren, schaden; 4, gebieten, befehlen, hören, gehorchen, folgen; 5, weichen, willfahren, widerstehen, widerstreben, trotzen; 6, antworten, erwiedern, gehören, eignen, beistimmen, zureden, trauen, glauben, vertrauen.

Ex.: Des Lebens ungemischte Freude ward keinem Sterblichen zu teil (Sch.). Straflose Freiheit spricht den Sitten Hohn (id.). Du redest ihm das Wort, anstatt ihn anzuklagen (id.). Das Stehen wird ihm sauer, It is hard work for him to stand. 1. Du gleichst dem Geist, den du begreifst, nicht mir (F. 512). Das zwingst du ihr (der Natur) nicht ab mit Hebeln und mit Schrauben (F. 675). 2. Einem Wirte läßt nichts übler als Neugierde (Le.), Nothing looks worse in a host than curiosity. So fluch' ich allem, was die Seele mit Lock- und Gaukelwerk umspannt (F. 1587). Der Landvogt grollte dem Tell. 3. (Sie) wehret den Knaben, she restrains the boys (Sch.). Der Knappe folgt dem Ritter. Gott hilft denen, die sich selber helfen. 4. Soll ich gehorchen jenem Drang? (F. 631). Du folgst mir doch bald nach (Sch.). Gehörst du dir? (id.). 5. Und die Gebilde der Nacht weichen dem tagenden Licht (id.). Wohl weißt du, daß ich deinem Zorn nicht trotze (id.). 6. Traue, schaue wem. Wem eignet Gott (Le.), To whom does God belong, = Who possesses him exclusively? Compound verbs: Ich habe dir nicht nachgestellt (F. 1426). Sehr gern steht Karlos dem Mini'ster nach (Sch.). Die Königin sah dem Kampfe zu (id.).

191. After transitive verbs the indirect object stands in the dative and the direct in the accusative (see **198**): Verhülle mir das wogende Gedränge (F. 61). Das Menschenrecht, das ihm Natur vergönnt (F. 136).

192. A dative still farther removed from the verb is the ethical dative, or dative of interest (on the part of the speaker or hearer). It is generally a personal pronoun.

Ex.: Geht mir, nichts weiter davon (Sch.), "Go, I tell you, no more of that." Mir zu Liebe, for love of me. Ihm zu Ehren. (Sie) sind dir gar lockere, leichte Gesellen (Sch.). Die Uhr schlägt keinem Glücklichen (id.).

193. After impersonal verbs: es ahnt, beliebt, ekelt, geht, fehlt, gebricht, es graut, grauset, gelingt, liegt (mir) an etwas, kommt (mir auf etwas) an, schaudert, schwindelt, träumt, ziemt, and many verbs in **190** can be counted here: Dem Vater grauset's (G.). Es liegt mir viel daran, I care much for it. Dem Kaiser ward's sauer bei Hitz' und bei Kälte (Bü.).

Dative after Adjectives.

194. These have meanings similar to the verbs in **190**, *e. g.*, angenehm, ähnlich, eigen, feind, folgsam, dienstbar, gnädig, hold, nachteilig, verbunden, zuträglich. Ex.: Das steht ihm ähnlich, = that's like him. Auch war der Anfang ihren Wünschen hold (Sch.). Die meisten sind mir zugethan (id.), "devoted."

195. Substitution of preposition + case, both after verbs and adjectives.

Für, auf, an, gegen, über + accusative, mit and von + dative may replace the dative: Ich zürne auf dich, ich glaube an dich, vertraue auf ihn; bin freundlich gegen die Armen. Der Anzug (suit) ist sehr passend für dich, etc.

196. Verbs with unsettled constructions.

With a number of verbs usage is either unsettled or the classics still show two cases, while the spoken language has settled upon one, *e. g.*, now only es däucht mir, but es dünkt mich, classics have D. or A. after either. Glauben with D. only, or an + A.; but F. 3438: Ich glaub' ihn (Gott) nicht. Es ekelt mir and mich. Man bezahlt den Knecht (person), das Brot (thing), dem Bäcker das Brot. Ich rufe dir, I call out to you; ich rufe dich, I call you, etc.

197. The few reflexive verbs after which the reflexive pronoun stands in the dative are really transitive verbs, and the pronoun is the indirect object: Er bildet sich etwas ein, "he imagines something," "is conceited." Ich darf mir schmeicheln (Le.); but see **190**, sub 2: Ich denke mir die Sache so.

Accusative.

198. The accusative is the case of the direct object after transitive verbs, including many inseparable compounds of intransitive verbs with be-, ent-, er-, ver-, zer-, durch-, hinter-, über-, unter-, um-, voll-, wieder-; such as befahren, befolgen, befeuchten, entkräften, entscheiden, erfahren, erfinden, verlachen, vertreiben, zerstreuen, durchse'geln, hinterge'hen, überse'tzen, umge'ben, vollbri'ngen, wiederho'len.

Ex.: Ihr seht einen Mann wie andere mehr (F. 1874). Verachte nur Vernunft und Wissenschaft (F. 1851). Die Rüben haben mich vertrieben (Folk-song). Cook hat die Welt umsegelt. B. Taylor hat den Faust übersetzt.

199. Two accusatives may stand, one of the person and one of the thing, after verbs meaning to ask for, to inquire, teach, to cause to do a thing or have a thing done, and similar ones, *e. g.*, fragen, lehren, laſſen, bitten. Ex.: Wer lehrte dich dieſe gewaltigen Worte? (Le.) Lehre mich thun nach deinem Wohlgefallen (B.) (thun = second acc.). Wollen Sie den Arzt nicht kommen laſſen?

1. After fragen, bitten, überreden, bereden, the two accusatives stand, as a rule, only when the accusative of the thing is a neuter pronoun, *e. g.*, ich bitte, frage dich etwas, nichts, viel. If the pronoun is lacking, then fragen nach + D., bitten um + A., überreden von or zu + D. or the G. without preposition is the prevailing construction: Haſt du nach ihm gefragt? Ich habe ihn darum gebeten.

Lügen ſtrafen, Wunder nehmen govern an A. of the person: Das nimmt mich Wunder, "I wonder at that."

2. But these pronouns, das, nichts, viel, stand for old genitives which were felt as accusatives. The construction was: Wunder nimmt mich des or deſſen, wonder seizes me on that account. (See 186.) Lügen is probably a G. of cause: Jemand wegen der Lügen ſtrafen. Lernen for lehren, though found in Goethe, is wrong.

200. Notice a choice of construction in certain cases, when the personal object is further defined by another case or preposition and case. The verbs that concern us here are such as ſchlagen, treffen, treten, ſtechen, and similar ones.

1. Dative of the person and accusative of the affected part: Ich waſche mir die Hände or meine Hände.

2. Dative of the person and preposition + A.: Ich trete ihm auf den Fuß, ſchlage ihm in's Geſicht.

3. Accusative of the person and preposition + A.: Wir ſchlagen den Feind auf's Haupt. Wir treten die Schlange auf den Kopf. The choice is between 2 and 3. But 2 is preferable after intransitive verbs; 3 after transitives.

201. These accusatives are both object-accusatives, but after verbs meaning to name, scold, regarding, and others of similar meaning, the second accusative is a predicate or factitive accusative, while the first is direct object, *e. g.*, after nennen, ſchelten, ſchimpfen, glauben, taufen, heißen (trans.).

Ex.: In tiefster Seele schmerzt mich der Spott der Fremdlinge, die uns den Bauernadel schelten, "who call us by the nickname of 'peasant nobility'" (Sch.). Die Treue . . . ist jedem Menschen wie der nächste Blutsfreund, als ihren Rächer fühlt er sich geboren (id.). Noch fühle ich mich denselben, der ich war (id.). Ich achte ihn als einen Ehrenmann.

202. 1. After lassen + sein and werden a predicate A. by attraction is found instead of the predicate nominative, but the latter is the preferable construction, *e. g.*, Laß das Büchlein deinen Freund sein (G.). Laß diese Halle selbst den Schauplatz werden (Sch.).

2. For the passive construction, see **179**, 2. The verbs in **199**, 1, may retain the accusative (pronoun), also lehren. This would also admit an accusative predicate noun in the passive: Das Schlimmste, was uns widerfährt, das werden wir vom Tag gelehrt (G.). Ich werde den Tanz gelehrt. But it is best to avoid all these predicate accusatives. They sound pedantic. Better say: Ich habe Tanzunterricht, Tanzstunde. Ich werde immer wieder darnach gefragt, darum gebeten.

203. The inner or nearer object stands in the accusative called the "cognate." The noun has the same meaning as the verb. Its idea is generally included in the verb: Einen guten Kampf habe ich gekämpft (B.). Eine Schlacht schlagen, heiße Thränen weinen, etc.; Karten spielen, Schlittschuh laufen. Gar schöne Spiele spiel' ich mit dir (G.).

204. Notice that the noun is sometimes replaced by an indefinite pronoun, was, es, eins, etc. Compare Eng. "to lord it," the unclassical "to come it over somebody." Aber die Eifersucht über Spanien gewann es diesmal über diese politische Sympathie (Sch.). Die Götter halten es mit den Tapfersten (id.); sich was rechtes (zurechte) laufen, springen, tanzen, "to run, etc., a great deal." Lügen Sie mir eines auf eigene Rechnung vor (Le.). Ich schwatze eins mit (Le.). See also F. 3416.

205. After many impersonal verbs and some other verbs the logical subject stands in the accusative (see **186**). The verbs denote states of the body and mind: es dürstet, hungert, schläfert, wundert, kränkt, verdrießt mich.

Here belong also es giebt, es hat, es setzt, es gilt: Dergleichen Stimmen giebt's (Sch), "There are such voices." Es hat Gefahr, wenn wir nicht gehen, "There is danger . . . ". Es setzt Hiebe, Händel, Schläge, There is a fight, a quarrel going on, somebody is being whipped. Comp. French *il y a.* See **236**,4.

206. After reflexive verbs the pronoun generally stands in the accusative: Entschließe dich. Besinne dich wo du bist (Sch.). But see **185** and **197**.

Adverbial Accusative.

207. It denotes measure (amount), time, and place.

1. It denotes measure after verbs like wiegen, kosten, gelten; after adjectives like lang, breit, hoch, alt, wert, etc.

Ex.: Die Ruhe deines Freundes gilt es, "is at stake" (Sch.). Die Kiste wiegt drei Kilogramm, zwei Zentner, fünf Lot, etc. Die Brücke ist mehrere Tausend Fuß lang, hundert sechzig hoch und achtzig Fuß breit. Das Dorf liegt eine Stunde (an hour's walk) von der Stadt. Friedrich ist einen halben Kopf größer als Dietrich.

The usage as to the case of the person with „kosten" is unsettled: Der Scherz kostet mich or mir viel Geld. Grimm's Dictionary favors the A.

2. It stands with verbs of motion to express the distance and the way, the noun being often followed by an adverb.

Ex.: Weiche keinen Schritt zurück. Zwei Wanderer sieht er die Straße ziehn (Sch.). Es zieht ein Haufe das ob're Thal herab (Uh.). Der Fels rollte den Berg hinab. Mit leisen Schritten schlich er seinen bösen Weg (Sch.).

The A. of measure and distance supplanted the G. of an older period; that denoting the way is old. The G. still occurs frequently. See **181**.

208. The accusative of time denotes the duration and the moment of an action. The former is often followed by an adverb, lang, durch, über. Ex.: Der Bote kann den Augenblick hier sein (Sch.). Er schläft den ganzen Morgen. Du hast es Jahre lang bedacht.

1. Compare the G. of time (see **187**), which denotes a repetition of the action or a custom. The A. denotes a definite point of time or fixed period: (Der) ließ Betstund' halten des Morgens gleich (Sch.). Sonnabends Nach= mittags haben wir keine Schule (= custom). Nächsten Mittwoch haben wir keine Schule. Noch diese Nacht muß er Madrid verlassen (Sch.). The G. denoting duration of time is rarer now: Ein Gift das neun ganzer Jahre dauert (Le.). This may be partitive G.

Absolute Accusative.

209. This is generally accompanied by an adverbial phrase, and denotes that with which the subject is provided. Ex.: Zu Dionys, dem Tyrannen, schlich Möros, den Dolch im Gewande (Sch.). Schon den Hals entblößt, kniet' ich auf meinem Mantel (Le.).

SYNTAX OF THE ADJECTIVE.

210. The adjective may be used attributively, predicatively, and substantively: der reiche Nachbar; der Nachbar ist reich; der Reiche.

Attributive Use of the Adjective.

211. Some adjectives are only or mostly used attributively, as: 1, the superlatives and ordinals; 2, certain adjectives derived from adverbs: hiesig, dortig, seitherig, bisherig, e. g., die hiesige Zeitung, but not die Zeitung ist hiesig; 3, many adjectives in –isch, –lich –en: nordisch, irdisch, täglich, anfänglich, endlich, golden, seiden, silbern, gläsern; 4, the comparatives and superlatives in **76, 2**.

1. If they do stand in the predicate, they must be inflected, and the noun may be understood, e. g., die Lieferung ist eine stündliche, not stündlich.

For the adjectives in –en and –ern, von + noun is substituted, e. g., ein Becher von purem Golde. But in poetry the adjective is found: Der Stuhl ist elfenbeinern (R.).

212. The attributive adjective is inflected and agrees with its noun in gender, number, and case: Mit süßer Kost und frischem Schaum hat er mich wohl genähret (Uh.). It may stand uninflected, however: 1. Before a neuter noun in N. (and A.) (very rarely before a masc. or fem.): Meine Mutter hat manch gülden Gewand (G.). Es ist ein pudelnärrisch Tier (F. 1167). Frequently in certain phrases like „bar Geld", "cash"; „auf gut Glück". Rare: Groß Macht und viel List (Lu.). Das Alter ist ein höflich Mann (G.); „fremd und fremder Stoff" (F. 635.). 2. When it stands after the noun, mainly in poetry; commonly after coins, weights, and measures: Der Hauptmann führt im Schild ein

Röslein rot von Golde und einen Eber wild (Uh.). Ein Schwarm von Gästen groß und klein (Bü.). Zehn Fuß rheinisch, fünf Pfund flämisch. In prose also, when the adjective or participle has adjuncts: Dort ein gutartiges, gesittetes Handelsvolk, schwelgend von den üppigen Früchten eines gesegneten Fleißes, wachsam auf Gesetze, die seine Wohlthäter waren (Sch.). 3. Of two adjectives the first stands uninflected in certain set phrases; when the two express one idea; in poetry, very frequently in Schiller: Die großherzoglich badische Regierung; das königlich preußische Zollamt. Weh dem, der an den würdig alten Hausrat ihm rührt (Sch.). Den falsch verräterischen Rat (id.). „In die weit und breite Welt" (G.). Schiller has „traurig finstrer Argwohn"; „weltlich eitle Hoheit"; „O unglückselig jammervoller Tag"; „mit grausam teuflischer Lust," etc.

1. Lauter, and generally eitel, both in the sense of "pure," "nothing but," also the adj. in -er, 507, 2, are undeclined: Das ist lauter Unsinn. Esset eitel ungesäuert Brot (B.). Der Kölner Dom.

213. The attributive adjective is inflected weak after certain limiting words, viz., after the definite article and pronouns declined like it; after ein, kein, and the possessives, excepting the N. sg. of all genders and the A. sg. neut. and fem. Ex.: der gute Apfelbaum (Uh.); zur glücklichen Stunde; zu jenem frohen Feste; eines schönen Tages; an einem langen Aste (Uh.); sein grünes Haus (id.); eine arme Bäuerin (N. and A. sg.); ein seidenes Kleid (N. and A. sg.).

214. The adjective is therefore declined strong, when not uninflected (see **218**) and when not preceded by any of the above limiting words, mentioned in **213**, e. g., Holde Sehnsucht, süßes Hoffen (Sch.). Stumme Hüter toter Schätze (Platen?). Also after the uninflected pronouns welch, solch, viel, wenig, mehr, etwas, nichts, and after uninflected numerals. Ex.: Er gibt dem treuen Hirten manch blankes Stück (piece of money) davon (Uh.). Welch reicher Himmel (G.). Solch trefflicher Monarch (Sch.) (see **216**, 4; **221**).

215. The syntactical distinction between strong and weak inflection of the adjective, though very old, is by no means clearly drawn even now. The oldest inflection of the adjective is the so-called "uninflected," identical with the strong noun declension. When the pronominal endings spread over the adjective declension, forming the present strong adjective declension, the adjective probably was still declined strong even after a pronoun (ind. article). Of this there are traces from O. H. G. down to the 17th century. The n-declension of the adjective is a characteristic of the Germanic languages. Having less distinctive and fewer endings than the strong, it is natural that the adjective should be declined according to it, when preceded by a word which had the strong endings. This has given rise to the syntactical distinction and to the feeling that two strong forms should not stand side by side. When an adjective became a substansive or was used as such, it was always inflected weak, with or without article. This explains 221, 1. In Gothic the present participle and the comparatives were always inflected weak. In O. H. G. appear only a few strong comparatives and superlatives.

216. Unsettled usage as to strong and weak forms.

1. The strong genitive sg. m. and n. turned weak in the 17th century, and this is now the prevailing form: „Hohes Muts" (Bü.); blut'gen Ruhms (Uh.). „Worte süßen Hauchs" (Sch.). The pronouns always remain strong, except jener, jeder, of which a weak form is rare, e. g., jeden Volks (Uh.); jenen Tags (Bü.). This weakening is due to the feeling, that two strong forms should not stand together. See 215, 217.

2. After personal pronouns the rule is strictly the strong form, as the pronoun is not a limiting word. But as early as M. H. G. weak forms begin to appear. Usage now favors: after ich, du, er (in address), mich, dich *only* the strong form, e. g., „du starker Königssohn" (Uh.); ich armer Mann; after mir, dir mostly the strong form; after wir, ihr the weak (if fem. always), e. g., Wer nie sein Brot mit Thränen aß . . . der kennt euch nicht, ihr himmlischen Mächte! (G.). In „Gegrüßt ihr, schöne Damen! (G.), the comma makes a difference. After uns and euch (A.) strong and weak are equally frequent. After uns and euch (D.) strong and weak coincide of course: Man sollte euch schlechte Kerle beistecken (arrest) lassen. Euch faulen Burschen ist jetzt der Brotkorb höher gehängt.

3. In the vocative the rule now is strong form both in sg. and pl., e. g., Unverschämter! wenn dich jemand gehört hätte (G.). Du, armer Geist (Sh.). The plural is still found weak, but rarely, as: Lieben Freunde, es gab beff're Zeiten als die unsern (Sch.).

In O. H. G. the weak form was the rule; in M. H. G., the strong in the sg.

4. After certain pronouns, pronominal adjectives, and indefinite

numerals, such as solche, welche, einige, etliche, alle, manche, keine, and others, there stands in the N. and A. pl. very frequently the strong form against the rule, but rarely in the G. pl. This strong form is the older. Even after diese and jene strong adjectives may be found in the classics. Ex.: Der Blumenhändler hat keine schöne Rosen mehr. Wo hast du solche halb-verfaulte Birnen gekauft? After the G. pl. zweier and dreier the weak adjective is frequent, but in the spoken language these genitives are very rare: der Ankauf von zwei neuen Häusern or zwei neuer Häuser, and not zweier neuen (or -er) Häuser.

217. If two or more adjectives hold the same relation to the noun, they have the same inflection. If the second adjective, however, be more closely related to the noun, forming a joint idea, then it usually stands in weak form in G. and D., not in N. and A. It can often be formed into a compound noun, and has less accent than the first adjective: Er traktierte uns mit schlechtem roten Weine (= Rotwein); die Folgen blutiger bürgerlichen Kriege (= Bürgerkriege).

1. After certain adjectives like folgender, obiger, erwähnter, gedachter, etc., the second adjective, as a rule, is inflected weak in all cases: Genanntes umumstößliche Prinzip, obiger anerkannte Satz.

The Adjective in the Predicate.

218. The predicate adjective is uninflected. If it stand inflected in the predicate, the noun is supplied and the adjective is looked upon as attributive: Die Kraft ist schwach, allein die Lust ist groß (F. 2203). Dein Geschäft ist ein schwieriges (supply "one"); „des Polizisten Los ist kein glückliches."

The adjective (or participle) is also uninflected when it is an appositional or factitive predicate: Wir kamen glücklich an. Nun, das sind ich dumm (F. 961). Der Glaube macht selig (B.).

219. Certain adjectives are only used predicatively. Some of these are really nouns, like feind, freund, heil, schade, not, nütze, schuld. Others, originally adjectives or past participles, have been restricted to this use, like habhaft, abhold, getrost, ansichtig, verlustig. All of them have not yet become full adjectives; and many, if with adjective form, are of late derivation: abspenstig, abhold, abwendig, ausfindig, handgemein. Ex.: Ottilie konnte dem Märchen nicht feind sein (G.). Ein schöner Mann, eine schöne Frau! ist der Direktor glücklich genug, ihrer habhaft zu werden, so . . . (id.). Die Knechte wurden handgemein.

1. In O. H. G. the adjective in the predicate is still inflected, though not always. In M. H. G. it is rarely inflected. In N. H. G. voller and halber are stereotyped strong forms used for both numbers and all genders: Die Nacht ist halber hin (coll.); „des Nachts um halber Zwölf" (student song). Voller Schmerzen und Krankheit (B.).

Substantive Use of the Adjective.

220. The adjective when used as a noun is inflected according to the rules already given for the adjective proper: Mit Kleinem fängt man an, mit Großem hört man auf (Prov.). Du Schwert an meiner Linken (Körner). Die Ersten werden die Letzten sein (B.). For gender see **160**, 3. No inflection is the rule in certain set phrases: Gleich und Gleich gesellt sich gern (Prov.). Jung und Alt, Groß und Klein, Reich und Arm, von Klein an, von Jung auf; also in the names of languages: Englisch, Französisch; mein geliebtes Deutsch (F. 1223). Wie heißt dies auf Italienisch? Er hat von Kind auf Norwegisch gekonnt. Also of colors: Grün, Blau.

221. Usage admits of many irregularities.

1. The weak form in the plural when no article precedes as Bedienten, Beamten, Schönen, Jungen, or rarely the strong form in the singular like any feminine noun, invariable in the sg.: der Schöne, instead of der Schönen (G. sg.). See **215**.

2. The strong or weak plural after alle, einige, etliche, etc.: alle Gelehrte, einige Gesandte.

3. After was, etwas, viel, etc., the weak form is rare. See **214**.

4 If an adjective precede an adjective-substantive and is inflected weak, the latter is of course weak; if the adjective is inflected strong, then the substantive may be either strong or weak. The latter form is perhaps more common for the neuter, the strong certainly for the masculine nouns: Nein, sie (das Weib) ist, o holde Schönen, zur Geselligkeit gemacht (G.). Die armen Verwandten sind gewöhnlich nicht willkommen. Hochgestellte Beamte sind entlassen. Der neue Bediente hat ein angenehmes Äußere. See F. II. 6842.

a. Do not confound das Recht, law—das Rechte, the right thing; das Gut, property—das Gute, the good (abstract); (das) Schwarz, black (the color) —das Schwarze (the bull's eye of a target), etc.

Syntax of Comparative and Superlative.

222. These may be used just like the positive, only that the superlative is never used predicatively, *i. e.*, uninflected, excepting allerliebst, *e. g.*, die Blume ist allerliebst. If it stands in the predicate, it is always weak, being preceded by the definite article: Dieser Baum ist der höchste or dieser Baum ist am höchsten. These two should not be used indiscriminately, however, as they too generally are in the spoken language. The first is the strictly relative comparison; it can be strengthened by aller–, *e. g.*, der höchste von allen, der allerhöchste. The prepositional superlative should only be used when not so much the objects themselves or different objects are to be compared, but the same objects under different circumstances of time and place. This is generally the "absolute" superlative, expressed by an adverbial phrase: Der Starke ist am mächtigsten allein (Sch.), "The strong man is most powerful standing alone, unimpeded by the weak." Die Äpfel sind auf der sonnigen Seite des Gartens am reifsten. Als Booth Richelieu spielte, war das Theater am vollsten.

1. The "relative" superlative is generally preceded by the definite article, the "absolute" has, as a rule, ein or no article. Goethe is very fond of such an absolute superlative: Ein allerliebstes Kind, a most lovely child. Dies deutet auf ein spätestes (a very late) Naturereignis (G.). Notice also: weil's die Wenigsten können (G.), because very few know how; der Fürst, die Eltern, die neueren Sprachen, and other examples. They show absolute comparison with the definite article. The absolute superlative is best expressed by an adverb + adjective in the positive. The more common adverbs used are: sehr, recht, höchst, äußerst, überaus, *e. g.*, eine höchst angenehme Überraschung, ein recht dummer Junge.

223. Any adjective can be compared by –er, –est, except those that are never used attributively (see **219**) and a few whose form seems awkward, like knechtisch, herrisch, but the latter are not absolutely excluded. Allein, weiß Gott, sie war mehr schuld als ich (F. 2960).

224. When two qualities belonging to the same object are compared, mehr, weniger, minder are now used, but the classics are still full of the comparatives in –er.

According to Lehmann (L. Sprache, p. 206) Lessing uses mehr only once: Diese Ausrufungen sind rhetorischer als grünblich (Le.). Present usage: Der Geselle ist weniger heimtückisch als dumm. Der Soldat ist mehr tapfer als klug.

225. Logically the superlative cannot be used of two objects, but it is so used much more frequently in German than in English, e. g., Zwei Söhne, wovon sie den ältesten . . . mit einem Pfeile erschoß (Le.).

1. For the conjunctions benn, als, after the comparative, see **333**.
2. Notice the bold comparative in H. and D., IX. 811 : Nun, ist das Meine meiner als jemals. Such forms as der Deinigste, etc., at the end of letters are rare. Leiber is a comparative of leib (adj.), which became a noun very early. Öfterer occurs in Lessing.

SYNTAX OF THE NUMERALS.

226. The cardinals, used attributively, are indeclinable now, except ein, eine, ein. The G. and D. of zwei and drei now and then occur still : Zweier Zeugen Mund macht alle Wahrheit kund (Prov.). (Here „zweier" shows the case; zwei Zeugen Mund would not be clear.) Zähle von eins bis hundert.

1. To express the year the cardinal is merely added to „im Jahr(e)" or to „in," as im Jahre achtzehn hundert ein und achtzig, or shorter, in 1813. The cardinal shows the year, the ordinal the month: Göthe starb den 22ten März 1832. Hannover, den (1.) ersten August 1881. The ordinals used only attributively, see **211**.

2. The time is expressed in various ways. Answering to such questions as: Wieviel Uhr ist es, welche Zeit ist es or haben wir? wie ist es an der Zeit? we say : Es ist zwölf vorbei, aber noch nicht eins. Es ist ein Viertel drei or auf drei, or ein Viertel nach (über) zwei (all mean a quarter past two). Es ist drei Viertel drei or auf

drei or ein Viertel vor drei, = a quarter of three. Es ist halb zwölf, = half past eleven, on the same principle as viertehalb (see **229**). We can say: 20 Minuten nach zehn (past ten), zwanzig vor zehn (of ten). Der Zug fährt 3 Uhr 20 Minuten nachmittags ab. Wir wollen uns um fünf treffen.

227. Used substantively the cardinals are more frequently inflected, having a plural in -e (see **429**) and a dative in -en (see **79**): Es waren ihrer fünf(e), zwölf(e).

1. Colloquially this -e is very commonly used as far as 19 incl., even when the figure itself be meant, which stands in the feminine singular: Diese Acht(e) ist nicht gut gemacht. Diese Neun(e) steht schief. Elf ist die Sünde. Elfe überschreitet die zehn Gebote (Sch.).

2. Die Million, die Billion, die Milliarde are regular nouns, and, unlike hundert and tausend, stand in the plural after the cardinals, e. g., drei Millionen, but fünf hundert, sechs tausend. Das Hundert, das Tausend are common nouns, pl.: Hunderte + hundreds, Tausende + thousands: e. g., zu Hunderten, a hundred at a time; bei Hunderttausenden die Menschen drücken (Le.).

228. „Beide" corresponds to Eng. "both" in form and use: Ist das Pferd an beiden Augen blind? It may have the definite article before it: die beiden Kühe, "both the cows."

1. The singular beid- means "either," "each" (of two). Beides läßt sich hören = either statement is reasonable; das Abendmahl unter beider Gestalt, the communion in either form; but the masc. and fem. are archaic. Denn zu einem großen Manne gehört beides: Kleinigkeiten als Kleinigkeiten und wichtige Dinge als wichtige Dinge zu behandeln (Le.). Beides has supplanted beide, *beidiu* (pl.), which are still common in the 16th and 17th centuries. Notice beides — und = both — and. Beides, ein löblicher König und mächtiger Schwinger der Lanze (Bü.).

229. 1. Peculiar are the compounds of the ordinals with halb following them and selb preceding them: Viert(e)halb (3½), neunt(e)halb (8½), meaning das vierte nur halb or weniger ein halb, das neunte nur halb. Dreizehntehalb Faß = 12 Faß aber das 13te nur halb. Ags., Icelandic, Danish, and L. G. have the same forms, though in the two latter "half" precedes the ordinal. It does not go back to O. H. G. Selbander = er(selbst) der zweite, two of them; selbdreizehnt, himself the 13th, thirteen of them (G.); selbbritt, selbviert generally uninflected. Selbst zwanzigster (Le.). The cardinal is not common, but Lessing has „ſelb fünfziger." This composition is more common than halb- in the modern dialects.

2. Notice also the cardinals in -er, as in ben fünfziger Jahren—either "from 1850-60" or "from 50-60 years old." It is now classical. This -er occurs in the names of the unit, ten, etc.: ber Einer, ber Zehner, etc. See 507, 1. Zu zweit, britt also occur for zu zweien, breien.

SYNTAX OF THE PRONOUNS.

Syntax of the Personal Pronoun.

230. 1. Du, sg., ihr, pl., are used in familiar intercourse in the family and among intimate friends, in addressing God, in sermons, in solemn discourses and in poetry. Ex.: Kennſt du das Land, wo die Citronen blühn? (G.). Blinder, alter Vater! du kannſt den Tag der Freiheit nicht mehr ſch a u e n ; du ſollſt ihn h ö r e n (Sch.). Erhab'ner Geiſt, du gabſt mir, gabſt mir alles, warum ich bat (F. 3218).

2. Sie, 3. p. pl., is used everywhere else, even among relatives in some families; also when grown children address the parents: Wo wohnen Sie, wenn ich fragen darf?

<small>3. This peculiar use of Sie sprang up early in the 18th century. It is due, no doubt, to the use of the singular Er and Sie in address, which were the height of politeness in the 17th century. Er and Sie are due to the use of Herr and Frau in direct address. In Chamisso's „Peter Schlemihl" the gray-coat always addresses Peter with „ber Herr," e.g., „Möge der Herr meine Zudringlichkeit entſchuldigen . . . ich habe eine Bitte an ihn." Herr, Frau, Ihre Gnaden, Eure Excellenz, Seine Majeſtät were followed by the "plural of majesty" (see 311, 2): Herr Doktor wurden da katechiſiert (F. 3524). Fürs erſte wollen Seine Majeſtät, daß die Arme'e ohn' Aufſchub Böhmen räume (Sch.). Herr was reduced to mere „er" as early as M. H. G., e.g., er Sigfrid ; in the 16th century, „Werter er Pfarrer." This form encouraged the use of the pronoun er in direct address.

4. Ihr, in addressing one person, was early very respectful and has maintained itself in the drama, except in comedy, to this day, and might be called the "stage-address," and is due to Eng. and Fr. influence. See Schiller's Maria Stuart.</small>

231. The gradation as to politeness and etiquette now is about as follows: 1. For princes and all persons of high standing, Ihre Gnaden, Eure Excellenz, Eure Majeſtät, with the verb in the pl. 2. Sie, addressing one or more persons, verb always in the pl., e.g., dürfte ich Sie begleiten? 3. Ihr, pl. of du, and Ihr in the drama addressing one or more persons, *e. g.*, Spät kommt Ihr, doch Ihr kommt (Sch.). See F. 981, 988. 4. Er, Sie, addressing one person, now rare. 5. Du, ihr, as in **230**, 1.

232. The genitive of the pronouns of the 1. and 2. persons stands very rarely after nouns. Goethe has it once, „mein, des Geognost'sten," "of me the geognost," but it is common as the object of verbs, after adjectives and numerals: Ich bitt' euch, nehmt euch meiner an (F. 1875). The uninflected possessive mein, dein are by some interpreted as predicate genitives, *e. g.*, der Becher ist dein (Sch.). As it is much more probable that the possessive adjectives were used as genitives of the personal pronoun than *vice versa*, this interpretation is hardly correct. (See **441**, *a*.)

233. The personal pronouns always accompany the verb. In the imperative „Sie" always stands, but du and ihr only for emphasis: Liebet eure Feinde (B.). Bleiben Sie gefälligst. See F. 1908.

1. In poetry, colloquially, and in merchants' letters the pronoun is often not put: Bin weder Fräulein, weder schön, kann ungeleitet nach Hause gehn (F. 2608). See F. 3429. Ihr Wertes (viz., Schreiben) vom 18ten dieses (viz., Monats), habe empfangen. Notice the set phrases bitte, I pray; danke, thank you; geschweige (conjunction, "say nothing of"), before which ich has to be supplied. Thut nichts, der Jude wird verbrannt (Le.), no matter, the Jew ...

2. Colloquially the subject, if a noun, may be repeated in the shape of a pronoun, as in Eng.: der Kirchhof, er liegt wie am Tage (G.). See **244**, 3.

234. The pronouns of the third person have demonstrative and determinative force. (Compare the cognate Latin *is, ea, id*.) Hence if they refer to lifeless objects or abstract nouns, they rarely stand in the G. and D. cases, but they are supplanted by the regular demonstrative pronouns or, if governed by prepositions, by da(r), hin, her + the preposition. Ex.: Dem Liebchen keinen Gruß! Ich will davon nichts hören (F. 2104). Habt euch vorher wohl präpariert (F. 1958). Allein ich glaub', du hältst nicht viel davon (viz., von der Religion) (F. 3418).

1. Also es (A.) is thus supplanted, when referring to an individual object: Wo liegt Paris? ... Den Finger drauf (not auf es) das nehmen wir (Arndt). Nenn's Glück! Herz! Liebe! Gott! ich habe keinen Namen dafür (F. 3455–6), Kennst du London? Besuche dasselbe jedenfalls.

Concord of Pronoun and Noun.

235. The pronoun of the third person agrees with the noun which it represents in gender and number. The concord of the pronoun with the natural and grammatical gender has been treated, see **165, 166**; also the neuter sg. es representing a plural and any gender, see **168**.

On the use of „es".

236. 1. Es is the *indefinite* subject of impersonal verbs denoting states of the weather and other natural phenomena, *e. g.*, es regnet, donnert, blitzt, schneit, hagelt, es hat gegla'tteist, es tagt, es wintert, es dunkelt, dämmert, taut, etc.

2. Es is made the *indefinite* subject of verbs, not really impersonal: Es schlägt elf; es brennt, es klopft, klingelt, es geht los, läutet; also in the passive and reflexive: es wird getanzt, gesungen, gespielt; compare man tanzt, man ruft. Es geht, spielt sich hier gut = it is good walking, playing here. Wohin soll es nun gehn (F. 2051).

a. Such an es is used by poets to give a vague, mysterious, ghostly impression. Schiller's „Taucher," Goethe's „Hochzeitlied" and „Totentanz" are full of them: Und als er im willigen Schlummer lag, bewegt es sich unter dem Bette (G.). The es (treated so far) except in the passive and reflexive verb-forms cannot be omitted like, for instance, the expletive „es" sub 3, 5.

3. Es is made the *grammatical* subject of a verb, when the *logical* subject follows later: Es zogen drei Bursche wohl über den Rhein (Uh.). Es schritt ihm frisch zur Seite der blühende Genoß (Uh.). See F. 3490-1; 3674-77.

The logical subject cannot be another pronoun, *e g.*, es war ich, es waren Sie, as in Eng. "it was I," "it was you," which is a late construction.

a. In ballads and other folk-lore this es is not required and inversion is still possible, as was the rule in O. H. G., without es at the head of the sentence. For after all, es was here used not merely to denote an indefinite subject, but to account for an inversion which had no apparent cause. It is an "*expletive*" and superfluous as soon as any other part of the sentence stands at the head bringing about the inversion. It is oftenest translated by "there." German tales begin „Es war einmal . . . ", "There was once ... ". Sah ein Knab' ein Röslein stehn (G.). Stellt' ein Knabe sich mir an die Seite (id.). The construction ich bin es, Ihr seid es, "you are it," as in Ags. and as English-speaking children still say, is already the rule in O. H. G. Nor can we say in German „ich bin er" and „Sie sind er," but ich bin es, das bin ich, der bin ich, ich bin derjenige, welcher ..., I am he who ...

4. Peculiar is the impersonal „es giebt," "there are" or "is," which is not a very old phrase, but rare in M. H. G., in which es with pl. verb was even possible.

„Es" is here the indefinite subject and has taken the place of the more definite „das" or a noun, which "gave," "furnished," "produced" a certain thing. Hence „es giebt" is always followed by the accusative: „es giebt Schläge," "Somebody is giving or will give somebody a whipping." Ei, da gab's westfäl'schen Schinken (Scheffel). „Es giebt" is not well followed by a noun in the sg. denoting one object or individual, e. g., Es giebt hier einen Hund, but by nouns in the pl., by abstract and material nouns: Es giebt keinen Zufall (Sch.). See F. 1118.

5. Es is used as the subject of impersonal verbs followed by an objective personal pronoun (D. or A.), denoting states of mind and body: Es dürstet mich, es hungert ihn, es reut mich, es ist ihm bange.

If the objective pronoun or any other part of speech precede the verb, es is not necessary, but it may be retained. Ex.: Ich schwöre euch zu, mir ist's als wie ein Traum (F. 2040). Dir wird gewiß einmal bei deiner Gottähnlichkeit bange (F. 2050). Mir ist schlecht zu mute, "I do not feel well."

6. Es stands further as indefinite predicate and as indefinite object. See **204**. In diesem Sinne kannst du's wagen (F. 1671). See further, F. 2012–14; 2080. Sie meint, du seist entflohn; und halb und halb bist du es schon (F. 3331–2).

In the last illustration and in similar ones es, if translated at all, may be rendered by "so": Sie sind wohl müde? O nein, aber ich bin es gewesen, = I was (so).

Syntax of the Reflexive Pronoun.

237. The reflexive pronoun always refers to the subject: Es ist der Lohn der Demut, die sich selbst bezwungen (Sch.). Die hat sich jegliches erlaubt (id.).

1. The dative was already lost in O. H. G. In M. H. G. the use of
fich as dative is very rare. Luther's Bible is still full of the dative of the
personal pronoun for the reflexive, e. g , Die Heiden, da fie das Gefetz nicht
haben, find (fie) ihnen felbft ein Gefetz. Die Weisheit läffet ihr fagen, = wisdom
will take advice. Gott fchuf den Menfchen ihm zum Bilde. Lessing has: Wer
fich Knall und Fall ihm felbft zu leben nicht entfchließen kann, der lebet anderer Sklav'
auf immer. But this „ihm" stands also because there is already one fich. It
is very rare in the classics and does not occur in the spoken language.

2. Selbft, felber strengthens the reflexive pronoun and prevents its confounding with the reciprocal. For examples see above. But felbft (felber)
is far from as common as the Eng. self (selves).

Syntax of the Reciprocal Pronoun.

238. As such are used uns, euch, fich, both in the accusative
and dative: Und (fie) nickten fich (D.) zu und grüßten fich (A.)
freundlich im Spiegel (H. and D., VII. 42). Wenn fich die Fürften
befehden, müffen die Diener fich morden und töten (Sch.).

But if any ambiguity arises, as is frequently the case, the unvarying
form einander or the inflected einer (der eine) den andern referring to masc.
nouns, die eine die andere referring to fem. nouns, die einen die andern pl. of
both, are used instead of them and even, though tautologically, in addition
to them. Ex.: und lieben uns unter einander (B.). Sie fpotten der eine des andern.

Syntax of the Possessive Pronouns.

239. The possessive pronoun used adjectively agrees with
the noun like any other adjective. See **212**. The uninflected
forms mein, dein, fein stand in the predicate and can be subjects
only when used as nouns with or without the article, e. g.,
Mein und Dein ift alles Zankes Urfprung (Prov.).

1. Standing in the predicate, therefore, it is right to say: Das Buch
ift mein, meines, das meine, das meinige. As subjects referring to das Buch:
Meines, das meine, das meinige ift verloren, = mine is lost.

2. Care should be taken that the right possessive be used when persons are addressed with Sie, du, ihr (Ihr). Ihr refers to Sie, dein to du,
euer (Euer) to ihr (Ihr), e. g., Sie haben Ihre Frau Mutter verloren? Wohin

wird dich deine Vermessenheit noch führen? Durch des Mannes Übermut, den Ihr durch Euer Brautgemach zum Throne geführt (Sch.).

240. Of der, die, das meine (der, die, das meinige), when used substantively, der, die Meine, pl. die Meinen (with capital letters), denote persons, viz., friends, relatives, etc.; das Meine or das Meinige denote my property, duty, share, deserts.

Ex.: Der Herr kennet die Seinen (B.). Sie hat das Ihrige erhalten (her dowry). Kardinal! Ich habe das Meinige gethan. Thun Sie das Ihre (Sch.). Diesen Morgen, als ich Sie im Kreise der Ihrigen fand . . . (id.). „Ganz der Ihrige," „die Deinige," „die Deine" are proper letter-endings.

241. The possessive pronoun must be repeated like the article with nouns of different gender: Sein hoher Gang, seine edle Gestalt, seines Mundes Lächeln, seiner Augen Gewalt . . . (F. 3395–8).

242. 1. As sein and ihr are both reflexive (referring to the subject of the sentence) and non-reflexive (referring to another noun) an ambiguity may arise, which should be avoided by using the demonstrative pronouns instead; either dessen, deren always preceding, or desselben, derselben either preceding or following the noun. Ex.: Roland ritt hinterm Vater her mit dessen Schild und Schwerte (Uh.). „Mit seinem Schild" would have meant Roland's shield. Compare the following lines of the same poem, in which ihm prevents ambiguity: R. ritt hinterm Vater her und trug ihm seinen starken Speer zusamt dem festen Schilde. Compare Frau N. N. ging mit der Haushälterin und ihrer Nichte nach dem Markte, *i. e*, Mrs. N. N.'s niece; but mit der Haushälterin und deren Nichte, *i. e.*, the housekeeper's niece. Es eifre jeder seiner (the father's) unbestochenen, von Vorurteilen freien Liebe nach (Le.).

2. The possessive of the 3. person is in the people's language often repeated for emphasis after a genitive of possession and also after a dative: „Meinem Vetter sein Garten." Comp. "John his mark." This is not to be imitated though it occur now and then in the classics and quite frequently in the 18th century: Auf der Fortuna ihrem Schiff (Sch.); des Illo seinem Stuhl (id.). Ihr artet mehr nach eures Vaters Geist als nach der Mutter ihrem (id.). See **180, 4.**

3. The definite article cannot precede the attributive possessive pronoun. Jener, dieser and such adjectives as obgedachter, erwähnter seemingly do, but such constructions as dieser dein Sohn, obgedachter mein Schreiber are rather appositional.

243. 1. By a license the possessives lose inflectional endings in such set phrases as occur in Jch möchte brum mein Tag nicht lieben (F. 2920). Mein Lebtag benf' ich bran (Sch.). Hab' ich bich boch mein Tage nicht gefehen (F. 4440). These phrases are in the transition stage to adverbs and the apostrophe may stand or not.

2. Sein is in proverbs and in one phrase „feiner Zeit" = "in due time," "in — time," still used for the feminine ihr, a remnant of the earlier periods, when ihr could not be used as the reflexive possessive: Sein Thor kennt jebe Kuh (Prov.). Untreue schlägt seinen eigenen Herrn (Prov.). „Seiner Zeit" is an adverbial genitive, in which feiner has become non-reflexive so that it apparently stands at times for ihrer, unseres, etc. Reflexive: „Alles Ding währt seine Zeit" (Hymn); but non-reflexive: Sie war seiner Zeit (once) eine große Sängerin.

Compare the relation of Eng. "his" and "its." The latter sprang up in Shakspere's time. "Its" is the genitive of "it." In Sh. "his" stands frequently where later "its" is used.

3. The use of the German definite article where in Eng. the possessive is used, is by no means as strict and as common in the spoken language as the grammarians would have us believe. Take for instance: Mein armer Kopf ist mir verrückt. Mein armer Sinn ist mir zerstückt (F., I. 3383–6). Solang ich mich noch frisch auf meinen Beinen fühle, genügt mir dieser Knotenstock (F. 3838–9). See **154**.

In the 17th century „fich" was used also for all persons. "Simplicissimus" is full of this misuse.

Syntax of the Demonstrative Pronoun.

244. Der, die, das, always accented, points out without reference to nearness in time or space. It is generally well translated by "that," also by "this," and by a personal pronoun.

Ex.: Dem Volke hier (this) wird jeder Tag ein Fest (F. 2162). Aber, wie ich mich sehne dich zu schauen, habe ich vor dem (that) Menschen (Mephistopheles) ein heimlich Grauen (F. 3480–1). O glücklich der (he), den ihr belehrt! F. 1981). Der (for her) hab' ich die Freude verbittert (Bo.). Wehe dem, der Voltair(en)s Schriften überhaupt nicht mit dem skeptischen Geist liest, in welchem er einen Teil derselben geschrieben (Le.).

1. The genitives des, dessen, deren sg. fem., derer and deren, pl., are used substantively as follows:

SYNTAX OF THE DEMONSTRATIVE PRONOUN.

a. Des is archaic, but occurs in compounds like deshalb, deswegen, dergestalt, etc., *e. g.*, Des freut sich das entmenschte Paar (Sch.). Wir sind der keines wert, das wir bitten (Lu.), We are worthy of none of those (things), etc.

b. Dessen, deren G. sg. fem. and G. pl., are used when they have the force of possessives (see **242**).

c. The present usage favors derer, G. pl., referring to persons and deren, dessen referring to things. But the classics do not agree with this. Generally these forms are antecedents of relative pronouns. Ex.: Jetzo sag' mir das Ende derer, die von Troja kehrten (G.). Hat das Kind schon Zähne? Es hat deren vier. Dort sieht man die Güter derer (of the gentlemen, lords) von Webeloh.

2. The lengthened forms in -en and -er sprang up as early as the 15th century both in the article and in the pronoun. Luther has „denen," D. pl., but the short genitives „des" and „der." In the 18th century they lost -er and -en again, owing, no doubt, to the desire of distinguishing between article and demonstrative, and between the substantive and adjective uses of the latter. Goethe has still „und von denen Menschen die sie besonders schätzen." Present usage, however, requires the short forms of the pronoun, when used adjectively.

3. Notice the frequent emphatic force of the pronoun, *e. g.*, Vom Rechte, das mit uns geboren ist, von dem ist leider nie die Frage (F. 1978-9).

Dieser, jener.

245. Dieser points out what is near in time and space, jener what is remoter. Dieser is "the latter," jener, "the former." They are used substantively and adjectively: Dieses junge Frauenzimmer hat Gefühl und Stimme (Le.). Dieser will's trocken, was jener feucht begehrt. Dies Blatt hier — dieses willst du geltend machen? (Sch.).

1. Das, dies like es, but less frequently, can be the indefinite subjects of neuter verbs. See **236**. *E. g.*, Das ist die Magd des Nachbars. Das ist ein weiser Vater, der sein eigen Kind kennt (Sch.). Dies ist die Art mit Herren umzugehn (F. 2518).

2. Dies und das, dies und jenes have the force of „irgend ein," *e. g.*, Wir sind nicht mehr beim ersten Glas, drum denken wir gern an dies und das (Song). Und er streckte als Knabe die Hände nicht aus nach diesem und jenem (H. and D. V. 64).

3. Dieser is strengthened by hier; der, jener and das by da, *e. g.*, Mit dem da werden Sie nicht fertig (Sch.). Jener, in the sense of "the other" and

" to come," „in jener Zeit", in jenem Leben. Shakspere's Gespenst kömmt wirklich aus jener Welt (Le.).

246. When not referring to persons hier + preposition may take the place of dieser, and da + preposition the place of der and jener, *e. g.*, Wer sonst ist schuld daran als ihr in Wien? (Sch.). Davon schweigt des Sängers Höflichkeit (?). Hiernach (according to this) muß die Lesart eine ganz andere gewesen sein.

1. Notice the two strong forms in Lessing's Alles dieses, seine Erfindungen und die historischen Materialien, knetet er denn in einen fein langen, fein schwer zu fassenden Roman zusammen. For an das, was ..., von dem, was ... no daran was ..., davon was ... should be substituted, though this is done colloquially. „Wir dachten daran, was du jetzt anfangen würdest" is not elegant.

247. D e r –, d i e –, d a s j e n i g e is generally used substantively followed by a relative clause or a genitive. Used adjectively it stands for der, die, das when a relative clause follows, *e. g.*, diejenigen Menschen, welche ... The best usage accents der, die, das. Used adjectively it has only medium stress.

Ex.: Diejenigen der Knaben, welche ihre Aufgaben nicht gemacht hatten, mußten nachsitzen (stay after school). Liebet diejenigen, welche euch verfolgen (B.).

248. D e r –, d i e –, d a s s e l b e denotes identity. It refers to something known or mentioned. It is used equally well substantively or adjectively. It can be strengthened by „eben": Mit aller Treue verwend' ich eure Gaben; der Dürftige soll sich derselben erfreuen (H. and D. II., 74–5).

1. Der nämliche also denotes identity, but is not written as one word. „Derselbige" is rarer than derselbe. War das nicht der Dienstmann (porter), der die Auswanderer betrogen hat? Der nämliche.

2. Selbig without der is rare, *e. g.*, Selbiges weiß ich gewiß (Heyse).

249. S e l b, s e l b e r, s e l b s t distinguishes one object from another. It strengthens personal and reflexive pronouns. It is made emphatic by eben, also in the phrase ein(er) und derselbe. Selber and selbst do not differ in meaning, but in use. Selber is never made an adverb as ſelbſt is. Selber always follows the word it qualifies, though it need not stand necessarily directly after it: Ich ſelber or ſelbſt habe ihn geſehen. Wer zweifelt Nathan, daß ihr nicht (see **309, 2**) die Ehrlichkeit, die Großmut ſelber ſeid? (Le.) Wer andern eine Grube gräbt, fällt ſelbſt hinein (Prov.).

1. Selbſt has become also an adverb with the force of „ſogar," and then stands best at the beginning of the sentence, unaccented: Selbſt ein ſo himmliſches Paar (viz., Psyche and Amor) fand nach der Verbindung ſich ungleich (G.).

2. Notice the compounds daſelbſt, hie(r)ſelbſt, in that or this very place; also the force of „von ſelbſt" in: Die Mühle geht nicht von ſelbſt (of its own accord).

For ſelb with ordinals see **229**. Alone it is very rare, *e. g.*, weil er in ſelbem (im Pala'ſte) alle um ſich verſammelt hatte (Le.).

250. S o l ch means + " such." It describes what is pointed out. It is used adjectively and substantively: Hilfreiche Mächte! einen ſolchen (Weg) zeigt mir an, den ich vermag zu gehen (Sch.). Wo war die Überlegung, als wir . . . ſolche Macht gelegt in ſolche Hand (id.).

1. The use of ſolch for the personal pronoun or der–, die–, daſſelbe is not good although found now and then in the classics, *e. g.*, Als ſie die Moos- hütte erreichten, fanden ſie ſolche auf das luſtigſte (see **300, 2**) ausgeſchmückt (G.).

2. For ſolch ein, ſo ein is a frequent equivalent. It is more common in the spoken language than ſolch ein. Lessing and Goethe are very fond of it, *e. g.*, So ein Dichter iſt Shakſpere und Shakſpere faſt ganz allein (Le.). Ich kann mich nicht, wie ſo ein Wortheld, ſo ein Tugendſchwätzer, an meinem Willen wär- men und Gedanken (Sch.).

„So ein" does not come from „ſolch ein," but from ein ſo before adjective and noun: „ein ſo hoher Turm" — „ſo ein hoher Turm," then „ſo ein Turm."

Syntax of the Interrogative Pronoun.

251. Wer, + " who," " which," and was, + " what," are used substantively only: Was kümmert es die Löwin, der man die Jungen raubt, in weſſen Walde ſie brüllt (Le.). Nun, wen lieben zwei von euch am meisten (id.). Was ist der langen Rede kurzer Sinn? (Sch.).

1. Once the genitive after wer and was was common. Wer is almost entirely supplanted by welcher, and was by was für ein. But was + genitive, which generally looks like an accusative, still remains in phrases like Was Wunder(s) (Le.). Was des Teufels, Was Henkers. Was ist Weißes dort am grünen Walde (G.). See 181, 188.

2. Wem only refers to persons. When it refers to things or whole sentences wo(r) + preposition is substituted. Wozu der Lärm? (F. 1322). Woran erkennst du den Dieb. Wor before a vowel, wo before a consonant.

3. In the spoken language „was" is preceded by a preposition that does not govern the accusative: zu was, mit was; but womit, wozu are preferable. The classics have it too. Even für was, um was, durch was are supplanted by wofür, worum, wodurch. Zu was die Posse? (G.) Mit was kann ich aufwarten?

4. Was in the sense of warum and wie is originally an absolute accusative, e. g., Was steht ihr und legt die Hände in (= in den) Schoß (Sch.). Was wird das Herz dir schwer (F. 2720).

5. Mark the interrogative adverbs: wo, + where; wann, + when; wie, + how; wo(r)- with preposition; warum, + wherefore, + why, only interrogative. For their etymology see 551.

252. Welch means + "which" and singles out the individual, though etymologically it inquires after the quality. It stands adjectively and substantively: Und welcher ist's, den du am meisten liebst? (Sch.). Welches Ungeheure sinnet ihr mir an? (id.).

In exclamatory sentences welch is originally interrogative, often followed by ein: Welch ein Jubeln, welch ein Singen wird in unserm Hause sein! (Song). See F. 742.

253. Was für, was für ein inquires after the nature and qualities of a person or thing. Was für always stands adjectively, was für ein adjectively and substantively. Was is separable from für ein. Lessing is particularly fond of this separation. Was für stands before the singular of a noun denoting material and before a collective noun; before the plural of any noun. Was für ein inquires also after an individual.

Ex.: Was für Wein ist dies? Was für Berge . . . trennen uns benn noch? (Le.). Was in Babylon ich bir für einen schönen Stoff gekauft (id.).

Syntax of the Relative Pronouns.

254. There being no original relative pronouns, the other pronouns were used as such or conjunctions like *so, dar, da, unde* (see below) connected coordinate sentences, one of which later became subordinate. The first pronoun used as a relative was ber, bie, bas, in O. H. G. Welcher, wer, was developed into relative pronouns gradually. First they were made indefinite pronouns by means of the particle *so*, O. H. G. *so hwelich(so), so hwer(so), so hwas(so)* > M. H. G. *swelich, swer, swas* = whosoever, whatsoever > N. H. G. welcher, wer, was, which can be strengthened by nur, auch, immer (= ever). To say therefore that the interrogative is used as the relative is hardly correct, though, no doubt, the indirect question had its influence in the coincidence of the forms of the interrogative and indefinite relative pronouns. The demonstrative ber, bie, bas introduced the coordinate clause, which afterwards became subordinate; and clause and pronoun were then called *relative*. Welcher is only of the 16th century.

255. Der and welcher are equivalent. After personal pronouns ber is preferable. Euphony should decide which is to be used. Ein Frauenzimmer, das benkt, ist eben so ekel als ein Mann, der sich schminkt (Le.). Welcher is preferable after derjenige. The following sentence is bad: Die, die die Mutter der Kinder war, ist gestorben.

1. Of the four relatives ber, welch-, wer, was only welch- can also be used adjectively, the other three only substantively. The genitive of ber, bie, bas is always bessen, beren, sg. and pl., never berer. Ex.: Wer kein Gesetz achtet, ist eben so mächtig als wer kein Gesetz hat (Le.) Am Montag, an welchem Tage wir abreisten . . . But this is not very elegant.

256. Der and welcher will take any antecedent soever. But wer, was, having sprung from indefinite and compounded pronouns, require none. Wer admits of no antecedent at all; was may have any other neuter pronoun, an adjective (preferably in the superlative), or a whole clause, *e. g.*, Für was brein geht und nicht brein (ins Gehirn) geht, ein prächtig Wort zu

dienſten ſteht (F. 1952–3). Alles was iſt, iſt vernünftig (Hegel). Was du ererbt von deinen Vätern haſt, erwirb es um es zu beſitzen (F. 682–3). Dem Herrlichſten, was auch der Geiſt empfangen, drängt immer fremd und fremder Stoff ſich an (F. 634–5).

 1. Er, wer; der Mann wer; der, wer are impossible. But Goethe has (in the "Walpurgisnacht"), F. 3964: So Ehre dem, wem Ehre gebührt. The proverb says: „Ehre, dem Ehre gebührt," the Bible „Ehre, dem die Ehre gebührt."

 2. Was referring to a substantive and welches referring to a whole clause are not present usage, though the classics use them so. Die Alten kannten das Ding nicht, was wir Höflichkeit nennen (Le.). Von früher Jugend an hatte mir und meiner Schweſter der Vater ſelbſt im Tanzen Unterricht gegeben, welches einen ſo ernſthaften Mann wunderlich genug hätte kleiden ſollen (G.).

 3. If wer has a seeming antecedent the latter stands after the clause. The antecedent is nothing but the subject of the main clause repeated for emphasis in the shape of another pronoun. If, however, wer and its seeming antecedent do not stand in the same case, the latter is indispensable. Ex.: Wer Pech angreift beſudelt ſich (Prov.). Wer über gewiſſe Dinge den Verſtand nicht verliert, der hat keinen zu verlieren (Le.). Wer vieles bringt, wird manchem etwas bringen (F. 97). But Wer ein Mal lügt, dem glaubt man nicht und wenn er auch die Wahrheit ſpricht (Prov.). Wer da hat, dem wird gegeben (B.). The same is true of was: Was man nicht weiß, das eben brauchte man und was man weiß, kann man nicht brauchen (F. 1066–7). Früh übt ſich, was ein Meiſter werden will (Sch.). For the gender in this illustration see **168**.

 4. The old short form wes is now archaic except in **weshalb, weswegen**: Wes Brot ich eſſe, des Lied ich ſinge (Prov.).

257. If the dative and accusative, governed by a preposition, do not refer to a person, wo, now rarely da, with that preposition, are generally substituted: Nichts iſt Zufall; am wenigſten das, wovon die Abſicht ſo klar in die Augen leuchtet (Le.).

 1. So, the oldest relative conjunction, has now been crowded out from the spoken language, though it was very common in the 16th and 17th centuries: Die linke Hand, dazu das Haupt, ſo er ihm abgehauen (Uh.). Von allen, ſo da kamen (Bü.).

258. The relative adverbs wo, "where" and da (colloquially); da, wann, wenn, wo, "when"; wie, "as" take the place of a relative pronoun governed by a preposition when they refer to nouns denoting time, place, and manner.

Ex.: Kennſt du das Land wo die Citronen blühn? (G.). Es gibt im Menſchenleben Augenblicke, wo er dem Weltgeiſt näher iſt als ſonſt (Sch.). In dieſem Augenblicke, da wir reden, iſt kein Tyra'nn mehr in der Schweizer Laude (id.). „Die Art und Weiſe wie," "the manner in which." („Wie" is more forcible than „in welcher.") O ſchöner Tag, wenn endlich der Soldat ins Leben heimkehrt (Sch.).

1. This construction is old only with the demonstrative adverbs used as relatives, viz., *da, dâr, danne.* Allwo, allda, woſelbſt are archaic.

Syntax of the Indefinite Pronouns.

259. Ein and einige can precede a numeral generally followed by a noun. They mean "some," "or so," "odd": ein acht Tage, a week or so; einige vierzig Jahr, forty odd years. The order may also be: „ein Jahr fünfzehn."

1. Grimm thinks this phrase has lost „ober," as if it meant einen Tag ober zehn, ein Jahr ober fünfzehn. No doubt „einige vierzig Jahr" has lost „und" and stands for einige und vierzig Jahr, forty (and) odd years.

260. Ein, etwas, was, wer, jemand, welche, einige can be strengthened by irgend (compounded of *io + hwar* and *gin =* "ever," "where," "you please," *gin* corresponding to L. *-cun*). For the origin of was, wer, welch, see **254.** Ach, wenn ich etwas auf dich könnte! "if I could influence you at all (F. 3423). Was anders ſuche zu beginnen (F. 1383). Die Jagd iſt doch immer was und eine Art von Krieg (G.). Hier ſind Kirſchen zu verkaufen. Willſt du welche? Haſt du irgend was verloren?

1. They stand generally only in the nominative and accusative. Einig is rare in the singular, and for it irgend ein is better used.

261. All-. The following examples show the many various forms of all-: all das Geld, all des Geldes, alles das Geld, was ſoll das alles?

1. Alle stood in M. H. G. only after prepositions as still now, *e. g.*, bei alle bem, "withal." Mir wird von alle dem so dumm (F. 1946). The form alle before the article and not preceded by a preposition, though very common in the classics and in the spoken language, is not so good as all or all with strong endings, *e. g.*, All der Schmerz (G.). All or alle in such phrases as der Wein ist all, "there is no more wine," has hardly been satisfactorily explained yet.

2. Notice the following meanings: Alle Stunden einen Theelöffel voll, "a teaspoon full every hour." The singular in the sense of "every" is rarer, auf allen Fall, in every case. Aller Anfang ist schwer (Prov.). Alles Ding währt seine Zeit, Gottes Lieb in Ewigkeit (Hymn). The singular in the sense of Eng. "all" is archaic, allen Winter (Logau, quoted in Grimm's Dict.), all winter. For all day, all night, we say best die ganze Nacht, den ganzen Tag. Notice also in aller Früh, "very early," in aller Stille, in alle Welt.

3. The plural of jeder, jedweder, jeglicher is rare. It is expressed by „alle." Even the singular of the last two is now archaic and rare.

262. M a n ch e r does not differ from the Eng. "many" in use and force. Compare ein mancher, manch einer, mancher gute Mann, manch ein guter Mann, manche schöne Blume.

263. V i e l and w e n i g, denoting the individual and used substantively denoting persons, must be inflected; if they denote an indefinite number, quantity, mass, they are generally uninflected. Denn viele sind berufen, aber wenige sind auserwählet (B.). Viel noch hast du von mir zu hören (Sch.). Zwar weiß ich viel, doch möchte ich alles wissen (F. 601). Es studieren viel Amerikaner in Deutschland.

1. Vieler, -e, -es denotes "various sorts," *e.g.*, vieler Wein; in composition vielerlei Wein, "many kinds of wine."

A fuller treatment of the large number of indefinite pronouns and numerals belongs rather to the Dictionary.

SYNTAX OF THE VERB.

CLASSIFICATION OF VERBS.

264. According to meaning and construction the verbs may be variously divided: 1, into independent verbs; 2, into the small class of *tense* auxiliaries and the *modal* auxiliaries. See **267**. Again: 1, into *personal* verbs, which can have any person, the 1., 2., or 3., as subject; 2, into *impersonal* verbs, which have the indefinite subject es, „es regnet." See **236**.

The personal verbs again divide: 1, into neuter or subjective verbs, as die Sonne scheint (see **179**); 2, transitive or objective verbs, the direct object of which stands in the accusative (transitive proper, see **198**) or in the genitive or dative (called also intrans., see **184, 190**).

As subdivisions of transitive verbs may be regarded: 1, the reflexive verbs; 2, the causative.

The reflexives again: 1, into reflexives proper, which occur only as reflexives, *e. g.*, sich grämen, to pine; sich erbarmen, to feel pity; 2, into both transitive and intransitive verbs used reflexively, *e. g.*, sich waschen, sich vereinen, sich tot lachen.

The pronoun is always in the accusative, but see **197**.

1. Transitive verbs have often intransitive or neuter force, but there can be no direct object then. Das Pferd zieht den Wagen, but Die Wolken ziehen am Himmel. Personal verbs can also be used without a logical subject: Das Wasser rauscht, but Es rauscht im Rohre. Also the modal auxiliaries occur still as independent verbs: Was soll das? but Wohin soll der Dieb geflüchtet sein? See **267**.

Syntax of the Auxiliaries.

I. Haben and sein.

265. Haben forms the compound tenses, active voice:

1. Of all transitive verbs: ich habe getragen, ich habe bedeckt, ich habe angeklagt.

2. Of the modal auxiliaries, of reflexive and impersonal verbs proper. Er hat es nicht gemocht, hat sich gewaschen, es hat geregnet, es hat mich gereut.

3. Of intransitive verbs which have no direct object, at most the object in the G. or D. Er hatte mein gespottet, er hat mir geschadet, er hatte gelacht, geweint, geschlafen.

4. Of (intransitive) verbs of motion when the mere action within a certain space, the effort, and its extent are to be emphasized, without reference to direction, point of departure or destination. A. von Humboldt hat viel gereist, = was a great traveler. Der Stallknecht hat eine Stunde hin und her geritten. Er hatte in Wien zehn Jahre gefahren (Le.). Das Lämmchen hat gehüpft, der Fisch hat geschwommen. Das Kleine (the little one) hat noch nie gegangen (has never walked). Sophie hat geklettert und sich die Schürze zerrissen. Der Schnellläufer hat schon längst gelaufen (finished running long ago). Good usage favors: Die Uhr hat einmal gegangen, aber jetzt steht sie still. Die Mühle, die Maschine, das Rad hat gegangen, but ist is frequently used.

5. Of sitzen, stehen, liegen, anfangen, beginnen, aufhören. But in S. G. sein is more common and it is also found in the classics. Wo habt ihr gesessen, gestanden? Wann hat die Schule angefangen?

266. Sein forms the compound tenses:

1. Of all verbs of motion, except some, which take haben, when action simply is denoted. See **265**, 4. These take sein when the direction, points of departure, destination and arrival are mentioned. These circumstances are often expressed by inseparable and separable prefixes in compound verbs. Ex.: „Der Mai ist gekommen." Er wird gefallen sein, = he probably fell. Wir sind schnell hinabgestiegen. Die Seefahrer sind auf der Insel Skye gelandet. Die Störche sind nach Süden gezogen. Der Stallknecht ist in einer Stunde hin und her geritten, = he rode to a certain place (there) and back. Die Feinde sind entflohen, entlaufen, eingetroffen. Wir sind schon mehrere Male umgezogen (moved).

2. Of certain verbs denoting a springing into being or passing away, a transition and development, growth and decay, often expressed by er-, ver-, zer-, and separable prefixes. Die Milch ist gefroren (< gefrieren, but es hat gefroren < frieren, there was a frost). Das Seil ist zerrissen. Der Schnee ist geschmolzen. „Der Bruder wäre nicht gestorben." Das Bäumchen ist gewachsen. Die reichen Leute sind im Kriege verarmt. Das Licht ist erloschen. Die Schale ist gesprungen (cracked). Der Lehrling war eingeschlafen (had fallen asleep). In the compound verbs it is just this prefix that called for sein. Compare trinken — ertrinken, scheinen — erscheinen, wachen — erwachen, hungern — verhungern, frieren — erfrieren.

3. Of sein, bleiben, begegnen, folgen, gelingen, geschehen, glücken, for which it is hard to account by meaning, but see **283**, 2. Ex.: Es ist ihm nicht gelungen, geglückt. Das ist schon alles dagewesen. Ein süßer Trost ist ihm geblieben (Sch.).

4. Haben has gained upon sein in German, but not so much as English "to have" upon "to be." Folgen and begegnen were once generally compounded with haben. Also the tendency to use intransitive verbs as transitives, so strong in Eng., has increased in German. While in Eng. one can "run" a locomotive, a sewing machine, a train, a ship, in German führen, leiten, in Gang bringen, gebrauchen, or the verb of motion + lassen or machen, will have to be used. Der Kutscher hat uns schnell gefahren. Der Postillion hat den Wagen vorgefahren. Man konnte die Feuerspritze nicht in Gang bringen.

5. The difficulty as to the use of haben and sein lies after all mainly in the way in which a verb is used, transitively or intransitively, and in the meaning. The student should attend particularly to these points and not be too timid, as in many cases usage is by no means settled.

As to the omission of haben and sein in dependent clauses, see **346**.

II. Special Uses of the Modal Auxiliaries.

This subject belongs really rather to the Dictionary, but the appreciation and translation of these verbs is so difficult that a brief treatment of them is given here.

267. 1. Können denotes ability: Der Fisch kann schwimmen. Hier steh' ich, ich kann nicht anders (Lu.). Possibility: Ihr könntet ihr Werkzeug sein, mich in das Garn zuziehen (Sch.). Knowledge, "to know how," its oldest meaning: Kannst du Italie'nisch? Compare können, "to have learnt," then "to be able"; kennen (< *kanjan*, causative of kann—können), "to be acquainted with"; wissen, "to know."

2. Dürfen denotes: 1. Permission and authorization: Du darfst auch

ba nur frei erscheinen (F. 336). Ohne Jagbschein barf niemand auf die Jagd gehn. 2. "To have occasion to," "reason for," "need": Man barf den Schlüssel nur zwei Mal umdrehen und der Riegel springt zurück, "You need . . ." Du barfst hinausgehen, die Luft ist hier sehr schlecht, "You have good reason to go out . . ." This force is the oldest, but rather rare now. 3. "To trust one's self to": Wer barf ihn nennen und wer bekennen: Ich glaub ihn (Gott) (F. 3433–5). This force has sprung from 1 and 2 and from the verb tar — türren + dare, whose meaning was embodied in barf — bürfen. On the other hand, it has nearly given up the original force of "need," "want," still apparent in 2, to its compound bebürfen. In some editions of the Bible bürfen, "to want," and tar — türren, "to dare," are still the rule. In later editions bebürfen and bürfen have been substituted for them. 4. The preterit subjunctive (potential, see **284**, 3) bürfte is used for a mild assertion: Die Nachwelt bürfte Bedenken tragen, dieses Urteil zu unterschreiben (Sch.), "Posterity very likely will . . ." Das bürfte zu spät sein, "I fear very much, that is too late." Etiquette admits such redundant phrases as: Dürfte or barf ich mir erlauben, etc.

3. M ö g e n denotes: 1. In its oldest, but now rare sense except in dialect, "ability" and "power." This it has given up to „können." Compare its cognates "may" and "can" in Eng.: Ihr Anblick gibt den Engeln Stärke, wenn keiner sie ergründen mag (F. 247–8), "although no one is able . . ." 2. Concession, no interference on the part of the speaker: Der Bursche mag nach Hause gehn (It lies with him, I have no objection). Wer mir den Becher kann wieder zeigen, er mag ihn behalten (Sch.). 3. Possibility, the action does not concern or influence the speaker; können means a possibility that lies in the ability of another person or object. Was für Grünröck' mögen das sein (Sch.). Er mag das gesagt haben, er mag das thun, It is possible he said so, he may do it. Das Tier mag zehn Jahre alt sein. With this force it supplants the potential and concessive subjunctives; if it stands itself in the subjunctive of the present or preterit, it supplants also the optative subjunctive. Ich wünsche daß die ganze Welt uns hören mag, hören möge. Möchte auch doch die ganze Welt uns hören (Le.). 4. From 2 springs the force of "inclination," "liking," "wishing." Was sich verträgt mit meiner Pflicht, mag ich ihr gern gewähren (Sch.). Ich möchte, daß er es nicht wieder erführe. Ich esse was ich mag und leide was ich muß (Prov.).

4. M ü s s e n, + must, denotes: 1. In its oldest sense, "to have occasion, room," "to be one's lot," "it is the case." A trace of this is left in the following uses: Mein Hund war ohne Maulkorb hinausgelaufen. Nun mußte auch gerade ein Polizist daher kommen (as luck would have it, a police-

man came along). Der Zufall mußte ihn grade hin bringen. Zum zweiten Mal soll mir fein Klang erschallen, er müßte denn (unless it should) besondern Sinn begründen (G., quoted in Sanders' Dict.). 2. Necessity of various kinds: Alle Menschen müssen sterben. Der Senne muß scheiden (Sch.). Ein Oberhaupt muß sein (id.). Das muß ein schlechter Müller sein, dem niemals fiel das Wandern ein (Song). Er muß sehr krank gewesen sein; er ist noch so schwach. The force of dürfen: Ich muß nicht vergessen, "I must not forget."

    Brauchen + negative generally takes the place of müssen + negative when it denotes moral necessity. Das brauchst du nicht zu thun, wenn du nicht willst. Wohl dem, der mit der neuen (Zeit) nicht mehr braucht zu leben (Sch.).

    5. Sollen, + shall, denotes: 1. Duty and obligation: 'Du sollst Gott deinen Herrn lieben von ganzem Herzen, von ganzer Seele und von ganzem Gemüte (B.). Du hättest da sein sollen, You ought to have been there. 2. Necessity and destiny: Diese Furcht soll endigen! ihr Haupt soll fallen. Ich will Frieden haben (Sch.). Ich weiß nicht was soll es bedeuten (Heine). Was soll das? What (is that) for? Darin sollte er sich täuschen, In that he was bound to be deceived, disappointed. 3. It denotes the statement and claim of another, "is to," "is said to": Das Meter soll acht Thaler kosten. Der Schatz der Nibelungen soll im Rheine liegen. Sieben Sträflinge sollen entkommen sein. 4. Sollte approaches the force of the conditional, + "should." Sollte er noch kommen, sag' ihm, ich hätte nicht länger warten können. Sollte er auch wohl krank sein? Is it possible that he is sick?

    6. Wollen, + will, denotes: 1. The will and purpose of the subject. Was wolltest du mit dem Dolche? sprich (Sch.). Ich will es wieder vergessen, weil Sie doch nicht wollen, daß ich es wissen soll (G.). Wolle nur was du kannst und du wirst können was du willst. 2. "To be about," "on the point of." Ein armer Bauer wollte sterben (Nicolai). Es will regnen. Frequent in stage-directions, „will gehen," „will abgehn." Will sich Hector ewig von mir wenden? (Sch.). 3. The claim and statement of another, who "says" or "claims to": Der Zeuge will den Angeklagten gesehen haben. Du willst ihn zu einem guten Zwecke betrogen haben. Notice the ambiguity of such a sentence as Der Herr will es gethan haben, "claims he did it," or according to 1, "wills or wishes that it be done."

    Wollen is really the most difficult to understand and use. It occurs in a great many more idioms with ever varying shades of meaning. Notice, e. g., Es will verlauten, "it is spread abroad." Was will das sagen? = "What does that amount to?" "that is nothing." Ich will es nicht gesehen haben, I will act as if I had not seen it or "nobody shall see it," according to 1. Wenn der Schüler doch diese Regel lernen wollte, "if he only would . . . = conditional. Wollte Gott daß . . ., would to God that . . . Diese Feder will nicht, this pen does not write (well). But it is impossible to give all these meanings.

Still Eng. "will" is not far behind the German. Sollen and wollen should not be confounded with Eng. "shall" and "will" of the future, see **279, 3.**

7. Laſſen, sometimes classed here, is really a causative auxiliary and never used as such without an inf., which stands as a further object. Keine Klage läßt ſie ſchallen (Sch.). Unverzüglich ließ er drei Batterien aufwerfen (id.). See **202, 1.** A second force is "to allow," "not to hinder." Der Gefangenwärter ließ den Gefangenen entwiſchen. Laſſen Sie das bleiben (= to leave a thing undone. Laſſen, to look, is a neuter verb.

For laſſen + reflexive, see **272**; in the imperative, see **287, 4.**

REMARK.—Verbs of motion can be omitted, particularly when an adverb expresses the direction. Willſt du mit? Ich muß hin. Das Packet ſollte fort (ought to be sent). Der Hut muß in die Schachtel. But all except müſſen and dürfen can be used as independent verbs, i. e., no other verb need be supplied. There is no call for a verb in Was ſoll der Hut? (Sch.), "What is this hat (here) for? Notice that ſollen, mögen, and wollen are really the only ones that deserve the term modal auxiliaries, since they assist in expressing the mood. See **287.**

THE PASSIVE VOICE.

268. The active voice needs no comment. Only transitive verbs form a complete passive. But transitives whose meaning admits only of an object of the thing, also intransitives and subjective verbs, form only the third person singular with the grammatical subject es or without it. Ihnen wird geholfen. Es wird gelacht und geſungen. Geſtern wurde geſpielt. Bei uns zu Hauſe (where I come from) wird viel Whiſt geſpielt.

269. In the transformation of the active into the passive voice, the direct object in the accusative becomes subject-nominative and the former subject is expressed by von + dative denoting the agent and by durch + accusative denoting means and instrument. Baumgarten erſchlug den Wolfen-ſchießen. W. wurde von B. erſchlagen. Der Brief wurde durch einen Dienſtmann beſorgt (through a porter). See prepositions, **304, 2.**

270. When a verb governs two accusatives both accusatives become nominatives with the verbs of naming, calling, scolding. Er wurde ſein Freund genannt. See **179, 2.**

1. With lehren and fragen the accusative of the thing may be retained, particularly if that accusative be a pronoun, e. g., Das Schlimmste, was uns widerfährt, das werden wir vom Tag gelehrt (G.). For etwas gelehrt werden it is better to use unterrichtet werden; for etwas gefragt werden, better nach etwas gefragt werden. The accusative of the noun now sounds pedantic, though lehren in M. H. G. always retained the accusative in the passive. See 202, 2.

271. With a verb governing an accusative, a genitive, or a dative, the accusative becomes nominative in the passive, but the genitive and dative are retained. H. wurde des Hochverrats angeklagt. Deiner wurde gedacht (no grammatical subject) or es wurde deiner gedacht. Mir wurde gefolgt, *I* was followed.

1. The verbs folgen, helfen, gehorchen, schmeicheln, widersprechen, danken often form a personal passive in the classics and in the spoken language, but it is very questionable whether this use should be imitated; certainly not by foreigners who are accustomed to this construction in their own language and are apt to make mistakes in the active and say „ich folge dich" if they hear or say „ich werde gefolgt, geschmeichelt." Those who defend the personal passive appeal to the older accusative after helfen and schmeicheln.

272. The reflexive, encouraged by French influence, and man, es + active often replace the passive. For Es wird gesungen, gepocht stands Man singt, pocht. Da öffnet sich das Thor, Then the gate is opened. Der Schlüssel wird sich finden, The key will be found. More frequent than the reflexive alone is sich . . . lassen, e. g., Er wird sich bestimmen lassen zu . . ., He will let himself be influenced to . . ., He can be induced to . . . Das läßt sich leicht machen, That is easily done. Das läßt sich hören, That is plausible. See **290,** 3, *b.* It is clear from this that the German passive is less frequent than the English. The grammars boast more of the full and long compound tenses than actual usage justifies.

273.   Origin of the Passive Voice.

1. In O. H. G. sein (*sin, wesan*), werden (*werdan*) were used to express the passive. Gothic alone shows traces of anything like a Latin passive, but even there the periphrastic form had to be resorted to. In M. H. G. the present is *ich wirde gelobet;* preterit, *ich wart gelobet;* perfect, *ich bin gelobet;* pluperfect, *ich was gelobet*. *Worden* was added to the perfect from the 13th century downward, but was not considered essential until the 17th century. The passive idea lies originally only in the past or passive participle and not in werden, which means only "I enter into the state of being „geliebt," „geschlagen," etc. Compare the future, ich werde lieben, "I enter into the state of loving." The M. H. G. *ich bin geliebet, ich was* (*war*) *geliebet* are by no means lost. Only they are not called tenses now. Ich bin geliebt, das Zimmer ist gefegt mean "I am

in the state of being loved," "the room is in a swept state," "has been cleaned," "is clean." The participles are felt as adjectives. Ich bin geliebt worden, das Zimmer ist gefegt worden mean 'I have passed into the state of being loved," "the room has passed into the state of being swept." The transition into this state, and not the present state, but the fact or action are emphasized, hence the idea of *tense* is prominent. The fitness of the name of perfect passive for this form and not also for ich bin geliebt is apparent because ich bin geliebt worden is composed of ich bin (ge)worden (the perfect) + geliebt. In O. H. G. sein still formed the present as "to be" now in Eng., but already in M. H. G. werden was the prevalent auxiliary (see above), while sein was prevalent in the perfect.

2. Perhaps the following examples will illustrate the force of the various forms:

Die Tochter ist verlobt, is engaged to be married. Vom Eise befreit sind Strom und Bäche (F. 903). Dieser Kessel ist von Bergen begrenzt (Hu.) These three are not passive tenses. But compare: Zu dem Lächerlichen wird ein Contra'st von Vollkommenheiten und Unvollkommenheiten erfordert (Le.) (present tense). Dieser Punkt ist viel bestritten worden (perf. pass.). The same difference between wurde + participle (= imperfect pass.) and war + participle (no tense), e.g., Home'r war vor Alters unstreitig fleißiger gelesen als jetzt (Le.). Die Häuser waren festlich geschmückt (no tense). Der Räuberhauptmann war schon gefangen genommen worden, als seine Leute herbeikamen (pluperfect pass.). Der Spio'n wurde ohne weiteres an einen Ast geknüpft und erhängt (imperfect pass.).

Examples of the future and conditional perfects passive are very rare in the classics.

Syntax of the Tenses.

Simple Tenses.

274. The Present.

1. It denotes an action as now going on. Wie glänzt die Sonne, wie lacht die Flur (G.).

2. It is the tense used in the statement of a general truth or fact or custom, in which the idea of time is lost sight of. Dreimal drei ist neun. Gott ist die Liebe (B.). Borgen macht Sorgen (Prov.).

3. The **historical** present is used in vivid narrative for a past tense. Das zu Linz gegebene Beispiel findet allgemeine Nachahmung; man verflucht das Andenken des Verräters; alle Arme'en fallen von ihm ab (Sch.).

4. For the English perfect German (also French) uses the present when the action or state continues in the present time, but there is generally an adverb denoting duration of time qualifying it. Ex.: Nun bin ich sieben Tage hier (G.). Zwei Tage gehen wir schon hier herum (id.). Ich bin allhier erst kurze Zeit (F. 1868).

This use is by no means new in German or unknown in English, e.g., "I forget why." "The world by what I learn is no stranger to your generosity" (Goldsmith, quoted by Mätzner). It is closely related to the present sub 2 and 3, and generally translated by "have been" + present participle.

5. **The future present**, that is, the present with the force of the future, is much more frequent in German than in English. Ex.: Nein, nein, ich gehe nach der Stadt zurück (F. 820). Wer weiß, wer morgen über uns befiehlt (Sch.).

It is a very old use of the present, from a time when the periphrastic future was not yet developed.

6. The English periphrastic present in "I am writing," "I do write" rarely has corresponding German phrases. For instance, thun is dialectic and archaic. Und thu' nicht mehr in Worten framen (F. 385). A large number of present participles are looked upon as adjectives and stand in the predicate after sein, but they do not form a tense (see **273**, 1). There is a difference between the simple present and sein + pres. part. The former, if it occur at all, denotes an *act* of the subject, the latter denotes a *quality* of the same or of another subject. Ex.: Man nimmt teil an etwas, one takes part in something. Jemand ist teilnehmend, one is sympathetic. Die Farbe schreit is hardly used, but die Farbe ist eine schreiende, the color is a loud one. Die Aussicht reizt einen, immer höher zu steigen, the prospect entices one to climb higher and higher, but die Aussicht ist reizend, the prospect is charming. Compare the Eng. "charming," "promising," etc.

275. The Preterit.

1. It is strictly the "historical" tense, used in narration, when one event is related in some connection with another event, as following it or preceding it. Ex.: Cäsar kam, sah und siegte. Er ward geboren, er lebte, nahm ein Weib und starb (Gellert).

In the story of the creation in Genesis only the pret. is used until chapter 2, verse 4, when the account is summed up Also ist Himmel und Erde geworden, which has the perfect as it should have. See **276**.

2. It represents a past action as lasting, customary; also as contemporaneous with another action. Gestern kam der Medicus hier aus der Stadt hinaus zum Amtmann (connect „hinaus" with „zum," not with „aus der Stadt") und fand mich auf der Erde unter Lottens Kindern, wie einige auf mir herumkrabbelten, andere mich neckten (G.). Kühn war das Wort, weil es die That nicht war (Sch.).

Compound Tenses.

276. The Perfect.

It is used to denote a past event as a separate act or independent fact. The act is completed, but the result of it is felt in the present and may continue in the present. Ex.: Ich habe genossen das irdische Glück (Sch.). Gott hat die Welt erschaffen = God is the creator of the world, but Im Anfang schuf Gott Himmel und Erde (B.). Du hast's erreicht, Octavio (Sch.). See **279, 2**.

1. In the best writers this distinction is generally observed, but not in the spoken language, in which the perfect is crowding out the preterit. As an illustration of the exact use of the tenses, particularly of the preterit and perfect, may be recommended the introduction to Schiller's Geschichte des Abfalls der vereinigten Niederlande.

277. The Pluperfect.

It denotes a past action which was completed before another past action began. Ex.: Tilly hatte kaum seinen Rückmarsch angetreten, als der König sein Lager zu Schwedt aufhob und gegen Frankfurt an der Oder rückte (Sch.).

278. The Future.

1. It denotes an action yet to take place. Ex.: Was wird aus dem Kindlein werden? (B.). Der Kaiser wird morgen abreisen.

2. It denotes probability and should then not be translated by an English future as a rule. Ex.: Der Hund wird sechs Jahre alt sein (= ist wohl or wahrscheinlich), the dog may be or is prob-

ably, six years old. Wer klopft? Es wird ein Bettler sein, it is probably a beggar.

3. In familiar language it stands for the imperative implying confident expectation of the result. Du wirst hier bleiben, You shall stay here. Du wirst dich hüten, Take good care not to do it.

For the present with the force of the future, see **274, 5**.

279. The Future Perfect.

1. It is the perfect transferred to the future. Vergebens werdet ihr für euren Feldherrn euch geopfert haben (Sch.). More frequently than the future, the future perfect denotes probability: Wo wird er die Nacht zugebracht haben? (Le.), Where can he have spent the night? Es wird was andres wohl bedeutet haben (Sch.), It probably meant something else.

2. As the present can have future force, so the perfect can have future perfect force. Nicht eher denk ich dieses Blatt zu brauchen, bis eine That gethan ist, die unwiterspechlich den Hochverrat bezeugt (Sch.).

3. In M. H. G., the future perfect is unknown and its force is expressed by *ge* prefixed to the present, and by the perfect.

a. Guard against confounding the modal auxiliaries in German with the Eng. future. Approach to a future might be felt in wollen and sollen, *e. g.*, Was wollen sie denn herausverhören, wenn einer unschuldig ist? (G.). Der Reichstag zu Augsburg soll hoffentlich unsere Proje'kte zur Reife bringen (G.). See **283, 4**.

280. The Conditionals.

They are future subjunctives corresponding to the preterit and pluperfect subjunctive as the future corresponds to the present. As in all subjunctives, the idea of tense is not emphasized. Preterit subjunctive and I. conditional, pluperfect subjunctive and II. conditional are nearly identical in force, but preterit and pluperfect deserve the preference, particularly in the passive. In dependent conditional clauses the preterit or pluperfect subjunctive only can stand. In the main sentence there is no choice between them and the conditionals. Ex.: Ohne deinen Rat würde ich es nicht gethan haben or hätte ich es nicht gethan. Was würdest du an meiner Stelle thun? Wärest du hier gewesen, mein Bruder wäre nicht gestorben (B.).

281. The conditionals should be substituted for the subjunctive of the preterit and of the pluperfect: 1. When the force of the future is to be emphasized as in: Nähme der Kranke die Medizin regelmäßig ein, so würde das Fieber von dieser Stunde an allmählich verschwinden. Sie glaubten, sie würden sich leicht als Helden darstellen (Sch.). 2. When the indicative and subjunctive forms coincide as is the case with certain persons in weak verbs: Auf einen Eid würde ich ihm nicht glauben. „Glaubte" might be pret. ind. Ihr würdet dies Rätsel mir erklären, sagte sie (Sch.). „Ihr werdet" could also be indicative future.

The Tense of Indirect Speech.

282. The rule is: The indirect speech retains the tense of the direct. Ex.: Die Bäume seien gebannt, sagt er, und wer sie schädige, dem wachse seine Hand heraus zum Grabe (Sch.). Egmont beteuerte, daß das Ganze nichts als ein Tafelscherz gewesen sei. Der Knabe behauptete, er hätte es nicht gethan, wenn er nicht von seinen Gefährten dazu verleitet worden wäre. Er sagte auch, er wolle es nicht wieder thun, wenn man ihm jetzt vergebe. Der Zeuge konnte nicht schwören, daß er den Angeklagten je gesehen habe.

1. But this rule is not strictly observed. If the main clause contains, for instance, a past tense, the other clause may take a preterit for the present, a pluperfect for the perfect, or a conditional for the future: Das wären die Planeten, sagte mir der Führer, sie regierten das Geschick (Sch.). Ihr würdet dies Rätsel mir erklären, sagte sie (id.). Mir meldet (pres. for perf.) er, er läge krank (id.). If any ambiguity arises, as is not unfrequently the case, this license should not be indulged in. If the main verb is in the present, it is not well to substitute the preterit or pluperfect in the subordinate clause, because this license is due to attraction of tenses, viz., preterit in one — preterit or pluperfect in the other. Compare: Er beteuert, er sei dagegen, he asserts, that he is opposed. Er beteuert, er wäre dagegen might be construed as meaning er würde dagegen sein, which means "he would be opposed." Er beteuert, er sei dagegen gewesen, he had been

opposed; er wäre bagegen gewesen might moreover be understood as having the force of the II. Conditional.

For the mood of the indirect statement, see 285. For further remarks on the use of tenses, see 284, also the General Syntax.

283.   Origin of the Compound Tenses.

1. The compound tenses in all the living languages are products of the development of so-called *periphrastic* conjugation, which uses certain independent verbs denoting existence, possession, transition, or the beginning of an action, in connection with an infinitive, participle, or gerundive. The more the inflectional endings of the simple tenses of the earlier periods weathered, the more favorable were the chances for the growth of analytical and circumlocutory tenses. Compare the Latin *amor, amatus sum* or *fui; excusavi, excusatam, -um habeo* or *teneo* with French *je suis aimé, -ée, je fus aimé, -ée; je l'ai excusé, -ée, je l'avais excusé, -ée*. The Germanic languages have only two simple tenses. Gothic shows still a mutilated passive. But the future perfect and pluperfect active and passive sprang up within historic times from a combination of an independent verb with an infinitive or participle, which were at first felt only as predicate noun or adjective. The participle in O. H. G. could be inflected like any predicate adjective.

2. At different periods of High German there were different verbs which could be thus employed. Besides the modern auxiliaries haben, sein and werden, in O. H. G. eigan, +to own. In Gothic *haban* + inf. was made to express the future, in O. H. G. suln (shall) and *werdan* + pres. part.; in M. H. G. besides these, wellen, müezen. Ich habe den Hut abgenommen or aufgesetzt means originally I have, possess the hat in some state or position, viz., in my hand (taken off) or on my head (put on). The German order, too, shows this early construction much better than the English "I have taken off my hat." Compare the Latin *Excusatum habeas me rogo*, "Have me excused, pray," „Bitte, habe (halte) mich (für) entschuldigt." Haben could only be used with transitive verbs, but losing the distinctive meaning of possession, it could combine with verbs having an object in the G. and D. and even with no object, viz., with intransitive verbs. Haben required the past participle in O. H. G. in the A., but sein required it in the N. Sein could not, from the nature of its meaning, form the perf. or pluperf. active of any transitive verb, but only of intransitives denoting a continuance of a state (bleiben, sein) or transition into another state, where it, however, collided with werden, used in the future. But notice that the idea of transition and change is in most verbs, here in question, due to the prefix. Sein + past participle could only mean existence in a certain state, at most the beginning or ceasing of an existence.

3. As to verbs of motion, their relation to these verbs is very intimate. When it is not, haben becomes the rival of sein, as soon as the activity of motion is to be brought out and not the result. That sein could be used with a past participle of a verb of motion at all, was partly brought about by its use with a present participle and infinitive. Such forms as vermutend, vermögend, nachgebend sein, vermuten sein are remnants of the use of *sîn* + pres. part. or inf. in M. H. G. We do not feel the participle or infinitive as such now. They form no tense.

4. Werben + pres. part. was in M. H. G. more common than werben + inf., but the

latter was the established future in the 16th century. From "I pass into the state of praising" to "I shall praise" is not a long step.

5. The conditionals formed with wûrbe sprang up in the 14th century and were settled in the 16th, according to Grimm. In M. H. G. before the 13th century "*solde*," "*wolde*" were used as in the other Germanic languages, but these lacked the umlaut, and therefore were not easily distinguishable as subjunctives.

THE MOODS.

Subjunctive.

284. The indicative is the mood of reality, the subjunctive is the mood of unreality, contingency, possibility.

1. The **imperative** subjunctive helps to fill out the imperative for the third persons sg. and pl. and the first person pl. It is a strong optative, see sub 2.

Ex.: Alles schweige, jeder neige ernsten Tönen nun sein Ohr (Song). Sehe jeder wie er's treibe, sehe jeder wo er bleibe (G.). Seien Sie mir willko'mmen. Lassen wir das, let us not do this. Gehen wir diesen Paragraph(en) noch mal durch, let us go over this paragraph once more. Gehen Sie. Treten die Herren gefälligst ein (rare).

Werbe and sei, seid really subjunctives, are used as imperatives in the second person. Werbe munter, mein Gemüte (Hymn). Sei mir gegrüßt, mein Berg (Sch.).

2. The **optative** subjunctive expresses a wish or request. The present subjunctive implies confidence of fulfilment. Only the third person is used.

Ex.: Dich führe durch das wildbewegte Leben ein gnädiges Geschick (Sch.). Dein Name sei vergessen (Uh.). Gott vermehre die Gabe (G.).

The preterit subjunctive implies less assurance, and, like the pluperfect subjunctive, even no expectation of realization.

Ex.: O wären wir weiter! o wär ich zu Haus (G.). O sähst du, voller Mondenschein... (F. 386). Wäre er nur noch am Leben! (Implying „er ist aber tot"). Frommer Stab, o hätt' ich nimmer mit dem Schwerte dich vertauscht (Sch.). See also F. 392-7.

3. The **potential** subjunctive expresses an opinion as such, a possibility, a mild assertion of an undoubted fact (*diplomatic* subj.); it stands in questions, direct and indirect; in exclama-

tions. The preterit and I. conditional are the potential subjunctives of the present; the pluperfect and II. conditional, of the past.

Ex.: Ich reime, däcdt' ich, doch noch so ziemlich zusammen, was zusammen gehört (Le.). Das ginge noch, "that might do yet" (id.). Wer wüßte das nicht? Everybody knows that. Hätte ich doch nimmermehr gedacht, daß er so groß werden würde (Le.). Wie ließe sich alles schreiben! (G.) (Implying „es ist unmöglich"). Fast hätte ich das Beste vergessen (id.). Beinahe wäre ich gegen einen Baum gerannt. Du hätteſt das gewußt? (Implying „ich glaube es nicht). Nicht, daß ich wüßte, not as far as I know.

See also the modal auxiliaries, **267**.

4. The **concessive** subjunctive denotes an admission, yielding, and supposition. Generally only in the third person of the present and perfect. It borders closely upon the optative and conditional.

Ex.: Es koste was es wolle (Le.). Es sei, "(it is) granted." Gesell, du seiſt ein guter oder schlimmer, leg' dich aufs Ohr (Uh.). See mögen, **267, 3**.

5. The **unreal** subjunctive stands in conditional sentences both in the premise and the conclusion, *i. e.* in the dependent clause and in the main clause, when the premise is not true. The preterit and pluperfect stand in the premise; the preterit, pluperfect, and the two conditionals in the conclusion. The preterit has present and future force, the pluperfect has future force only.

Ex.: Es ließe sich alles trefflich schlichten, könnte man die Sachen zweimal verrichten (G.). Ich wäre nichts, wenn ich bliebe was ich bin (id.). Wenn wir Geld bei uns gehabt hätten, so würden wir den Armen was gegeben haben.

The premise omitted or represented by an adverb, etc.: Ich thäte das nicht an Deiner Stelle = wenn ich an Deiner Stelle wäre. Wir wären des Todes. Ohne Alpenstock wäre der Wanderer in die Tiefe hinabgefallen.

The conclusion omitted: Ja wenn wir nicht wären, sagte die Laterne zum Mond. Da ging sie aus (Folk-lore).

285. The subjunctive is the mood of the indirect statement, in which the speaker expresses the ideas of another in his own words without sharing the responsibility for, and belief in, the statement. For the mood in the dependent clause included in the statement notice especially the 3. and 4. sentences of **282** and the last of **328**. For examples and tense see **282**.

Imperative.

286. It expresses a command and occurs only in the 2. p. sg. and pl. For the 1. and 3. p. pl., see **284**, 1. Eile mit Weile, Make haste slowly. Lehre du mich meine Leute kennen (Sch.). Bindet ihn (id.). Wartet ihr, indem wir voran laufen.

1. The pronoun is quite optional; only when there is a contrast, as in the last sentence (ihr — wir), it should stand. In the subjunctive it always stands.

The imperative is only used in the present and has future force, but by a license also a perfect imperative occurs: Besen! Besen! Seib's gewesen! says the apprentice when he wants the brooms to cease being watercarriers (G.).

287. Other verbal forms that take imperative force and a very strong one, are:

1. The infinitive: Maul (Mund) halten! Hold your tongue. Nicht anfassen! Do not touch.

2. The past participle: Die Trommel gerührt (G.). Frisch auf Kameraden, auf's Pferd, auf's Pferd! in das Feld, in die Freiheit gezogen (Sch.).

3. The present and future indicative: Georg, du bleibst um mich (G.). Du wirst den Apfel schießen von dem Kopf des Knaben (Sch.). See **278**, 3.

4. The modal auxiliaries denoting a necessity, duty, can express imperative force, also lassen. Du sollst nicht stehlen (B.). Kein Mensch muß müssen (Le.), no man ought to be compelled.

Since the Eng. "let" shows no inflection, notice the German forms: Laß uns gehen, to a person addressed as du; plural Laßt uns gehen. Lassen Sie uns gehen, to a person addressed as Sie.

Infinitive.

288. It is a verbal noun and the present infinitive has neither voice, tense, nor inflection. The compound infinitive arose like the compound tenses (see **283**): gelobt werden, to be praised; gelobt worden sein, to have been praised; gelobt haben, to have praised.

1. Notice the marked difference in meaning between the present of some of the modal auxiliaries + perfect infinitive, and the perfect or pluperfect + present infinitive. Ex.: Der Kutscher will den Gefangenen gesehen haben = claims to have seen him, but hat ihn sehen wollen = wanted to see him. Der Hausirer muß vorbeigegangen sein = must have passed by, but hat vorbeigehen müssen, was forced to pass by, etc.

289. We distinguish between the infinitive *without* zu and *with* zu.

The former is the older construction. Being a noun, the infinitive always stood in the D. after zu in O. and M. H. G. But in early N. H. G., when it was no longer inflected, the prepositional infinitive gained ground and gave also rise to the gerundive (see **298**). Usage is in many cases still unsettled as to the use of zu. Its frequent use is the source of much bad style (see Sanders' „Hauptschwierigkeiten" . . . sub Inf.). The cases where the infinitive has taken the place of the present participle are mentioned below under each head. In the gerundive alone the participial form has taken the place of the infinitive. See **298**.

The Infinitive without zu.

290. 1. It is dependent upon the modal auxiliaries. Der Bote will es aus aller Leute Mund erfahren haben. Man soll den Tag nicht vor dem Abend loben (Prov.). Also upon thun in quaint and dialect style, *e. g.*, Da thäten sie sich trennen (Uh.). See the speeches of Marthe and Margarete in F., I. Upon haben in the phrase gut haben. Du hast gut reden, it is easy enough for you to talk. Er thut nichts als . . . , he does nothing but . . .

2. In certain phrases dependent upon some verbs of motion; also upon helfen, heißen (command), lassen, lehren, lernen, machen, nennen. The verbs of motion are: spazieren reiten, fahren, gehen; schlafen gehen, sich schlafen legen, etc. Heißt mich nicht reden,

heißt mich schweigen; denn mein Geheimnis ist mir Pflicht (G.). Lehre mich thun nach deinem Wohlgefallen (B.). See Schiller's Tell, 1549.

3. Dependent upon certain verbs of rest: bleiben (most frequently), liegen, stehen (rarely); and upon verbs of perceiving: finden, fühlen (rarely), hören, sehen; also haben. Stecken bleiben, to stick fast (intr.). Schlafen liegen. Wir fanden den Leichnam im Walde liegen. Wir sahen den Führer über dem Abgrunde schweben. Der Tyroler hat gewöhnlich Federn am Hute stecken, der Engländer Bänder herunterhangen. Ich hab' es öfters rühmen hören, ein Komödia'nt könnt' einen Pfarrer lehren (F. 526–7).

<small>a. Sein is still so used in dialect. Er ist fischen, jagen, he has gone afishing, ahunting; er ist fischen gewesen, he has been afishing. With all the verbs sub 3 and several sub 2 the present participle was once the rule in older German. Compare the participle in the predicate, 294, 2.</small>

<small>b. After fühlen, hören, lassen, sehen the infinitive has either passive or active force, and often an ambiguity arises which should be avoided by a different construction. Wir haben es sagen hören, We have heard it said. Die Dogge läßt sich nicht necken, The bulldog will not be teased. Wir hören den Knaben rufen, calling and called (generally the first). Der Lohnkutscher ließ uns nicht fahren, the hackman did not let us go, did not allow us to drive, did not have us driven Der Meister ließ die Tochter nicht malen, did not allow her to paint and did not have her portrait painted.</small>

4. As subject or predicate with sein and heißen, to be, to amount to: Noch ei'nmal ein Wunder hoffen hieße Gott versuchen (Sch.). Ein Vergnügen erwarten ist auch ein Vergnügen (Le.).

The Infinitive with zu.

291. 1. It expresses the purpose of an action and in general the indirect object; also necessity and possibility after neuter verbs, e. g., sein, bleiben, stehen, when it has passive force. Die Sache ist nicht zu ändern. Es bleibt noch viel zu thun. Das steht noch zu überlegen. Da treibt's ihn, den köstlichen Preis zu erwerben (Sch.).

This is the old and proper use of the infinitive, originally a noun in the D. governed by zu. In N. H. G. um was added to express purpose, but it was really superfluous, though common in the spoken language. Um die Strömung abzuleiten gruben sie ein frisches Bette (Platen). Wir leben nicht um zu essen, sondern wir essen um zu leben. The force of zu was much weakened when um could thus be added. Besides um, anstatt and ohne can precede zu: anstatt weg zu laufen, kam der Bär näher heran. Ohne sich umzusehen, lief der Dieb davon. But „um" should never be used except to express purpose. It is used too frequently. See sub 4.

2. It stands as direct object of verbs, often preceded by, or in apposition to, a pronoun or pronominal adverb + preposition. Ex.: Fang an zu hacken und zu graben (F. 2355). Niemand säume zu geben. Ich denke nicht daran, dir das zu gewähren.

In older periods of the language there was no zu in this case.

3. It stands as subject, in the spoken language, more frequently than without zu; there is no choice. Gefährlich ist's den Leu zu wecken (Sch.). Eine schöne Menschenseele finden ist Gewinn (He.).

4. As adjunct of nouns and adjectives, the latter often being qualified by zu and genug. „Die Kunst sich beliebt zu machen." Zu stolz, Dank einzuernten, wo ich ihn nicht säete (Le.). Du wärest blind genug, das nicht einzusehn? ... Bereit, dir zur Gesellschaft hier zu bleiben (F. 1431).

After adjectives „um zu" is now far more common than zu alone. Ich bin zu alt, um nur zu spielen, zu jung, um ohne Wunsch zu sein (F. 1546-7). Quite rare is als zu + infinitive.

5. For the independent use of infinitive, see imperative, **287, 1.** With or without zu in elliptical expressions: Was thun, spricht Zeus (Sch.). Was, am Rand des Grabs zu lügen! (F. 2961).

ACCUSATIVE WITH THE INFINITIVE.

292. In this construction the logical subject of the infinitive stands in the accusative. The infinitive stands with or without zu. Ex.: Hier ruhet Martin Faulermann, wenn man den ruhen sagen kann, der seinen Lebtag nichts gethan (Weckherlin, quoted by Blatz). Lügen, die man Lügen zu sein weiß (Le.).

1. Accusative with infinitive was not rare in O. H. G. in the translations from Latin and Greek. It is largely due to foreign influence. In M. H. G. it is very rare. In

modern German it is discouraged by the best authorities, though Lessing uses it quite frequently.

2. The corresponding English constructions must therefore be rendered freely into German. I believe him to be my friend, Ich glaube daß er mein Freund ist or Ich halte ihn für meinen Freund. German loses thus a compact construction.

The Infinitive as a Noun.

293. Some infinitives are felt as nouns only, *e. g.*, das Leben, das Ansehen, das Leiden. The infinitive used as noun generally has the article. Das Rauchen ist hier verboten. Beim Überse'tzen muß man bis an's Unüberse'tzliche herangehn (G.). Der Erben Weinen ist ein heimlich Lachen (Prov.).

Participles.

294. The participles are really adjectives derived from verbal stems. The present participle retains more of the verbal construction and force than the past, in which the idea of tense only appears in intransitive verbs.

The **present participle** has active force in all verbs and the noun is the subject of the action. Der lächelnde See, die aufgehende Sonne, das schlagende Wetter, "fire-damp." Both participles can be used as nouns, adjectives, and adverbs very much as in English. They stand in apposition, in the predicate and as attributes.

1. Participles in which the noun is not the subject of the action, and those in which lies passive rather than active force, are still current, but not so frequent as in early N. H. G. They are not generally countenanced, *e. g.*, bei schlafender Nacht, "at night time," "when everybody sleeps"; eine sitzende Lebensart, a sedentary habit of life; essende Waaren, eatables (better Eßwaaren); eine vorhabende Reise, an intended journey. Some of these can be defended: fahrende Habe, movables, chattels (intrans. verb); erstaunende Nachricht, astonishing news (trans. verb); eine melkende Kuh (intrans. like „milchen"); die reitende Post, postman on horseback. Poetic are der schwindelnde Fels, the giddy rock. Von des Hauses weitschauendem Giebel (Sch.).

2. In the predicate appear now only such present participles as have become regular adjectives: bedeutend, important; reizend, charming; hinreißend, ravishing; leidend, in pain, ill health; dringend, urgent. See **274, 6.**

3. In apposition: Kochend, wie aus Ofens Rachen, glühn die Lüfte (Sch.). Ich empfange knieend dies Geschenk (id.).

4. The participial clause with the present participle is only in very restricted use in German compared with English. It cannot express an action preceding or following another action, a cause, purpose, etc. It has usually the value of an adjective clause and can often be explained as in apposition. Der Arme, sich an mich wendend, sprach: Haben Sie Mitleid, mein Herr.

295. The past participle of a transitive verb has passive force; that of a verb which forms its compound tenses with sein has active force: der laubumkränzte Becher (Sch.); das hergeführte Volk (id.); die abgesegelten Schiffe; der durchgefallene (unsuccessful) Candida't.

1. But not all verbs that have sein in compound tenses can be thus used; the participle must denote the state produced by the action of the verb. Die gesegelten Schiffe, der gelaufene Knecht would not do. Der entlaufene Sklave means "the runaway slave." This force is clear from the origin of the compound tense with sein (see **273, 283**).

2. Seemingly a large number of past participles have active force, but they are either quite wrong or they can be explained as having had originally passive force. Thus: „Ungebetet ißt man nicht" (Gerok) ; „ungegessen zu Bette gehn" are as wrong as their English equivalents: One does not eat unprayed, go to bed uneaten. „Bedient" means "in service," "invested with an office," hence a servant, ein Bedienter. „Verdient," one who has merits, weil er sich um etwas or jemand verdient gemacht hat; eingebildet means conceited, taken up with one's self; ein verlogener Mensch, a man given to lying; versoffener Mensch, given to drinking, and many other compounds with ver–: verweinte Augen, eyes red with weeping.

a. That some are now felt as having active force cannot be denied, else the wrong use mentioned could not have sprung up: gott-, pflichtvergessen, forgetful of one's duty, of God; verschlafen, "one who slept too long"; vermessen, "presumptuous"; verlegen, embarrassed; besides the above.

296. The peculiar past participles of verbs of motion, which seemingly have active force, stand in a sort of apposition or as predicates with kommen, rarely with gehen. Ex.: Kam ein Vogel geflogen (Song). Da kommt des Wegs geritten ein schmucker Edelknecht (Uh.).

1. This use is by no means modern. Kommen and gehn are felt as auxiliaries. Compare verloren gehen.

2. Special notice deserves the past participle with heißen, sein, and nennen, which has the force of an infinitive, but belongs under this head. Das heißt schlecht geworfen, That is a bad throw. Unter ehrlichen Leuten nennt man das „gelogen." Frisch gewagt ist halb gewonnen (Prov.).

297. The participle appears in an absolute construction. The logical subject is left indefinite (Lessing is very fond of this). The logical subject stands in the accusative and with a few, like ausgenommen, eingeschlossen, abgerechnet, even in the nominative. Alle waren zugegen, der Pfarrer ausgenommen. Und dieses nun auf Laokoon angewendet, so ist die Sache klar (Le.).

1. Closely related to this construction is the absolute accusative + a past participle (see 209) and in some cases there may be doubt as to which is meant. Und sie singt hinaus in die finstere Nacht, das Auge von Weinen getrübet (Sch.).

The past participle is in elliptical construction in the imperative, see **287, 2.**

The Gerundive.

298. It stands only attributively. In the predicate the old infinitive stands, which it has supplanted. Der noch zu verkaufende Schrank, the wardrobe which is still to be sold; but der Schrank ist noch zu verkaufen, the wardrobe is still to be sold. See **289, 452.**

Though the form is rather that of the gerund than of the gerundive, in construction it closely resembles the Latin gerundive. Hence the name in German.

SYNTAX OF THE ADVERB.

299. The adverb qualifies a verb, an adjective or another adverb. Ex.: Du hast mich mächtig angezogen (F. 483). Die unbegreiflich hohen Werke sind herrlich wie am ersten Tag (F. 249–50). Das ist sehr schön geschrieben.

1. The adverbs of time and place often accompany a noun with the force of an attribute: Vor Jenem droben steht gebückt, der helfen lehrt und Hilfe schickt (F. 1009–10). Georg V. (der Fünfte), einst König von Hannover, starb im Auslande.

2. The adverb stands as a predicate: Die schönen Zeiten von Aranjuez sind nun vorüber (Sch.). Die Thür ist zu (one can supply „gemacht"). Der or dem Mini'ster ist nicht wohl.

a. Do not confound gut and wohl. Except in a few cases, as in wohl thun, to do good, wohl does not qualify a transitive verb. We do not say in German wohl schreiben, wohl antworten, wohl anfangen in the sense of English "well." Er hat es wohl geschrieben means "he wrote it, indeed, (I assure you)"; or it is concessive and can mean: "to be sure he wrote it, but then —." In the last sense wohl has no stress.

3. With adjectives or participles used as nouns that are felt rather as substantives than as adjectives or as derived from a verb, the adverb changes to an adjective: ein nah Verwandter > ein naher Verwandter; ein intim Bekannter > ein intimer Bekannter. But compare Goethe's famous line: Das Ewig-Weibliche zieht uns hinan.

300. An adverb may strengthen the force of a preposition by standing before or after the preposition + case. This is always the case when the adverb is the prefix of a separable compound verb: rings um die Stadt (herum), mitten durch den Wald, in das Dorf hinein, aus dem Garten heraus. Es ritten drei Reiter zum Thore hinaus (Uh.).

1. Mark the adverbs which are only adverbs and not adjectives: wohl, fast, schon, sehr, neulich, freilich, früh (rare), spät (rare), bald, and others.

2. The uninflected comparative and superlative of adjectives serve also as adverbs. Notice the difference between auf + A. and an + D. Sie sangen auf das beste (Uh.), they sang as best they knew how. This is *absolute* superlative. Sie sangen am besten, they sang best of all, any. This is *relative* superlative.

SYNTAX OF THE PREPOSITION.

301. The prepositions express the relations of a noun to a verb or to another noun.

1. Prepositions are originally adverbs, and the distinction between prepositions, adverbs and conjunctions is only syntactical. Denn is, for instance, a conjunction = for, and an adverb = then, than; während is a conjunction = while, and a preposition = during. Prepositions could not originally "govern" cases. A certain case was called for independently of the preposition, then still an adverb. In Greek there are prepositions governing three cases, which shows how loose the connection between case and preposition was. In fact nearly all adverbs, old and new, can be traced back

to cases of nouns or pronouns. They are isolated or "petrified" cases, and as such could only stand in the loosest connection with the living cases, which they gradually began to "govern."

2. Prepositions can govern different cases in different periods of the language. The preposition has been partly the cause of the loss of case-endings. Its function becomes the more important the more uninflectional (analytical) a language becomes. It is one of the most difficult and subtle elements to master in the study of a living language. For another reason the preposition is very important, viz., the preposition + case has supplanted and is continuing to supplant the case alone, directly dependent upon a verb or noun. The two together are much more expressive and explicit than a case alone. In Die Liebe des Vaters, the genitive may be subjective or objective, but there is no ambiguity about die Liebe zum Vater, des Vaters Liebe zum Sohne.

CLASSIFICATION AND TREATMENT OF THE PREPOSITIONS ACCORDING TO THE CASES THEY GOVERN.

302. Prepositions governing the Genitive:

Unweit, mittels, kraft und während; laut, vermöge, ungeachtet; oberhalb und unterhalb; innerhalb und außerhalb; diesseits, jenseits, halben, wegen; statt, auch längs, zufolge, trotz.

These are all cases of substantives or adjectives (participles) and their number might be easily increased, *e. g.*, by bezüglich, with reference to; angesichts, in the face of; seitens, on the part of; inmitten, in the midst of, etc.

(The order is the one in which they are given in German grammars. The semicolon shows the ends of the lines of the doggerel.)

We comment in alphabetical order briefly upon those that seem to require comment. Often a mere translation will suffice.

1. Anstatt, an — statt, statt, + instead of. Draus (from which, from whose breast) statt der goldenen Lieder ein Blutstrahl hoch auf springt (Uh.). An Tochter statt, in daughter's stead. Statt sometimes with the dative. It also governs an infinitive like ohne, translated by "without + participle." See Infinitive, **291, 1.**

2. Außerhalb + outside of; innerhalb + inside of; oberhalb, above; unterhalb, on the lower side of, below. They are all more expressive than the simple forms. They rarely govern the dative.

3. Diesseit(s), jenseit(s), this side of, on the other side, beyond. Rarely with the dative.

4. Halben, halber, halb, on account of, + in behalf of. Follows

its case. Frequent in composition: deshalb, therefore; meinethalben, on my behalf; Alters halber, on account of age. Comp. wegen and willen.

5. **Kraft**, according to, by virtue of. Kraft des Gesetzes; kraft des Amtes. Formerly only in Kraft, e. g., daß stets der liebste (Sohn) . . . in Kraft allein des Rings, das Haupt, der Fürst des Hauses werde (Le.). Comp. laut.

6. **Laut**, from, „nach Laut," lautes (Luther), means "according to,' "by." Laut Befehls, by command; laut des Testamentes, according to the last will and testament.

Plural nouns without articles in which the genitive could not be distinguished stand in the dative: laut Briefen, according to letters. Laut means literally according to a verbal or written statement; kraft gives a moral reason.

7. **Mittels**, mittelst (most common), vermittelst, by means of, with. Mittelst eines Hammers, eines Bohrers. It is more expressive than mit or durch. Rarely with the dative.

8. **Ob**, rare and archaic. With genitive if causal (on account of); with dative if local (above), and temporal (during). Da weinten zusammen die Grenadier' wohl ob der kläglichen Kunde (Heine). Ob dem Wald; nid bem Wald (Sch., *Tell*); ob dem Altare (id.).

9. **Trotz**, with genitive and dative, in defiance of, in spite of; in the sense of "in rivalry with," "as well as," always with the dative. Trotz des heftigen Regens fuhren wir ab. Die Sängerin singt trotz einer Nachtigall, as well as a nightingale. Comp. the forms zu or zum Trotze preceded by a dative: Mir zum Trotze fuhr er fort zu lesen, in defiance of me or to defy me he continued reading.

10. **Unangesehen**, setting aside, unbeschabet, without detriment to, ungeachtet, notwithstanding (very frequent). The last two also with a preceding dative; bemungeachtet is felt as an adverb. These are very modern prepositions. Unweit, unfern, not far from, occur also with dative.

11. **Vermöge**, in virtue of, through, in consequence of, by dint of. Denotes a reason springing from a quality of the subject: vermöge seiner Redlichkeit, through his honesty. We could not say kraft seiner R.; vermöge (and not kraft) großer Anstrengungen, by dint of great efforts. (Perhaps from „nach Vermögen.")

12. **Während**, during. Sometimes with the dative: währenddem, meanwhile.

13. **Wegen**, on account of, both preceding and following the noun;

also with the dative. Wegen denotes also a motive and an impediment. Seiner Größe wegen konnte das Schiff nicht durch den Kanal. Der Müller war wegen seiner Stärke berühmt. Wegen from von — wegen, still common in „von Rechts wegen," strictly, in justice.

14. Willen, generally um — willen, denotes the purpose, the advantage or interest of a person. Um meiner Ruhe willen erklären Sie sich deutlicher (Sch.). Um des Sohnes willen, um meinetwillen, for the sake of or in the interest of the son, for my sake. Wegen, halben, and willen all appear with pronouns, and are used promiscuously.

15. Zufolge, as frequently with the dative, denotes the result, " in consequence of." Zufolge des Auftrages, in consequence of the commission; den Verabredungen zufolge, in accordance with the verbal agreements.

Prepositions governing the Dative.

303. Schreib: mit, nach, nächst, nebst, samt; seit, von, zu, zuwi'der; entgegen, außer, aus — stets mit dem Dativ nieder.

1. Ab, still used in the Alemanic dialect (Baden, Switzerland) as a preposition. In business style it denotes the place from which merchandise is delivered or the time after which anything is to be had: ab Hamburg, ab Neujahr, ab = "all aboard."

2. Aus denotes the starting point of a motion, the opposite of in +. accusative, = "out of," "from": Aus den Augen, aus dem Sinn, "out of sight, out of mind": aus dem Fenster sehen, to look out of the window. Origin and descent: aus alten Zeiten, from olden times; aus Hannover, from Hanover. Material: aus Lehm, of clay; aus Mehl, of meal. Motive: aus Mitleid, Haß, from pity, hatred. Origin also in aus Erfahrung, from experience; aus Versehen, by mistake. Notice the idiom: aus Köln gebürtig, a native of Cologne, born in C.

3. Außer, outside of, beside, the opposite of in + dative. Denotes also exception and "in addition to." More frequent in the figurative than in the local sense, because außerhalb is more precise. Außer dem Hause, not at home; außer Hause speisen, to dine out; außer sich sein, to be beside one's self. Nur der Vetter war außer mir da. Mark once the genitive außer Landes gehen, to go to foreign parts; also the accusative in außer allen Zweifel setzen, to put beyond all doubt. (Setzen being a verb of motion.)

4. Bei. Original meaning is nearness, hence by, near, with: bei der Scheune, near (by) the barn; bei der Tante, near the aunt or at the house of

the aunt; beim Zeus, by Jove; die Schlacht bei Wörth, the battle of W.; bei Tisch sein, to be at dinner; bei Tag und bei Nacht, by day and by night; bei (einem) Namen nennen, to call by name (but Friedrich mit Namen, Frederic by name); bei (rare) neunzig Gefangenen, about ninety prisoners; bei Strafe von zehn Mark, ten marks fine. Ich habe kein Geld bei mir, I have no money about me. The accusative stands in bei Seite legen, bringen, stellen, to lay, put aside. In M. H. G. after verbs of motion regularly the accusative, but in the spoken language now discarded, though still found in the classics.

5. **Binnen**, sometimes with genitive, expresses now time only, "within": binnen drei Jahren, within three years. < be — innen.

6. **Entge′gen** denotes approach, both friendly and hostile, towards and against; stands generally after its case. Wir gingen dem Freunde entgegen; fuhren dem Winde entgegen. With verbs of motion it frequently forms separable compounds and is really more adverb than preposition.

7. **Gegenü′ber**, opposite, facing; generally after its case; rarely gegen — über. Dem Schlosse gegenüber.

8. **Gemäß**, preceding and following its case, according to, in accordance with; really an adjective. Dem Versprechen gemäß, according to the promise; gemäß dem Gesetze, according to the law. It is more definite than nach.

9. **Mit** means "in company with," "with"; denotes presence, accompanying circumstances and instrument. Arm in Arm mit dir, so forb're ich mein Jahrhundert in die Schranken (Sch.). Mit Freuden, gladly; eile mit Weile, hasten slowly; mit Fug und Recht, justly (emphatic); mit der Zeit pflückt man Rosen, in due time . . . ; mit Fleiß, intentionally; mit dem Pfeil, dem Bogen (Sch.). (See mittels, 302, 7.)

10. **Nach** denotes originally a "nearness to," being an adjective (nahe); then "a coming near to," and generally corresponds to Eng. "after" in point of time, order. With verbs of motion (literal and figurative) "to" and "after." Nach etwas streben, sich sehnen, to strive after, long for; nach Mitternacht ; nach dir komme ich, it is my turn after your; nach Berlin reisen. "In accordance with," not so expressive as „gemäß," in this sense often after its case. Nach den Gesetzen verdient er den Tod; dem Wortlaute nach, literally. Aim: nach etwas schlagen, schießen, to strike at, shoot at. Nach etwas schmecken, riechen, etc., something has the smell, taste of; nach etwas urteilen, to judge by; nach etwas or jemand schicken, to send for. (See zu and gemäß.)

11. **Nächst** is the superlative of nahe (nach), and denotes very close nearness to in place, order, = + "next to." Zunächst has no different force. Und nächst dem Leben was erflehst du dir? (G.).

12. **Nebst** denotes very loose connection and connects also things and persons not necessarily belonging together; samt, on the other hand, only what naturally belongs together. Auf einer Stange trägt sie einen Hut nebst einer Fahne (Sch.) (a hat *and* a banner). < nebenst < L. G. *nevens*.

13. **Samt, mit samt, zu samt,** "together with." Mich samt meinem ganzen Heere bring' ich dem Herzog (Sch.). See nebst. It implies a close union, which does not lie even in mit.

14. **Seit**, older sint, = + since, denotes the beginning of an action and its duration to the present moment. Seit diesem Tage schweigt mir jeder Mund (Sch.). Er ist herein seit mehreren Stunden (id.), it is several hours since he came in (into the city). Seit einigen Jahren zahlt er keine Zinsen, For several years he has paid no interest.

15. **Von**, "from," denotes the starting point of a motion or action in time and place. Its case is often followed by another preposition or by her. Von der Hand in den Mund; von Worten kam's zu Schlägen, from words they came to blows. Von Ostern bis Pfingsten ist fünfzig Tage. Origin: Walther von der Vogelweide. Fürst von Bismarck. Herr von Schulemburg. Hence von in the names of persons denotes nobility: Herr von So und So. Von Jugend auf; von Grund aus, thoroughly; von Osten her. Separation: frei, rein von etwas. Supplants the genitive: ein Mann von Ehre, von großen Kenntnissen; der Pöbel von Paris. Denotes the personal agent: Wallenstein wurde von Piccolomini hintergangen und von vielen Generalen im Stiche (in the lurch) gelassen. Notice: Schurke von einem Wirt (Le.). Cause: naß vom (with) Tau, vom Regen.

16. **Zu** denotes first of all the direction toward a person (but nach toward a thing) + "to": zu jemand gehen, kommen, sprechen, etc. Sie sang zu ihm, sie sprach zu ihm (G.). Zu sich kommen, "come to"; etwas zu sich stecken, to put something in one's pocket. (This is its only use in O. H. G. In M. H. G. its use spread.) In dialect and in poetry it stands before names of cities and towns (= at). Zu Straßburg auf der Schanz (Folk-song). Ihr seid mein Gast zu Schwyz (Sch.).

In certain very numerous set phrases and proverbs zu stands before names of things. Direction: von Ort zu Ort, from place to place; zu Bett(e), zur Kirche, zur Schule, zu Grunde, zu Rate gehen = "take council";

many loose compounds with fahren; zu Fall, zu Statten, zu Schaden, zu Ende, zu Ehren kommen; zu Schanden, zu Nichte; zum Schelme werden.

Place where?: „zu beiden Seiten des Rheins" (Song); zu Hause, zur Hand sein; zu Füßen liegen. Manner of motion: zu Land, zu Wasser, zu Pferd (zu Roß), zu Wagen, zu Fuß = Eng. "by" and "on." Transition or change: zum König machen, wählen, ernennen; zum Narren, zum besten haben, to make a fool of. Degree or size, numbers: zum Teil, in part; zu Hunderten, by the hundred; zu dreien waren wir im Zimmer, there were three of us in the room; zum Tode betrübt (G.), sad unto death. Combination of things: Nehmen Sie nie Pfeffer, Salz oder Senf zu (with) dem Ei? Oft hatt' er kaum Wasser zu Schwarzbrot und Wurst (Bü.). Notice the use of zu before nouns followed by hinein, heraus, etc.: zum Thore hinaus; zum Fenster heraus. Time (rare): Und kommt er nicht zu Ostern, so kommt er zu Trinita't (Folk-song). After the noun = "in the direction of," "toward": dem Dorfe zu, toward the village; nach dem Dorfe, to the village.

Prepositions governing the Accusative:

304. Bis, durch, für, gegen, ohne, sonder, um, wider.

1. Bis, till, until, denotes the limit in time and space. When denoting space it is followed by other prepositions, except before names of places. The nouns of time rarely have an article or pronoun. Bis Fastnacht; bis ans Ende aller Dinge; bis hierher und nicht weiter; bis an den hellen Tag; neunzig bis hundert Mark; bis Braunschweig. (Bis < $bi + az$, + Eng. by + at.)

2. Durch, + "through," denotes a passing through: durch den Wald, durchs Nadelöhr. Extent of time (the case often followed by hindurch): durch Jahrzehnte hindurch; die ganze Zeit (hin)durch. Cause and occasion, very much like aus: durch Nachlässigkeit, durch eigene Schuld. Means: durch einen Pfeil verwunden, durch einen Dienstmann besorgen, attend to through a porter. (Durch more definite than mit. See this and mittels. It denotes now no longer the personal agent.)

3. Für, + for, denotes advantage, interest, destination: Wer nicht für mich ist, ist wider mich (B.). Er sammelt für die Armen. Die Scheere ist kein Spielzeug für Kinder. Die Wahrheit ist vorhanden für den Weisen, die Schönheit für ein fühlend Herz (Sch.). Substitution and price: Da tritt kein anderer für ihn ein (Sch.). Mein Leben ist für Gold nicht feil (Bü.). Limitation: Ich für meine Person. Genug für dieses Mal. Ihr zeigtet einen kecken Mut . . . für eure Jahre (Sch.). Stück für Stück, point by point. In its old sense (local) only in certain phrases: Schritt für (by) Schritt, Tag für (by) Tag, Satz für (after) Satz. (See vor.)

4. **Gegen** denotes "direction toward," but with no idea of approach that lies in zu and nach. It implies either friendly or hostile feeling if persons are concerned = "towards," "against." Gegen die Wand lehnen; gegen den Strom schwimmen. Wenn ich mich gegen sie verpflichten soll, so müssen sie's auch gegen mich (Sch.). Gibt es ein Mittel gegen die Schwindsucht? Gegen Dummheit kämpfen Götter selbst vergebens. Exchange, comparison: Ich wette hundert gegen eins. Roland war ein Zwerg gegen den Riesen. Indefinite time and number: "towards." Der Kranke schlief erst gegen Morgen ein. Der Feldherr hatte gegen dreihundert tausend Soldaten. Gegen drei Uhr. Gegen once governed the dative almost exclusively and traces of it are still found in Goethe.

Gen is still preserved in „gen Himmel." Gen < gēn < gein < gegen, + again. See entgegen, which implies a mutual advance.

5. **Ohne**, "without," the opposite of „mit," „bei." Mit oder ohne Klausel, gilt mir gleich (Sch.), "With or without reserve, it is all the same to me." Ein Ritter ohne Furcht und Tadel. In „ohnedem" is a remnant of the D. in M. H. G.; zweifelsohne of the G. occurring after the M. H. G. adverb âne, from. Etwas ist nicht ohne, there is something in it (Coll.). Ohne in Composition, see **489**, 3; + infinitive, see **291**, 1.

6. **Sonder**, "without," is now archaic except in set phrases like „sonder Gleichen," „sonder Zweifel," "without compare," "no doubt," + Eng. asunder. Once governed the accusative and genitive.

7. **Um**, "around," "about." Und die Sonne, sie machte den weiten Ritt um die Welt (Arndt). Und um ihn die Großen der Krone (Sch.). Her or herum often follows the case: In einem Halbkreis standen um ihn her sechs oder sieben große Königsbilder (Sch.). It denotes inexact time or number: Um Mitternacht begrabt den Leib (Bü.). Um drei hundert Hörer, an audience of about three hundred. (Gegen is rather "nearly," um means more or less.) But „um dreiviertel fünf" means "at a quarter to five." "At about" would be „ungefähr um" or „um ungefähr," e. g., ungefähr um 6 Uhr. It denotes further exchange, price, difference in size and measure: Aug' um Auge, Zahn um Zahn (B.). Alles ist euch feil um Geld (Sch.). Um zwei Zoll zu klein. Er hat sich um zwei Pfennige verrechnet. Loss and deprivation: um's Leben bringen, to kill; um's Geld kommen, to lose one's money. Da war's um ihn geschehn (G.), He was done for. Wer brachte mich drum? (um deine Liebe) (F. 4496), Who robbed me of it? It denotes the object striven for: um etwas werben, spielen, fragen, bitten, streiten, beneiden, etc. The object of care, mourning, weeping: Wein' um den Bruder, doch nicht um den Geliebten weine (Sch.). Schade wär's um eure Haare (id.). Nicht um diese thut's mir leid (id.).

8. **Wider,** "against," always in the hostile sense. Denotes resistance and contrast: Was hilft uns Wehr und Waffe wider den? (Sch.). Es geht ihm wider die Natur, It goes against his grain. + Eng. "with" in withstand.

Prepositions governing the Dative and Accusative.

305. An, auf, hinter, in, neben, über, unter, vor, zwischen.

1. In answer to the question whither? they require the accusative. In answer to the question where? the dative. Pflanze die Bäume vor das Haus. Die Bäume stehen vor dem Hause.

2. In answer to the question how long and until when? they require the accusative. In answer to the question when? the dative: Im Jahre 1872 wurde Straßburg wieder als deutsche Universität eröffnet. Wir reisen auf vierzehn Tage ins Bad.

3. When an, auf, in, über, unter, vor denote manner and cause, then auf and über always require the accusative, but an, in, unter, vor generally the dative, in answer to the questions how and why? Wir freuen uns über (= over) and auf (= looking forward to) seine Ankunft. Auf diese Weise, but in dieser Weise. Der Bettler weinte vor Freuden über die herrliche Gabe.

The above general rules, as given in Krause's grammar, will be found of much practical value.

306. 1. **An + Dative.**

After nouns and adjectives of plenty and want: Mangel an Geld, reich an Gütern. After adjectives when the place is mentioned where the quality appears: an beiden Füßen lahm, an einem Auge blind. After verbs of rest, increase or decrease, and after those denoting an immediate contact or a perception: An der Quelle saß der Knabe (Sch.). Es fehlt an Büchern. Der Auswanderer litt am Wechselfieber. Der Zigeuner führt den Bären an einer Kette. Den Vogel erkennt man an den Federn (Prov.). It denotes an office and time of day: am Theater, an der Universität, am Amte angestellt sein, to hold an office at . . . ; am Morgen, Abend; es ist an der Zeit . . ., it is time . . . .

2. An + Accusative.

After denken, erinnern, mahnen and similar ones, and verbs of motion. Denket an den Ruhm, nicht an die Gefahr. Setzen Sie sich doch ans Fenster (near the window). Inexact number: an die drei mal hundert tausend Mann (as many as). From its English cognate "on" an differs very much in meaning. "On" generally is auf. See also **300**, 2.

3. Auf + "upon." For auf + Dative, see **305**, 1, 2, 3.
It denotes rest or motion upon the surface.

Auf + Accusative.

Stands after verbs of waiting, hoping, trusting, etc., *e. g.*, auf etwas warten, hoffen, sich besinnen (recall), gefaßt sein, sich freuen (see **305**, 3), verzichten, (es) auf etwas wagen, hören. Here it stands generally for the old gen. without preposition. Ich kann mich auf die genauen Umstände nicht besinnen, I cannot recall . . . Der Hund wartet auf sein Fressen. Merke auf die Worte des Lehrers. Trotzt nicht auf euer Recht (Sch.). After adjectives denoting pride, envy, anger, malice, *e. g.*, eifersüchtig, neidisch, stolz, böse, erbost: eifersüchtig auf seine Ehre (Sch.); stolz auf seine Unschuld; erbost auf den Gefangenen (über would mean cause). Exact time, limit, and measure; often with „bis." Here belongs the superlative, see **300**, 2. Bis auf's Blut. Bis auf Speis' und Trank (Le.). Es ist ein Viertel auf drei, a quarter past two. Auf die Minu'te, Seku'nde, auf Schußweite, at shooting distance. Bis auf die Neige, to the last drop. Auf sieben schon eines wieder (Le.). (Nathan had "toward" or "as a return for" his seven dead sons one child in Recha.) Auf eine Mark gehen hundert Pfennige.

4. Hinter + "behind," opposite of „vor." See **305**, 1, 2.

It denotes inferiority: Die französische Artillerie stand weit hinter der deutschen zurück (ambiguous, either stood far back of the G. or was much inferior to the G.). Notice the following idioms: sich hinter etwas machen, to go at with energy. Ich kann nicht dahinter kommen, I cannot understand it. Es hinter den Ohren haben, to be sly (coll.); hinter die Ohren schlagen, to give a box on the ear; sich etwas hinter die Ohren schreiben, to mark well.

5. In + in, into (A.).

The German and English prepositions are more nearly identical than any other two. See **305**, 1, 2.

In + Accusative.

Denotes direction, including transition, change, division: Wenn der Leib in Staub zerfallen, lebt der große Name noch (Sch.). Deutschland zerriß auf diesem Reichstage in zwei Religio′nen und zwei politische Partei′en (id.).

6. **Neben**, near, by the side of. See **305**, 1, 2. < *eneben*, lit. "in a line with."

7. **Über** + over, above. See **305**, 1, 2, 3.

Über + Accusative.

After verbs denoting rule and superiority over, *e. g.*, herrschen, siegen, verfügen (dispose); laughter, astonishment, disgust, in general an expression of an affection of the mind, *e. g.*, über etwas lachen, erstaunen, sich . . . beklagen, sich . . . entrüsten, sich ärgern. (For an older simple genit.) Karl der Große siegte über die Sachsen. Das Testament verfügt über ein großes Vermögen. Wie stutzte der Pöbel über die neuen Livre′en (G.). Die Gefangenen beklagen sich über ihre Behandlung. Über sein Benehmen habe ich mich recht geärgert. It denotes time and excess in time, number, measure: Über′s Jahr, a year hence, only in certain phrases, duration: über Nacht, die Nacht über. Den Sabbath über waren sie stille (B.). Über ein Jahr, more than a year (ambiguous, either "more than a year" or "a year hence"). Über drei tausend Kanonen. Über alle Begriffe schön, beautiful beyond comprehension.

When it denotes duration or simultaneousness, or when the idea of place is still felt, then the dative follows; when it denotes the reason then the accusative follows. This is clear when the same noun stands in both cases, as in Ich bin über dem Buche eingeschlafen, means "while reading it I fell asleep." Ich bin über das Buch eingeschlafen means "it was stupid, therefore I fell asleep." Über der Beschreibung da vergeß′ ich den ganzen Krieg (Sch.). Schade, daß über dem schönen Wahn des Lebens beste Hälfte dahin geht (Sch.).

Notice von etwas and über etwas sprechen. Ich habe davon gesprochen, I have mentioned it. Ich habe darüber gesprochen, I have treated of it, spoken at length.

8. **Unter** + under. See **305**, 3.

In the abstract sense this rule holds good. It denotes protection, inferiority, lack in numbers (Dative, opposite of über), mingling with, contemporaneous circumstance (D.). It stands for the partitive genit. (= among). Unter dem Schutze. Der Feldwebel steht unter dem Offizier. Wer will unter die Soldaten, der . . . , he who wants to become a soldier (Folk-song). Er ist brunter geblieben, he did not reach the number. Cambrai öffnete seinem Erzbischofe unter (amid) freudigem Zurufe die Thore wieder (Sch.), Wer unter (among) diesen (D.) reicht an unsern Friedland? (Sch.) (von diesen would be "of these"). It denotes time when none of the exacter modes of expressing time is used: Wir sind geboren unter gleichen Sternen (Sch.). Unter der Regierung der Königin Victoria = in the reign; während implies not a single act, but a commensurate duration, = during. Der Sakristan schlief während der Predigt, but ging unter der Predigt hinaus. In „unterdessen," and other compounds of that class, indessen, etc., the gen. is probably adverbial and not called for by the preposition.

See zwischen.

9. Vor + before, in front of. See **305**, 1, 2, 3.

Vor + **Dative.**

Introduces the object of fear and abhorrence: Kein Eisengitter schützt vor ihrer List (Sch.). Vor gewissen Erinnerungen möcht' ich mich gern hüten (id.). Mir graut vor dir. Time before which anything is to happen or has happened: Der König ist gesonnen, vor Abend in Madrid noch einzutreffen (Sch.). Vor dreißig Jahren, thirty years ago. Vor acht Tagen, a week ago. Hindrance and cause: Die Großmutter wird vor Kummer sterben (Sch.). Den Wald vor lauter Bäumen nicht sehen (Prov.). Vor Hunger, vor Durst sterben. Preference: vor allen Dingen, above all things; herrlich vor allen.

Vor and für are doublets and come from *fora* and *furi* respectively. In M. H. G. *für* + A. answered the question whither? *vor* + D. the question where? In N. H. G. they were confounded, even in Lessing very frequently, but in the last seventy years the present syntactical difference has prevailed. Goethe and Schiller rarely confound them

10. Zwischen.

"Between" *two* objects in place, time, and in the figurative sense. Kein muß es bleiben zwischen mir und ihm (Sch.). Die Wolkensäule kam zwischen das Heer der Ägypter und das Heer Israels (B.). See **305**, 1, 2; also unter = among, sub 8.

SYNTAX OF THE CONJUNCTIONS.

307. The conjunctions are divided: 1. Into the coordinating, like und, denn, etc.; 2. Into the subordinating, *e. g.*, weil, da, als, etc. They are treated in the General Syntax, where see the various clauses.

GENERAL SYNTAX.

I. THE SIMPLE SENTENCE.

308. **Subject** and **verb** make up the **simple** sentence. This sentence may be expanded by complements of the subject and of the verb. The subject may be either a substantive, a substantive pronoun, or other words used as substantives. The attributes of the subjects may be adjective, participle, adjective pronouns, numerals. These are adjective attributes. Substantives, substantive pronouns, and the infinitive are substantive attributes. Their relation to the subject may be that of apposition and of coordination; or they may be connected by the genitive, or by preposition + case in subordination. Preposition + case is more expressive than the genitive alone, when the subject is to be defined as to time, place, value, kind, means, purpose.

The predicate is either a simple verb or a copula + adjective or substantive or pronoun which may be again expanded like the subject. The complements of the verb are object and adverb. The object is either a noun, substantive pronoun, or other words used as nouns. It stands in the accusative, dative or genitive, or is expressed by preposition + case. The adverb qualifies the verb, adjective, and other adverb. It is either an adverb proper or preposition + case of substantive or what is used as such. It may also be a genitive or an accusative.

309. As to form the main sentences may be divided as follows :

1. **Declarative sentences,** which either affirm something of the subject or deny something with regard to it. Affirmative : Kurz ist der Schmerz und ewig ist die Freude (Sch.). Du hast Diamanten und Perlen (Heine). Negative : Das Leben ist der Güter

höchstes nicht (Sch.). Sie sollen ihn nicht haben, den freien deutschen Rhein (Beck).

1. The double negative is still frequent in the classics and colloquially, but it is not in accordance with correct usage now: Keine Luft von keiner Seite (G., classical). Man sieht, daß er an nichts keinen Anteil nimmt (F. 3489) (said by Margaret, coll.). After the comparative it also occurs in the classics: Wir müssen das Werk in diesen nächsten Tagen weiter fördern, als es in Jahren nicht gedieh (Sch.).

2. After verbs of "hindering," "forbidding," "warning," like verhüten, verhindern, warnen, verbieten, etc., the dependent clause may contain „nicht„: Nur hütet euch, daß ihr mir nichts vergießt (G.). Nimm dich in Acht, daß dich Rache nicht verderbe (Sch.).

3. When the negative does not affect the predicate, the sentence may still be affirmative. Nicht mir, den eignen Augen mögt ihr glauben (Sch.). But nicht mir stands for a whole sentence.

2. **Interrogative sentences**: Hast du das Schloß gesehen? (Uh.). Wer reitet so spät durch Nacht und Wind? (G.). Double question: War der Bettler verrückt oder war er betrunken? Glaubst du das oder nicht? Willst du immer weiter schweifen? (G.). Wer weiß das nicht?

For the potential subjunctive in questions, see **284**, 3.
For the indirect question, see **325**, 2.

3. The **exclamatory sentence** has not an independent form. Any other sentence, even a dependent clause, may become exclamatory: O, du Wald, o ihr Berge drüben wie seid ihr so jung geblieben und ich bin worden so alt! (Uh.). Das ist das Los des Schönen auf der Erde! (Sch.). Was dank' (owe) ich ihm nicht alles! (id.). Wie der Knabe gewachsen ist!

For the imperative and optative sentences, see **284**, 2; **286**.

310. Elliptical clauses generally contain only the predicate or a part of it, including the object or adverb. Guten Morgen! Gelt! Truly! Getroffen! You have hit it! Langsam! Schnell! etc. It is very frequent in the imperative, see **287**.

Proverbs often omit the verb: Viel Geschrei und wenig Wolle. Kleine Kinder, kleine Sorgen; große Kinder, große Sorgen. See **309**, 3, in which the last examples are really dependent questions.

Concord of Subject and Predicate.

311. The predicate (verb) agrees with the subject in number and person.

Two or more subjects (generally connected by unb) require a verb in the plural: Unter ben Anwesenden wechseln Furcht und Erstaunen (Sch.). Doch an dem Herzen nagten mir der Unmut und die Streitbegier (id.).

1. If the subjects are conceived as a unit and by a license greater in German than in English, the verb may stand in the singular; also in the inverted order if the first noun is in the singular. Ex.: Was ist das für ein Mann, daß ihm Wind und Meer gehorsam ist (B.). Eh' spreche Welt und Nachwelt, etc. (Sch.). Da kommt der Müller und seine Knechte. By license: Sagen und Thun ist zweierlei (Prov.). Das Mistrauen und die Eifersucht . . . erwachte bald wieder (Sch.).

2. The plural verb stands after titles in the singular in addressing royalty and persons of high standing. In speaking of ruling princes the plural also stands. Servants also use it in speaking of their masters when these have a title. Ex.: Eure (Ew.) Majestät, Durchlaucht, Excellenz befehlen? Seine Majestät der Kaiser haben geruht, etc. Der Herr Geheime Hofrat sind nicht zu Hause. Die Herrschaft sind ausgegangen.

312. After a collective noun the verb stands more regularly in the singular than in Eng. Only when this noun or an indefinite numeral is accompanied by a genitive pl., the plural verb is the rule. In early N. H. G. (B.) this plural was very common. Die Menge floh. Alle Welt nimmt Teil (G.). Und das junge Volk der Schnitter fliegt zum Tanz (Sch.). Alle Menge deines Hauses sollen sterben (B.).

313. When the subject is a neuter pronoun, es, dies, das, etc., the neuter verb agrees with the predicate noun or substantive pronoun in number: Das waren mir selige Tage (Overbeck). Es sind die Früchte ihres Thuns (Sch.). Es zogen drei Jäger wohl auf die Birsch (Uh.). In this case es is only expletive. Wer sind diese?

314. When subjects are connected by entweder — oder, nicht nur — sondern auch, weder — noch, sowohl — als (auch), the verb has the person and number of the first subject and joins this one if the subjects are of different persons. The verb for the second subject is omitted. Entweder du gehst (or gehst du) oder ich. Teils war ich schuld, teils er. Subjects of the same person connected by the above correlatives ; by oder, nebst, mit, samt have as a rule a singular verb and the verb joins the second subject. Dem Volke kann weder Feuer bei noch Wasser (Sch.), Neither fire nor water can harm those people.

315. If the subjects are of different persons, the first has the preference over the second, the second over the third. Moreover, the plural of the respective pronouns is often added. Der da und ich, wir sind aus Eger (Sch.). Du und der Vetter, (ihr) geht nach Hause.

The adjective as a predicate or attribute has been sufficiently treated under the adjective, see **210-225.**

316. The noun as a predicate agrees with the subject in case ; if the subject is a person, also in number and gender, but in the latter only when there are special forms for masculine and feminine. See **167.** Ex.: Die Weltgeschichte ist das Weltgericht (Sch.). Die Not ist die Mutter der Erfindung (Prov.). Das Mädchen will jetzt Erzieherin werden, zuerst wollte sie Schauspielerin werden.

1. If one person is addressed as Sie or Ihr, the substantive stands of course in the singular. „Sie sind ein großer Meister im Schießen." Poetic and emphatic are such turns as : Regierte Recht so läget ihr vor mir im Staube jetzt, denn ich bin Euer König (Sch., spoken by Maria Stuart).

317. The substantive in **apposition** has the same concords as the substantive in the predicate, only the rule as to case is frequently found unobserved in the best writers. Was Venus band, die Bringerin des Glücks, kann Mars, der Stern des Unglücks ſchnell zerreißen (Sch.). Ihr kennet ihn, den Schöpfer kühner Heere (id.).

The apposition may be emphasized by nämlich and als: Ihnen, als einem gereiften Manne, glauben wir.

II. THE COMPOUND SENTENCE.

318. The compound sentence consists of two or more clauses, which may be **coordinate** (of equal grammatical value) or **subordinate** (one dependent upon the other).

Coordinate Sentences.

We may distinguish various kinds of coordinate sentences, which may or may not be connected by conjunctions.

319. Copulative Sentences. The conjunctions und, auch, desgleichen, gleichfalls, ebenfalls, and their compounds, desgleichen auch, ſo auch, ebenſo auch; nicht nur — ſondern auch; nicht allein — ſondern auch; ſowohl — als (auch); weder — noch indicate mere parataxis. Zudem, außerdem, überdies, ja, ſogar, ja ſogar, vielmehr emphasize the second clauses. Partitive conjunctions are teils — teils, halb — halb, zum Teil — zum Teil. Ordinal conjunctions are erſtens — zweitens, etc.; zuerſt — dann — ferner, endlich, zuletzt; bald — bald. Explanatory are nämlich, und zwar. Ex.: Die Müh' iſt klein, der Spaß iſt groß (F. 4049). Halb zog ſie ihn, halb ſang er hin (G.). Ich will weder leugnen noch beſchönigen, daß ich ſie beredete (id.). Nicht allein die erſten Blüten fallen ab, ſondern auch die Früchte (id.).

1. Notice that the adverbial conjunctions such as bald, zuletzt, dann, weder — noch, halb, teils, etc., always cause inversion. Some admit of inversion, but do not require it, *e. g.*, auch, erſtens, nämlich. The ordinal conjunctions and nämlich are frequently separated by a comma, then no inversion takes place. Erſtens iſt es ſo der Brauch, zweitens will man's ſelber auch (Busch).

320. Adversative Sentences. 1. One excludes the other (disjunctive-adversative): oder, or, entweder — oder, ſonſt (else), andernfalls, otherwise. Ex.: Er (Wallenstein) mußte entweder gar nicht befehlen oder mit vollkommener Freiheit handeln (Sch.). One contradicts the other (contradictory-adversative): sondern, vielmehr, sondern . . . vielmehr. The first clause contains nicht, zwar, freilich, allerdings, wohl. So wagten sie sich nicht in die Nähe der Feinde, sondern kehrten unverrichteter Sache zurück (Sch.).

2. The second sentence concedes the statement of the first in part or wholly. The first may contain nicht, etc., as above; the second has aber, often in the connection aber doch, dennoch aber, aber gleichwohl; allein, übrigens; nur. Allein is stronger than aber.

<small>Mark the contrast between aber and sondern, Eng. but. Aber concedes, sondern contradicts. Er war zwar nicht krank, aber doch nicht dazu aufgelegt. "but he did not feel like it." Er war nicht krank, sondern er war nur nicht dazu aufgelegt (he only did not feel like doing it). Viele sind berufen aber wenige sind auserwählet (B.). Den Ungeheuern, den Gigantischen hätte man ihn (Corneille) nennen sollen, aber nicht den Großen (Le.). Wasser thut's freilich nicht (It is not the water that is effective in baptism), sondern das Wort Gottes, so (which) mit und bei dem Wasser ist (Lu.).</small>

3. The second sentence states something new or different or in contrast with the first without contradicting or excluding or limiting the same. It occurs commonly in narrative and may be called "connexive- or contrasting-adversative." Conjunctions: aber, hingegen, dagegen, übrigens, trotzdem, gleichwohl, indessen, etc. Die Beleidigung ist groß; aber größer ist seine Gnade (Le.). Es scheint ein Rätsel und doch ist es keins (G.). Es ist die schönste Hoffnung; doch ist es nur eine Hoffnung (Sch.).

321. Causal Sentences. One gives the reason or cause for the other. Conjunctions: d(a)rum, deswegen, daher, denn, nämlich, etc. The clause containing the reason generally stands second, the one beginning with „denn" always. Notice denn, "for," always calls for the normal order. Ex.: Soldaten waren teuer, denn die Menge geht nach dem Glück (Sch.). Eine Durchlauchtigkeit läßt er sich nennen; drum muß er Soldaten halten können (id.).

322. Illative Sentences. One sentence is an inference or effect of the other. Closely related to the causal. Conjunctions: ſo, a'lſo, ſomi't, folglich, mithi'n, de'mnach, etc. Meine Rechte (right hand) iſt gegen den Druck der Liebe unempfindlich . . . ſo (then) ſeid ihr Göß von Berlichingen (G.). Die Sonnen alſo ſcheinen uns nicht mehr (Sch.).

SUBORDINATE SENTENCES.

323. We shall distinguish three classes of dependent clauses, according to the logical value of the part of speech they represent:

1. **Substantive clauses,** with the value of a noun.
2. **Adjective clauses,** with the value of an adjective.
3. **Adverbial clauses,** with the value of an adverb.

SUBSTANTIVE CLAUSES.

324. The clause is subject: Das eben iſt der Fluch der böſen That, daß ſie fortwährend Böſes muß gebären (Sch.). Mich reuet, daß ich's that (id.). Predicate (N.): Die Menſchen ſind nicht immer was ſie ſcheinen (Le.). Object (A.): Glaubſt du nicht, daß eine Warnungsſtimme in Träumen vorbedeutend zu uns ſpricht? (Sch.). Was man ſchwarz auf weiß beſißt, kann man getroſt nach Hauſe tragen (F. 1966-7). Dative: Wohl dem, der bis auf die Neige (to the very end) rein gelebt ſein Leben hat (He.). Genitive: Wes das Herz voll iſt, des geht der Mund über (B.). Apposition: Den edeln Stolz, daß du dir ſelbſt nicht genügeſt, verzeih' ich dir (G.).

325. As to their contents the substantive clauses may be grouped as follows:

1. Daß, or declarative clauses, always introduced by „daß." Schon Sokrates lehrte, daß die Seele des Menſchen unſterblich ſei, or die Lehre, daß die Seele . . ., or wir glauben, daß die Seele . . .

More examples in **324**.

2. **Clauses containing indirect questions**: *a.* Questions after the predicate always introduced by ob; in the main clause may stand as correlatives es, das, dessen, davon, etc. Er hatte nicht geschrieben, ob er gesund geblieben (Bü.). (See F. 1667–70). *b.* Questions after any other part of the sentence, introduced by an interrogative pronoun, by an interrogative adverb, simple or compounded with a preposition, viz., wer, was, wie, wo, wann, womit, woher, wohin, etc. Ex.: Fraget nicht, warum ich traure (Sch.). See F. 1971. Begreifst du, wie andächtig schwärmen viel leichter als gut handeln ist? (Le.). Noch fehlt uns Kunde, was in Unterwalden und Schwyz geschehen (Sch.). *c.* The question may be disjunctive, introduced by ob — oder; ob — oder ob; ob — ob. Ex.: Aber sag' mir, ob wir stehen oder ob wir weiter gehen (F. 3906–7). Und eh' der Tag sich neigt, muß sich's erklären, ob ich den Freund, ob ich den Vater soll entbehren (Sch.).

REMARKS.—1. The mood in 1 and 2, according to circumstances, is either the indicative or the potential subjunctive. See the examples sub 1 and in **324**.

2. In „daß"-clauses the other two word-orders are also possible, but without daß: Sokrates lehrte, die Seele sei unsterblich. Es wurde behauptet, gestern habe man ihn noch auf der Straße gesehen.

3. When the subject is the same in both clauses or when the subject of the dependent clause is the object of the main clause, in short, when no ambiguity is caused, the infinitive clause can stand in place of daß + dependent order. Man hofft, das untergegangene Schiff noch zu heben. Die Polizei hat dem Kaufmanne befohlen, sein Schild höher zu hängen.

3. **Clauses with indirect speech**—after verbs of saying, asserting, knowing, thinking, wishing, demanding, commanding. They either begin with daß with dependent order or they have the order of the direct speech. The subjunctive is the reigning mood. For examples and tense, see **282**.

4. **Clauses containing direct speech, a quotation**: Das Wort ist frei, sagt der General (Sch.). Der König rief: Ist der Sänger da?

ADJECTIVE CLAUSES.

326. The clause is introduced by a relative pronoun or by a relative adverb. Nothing can precede the pronoun in the clause except a preposition. Unless the personal pronoun is repeated after the relative, the verb stands in the third person. Ex.: Du sprichst von Zeiten, die vergangen sind (Sch.). Die Stätte, die ein guter Mensch betrat, ist eingeweiht (G.). Der du von dem Himmel bist, süßer Friede . . . (id.).

For use of the pronouns and more examples, see 255-258.

327. 1. The relative pronoun can never be omitted as in English. In several relative clauses referring to the same word, the pronoun need stand only once, if the same case is required; if a different case is necessary, the pronoun should be repeated. This is often sinned against, for instance by Schiller: Sieh da die Verse, die er schrieb und seine Glut gesteht, instead of worin er . . . gesteht.

2. The relative clauses beginning with wer, was without antecedents are really identical with substantive clauses, e. g., Da seht, daß ihr tiefsinnig faßt, was in des Menschen Hirn nicht paßt. Für was drein geht und nicht drein geht, ein kräftig Wort zu Diensten steht (F. 1950-3).

3. Case-attraction between relative and antecedent is now rare.

Als welcher, denoting rather a cause than a quality, is now archaic, but still quite frequent in Lessing's time. Äneas, als welcher sich an den bloßen (mere) Figuren ergetzet, = "Æneas, since he delights . . ." (Le.). Von der Tragödie, als über die uns die Zeit ziemlich alles daraus (of *Aristotle's Poetics*) gönnen . . . "about tragedy, in so far as time has favored us . . ." (id.). „Da" in the relative clause is no longer usage. Wer da stehet, sehe zu, daß er nicht falle (B.).

328. The mood depends upon circumstances. The potential subjunctive (of the preterit and pluperfect) is frequent after a negative main clause. Es ist keine große Stadt in Deutschland, die der Onkel nicht besucht hätte (= did not visit). The subjunctive of indirect speech also stands. Die Regierung der Vereinigten Staaten beschwerte sich über die Landung sovieler Armen, welche manche europäische Regierung fortschicke.

ADVERBIAL CLAUSES.

329. They are introduced by the subordinating conjunctions. The main clause often has an emphatic adverb, e. g., alfo, dann, da, dahin, jetzt, daher, darum. So does not, as a rule, stand after dependent clauses expressing time and place, and generally becomes superfluous in English after dependent clauses of manner.

330. Temporal Clauses. 1. *Contemporaneous action* implying either duration or only point of time. Conjunctions: während, indem, indes (indeffen), wie, da (all meaning "while," "as"); folange (als); fo oft (als); fo bald (als); da, wo (rare and colloquial) = when; wenn (wann is old) + "when," refers to the future; als, "when," refers always to the past with the preterit; weil, dieweil, derweil, = + "while," are archaic. Solange, fo oft, fobald are now much more common without „als."

Ex.: Ach! vielleicht indem (as) wir hoffen, hat uns Unheil schon getroffen (Sch.). Nur der Starke wird das Schicksal zwingen, wenn der Schwächling unterliegt (Sch.). Und wie (as) er sitzt und wie er laufcht, teilt sich die Flut empor (G.). Als des Sanctus Worte kamen, da schellt er dreimal bei dem Namen („Sanctus . . ." is part of the mass) (Sch.). Es irrt der Mensch, folang' er strebt (F. 317). Sobald die ersten Lerchen schwirrten (erschien) ein Mädchen schön und wunderbar (Sch.). Das Eisen muß geschmiedet werden, weil es glüht (Prov.). Will mir die Hand noch reichen, derweil ich eben lab (= while I am loading the musket) (Uh.).

2. *Antecedent action, i. e.,* the action of the dependent clause precedes that of the main clause. Conjunctions: nachdem, after; da, als, wenn, after, when; seitdem, seit, seitdem daß (all mean + since); fobald (als), fowie, wie, as soon as; the adverb kaum + inverted order.

Ex.: Nimmer (no more) fang ich freudige Lieder, seit ich deine Stimme bin (Sch.) Wenn (after) der Leib in Staub zerfallen, lebt der große Name noch (Sch.). Und wie er winkt mit dem Finger, auf thut sich der weite Zwinger (id.). Kaum war der Vater tot, so kommt ein jeder mit seinem Ring (Le.). (Notice the inversion.)

Der König verließ Nürnberg, nachdem er es zur Fürsorge mit einer hinlänglichen Besatzung versehen hatte (Sch.).

3. *Subsequent action.* The action of the dependent clause follows. Conjunctions: Ehe, bevor, + "ere", "before"; bis, until, with or without daß.

Ex.: Nie verachte den Mann, eh' du sein Inn'res erkannt haft (He.). Bevor wir's laffen rinnen, betet einen frommen Spruch (Sch.). Bis die Glocke sich verkühlet, laßt die strenge Arbeit ruhn (id.). Ehe wir es uns versahen (unexpectedly), brach der Wagen zusammen.

a. The main clause may be emphasized by dann, damals, bann, darauf, and so, if it follows the dependent clause.

In 2 and 3 the potential subjunctive can stand.

331. Local Clauses. They denote the place and direction of the action of the main clause. They begin with wo, wohin, woher, and the main clause may contain a corresponding da, dahin, daher, hier.

Ex.: Wo Menschenkunst nicht zureicht, hat der Himmel oft geraten (Sch.). Die Welt ist vollkommen überall, wo der Mensch nicht hinkommt mit seiner Qual (id.). Denn eben wo Begriffe fehlen, da stellt ein Wort zur rechten Zeit sich ein (F. 1995-6). Kein Wasser ist zu haben, wohin man sich auch wende.

a. The demonstratives da, dahin, daher in the local clause are now archaic. Do not confound the relative clauses and indirect questions with the local clauses which generally refer to an adverb.

The potential subjunctive may stand in them.

Clauses of Manner and Cause.

332. *Modal clauses* express an accompanying circumstance and are therefore related to contemporaneous clauses. Conjunctions: indem, daß nicht, ohne daß, without, indem nicht, statt or anstatt daß, instead of. Ex.: Der Ritter ging fort, indem er auf den Gegner einen verächtlichen Blick warf. Ich bin nie in London, daß ich nicht das Museum besuchte (subj.).

1. They may have the potential subjunctive. But these clauses occur more frequently in the form of participial and infinitive clauses with

„ohne zu," „anstatt zu" : Al-Hasi, anstatt zu empfangen, mußte zahlen. Er ritt fort ohne sich umzusehen.

333. *Comparative clauses* denote manner, degree, and measure. Conjunctions: wie, als, "as," "than" with the corresponding so, also, ebenso (= so) in the main clause. After the comparative als, denn, weder, "than." Other forms: gleichwie — so; so wie — so; just as — as, so. Wie denotes rather manner and quality, als the degree and quantity. When both clauses have the same predicate, contraction is common. Then wie denotes likeness, als identity.

Ex. : Ich singe wie der Vogel singt (G.). Danket Gott so warm als ich für diesen Trunk euch danke (id.). Wie du mir („thust" understood), so ich dir (Prov.). Du bist mir nichts mehr als sein Sohn (Sch.). Der träge Gang des Krieges hat dem König ebensoviel Schaden gethan als er den Rebellen Vorteil brachte (id.). Hatte sich ein Ränzlein angemäst't als wie der Doktor Luther (F. 2129–30) (als wie is colloquial). „Wie ein Ritter," "like a knight"; „als (ein) Ritter," "as a knight." Sein Glück war größer als man berechnet hatte (Sch.). Eines Hauptes (by one head) länger benn alles Volk (B.). Weder is very rare.

1. Specially to be noticed are the clauses with als ob, alswenn, generally followed by the potential or unreal subjunctive. For wenn + dependent order occurs also the inverted without wenn. Ex.: Ihr eilet ja, als wenn ihr Flügel hättet (Le.). Suche die Wissenschaft, als würdest ewig du hier sein; Tugend, als hielte der Tod dich schon am sträubenden Haar (He.). But the indicative is possible: Und es wallet und siedet und brauset und zischt wie wenn Wasser mit Feuer sich mengt (Sch.).

2. Denn is preferable after a comparative when several „als" occur. Wie is colloquial. Es fragt sich ob Lessing größer als Dichter denn als Mensch gewesen sei. Nicht in the clause after als is no longer good usage, though common in the 17th and 18th centuries. Lessing has it very frequently. Ich lebte so eingezogen, als ich in Meißen nicht gelebt hatte (Le.).

a. Nichts weniger als means "anything but," literally "nothing less than that," generally felt by English speakers as meaning "nothing but," *e. g.*, Aber ich darf sagen, daß diese Einrichtung der Fabel nichts weniger als notwendig ist, *i. e.*, that this arrangement of the plot is anything but necessary (Le.). In „nichts als" = "nothing but," as after all negative pronouns, „niemand als du" = nobody but you, als has exclusive force, = " but."

3. Other correlatives are so einer — wie; der nämliche — wie; derselbe — wie; solch-, so + positive adjective — wie (quality) and als (degree); after

zu, allzu + positive and after ein anderer stand als + daß or wenn, als and infinitive, e. g., Er denkt zu edel, als daß er so etwas von uns erwarten könnte. Er ist der nämliche wie er immer war. Eure Versöhnung war ein wenig zu schnell, als daß sie dauerhaft hätte sein sollen (G.).

Notice the potential subjunctive after „als daß."

334. Under this head comes really the *proportional clause*, which expresses the proportion of the decrease or increase of what is asserted in the main clause. The conjunctions are the following correlatives : je — desto, um so (or um desto, rarely); je — je, = the — the; je nachdem (or nachdem or wie, rarely), according as. If the main clause stand first, its correlative is dispensable.

Ex.: Je mehr der Vorrat schmolz, desto schrecklicher wuchs der Hunger (Sch.). Je länger, je lieber (Prov.). Je mehr er hat, je mehr er will. (Je) nachdem einer ringt, nachdem ihm gelingt (G.), "The success depends upon the effort."

1. Je = ever ; desto, "on that account," "hence," see **442**, *a*. Notice the dependent order in the first, the inverted generally in the second.

335. *Consecutive clauses* express the result or effect of the predicate of the main clause. Conjunctions: daß (sodaß), that; in the main clause, if any correlative, so, so sehr, dergestalt, derart, solch. Ex.: So verabscheut ist die Tyrannei', daß sie kein Werkzeug findet (Sch.). Er schlug, daß laut der Wald erklang und alles Eisen in Stücken sprang (Uh.).

1 The result may also be expressed in the form of a main clause or of an infinitive clause: Doch übernähm' ich gern noch ei'nmal alle Plage, so lieb war mir das Kind (F. 3123–4). Ich bin zu alt, um nur zu spielen, zu jung um ohne Wunsch zu sein (F. 1546–7).

2. Mark the potential and unreal subjunctives of the preterit and pluperfect which may stand in these clauses : Vermeint Ihr mich so jung und schwach, daß ich mit Riesen stritte? (Uh.). Das Pferd war so lahm, daß wir schneller zu Fuß heim gekommen wären.

336. *Restrictive clauses* limit the value and scope of the statement of the predicate and border closely upon the conditional and comparative clauses. Conjunctions: nur daß, only (that), außer daß, except that, in so fern (als), wofern, in wie fern, in so or in wie weit, in as far as, in as much as. The negative force is given also by the subjunctive and the normal order with the adverb denn or by es sei denn, es wäre denn, daß, which is now more common.

Ex. : Wir waren gar nicht so übel bran, nur daß wir nichts zu trinken hatten, We were not at all so badly off, only . . . In so fern nun diese Wesen Körper sind, schildert die Poesie auch Körper (Le.). Er entfernte sich niemals weit, er sagt' es ihr denn (H. and D., IV. 42–8). Ich lasse dich nicht, du segnest mich denn (unless thou bless me) (B.). Ruhig (gedenke ich mich zu verhalten); es sei denn, daß (unless) er sich an meiner Ehre oder meinen Gütern vergreife (Sch.).

1. This is a very old construction, quite common in M. H. G. The negative force lies not in denn, but in the lost *ne* + the potential or concessive subjunctive. Denn < M. H. G. *danne*, is unessential. Compare M. H. G. *den lip wil ich verliesen, si en werde mîn wîp* = my life will I lose, (she become not my wife) unless she, etc. *Swaz lebete in dem walde ez entrünne danne balde, das was zehant tot,* = Was im Walde lebte, das war auf der Stelle tot, es sei denn daß es bald davon lief or gelaufen wäre (quoted by Paul). *Ne* disappeared as early as late M. H. G., particularly after a negative main clause. It is left in nur < *ne waere* = (es) wäre nicht daß. See Paul's M. H. G. gram., § 335–40.

337. *Causal clauses* denote the cause, reason, and means. Conjunctions: da, since, weil, because, indem = by + present participle in Eng. Correlatives, if any: da'rum, da'her, so, deshalb etc. Da'durch daß, da'mit daß express rather the instrument. Weil expresses the material cause; da the logical reason; „in=dem" is a weak causal and borders rather closely upon the contemporaneous „indem." Denn + normal order expresses a known or admitted reason. It is emphatic. See **321**.

Ex. : Das Schlepptau (hawser) zerriß, weil der Schleppdampfer (tug) zu schnell anzog. Mit bem besten Willen leisten wir so wenig, weil uns tausend Willen kreuzen (G.). Jeden andern zu schicken ist besser, da ich so klein bin (G.). Dir blüht gewiß das schönste Glück auf Erden, da du so fromm und heilig bist (Sch.). Richelieu wußte sich nur dadurch zu helfen, daß er den Feindseligkeiten ein schleuniges Ende machte (Sch.).

1. Nun, dieweil, allbieweil, maßen, sintemal, and others, are rare and archaic.

2. The clauses with ba'burch baß, ba'mit baß border closely upon the substantive clause. Da, says Becker, denotes the real *and* logical reason, weil the logical only when the kind of reason is not emphasized. Weil stands in a clause that answers the question as to the reason. Warum wurde Wallenstein abgesetzt? Weil man ihn für einen Verräter hielt.

338. *Final clauses* express intention and object. Conjunctions: Dami't, baß, "in order that." Auf baß, und baß are archaic. In the main clause rarely stand barum, bazu, in der Absicht, zu dem Zwecke (both followed by baß).

Ex.: Darum eben leiht er feinem, damit er stets zu geben habe (Le.). Dazu ward ihm der Verstand, baß er im innern Herzen spüret, was er erschafft mit seiner Hand (Sch.). Ehre Vater und Mutter, auf baß dir's wohl gehe und du lange lebest auf Erden (B.).

1. The reigning mood of this clause is the subjunctive. If the object is represented as reached, the indicative may also stand. Um zu + inf. forms a very common final clause; Man lebt nicht um zu essen, sondern man ißt um zu leben.

339. *Concessive clauses* make a concession to the contradiction existing between the main clause and the result expected from it in the dependent clause. They are called also adversative causal clauses. Conjunctions: obglei'ch (ob . . . gleich), obscho'n (ob . . . schon), obwohl (ob . . . wohl), ob auch, ob zwar, wenn auch, wenn gleich, ob, all = "although." The main clause may contain be'nnoch, boch, nichtsbestoweniger, gleichwohl, but so only if it stands second.

Relative clauses with indefinite relative pronouns and adverbs, wer . . . auch (immer, nur), wie . . . auch, so . . . auch (noch); inverted clauses and those with the normal order, containing the adverbs schon, gleich, zwar, wohl, freilich, noch have also concessive force.

Ex.: Ist es gleich Nacht, so leuchtet unser Recht (Sch.). (Compare Obgleich es Nacht ist, ob es gleich Nacht ist . . .) Was Feuerswut ihm auch geraubt, ein süßer Trost ist ihm geblieben (id.). Mutig sprach er zu Reinekens besten (in favor of R.) so falsch auch dieser bekannt war (G.). Ein Gott ist, ein heiliger Wille lebt, wie auch der menschliche wanke (Sch.). Erfüll' davon dein Herz, so groß es ist (F. 3452).

Man kommt ins Gerede, wie man sich immer stellt (G.). Dem Bösewicht wird alles schwer, er thue was er will (Hölty). Zwar weiß ich viel, doch möcht' ich alles wissen (F. 601).

1. Mark also the form of the imperative and und + inversion: Sei noch so dumm, es gibt doch jemand(en), der dich für weise hält. Der Mensch ist frei geschaffen, ist frei, und würde er in Ketten geboren (Sch.).

2. Mood: if a fact is stated, the indicative; if a supposition, the concessive and unreal subjunctive. See examples above.

3. When certain parts of speech are common to both clauses, there may be contraction. Obwohl von hohem Stamm, liebt er das Volk (Sch.).

340. *Conditional clauses* express a supposition upon which the statement of the main clause will become a fact. If the supposition is real, the conditional clause has the indicative; if only fancied or merely possible, the potential subjunctive; if it implies that the contrary of the supposition is about to happen or has happened, then it has the unreal subjunctive of the imperfect or the pluperfect. Conjunctions: wenn, if; falls, im Falle daß, in case that; wenn anders, if . . . at all; also wofern, sofern (such often difficult to distinguish from a concessive clause); wo, so (rare). The main clause may have da, dann, in dem Falle, and if it stand second, generally begins with so.

Ex.: Wenn sich die Völker selbst befrein, da kann die Wohlfahrt nicht gedeihn (Sch.). Wenn du als Mann die Wissenschaft vermehrst, so kann dein Sohn zu höh'rem Ziel gelangen (F. 1063). Wer miede nicht, wenn er's umgehen kann, das Äußerste (Sch.). So du kämpfest ritterlich, freut dein alter Vater sich (Stolberg).

1. Other forms of the conditional clause are the inverted order, the imperative, and the normal order with denn + subjunctive (= if . . . not, unless; see **336**, 1). Sei im Besitze und du wohnst im Recht (Sch.), Possession is nine points of the law. Dem lieben Gotte weich' nicht aus, find'st du ihn auf dem Weg (Sch.).

2. Wofern nicht, außer wenn, es sei denn daß, if not, unless, denote an exception to a statement true in general. Der Wolf ist harmlos, außer wenn er Hunger hat. See **336**, 1.

3. Sometimes the preterit ind. is substituted for the unreal subjunctive in the dependent or in the main clause or in both. Its force is

assurance, certainty. Traf ein Kürbis mein Gesicht, ach, so lebt' ich sicher nicht (Gleim). Mit diesem Pfeil durchschoß ich Euch, wenn ich mein liebes Kind getroffen hätte (Sch.). O wärst du wahr gewesen und gerade, nie kam es dahin, alles stünde anders (Sch.).

4. Contracted and abbreviated forms: Entworfen bloß ist's ein gemeiner Frevel; vollführt ist's ein unsterblich Unternehmen (Sch.). Wenn nicht, wo nicht, wo möglich are very common. Wir versuchten ihn wo möglich zu beruhigen, wenn nicht ganz zu entfernen.

For the tenses see also 275-280.

WORD-ORDER.

341. We distinguish three principal word-orders according to the position of subject and verb:

1. **The normal,** viz., subject — verb.
2. **The inverted,** viz., verb — subject.
3. **The dependent,** viz., verb at the end.

(By "verb" we shall understand for the sake of brevity the personal part and by "predicate" the non-personal part of the verb, viz., participle and infinitive.)

342. The normal occurs chiefly in main sentences: Der Wind weht. It is identical with the dependent order if there is only subject and verb in the dependent clause. Die Mühle geht, weil der Wind weht.

343. The inverted order occurs both in main and dependent clauses: Geht die Mühle? Weht der Wind, (so) geht die Mühle. It occurs:

a. In a question.

b. In optative and imperative sentences.

c. In dependent clauses, mainly conditional and after als + subjunctive when there is no conjunction like wenn, ob, etc.

d. If for any reason, generally a rhetorical one, any other word but the subject, or if a whole clause, head the sentence.

e. For impressiveness the verb stands first.

Examples with adjuncts (objects, adverbs, etc.) added:

a. Schreibt der Freund? Bleibt der Diener nicht lange aus? Was schreibt dir der Freund?

But when the inquiry is as to the subject the normal order stands of course. Wer schreibt einen Brief? Was ist der langen Rede kurzer Sinn? (Sch.).

b. Möge nie der Tag erscheinen, wenn des rauhen Krieges Horden dieses stille Thal durchtoben (Sch.). For more examples, see **284**, 1, 2.

But the inverted order is not required: Die Zahl der Tropfen, die er hegt, sei euren Tagen zugelegt! (F. 989–990).

c. Willst du genau erfahren was sich ziemt, so frage nur bei edlen Frauen an (G.). Wird man wo (= irgendwo) gut aufgenommen, muß man nicht gleich wiederkommen (Wolff). (Er) Strich drauf ein Spange, Kett' und Ring', als wären's eben Pfifferling'; dankt' nicht weniger und nicht mehr, als ob's ein Korb voll Nüsse wär' (F. 2843–6).

Notice here the inversion after als alone, but dependent order after als ob. See **340**, 1; also F. 1122–25, 1962–3.

But for emphasis and to add vividness, the normal is still possible: Du stehest still, er wartet auf; du sprichst ihn an, er strebt an dir hinauf (F. 1168–9). This is mere parataxis.

d. Die Botschaft hör' ich wohl, allein mir fehlt der glaube (F. 765). Ernst ist das Leben, heiter ist die Kunst (Sch.). Mich hat mein Herz betrogen (id.). Wo aber ein Aas ist, da versammeln sich die Adler (B.). Deines Geistes hab' ich einen Hauch verspürt (Uh.). See also F. 860–1, 1174–5, 1236. Übersehen kann Caylus dies Gemälde nicht haben (Le.). Geschrieben steht: „Im Anfang war das Wort" (F. 1224). See also **236**, 3.

1. The main clause, inserted in any statement or following it, has inversion according to this rule. Das, spricht er, ist fein Aufenthalt, was fördert himmelan (Sch.). Wie seid ihr glücklich, edler Graf! hub er voll Arglist an (id.). For emphasis the speaker can insert a clause uninverted: Denn, ich weiß es, er ist der Güter die er bereinst erbt, wert (H. and D., III. 53).

2. The coordinating conjunctions aber, allein, denn, nämlich, oder, sondern, und standing generally at the head of the sentence, any adverb with the force of an elliptical sentence (zwar, ja, etc., having generally a comma

after them) call for no inversion. After entweder there is option. Ex.: Aber die Kunst hat in den neueren Zeiten ungleich weitere Grenzen erhalten (Le.). Zwar euer Bart ist kraus, doch hebt ihr nicht die Riegel (F. 671). Fürwahr! ich bin der einzige Sohn nur (H. and D., IV. 91). Ja, mir hat es der Geist gesagt (id., IV. 95). Denn die Männer sind heftig (id., IV. 148).

3. When the dependent clause precedes, the main clause can for emphasis and very frequently colloquially have the normal order. Ex.: Hätte er die Ursachen dieses allgemeinen Aberglaubens an Shakspere's Schönheiten auch gesucht, er würde sie bald gefunden haben (Le.).

e. Hat die Königin doch nichts voraus vor dem gemeinen Bürgerweibe (Sch.). Stehen wie Felsen doch zwei Männer gegen einander! (H. and D., IV. 229). Generally contains doch.

344. The **dependent order** occurs only in dependent clauses. The clause begins with a relative or interrogative pronoun which may be preceded by a preposition; with a relative or interrog. adverb; or with a subordinating conjunction. Ex.: Wenn ich nicht Alexander wäre, möchte ich wohl Diogenes sein. Je mehr er hat, je mehr er will (Claudius). So stolz ich bin, muß ich mir selbst gestehn: dergleichen hab' ich nie gesehn (G.). Wie solche tiefgeprägte Bilder doch zu Zeiten in uns schlafen können, bis ein Wort, ein Laut sie weckt (Le.). See also F. 2015–18, 2062.

345. The dependent order does not occur in main clauses, but it is not the only order of the dependent clause.

1. The verb precedes two infinitives. One may be the past participle of a modal auxiliary. Ex.: Kann ich vergessen, wie's hätte kommen können? (Sch.). Daß ein Mensch doch einen Menschen so verlegen soll machen können! (Le.).

a. But in this case and in other compound tenses the "verb" (*i. e.*, the personal part) may also stand between the participle and the other auxiliary or the infinitive, *e. g.*, weil der Kaufmann das Haus soll gekauft haben or gekauft soll haben (in poetry). Gekauft haben soll is the common order.

2. The normal order may stand:

 1. In dependent clauses containing indirect speech. Er

glaubt, Shakspere habe Brutus zum Helden des Stückes machen wollen (Le.).

2. See last sentence of **358**.

3. In certain clauses with negative force containing an enclitic „denn": es sei denn daß + dependent order. See **336**.

4. In substantive clauses: Gott weiß, ich bin nicht schuld (Le.). This is mere parataxis without conjunction.

346. The auxiliaries haben and sein are also frequently dropped in dependent clauses to avoid an accumulation of verbal forms, both in prose and poetry. Lessing, Goethe, and Klopstock, especially the first, drop the auxiliary very freely and skillfully.

Ex.: Wie unbegreiflich ich von ihm beleidigt worden (supply bin here or before beleidigt) und noch werde (Le.). Möglich, daß der Vater die Tyranne'i des e i n e n Rings nicht länger in seinem Hause (supply hat) dulden wollen (id.).

347. The dependent order in main clauses is archaic and poetic. Ex.: Siegfried den Hammer wohl schwingen kunnt (dialect for konnte) (Uh.). Urahne, Großmutter, Mutter und Kind in dumpfer Stube beisammen sind (Schwab).

348. 1. The inverted order in the conditional clause and in a main clause for the sake of impressiveness has sprung from the order of the question. Compare, for instance: 1. Ist der Freund treu? (question). 2. Ist der Freund treu? (question). Gut, so wird er mir beistehen. 3. Ist der Freund treu (conditional clause), so wird er mir beistehen. 4. Ist mir der Freund doch treu geblieben! (impressive inversion).

2. The main clause has inversion when the dependent clause precedes, because it generally begins with an adverb like so, dann, etc. Gehst du nicht, so thust du Unrecht. Without so, the inversion really ceases. Hence we say, the normal order may still stand for emphasis. But so, etc., were so frequent that inversion became the rule. Inversion is therefore limited originally to the question and to the choice of placing the emphatic part of the sentence where it will be most prominent.

349. 1. The dependent order was in O. H. G. by no means limited to the dependent clause. Toward the 10th century it begins to become rarer in the main clause. In early M. H. G. it became limited to the dependent clause, so that now we may justly call it the "*dependent-clause order.*"

2. The verb at the end is, no doubt, a great blemish of German style—second only to the separation of the little prefix of separable compound verbs, which may turn up after many intervening parts at the close of the sentence. According to Delbrück, the dependent order—subject, object, verb—was the primitive one, still in force in Latin.

General Rules for the Order of other Parts of the Sentence besides Subject and Verb.

Position of the Predicate.

350. The predicate, be it an adjective, a substantive, participle, infinitive, or separable prefix of a compound verb or the first element of a loosely compounded verb, stands at the end of a main clause in a simple tense. The adjuncts of the predicate, such as objects, adverbs, stand between verb and predicate.

Ex.: Der Senne muß scheiden, der Sommer ist hin (Sch.). Ihr seid ein Meister (id.). Er hat verlor'ne Worte nur gesprochen (id.). Kein Schild fing diesen Mordstreich auf (id.). Straflose Frechheit spricht den Sitten Hohn (id.). Gestern fand ein Wagner=Conce'rt statt.

In the dependent clause only the verb changes position, subject and predicate remain as in the main clause, and the adjuncts stand between them. For instance: Glaubt das nicht! Ihr werdet dieses Kampfes Ende nimmer erblicken (Sch.), becomes Glaubt nicht, daß ihr dieses Kampfes Ende je erblicken werdet.

351. In the compound tense the separable prefix immediately precedes the participle, be it in a main or in a dependent clause. Dreißig Jahre haben wir zusammen ausgelebt und ausgehalten (Sch.). Die Cholera will (is about to) ü'berhand nehmen. See **137**.

Order of Objects and Cases.

352. *a.* Case of a person before a case of the thing. Aber auch noch dann ... fuhr der Kaiser fort, den Ständen den Frieden zu zeigen (Sch.).

b. Case of a pronoun before a noun. Man bestimmte sie (them) dem allgemeinen Unwillen zum Opfer (Sch.).

c. The dative stands before the accusative; if both are persons, the accusative may stand before the dative. Er selbst hatte dem Dienste dieses Hauses seine ersten Feldzüge gewidmet (Sch.).

d. The accusative-object stands before remoter objects, a genitive or a preposition + case. But see also *a*. Man möchte sagen, Voltaire habe ein Gefühl von der Wichtigkeit dieser Persönlichkeit gehabt (H. Grimm). Die Schülerin schrieb einen Aufsatz über den Winter.

e. As to pronouns, sich stands generally before es, and both before every other pronoun. The personal pronoun stands before the demonstrative. The personal and sich may stand before the subject, if it be a noun, in the inverted and dependent orders. Er hat sich es angeeignet. Krummau (a proper name) nähert sich ihm (Sch.). Wer darf sich so etwas erlauben? Jenem den Weg zu dem böhmischen Throne zu verschließen, ergriff man die Waffen schon unter Matthias (Sch.). Was ihm die vergrößerte Macht der Stände (estates) an Selbstthätigkeit noch übrig ließ, hielten seine Agnaten (relatives) unter einem schimpflichen Zwang (id.). Hat sich die Flotte ergeben? Hast du es ihm wieder gegeben?

1. *c* also includes the personal pronouns: Wie könnt' ich ohne Zeugen mich ihr nahn? (Sch.). The rules *a, c, d* are by no means strict.

353. For the position of the adjective, see the use of the adjective, **194, 212.** Notice that what depends upon an adjective, participle, or infinitive precedes them. Die Engländer sind ihrem Herrscherhause ergeben. Zum Sehen geboren, zum Schauen bestellt, dem Turme geschworen, gefällt mir die Welt (G.). Wir baten ihn, den Brief auf die Post zu geben. (Shakspere's Werke sind) keine Tugendlehren, in Kapitel gebracht und durch redende Exempel erläutert (Le.).

Position of Adverbs.

354. In general, adverbs stand before the words they qualify. The modal adverbs nicht, etwa, zwar, schon, wol, etc., and the adverbs of time immer, schon, jetzt, nie, nimmer stand generally immediately before the predicate or in place of it if there is none. Dies Bildniß ist bezaubernd schön (Mozart's Zauber=

flöte). Ein sehr heftiger Husten greift den Kranken stark an. Das schwere Herz wird nicht durch Worte leicht (Sch.). Schon viele Tage seh' ich es schweigend an (id.). Ich habe euch noch nie erkannt (B.). Hast du ihn noch nicht besucht? (Notice the opposite of the English order in "never yet," "not yet.")

355. An adverb of time stands before one of place, and both before one of manner. Ex.: Viele Bauern waren gestern nach der Stadt zu Markte gefahren. Wir fahren morgen *per* Eisenbahn nach Rudolstadt. Es tanzt sich auf diesem glatten Fußboden nicht sehr gut.

1. Of several adverbs of time or place the more general precede the more specific. Wir reisen morgen früh um 6 Uhr 59 Minuten ab. Der Polizist fand den Betrunkenen auf der Fahrstraße im Drecke liegen.

2. Adverbs of time precede objects when these are nouns, but pronouns precede all adverbs. Wir feiern balb den 4ten Juli, den Tag der Unabhängigkeitserklärung. Wir hoffen ihn morgen auf dem Bahnhofe zu treffen.

356. Only aber, nämlich, jedoch, and a few others, can separate subject and verb. Ex.: Der Richter aber sprach (Le.). Die Nachtigall jedoch singt wunderschön.

357. As to the position of the prepositions, they, with very few exceptions, precede the noun; when they follow the noun has been stated under Prepositions. See, for instance, **303**, 7, 8, 10.

Position of Clauses.

358. Dependent clauses have, in general, the positions of those parts of speech and of the sentence which they represent, *i. e.*, the substantive clause standing for the subject or object has the position of the subject or the object in the sentence, etc. No special rules are needed for them. When there are several dependent clauses, the last often takes for variety the normal order introduced by und.

The following examples show well-placed dependent clauses: Kein Kaiser kann, was unser ist, verschenken (Sch.). Versiegelt hab' ich's und verbrieft, daß er mein guter Engel ist (id.). Die Ehr', die ihm gebürt, geb' ich ihm gern; das Recht das er sich nimmt, verweigr' ich ihm (id.). Als ich jünger war, liebte ich nichts so sehr, als Roma'ne (novels) (G.). Richelieu wußte sich dadurch zu helfen, daß er den Feindseligkeiten zwischen beiden ein schleuniges Ende machte (Sch.). Mein guter Geist bewahrte mich davor, die Natter an den Busen mir zu legen (mir before die Natter in prose) (id.). Der Mensch begehrt, alles an sich zu reißen (G.). Wie glücklich ist der, der, um sich mit dem Schicksal in Einigkeit zu setzen, nicht sein ganzes vorhergehendes Leben wegzuwerfen braucht (id.).

359. The rules given can hardly be abstracted from poetry. Even in prose they will be found frequently infringed. Rhythm, rhyme, and, in prose, emphasis control the order of words and allow of much choice. But students translating into German should adhere to the rules very strictly. It will be noticed that the German word-order coincides very nearly with the old English, and does not differ after all so much from the modern English word-order. The chief points of difference are the dependent order, the position of adverbs of time, which in English stand generally at the end, and the position of the adjuncts of adjectives, participles, and infinitives, which precede the latter instead of following them as in English.

1. The word-order required by certain conjunctions has been frequently mentioned in the General Syntax. See, for instance, 320.

LIST OF ABBREVIATIONS AND SYMBOLS THAT REQUIRE EXPLANATIONS.

Ags. = Anglo-Saxon.
(B.) = Bible.
(Bo.) = Bodenstedt.
(Bü.) = Bürger.
(Ch.) = Chamisso.
D. = Dutch or Dative.
(F.) = Hart's Edition of Goethe's Faust, Part I.
Fr. = French.
(G.) = Goethe.
Go. = Gothic.
Gr. = Greek.
G. T. = General Teutonic.
(H. und D.) = Hart's edition of Goethe's *Hermann and Dorothea*.
(He.) = Herder.
H. G. = High German.
(Hu.) = A. von Humboldt.
I.-E. = Indo-European.
L. = Latin.
(Le.) = Lessing.

L. G. = Low German.
(Lu.) = Luther's works excepting his translation of the Bible.
M. G. = Middle German.
M. H. G. = Middle High German.
N. G. = North German or North Germany.
N. H. G. = New High German.
O. Fr. = Old French.
O. H. G. = Old High German.
(Prov.) = Proverb.
(R.) = Rückert.
Rules = the official rules for spelling, see **37**.
(Sch.) = Schiller.
S. G. = South German.
(Sh.) = Shakespere translated by Schlegel and Tieck.
(Uh.) = Uhland.
V. L. = Vulgar Latin.

< means "derived from," "sprung from," "taken from."

> means "passed or developed into," " taken into."

+ between a German and non-German word denotes common origin or "cognates." In other positions it means "accompanied or followed by."

* before a word means that that form of the word does not actually occur, but is conjectured or reconstructed.

: = :, or : as :, means a relation as in a mathematical proportion.

I, II, III after verbs indicates the strong verb-classes.

— between letters means "interchanges with," *e.g.*, h — ch as in hoher — hoch or e — i as in nehmen — nimmst.

SUBJECT-INDEX.

The numbers refer to the paragraphs. The umlauts have a separate place, ä after a, ö after o, ü after u.

Ablaut: nature of, 393; four grades, 394, 463, 2; 496; 497.
Ablaut series: and verb-classes, 122–129; I.-E., 394, 1; G. T., > O. H. G. > N. H. G., 395–400; 459–467; grouping of, 459.
Abstract nouns: article before, 149; no article, 145; 155, 2; plural of, 171; 62, Rem.
Accent: 417, 418; degrees of, 419; chief on stem-syllable, 420; 420, 2; 478, 4; Eng. in Norman-Fr. words, 420, 3; in compounds, 421–423; secondary, 424; rhetorical, 426; "free" in I.-E., 420, 2; in foreign words, 427, 420, 1; 424, 4; 493, 2; 63, 2; characteristic of Germanic Lang., 478, 4; =intonation, 392, 1.
Accidence: 38–138; Historical Commentary on, 428–476.
Accusative: office of, 198; after verbs, 198–206; two A. after verbs, 199; predicate in passive, 202, 2; cognate, 203; logical subject in, 205; after reflexive verbs, 206; adverbial, 207; difference between A. and G. of time, 208, 1; after adjectives, 207, 1; 183; absolute, 209; 297, 1; by attraction in the pred. after laſſen, 202, 1; after prepos., 304–306; with Inf., 292.
Adjective: decl. of, 69–72; 436; origin of strong decl., 437; comparison of, 73–76, see comparison, compar. and superlat.; 438, 439; used as nouns, 220, 221, 181; gender of same, 160, 3; 169; 162, 3; G. after, 182, 183; D. after, 194; A. after, 183; 207, 1.
Attributive use of, 211–217; only used attributively, 211; uninflected used attributively, 212; in the predicate, 218, 220; as nouns declined strong, 214; G. sg. m. and n., 216, 1; declined weak, 213; 217, 1; as nouns 221, 1; origin of double decl., 215; unsettled usage as to strong and weak decl., 216, 221; after indef. pron., 214; 216, 4; 181; after person. pron., 216, 2; two or more adj., 212, 3; 217. In the predicate, 218, 219; only used in pred., 219; position of adjuncts of, 353; accent in certain compounds, 422, 1–7; derivation of, 522–528; used as adverb, 554.
Adjective Clauses: nature of, 323; 326–328; 339.
Adverbial Clauses: nature of, 323, 329; various kinds of, 330–340; see temporal, local, clauses of manner and cause (332–340), final (338), conditional, (340), etc.
Adverbs: origin of, 551-555; < G. of nouns, 187, 552; +prepos. supplanting the person. pron., 234; syntax of, 299, 300; after prepos. + noun, 300; adverbs which are only adverbs, 300, 1; 554, 2; adjective as, 300, 2; 554; comparison by, 223, 224; relative and absolute superl. of, 300, 2; nature of, 301, 1; interrogative, 251, 5; relative, 258, 326, 331; demonstrative, 327, 3; in local clauses, 331, a; position in a sentence, 354; order of adverbs of time, place, manner, 355; accent in compound, 423.
Adversative Sentences: coordinate, 320.
Affricate: 413, 5; 408, 1.
Alemanic: 483, 1.
Alphabet: printed and script, 1, 2; origin of the G. letters, 360; Latin letters in G., 360, 2; relation to G. sounds, 361.
Anglo-Saxon, see English.
Apposition: < G. of nouns, 181; 179, 1; 317.
Articles: inflect. of, 38; accent of, 39; contraction with prepositions, 40; spelling of, 39; 41; syntax of, 140–158; nature of 140; general cases of absence of, 141–146; before proper nouns, 147; before abstract nouns, 149; before names of materials, 150; before collective nouns, 151; repetition of, 158. See A., def. and indef.
Article, Def.: infl. of, 38; attraction to preceding words not prepositions, 41; contraction with preceding prepos., 40; relation to Eng. possessive pron., 154, 243, 3; distributive for Eng. "a," 156.
Article, Indef.: infl. of, 38; aphaeresis of, 41; after certain pronouns, 144, 252; before certain pronouns, 157.
Austrian: 483.

SUBJECT-INDEX. 267

Auxiliaries: of tense: infl. of, 110; use of, 265, 266; 283, 2; omission of, 346; in passive voice, 273.
    Modal: see pret. pres. verbs; special uses of, 267; verbs of motion omitted after, 267, Rem.; imperative force of, 287, 4; +perf. and pres. inf., 288, 1; 290; in future, 279, 3, *a*.

Bavarian-Austrian: 483, 2; 488, 5, *a*.
Bible: 486; 487.
Brechung: 405, Rem.

Capitals: initial, 364; in pronouns of address, 230; in article, 39.
Cardinals, see Numerals.
Cases: see individual cases, N., G., etc.; order of cases in the sentence, 352.
Causal Sentences: coordinate, 321; subordinate, 337.
Comparative: see comparison; use of, 222; by adverbs, 223, 224; conjunctions after, 333.
Comparative Clauses: 333, 1-3; with nicht, 333, 2.
Comparison: of adjectives, 73-76; 438; 439; irregular, 76, 1; defective and redundant, 76, 2; the suffixes, 73, 438; by adverbs, 223, 224, 222, 1; of two qualities of the same object, 224.
Compound words: accent of, 421-424; irregular accent of certain nouns, adjectives, and prefixes, 422; secondary accent in, 424; 521; see nouns, adj., etc.; 516; compared with Eng., 521, 2, *b*.
Compound tenses: 109-115; 283.
Concessive Clauses: 339.
Conditionals: formation of, 115, 283, 5; force of, 280, 281, 284, 5.
Conditional Clauses: tenses in, 280, 284, 5; nature of, 340; several forms of, 340, 1; word-order in, 343, *c*.
Conjugation: strong and weak, 101-103; 446, 476; weak, 117, 118, 447, 454, 455; strong, 120-133, 446, 456-469.
Conjunctions: classification of, 307; origin of, 301, 558.
    Coordinating: copulative, 319; adversative, 320; concessive, 320, 2; causal, 321; illative, 322.
    Subordinating: in temporal clauses, 330; in comparative clauses, 333; 334; in consecutive clauses, 335; in restrictive clauses, 336; causal, 337; final, 338; concessive, 339; conditional, 340.
Consecutive Clauses: 335.
Consonant-declension, see n-declension.
Consonant-stems: become *i*-stems, 54; 428, 2; 432, 1; 432-435.
Consonants: description of, 374-389; open, 374-381; shut, 382-385; nasals, 386-388; compound, 389; long, 389, 5; cons.-table, p. 107; see Grimm's and Verner's Laws; doubling or lengthening of, 389, 5; 413, 5; 488, 2, *c*; 535, 1, R. 2.
Coordinate Sentences: 318; various kinds of, 319-322.
Copulative Sentences: 310.

Danish: 479, II.
Dative: office of, 189; as nearer object after intrans. and certain compound verbs, 190; as indirect object after trans. verbs, 191; ethical, 192; after impers. verbs, 193; after adj., 194; 190; supplanted by prepos. + case, 195; after prepos., 303, 305, 306.
Declension: of articles, 38; of nouns, 42-68; 428-435; of foreign nouns, 64, 62, 3; of proper nouns, 65-68; of the adjective, 69-72; of pronouns, 81-100.
Demonstrative Pronouns: 88-91; use of, 244-250; origin of, 442; supplanted by hier and da + prepos., 251, 2.
Dependent Clauses, see Subordinate.
Dependent order of words: 341, 344; in main clauses, 347, 349; the oldest order, 349, 2.
Dialect: and written language, 390; in M. H. G., 485, 2; in N. H. G., 486, 487; in the pronunciation of the educated, 390; and the public school, 392, 5.
Diphthongs: pronunc. of, 32; analysis of, 372; become single vowels, 488, 4 · < long vowels, 488, 5.
Dutch: 481, 3; 493, 3.

East Frankish: 482, 3; 486.
Elliptical clauses and phrases: 310; 284, 5, Rem.; 287; 343, *d*, 2.
English: 479, III.; 492, 4; umlaut in, 402, 2.
Euphony: 418, 1.
Exclamation: G. in, 188, 309, 3; order of words in, 343, *e*; see interjections.

Final clauses: 338.
Flemish: 481, 3.
Foreign nouns: decl. of, 64; gender of, 163; verbs, 538.
Foreign words: spelling of, 365; accent, 427, 420, 1; 424, 4; in G. word-stock, 492-494.
Fractions: 533, 2.
Frisian: 481, 1.
Future: formation of, 114; force of, 278; imperative force of, 278, 3; 287, 3; present with future force, 274, 5; condit. for subj. of, 281; origin of, 283, 4; 279, 3.

Gender: of nouns and their distribution among the declensions according to, 43; syntax of, 159-169; grammatical and sex, 159, 160; concord of the

same, 165-168; according to meaning, 160; according to endings, 161; doubtful and double, 162; change of, 161, Rem., 163; of compound nouns, 164; concord of, 165-168; between subject and predicate, 313, 316.
Genitive: office of, 180; various kinds of G., 180, 1-7; partitive G. passed into apposition, 181, 251; supplanted by prepos., 181; dependent upon adj., 82, 182; dependent upon verbs as nearer object, 184; as remoter object, 185; after impersonal verbs, 186; adverbial G. of place, time, etc., 187; supplanted by A., 207, Rem.; difference between A. and G., 208; after prepos., 302; in exclamations, 188.
German Dialects: classification of, 480-483; 484.
German Language: see *Schriftsprache*; history of, 478-494; relation to other Germanic languages, 480-486.
German Sounds: analysis of, 366-389.
Germanic Languages: relation to other I.-E. languages, 477; characteristics of, 478; classification of, 479-484.
Gerundive: 107; 289, Rem.; 298; 452.
Gothic: letters, 360; language, 479, 1.
Grimm's Law: 407-415; G. T. shifting, 407-410; G. shifting, 413-415; modifications of, 412; in dialects, 480; in derivative verbs, 535, 1, R. 2.

Hessian: 482, 2.
High German: explanation of terms, 480, 3, a. See South German.
Hildebrantslied: 485, 1.

Icelandic: 479, II; 229, 1; 530.
Illative Sentences: co-ordinate, 322.
Imperative: 105, 450; in strong verbs, 121; personal pron. in, 286, 1; future with imperative force, 278, 3; 287, 3; force of, 286; other verbal forms with the force of, 287; conditional and concessive force of, 339, 1; word-order in, 343, b.
Indefinite Pronouns: 94-100, 445; use of, 259-263.
Indirect Speech: tenses in, 282; mood in, 285; 325, 3; 328.
Indo-European: 477.
Induitive: 106, 451; nature of. 288; 290, 3, b; perfect, 288, 1; imper. force of, 287, 1; without and with zu, 289-291; 291, 3-5; without zu, 289, Rem.; after certain groups of verbs, 290; with zu, do., 291, 1; as object and subject, 291, 2, 3; A. with, 292; as a noun, 293; governed by prepos. + zu, 291, 1; inf. clause, 325, 2, Rem. 3; 332, 1; 335, 1; position of two, in dependent clause, 345, 1; position of adjuncts of, 353.
Instrumental: 194.
Interjections: 559, 560.
Interrogative Pronouns: 92, 444; use of, 251-253; D. supplanted by we(r) + prepos., 251, 2.

Interrogative Sentences: 309, 2; indirect, 325, 2; disjunctive, 325, 2, c; word-order, 343, a.
Inverted order of words: 341, 343; in inserted main clause, 343, 1; origin of, in conditional and in main clauses, 348, 1; after certain co-ordinating conjunctions, 319; in a clause instead of obgleich, etc., 339.
I-stems: 52-55; 420.
Iteratives: 531, 2.

Jo-stems: 46, 2; 428; in adj., 437, 3; 496, 2; 522.

Kanzleisprache: 486, 487.

Labialization, 367, 1; 370, 4, Rem.
Language: written. See *Schriftsprache*.
Law of Finals: 478, 3.
Levelling: nature of, 491, 1; in the strong pret., 460; in the weak verbs, 454, 455.
Low Frankish: 481, 3.
Low German Dialects: 480, 1; 481; > H. G., 493, 3; their relation to the written language, 392, 1-3; 391.
Low Saxon: 481, 2.
Luther: 486, 487.

Middle Frankish: 482, 1.
Middle German Dialects: 480, 2; 482; 488, 3, a; 488, 4.
Middle High German: 485, 2; transition of sounds to N. H. G., 488-491.
Mi-verbs: 136; 449, 1, 2; 473-476.
Modal Clauses: 332.
Modal Auxiliaries. See Auxiliaries.
Mood: see subj., imper.; in adjective clauses, 328.
Multiplicatives: 531, 1.

N-declension: of nouns, 47, 61, 62, 432-435; of adjectives, 69, 213, 215.
Narrowness of vowels: 367, 2.
Negatives: 309, 1; double negative, 309, 1; in comparative clauses, 333, 2.
New High German: 485, 486.
Nominative: 178, 179; absolute, 297; predicate, 179; A. for, in pred., 202, 1.
Normal order of words: 341, 342; in subordinate clauses, 345, 2; after co-ordinating conjunctions, 343, 2; when the subordinate clause precedes, 343, 3; 348, 2; 343, c; 358.
North German: see Low G.
Norwegian: 479, II.
Nouns: decl. of, 42-68; systems of noun-decl., 42; distribution of nouns among the three declensions according to gender, 43, 433; general rules for noun-decl., 43; strong decl. of, 44-60, 428-431; weak decl. of, 61, 62, 428, 2;

SUBJECT-INDEX. 269

432; mixed decl. of, 63, 435, 1; use of cases, see individual cases; derivation of, 496-516; composition, 517-521. gender of compound, 164; accent of, 421, 422. See Number, Proper N., Foreign N., Abstract N., Compound.
Number: Singular and plural of nouns:
pl. the basis of classification of strong nouns, 44; no sign, 45, *a*; umlaut, 45, *b*; -*e*, 49-55; -*er*, 56-60, 431; (e)n, 61-63; pl. in -*s*, 60; irregular, 51, 172, 173; double forms, 58, 162, 4; 431, 2; of abstract nouns, 171; nouns only in pl., 174.
Sing. or pl. after nouns of quantity, etc., 175; why sing., 176; sing. where Eng. pl., 177; sing. neut. of pronouns refer to masc., fem., and plural nouns, 168, 313.
Sing. and pl. of verbs: 311; pl. after a collective noun, 312; " pl. of majesty," 311, 2.
Numerals: 77; infl. of, 78; when inflected, 226, 227; cardinals, 77-79; pl. in -*e*, 227; in -*er*, 228, 2; ordinals, 80, 211, 530, 532; infinitive, 100; derivation of, 529-533.

Old High German: 485.
Ordinals: see Numerals.
Orthography: division into syllables, 36; regulated by government, 37, 361, 2; historical notes on, 360-365; umlautsigns, 362; on the marks to show length, 363; on use of capitals, 364; of foreign words, 365; government rules, 37.
O-stems: lose sign of the pl., 47, 51, 428.

Participial Clauses: 294, 4; 332, 1.
Participles: 102, 107, 453; use of, 294 -297; position of adjuncts of, 353.
Past part. without ge-, 108, 113, 453, 2; 470, 528; isolated, 129, Rem.; 131, Rem.; 524, 4; imper. force of, 287, 2; passive force of, 295; active force of, 295, 2; 296; dependent upon kommen, bleiben, etc., 296; of verbs of motion, 296; absolute construction, 297.
Pres. part., 274, 6; 283, 3, 4; 294, 453; in compound tenses, 283, 1, 2; 351.
Passive: see Voice.
Perfect: formation of, 112; force of, 276; with future perf. force, 279, 2; Eng. perf. — G. pres., 274, 4; imperative, 286, 1; infinitive, 288.
Personal Pronouns: 81, 82, 440; syntax of, 230-235; gender of, 81; use of, in address, 230-233; repetition of, 233, 2; omission of, 233, 1; supplanted by other pronouns and prepositions, 234; in the imper., 286. 1.
Phonology: 360-427; orthography, 360 -365; analysis of sounds, 366-389;

as standard of pronunc., 390-392; phonetic laws. 393-417; accent, 418-427.
Plattdeutsch: 481, 2, *a*; 484.
Pluperfect: formation of, 112; force of, 277; relation to Condit., 280, 281, 284, 5.
Plural: see Number.
Popular Etymology: 494, 2, 3.
Possessive Pronouns: 85-87; syntax of, 239-243; origin of, 441; compounds with, 87; used substantively, 240; repetition of, 241, 242, 2; relation to def. article, 154, 243, 3; supplanted by demonstr. pron., 242, 1; uninflected, 239, 243, 1; after G., 180, 4.
Predicate, 308; concord of subj. and pred., 311-317; number of verb after collective noun, 313; when subjects are connected by conjunctions, 311, 314; person of verb when subjects are of different persons, 315; position of, 350, 351.
Prepositions: syntax of, 301-306; nature of, 301, 1, 2; 556; classification of, according to cases, and treatment of, in alphabetical order, 302-306; governing the G., 302; governing the D., 303; governing the A., 304; governing D. and A., 305; general position of, 357.
Present: infl. of, 103; of weak verbs, 118, 447; of strong verbs, 121, 456; O. H. G., 446; of pret.-pres. verbs, 134; uses of, 274; periphrastic, 274, 6; imper. force, 287, 3; formation of present-stem, 457.
Preterit: infl. of, 103; weak, 454; strong, 458; levelling in, 460; double subj., 125, 126, 464, 3; 129; of pret.-pres. verbs, 134, 470; force of, 275; relation to condit., 280, 281, 284, 5; ind. for unreal subj., 340, 3.
Pret.-pres. verbs: 134; 135; 108, 2; 267; 470-472.
Pronouns: inflection of, 81-100, 440-445; syntax of, 230-263; concord with noun, 165-168, 235; origin of, 496; position of, in the sentence, 352, *e*; neut. pron. refers to masc. or fem. nouns, 168; neut. pron. one of two accusatives, 199, 1, 2. See reciprocal, possessive, etc., separately.
Pronunciation: of letters, 1-37, 366; standard of, 390-392; disputed points in standard, 391; Hanoverian and N. G., 390, 4; 392, 1-3; dialect in, 390, 1-3.
Proper Nouns: decl. of, 65-68; article before, 147, 155, 1; gender of, 160, 2, with Rem.; 164.

Question: see Interrogative Sentences.

Reciprocal Pronouns: 84, 197, 206, 238.
Reduplication: nature of, 458; in VII. Cl.

of verbs, 130, 131; in the present, 457, 3.
Reflexive Pronouns: 83, 237; personal for, 237, 1.
Relative Clauses: see Adjective Cl.
Relative Pronouns: 93; use of, 254-258; origin of, 254; supplanted by adverbs and conjunctions, 257, 258, 326, 327.
Restrictive Clauses: 336.
Roundness of vowels: 367, 1; in S. G., 391, 5.
Runes, 492, 2.
Rückumlaut: 402, 2; 455.

Scandinavian, 479, II.
Schriftsprache: 390; 485, 2; 486, 487.
Sentence: structure of simple, 308; constituents of, 308; arrangement of, see word-order: various kinds of main, 309; 284, 2; 286; compound, see coordinate and subordinate.
Shifting of mutes: see Grimm's Law.
Shifting of spirants: see Verner's Law.
Silesian: 482, 6.
Singular: see Number.
Slavic: 477; 481, 2, Rem.; 482, 4-6.
Sonancy: 376.
South Frankish: 482, 2.
South German Dialects: 480, 3; 483; 488, 5, *a*; 489; 490, 1, *a*; relation to the written language, 391, 392, 4.
Suabian: 483, 2.
Subject: 308; concord of, and predicate, 311-317; position of subject and verb, 341, 356.
Subjunctive: kinds of, 284; potential, 284, 3; 325, 2. Rem. 1; 325, 2; 328; in conditional clauses, 340, 448.
Subordinate Sentences: 318, 323, 324-340; word-order in, 343, *c*; 344-346; 350, Rem.; omission of auxil., 346; position of, 358.
Substantive Clauses: 323-325; nature of, 323; various kinds of, 325; normal order in, 345.
Superlative: see Comparison; use of, 222-225; never uninflected, 222; absolute and relative, 222; applied to two objects, 225; of adverbs, 300, 2.
Surdness: 376.
Swedish: 479, II.
Swiss: 483, 1, *a*.

Temporal Clauses: 330.
Tenses: simple, 101, 103, 448; use of, 274, 275, 283.
Compound: 109, 112-116, 276-281; origin of, 283; position of separable prefix, 351. See the separate tenses.
Thuringian: 482, 4.
Time: modes of expressing time, 226; G. of, 187; A. of, 208.

Umlaut: signs of, 31, 362; as a sign of the pl., 45, *b*; 48; in comparison of adj., 74; in pret. subj. of strong verbs, 121; in the pres. of strong verbs, 127, Rem.; 129, Rem.; 130, Rem.; 131, Rem.; 404; nature of, 401; in Eng. 402, 2; spread of, 488, 1; in derived verbs, 535.
Upper Saxon: 482, 5.

Varintives: 533.
Verb: principal parts of, 102; infl. of, 103; personal suffixes of, 104, 118, 121, 449; classification of, 264; irregular weak, 119, 454, 455; weak verbs are derivative, 117, 1.
Reduplicating: 130, 131, 458; non-thematic, see mi-verbs; anomalous, 134-136.
Compound: 137; D. after, 190; A. after, 198, 547-550; accent in, 421.
Reflexive, 138; 197; 206; 236, 2; 264.
Impersonal: subject of, 236, 1, 2, 5; cases after, 186, 193, 205; G. after, 184-186; D. after, 189-193; D. or A. after, 196, 200; A. after. 198; two A., 199, 201; neuter, 179; trans., 191, 264; intrans., 264.
V. of motion: comp. tense of, 265, 4; 266; 283, 3; 290, 2; past part. of, 296; see Number, Predicate, auxil., pret. pres. verbs; person of, in relative clauses, 326; position of, 341, 350, Rem.; derivation of, 534-550.
Verner's Law: 411, 412, 416.
Voice: passive, infl. of, 116; construction in, 179, 2; 202, 2; 268-273; replaced by reflexive construction, 272; origin of, 273; in Go., 283, 1.
Vowel-declension: see Noun, strong; 428-431.
Vowels: quantity of, 33-35, 488, 2, *b*; analysis and description of, 367-373; vowel-table, p. 162; general remarks upon, 373; doubling of, 33, 363, 4; connecting v. in conjugation, 118; 449, 2; 454, 2, 3; in ablaut, 393-400; in umlaut, 401, 402, 404; interchanges of, 403-406; lengthening of, in W. H. G., 488, 2; shortening of, 488, 3; diphthongization of long v., 488, 5.
Vowel-stems: see Vowel-Declension.

Word-formation: 495-559; substantives, 495-521; pronouns, 496; adjectives, 522-533; verbs, 534-550; adverbs, prepositions, conjunctions, 551-558; interjections, 559.
Word-order: 341-350; normal, 342; inverted, 343; dependent, 344. See these separate heads; in poetry and prose, 359.
Word-stock: 492-494.

WORD–INDEX AND GERMAN–ENGLISH VOCABULARY.

The first contains a list of the German and English words, prefixes and suffixes specially treated in the grammar. Also the strong and irregular verbs with the principal parts, and the second or third pers. sing. of the pres. ind. and the imperative sing., if they are at all peculiar.

The umlauts have a separate place, ä after a, ö after o, ü after u.

The numbers refer to the paragraphs. I., II., III., etc., mean the strong verb-classes and ablaut series.

After the substantives the gender (*m.*, *n.*, *f.*) and the plural ending are always indicated of the strong nouns, the gender and *w.* (= weak) are given after the weak nouns. When there is no pl. sign at all, it is indicated by -. When the cognate Eng. word is rare, or when its meaning differs quite widely from the German word, it is placed after the common Eng. meaning.

The vocabulary is meant to cover all untranslated single words and illustrative sentences as far as § 147, except the foreign words 62, 3; 63, 2; 64.

If weak verbs must have the connecting vowel this is indicated by the preterit.
- after a word means a prefix in composition, before a word it means a suffix.

A.

a, pronunc. of, 3; description of, 371, 4; quantity of, before r, rt, rb, 33, 488, 2; in ablauts., VI., 459, 4; in ablauts. I.-V., 459.
a, in Engl. phrase "so much a pound," 156.
Aas, *n.*, *pl.* Äser, carrion.
ab, from, 303, 1; 516, 1.
aber, but, 60, + word-order, 343, 2; 356; compared with ſondern, 320, 2 R
Aber-, 516, 1.
abhanden, lost, 429, 1.
ab'ſchreiben, to copy, see ſchreiben.
Abt, *m.*, ⸚e, + abbot.
ach, alas, 60; 559, 1.
achten, with G., to attend to, in 82; (ach= tete).
ae, as sign of umlaut of a, 362, 2.
aeu as sign of umlaut, 362, 2.
After-, 516. 2.
-age, noun-suffix; fem. gender, 161, 2; 163, 5.
ai, pronunc. of, 32, 372. 1.
all, +all, 100; def. art. after, 144; neuter, 168; use of, 261; accent, 422, 5.
allein, *conj.*, but; + word-order, 343, c.
aller-, + superl., 222; accent, 422, 1, 5.
allerdings, certainly, 552, 1.
allerlie'bſt, charming, very lovely, 222; 422, + Shakspere's *allerliefest*.
allerwärts } everywhere, 552, 1.
allerwegen
allmählich, gradually, 526, 3, *c.*
als, before a predicate noun, 179; in apposition, 317; before a relative pronoun, 327, 3; in temporal clauses, 330, 1; in comparative clauses, 333, 343, *c*; after comparative, 333, 2; after adjectives, nichts, ander-, 333, 2, *a*, 3; + daß, 333, 3.
alt, + old, *etym.*, 453, 1.
Alter, *n..* -, age, old age.
am < an dem, + on the, 40.
-am, noun-suf., 501.
Amt, *n.*, ⸚er, *etym.*, 516, 3.
an, + on, 305, 3; 306, 1, 2; compared with auf, 300, 2.
an < an ben. 40.
an'binden, to tie, see binden.
-and, noun-suffix, 505.
ander-, + other, 94; accent in comp., 423, 1; *etym.*, 445, 3; in comp., 530.
anderthalb = 1½, 530.
Anmut, *f.*, *no pl.*, grace; gender, 164, *a.*
an'ſchreiben, to write down, charge, see ſchreiben.

anstatt, +instead of, 302, 1; +zu and inf., 291, 1, R.; 332, 1.
Ant-, 516, 3.
-ant, 505.
Antwort, f., w., +answer; gender, 164, e.
Arm, m., -e, +arm.
Armut, f., no pl., poverty; gender, 164, a.
-at, 511, 2, a; in neut. foreign nouns, 163, 1.
Atem, m., -s, no pl., breath, 47, 1; 501.
atmen, to breathe, 118, 1; (atmete).
au, pronunc. of, 32; analysis of, 372, 2; origin of, 488, 5; 490, 6.
auch, also, + eke; in relat. clause, 93, 4; with wenn, ob, 339.
auf, + upon, 303, 3; compared with an, 300, 2; +daß, in order that. 338.
auf'erste'hen, to rise again, 546, 2.
auf'richten, to erect, (-richtete).
Auge, n., -s, -n, +eye.
a-umlaut, see ä, e.
aus, +out of, 303, 2.
außer, besides, 303, 3; +daß, 336.
Axt, f., ̈, +axe, 491, 2; 512, 2.
ä, pronunc. of, 31; 362; 371, 2, R. 3; see umlaut.
ätzen, to bait, corrode, +etch, 535, 1, R. 2.
äu, pronunc. of, 32; 372, 3; origin of, 488, 5.
äußer-, +outer, 76, 2.

B.

b, pronunc. of, 4; description of, 385, 2; final, 385, 3; „hartes" b, 383, 1, R.; 392, 2; Eng. correspondents of, 408, 2; 413, 2; 490, 6.
b-, see be-; 557, 1; 414, 3.
backen, buk, gebacken, +bake, VI., 129; (bäckst, bükt); in comp., 528.
Bad, n. -es, ̈-er, +bath.
Balke(n), m., -; beam, 46, 4.
Band, n., 58; m., 162, 4; 496.
Bande, f., w., +band (of robbers, etc.).
-bar, adj.-suffix, 526, 1; accent, 424, 1, b.
barmhe'rzig, merciful; accent, 422, 3.
baß, more, very, +better, 76; etym., 439.
Bauer, m., w., farmer, 62, 2; 63; strong, -, builder; n., -; cage.
Bau, m., -e, see also 51.
Baum, m., ̈-e, tree, +beam.
Bär, m., w., +bear.
be-, +be-, by, 108, 3; 540, 1; see bei.
beben, tremble, etym., 457, 3.
bedarf, see bedürfen.
bedecken, to cover, +deck.
bedient, etym., 295, 2.
bedingt, past part., conditioned, 125, 1.
bedürfen, +G., to need; for infl. see 135, 2.
befehlen, befahl, befohlen, to command, IV., 127; (befiehlst, befiehl, beföhle).
Befestigung, f., w., fortification.
befleißen, befliß, befliffen, I., 122, 1; refl., to apply oneself to; (du befleißest, du or er befleißt).
befreunden, +befriend; (befreundete).

begeben, refl., +G., to give up, 540, 4; see geben.
beginnen, begann, begonnen, +begin, III., 125, 2; 454, 3; 457, 2; (begönne).
behaupten, to assert, 540, 4; (behauptete).
bei, +by, near, 303, 4; in comp., 516, 4.
beid-, +both, 100; use of, 228.
Bein, n., -e, leg, +bone.
beisammen, together, in the presence of.
beißen, biß, gebissen, +bite, I., 122, 1; (du beißest, du or er beißt).
beizen, + to bait, cauterize; etym., 535, 1, R. 2.
belesen, past part., well read, 540, 3.
bellen, boll, gebollen, + to bark, VIII., 133; (w. and billst).
benehmen, take away, 540, 4; see nehmen.
bequem, convenient, comfortable, +becoming; 409, 3.
bergen, barg, geborgen, hide, III., 125, 3; 397; (birgst, birg, bärge and bürge).
beritten, past part., mounted; 524, 4.
bersten, barst, geborsten, +burst, III., 125, 3; (du birstest, du or er birst, birst or berste; börste or bärste).
besagt(er), the afore+said 146, 1.
bescheiden, modest, past part., 524, 4.
besser, best, +better, best, 76, 1; 439; 300, 2.
besucht, frequented, 74.
beten, to pray; (betete).
Betrübnis, f. or n., -isse, sadness, grief.
Bett, n., -es, -en, +bed; zu — +to — or in —.
beugen, +bow 488, 5.
bewegen, bewog, bewogen, to induce, VIII., 133; (bewegst, bewege).
bid, Eng., 396.
biegen, bog, gebogen, bend, II., 124, 2; (du beugst, rare).
Biene, f., w., +bee, 455, 2.
bieten, bot, geboten, offer, II., 124, 2; 396; 408, 2; (er bietet and beut).
binden, band, gebunden, +bind, III., 125, 1; 496; (er bindet).
binnen, within, 303, 5; 557, 1.
Binse, f., w., +bentgrass, 490, 2.
Birne, f., w., +pear, 435, 3.
bis, till, until, prepos., 304, 1; conj., 330, 3; etym.. 557, 1.
bitten, bat, gebeten, ask, +bid; V., 128, 2; 199; 233, 1; 457, 1; 466; (er bittet).
blank, shining, 74.
blasen, blies, geblasen, blow, VII., 130, 1; (du bläsest, du or er bläst).
blaß, pale, 74.
Blatt, n., -es, ̈-er, leaf, +blade.
blau, +blue, 74.
blättern, to turn the leaves of a book.
Blei, n., no pl., lead.
bleiben, blieb, geblieben, remain, I., 122, 2; +inf., 290, 3.
bleichen, blich, geblichen, +bleach, I., 122, 1.
Blüte, +blowth, blossom; etym., 430, 1.
Bote, m., w., messenger.
Boot, n., pl. Böte, +boat.
Bösewicht, m., pl. -e or -er, rascal, 57, 3; 59.

WORD-INDEX AND GERMAN-ENGLISH VOCABULARY. 273

Branntwein, *m.*, -e, +brandy.
braten, briet, gebraten, roast, fry, VII., 130, 1; (brätst, brät).
brauchen, need, compared with müssen, 267, 4.
Braut, *f.*, ⁻e, +bride.
Bräutigam, *m.*, -e, +bridegroom, 429, 1.
brechen, brach, gebrochen, +break, IV., 127; (du brichst, brich).
brennen, brannte, gebrannt, + burn, 119, 1; 455; (brennte).
bringen, brachte, gebracht, + bring, 119, 1; 454, 2; (brächte).
Bronn, *m.*, for Bronnen, Brunnen, well, spring, +bourn, 489, 4; 46, 4.
Brosam, *m.*, -e, crumb; Brosame, *f.*, *w.*, 47, 1; 501.
Brot, *n.*, -e, sometimes ⁻e, +bread.
Bruder, *m.*, ⁻, + brother, 46, 48, 411, 415.
Brunnen, see Bronn.
Buch, *n.*, ⁻er, +book.
Bulle, + bull, see 162, 3.
bunt, variegated, 74, 5.
Burg, *f.*, *w.*, castle, 397; in comp., 164, *c.*
Bursch, *m.*, -e, and *w.*, fellow.

C.

c, pronunc. of, 5; in foreign words, 389, 3.
Casuslehre, *f.*, *w.*, theory of the cases (of nouns).
causeway, causey, +Chaussee, 494, 3.
ch, pronunc. of, 6; 375, 4; 378, 3; 383, 1; description of, 375; quantity of vowel before, 35; Eng. correspondents of, 410, 3; 414, 3; 415, 1, 3; 490, 3; ch—g, 416; ch—f, 493, 4; ch—t, 535, 1, R. 2.
ch. Ger. correspond. of, 414, 3; 535, 1, R. 2.
-chen, + -kin, 46, 1; 493, 4; 510; neuter gend., 161, 3; pronunc. of, 6; 375, 2.
-che(n), in verbs, 536, *a.*
Christ, *m.*, *w.*, +Christian, 435, 3.
choose, +kiesen, 416, 1.
chi, che, pronunc. of, 29, 383, 1; 490, 3, *a.*
d, 14; 383, 1; Eng. correspondents of, 413, 4; 414, 3; d—ch, 535, 1, R. 2.

D.

b, pronunc. of, 7, 385, 3; description of, 384, 2. Eng. correspondents of, 410, 1; 413, 1, *a*; 415; b—t, 416.
-b, 511, 1.
da, + there, *adv.*; before a prepos. beginning with a vowel, bar; in relat. clause, 258, 327, 2; in local clauses, 331, *a*; = because, since in causal clauses, 337; = as, when in temporal clauses, 330, 1, 2; *etym.*, 551, 1; after demonstr. pron., 245, 3.
Dach, *n.*, ⁻er, roof, +thatch.
dachte, see benken, also 417, 1.
Dame, *f.*, *w.*, lady, +dame.
damit, *conj.*, in order that, 338.

damit, +daß = by+part. clause, 337
Dank, *m.*, -es ; *pl.* of, see 173.
darf, see dürfen.
das, +that ; see der; peculiar use of, 168; for G., 183.
daß, + that, *conj.*; in substantive clauses, 325 ; + nicht = without + part. clause, 332 ; in other adverbial clauses, 335, 336, 338.
däucht, see deucht.
-be, noun-suffix, 511, 2.
Dehnungs=h, 363, 2. 3.
dein, G. of du, 81; possessive pronoun, 85.
deiner, G., see dein.
bemungeachtet, notwithstanding, *prep.*, 302, 10.
denken, dachte, gedacht, +think, 119, 2; 402, 2 ; 454, 3; (dächte). Inf. as noun, das Denken.
Denkmal, *n.*, monument; for *pl.* see 58.
denn, + then, for, 301, 1 ; causal conjunction, 321, 337; after comparative, 333, 2; in restrictive clauses, 336; origin of, 551, 1.
der, + the, def. art., 38–40; demonstr. pronoun 88, 442; lengthened forms in en, er, 244, 2; relat. pronoun, 93.
derart daß, so that, 335.
deren (G. *pl.*), 88, 93. 1; use of. 244, 1.
derein–, 87, 89.
dergestalt daß, in such a manner that, 335.
derer, see deren.
derjenige, he, that one, 91, 1; 247.
ders, 89, 442.
derselbe, -selbige, the same, 91.
derweil, + while, 330.
des, des, dessen, 89.
dessent–, 89.
desto, + the, 442, *a*; correlative of je, 334.
deucht < dünken, 119, 2 ; 454, 3.
deutsch, German (+Dutch), 413, 1, *a.*
Deutschland, *n.*, Germany.
-dge, Ger. correspondents of, 413, 4.
Dichter, *m.*, -, poet.
dich, +thee, Acc. of du, *q. v.*
die, +the, fem. def. art., see der.
dies, dies(er), + this, 90 ; *etym.*, 443 ; use of, 245, 246; dies und das, jenes, 245, 2; supplanted by adverb+prepos., 246.
dieweil, +while, 330; because, 337, 1.
Ding, *n.*, + thing; for *pl.* see 58.
dingen, dang or dung, gedungen, III., 125, 1.
dir, +thee, D. of du, *q. v.*
doch, *adv.*, yet, after all, +though, 343, *e.*
Doktor, *m.*, -s, *pl.* -o'ren, 63, 2.
doppel–, +double, 531, 1.
Drangsal, *f.*, -e, distress.
dreschen, drasch or dresch, gedroschen, +thresh, III., 125, 3, 132 ; (träsche or drösche; drischest, du and er drischt, drisch, also weak, dreschest, dresche).
bringen, drang, gedrungen, to penetrate, III., 125, 1; (dränge).
britt–, +third, 410, 1; 530.
drucken, to print } 535. 2.
drücken, to press }

bumpf, hollow (sound), + damp, musty (air), 74, 5.
bunfel, dark, compar. bunfler.
burch, + through, 304, 2; compar. with von, 269; with mittels and mit, 302, 7; separable and insep. prefix in comp. verbs, 549, 1.
Durchlaucht, *f., w.*, Serene Highness.
bünfen, bünfte, gebünft, *impers. verb*, it seems, +(me) thinks, 119, 2; 454, 3.
türfen, burfte, geburft, to be permitted; infl., 135, 2; past part., 108, 2; use of, 267, 2; *etym.*, 416.

E.

e, pronunc. of, 8; description of, 371, 1-3; unaccented, 371, 3; 485, 2; sign of length, 33, 363, 1; sign of umlaut, 362; before r, rt, rh, 33, 488, 2; sign of plural, 47, 49, 51, 52; in cardinals, 227; in the adj.-suffixes –el, –er, –en, 71; connecting vowels in conjugation, 118; in case-suffix, 43, 46; derivative e in verbs, 535, 536; secondary before r, 491, 2; e — i, ie, 127, 128, 403; e — ö, 489, 1.
-e in imperative, 105; 118, 3.
-e in nouns < adj., 498, 1; gender of such nouns, 161, 2.
-e in jo-stems. 46, 47, 51, 437, 3; 498, 2; gender of such nouns, 161, 3.
-e in adverbs, 554, 1.
echt, genuine, *etym.*, 488, 3, *a.*
Ede, *f., w.*, corner, + edge, 413, 4.
edel, noble, 404, 71.
ehe, before, + ere, 76, 2, *b*; 439, 2; *conj.*, 330, 3.
ei, pronunc. of, 32; analysis of, 372, 3; origin of, 488, 5.
-ei, noun-suffix, 498, 3; gender of such nouns, 161, 2.
Eidam, *m., -e*, son-in-law, 47, 1; 501.
-eien, verb-suffix < French verbs in *-ier*, 538.
eigen, +own, *adj.*, 470; 471, 6; 524, 4.
eigentümlich, accent and meaning, 422, 2.
eilen, to hasten.
eim < einem, D. of ein, *q. v.*, 41, 1.
Eimer, pail, *etym.*, 398.
ein, + a, one, indef. art., 38, 41; after welch, was für, 92, 2, 3; indef. pronoun, 72, 95, 259, 260; ein par, ein wenig, a few, a little, 100.
ein, *adv.*, + in; — und aus, + in and out; 528, 7.
einander, + one another; uninflected, 84.
eingeboren, for two meanings see 528, 5, 7.
einig–, *indef. pron.*, some, 95; *adj.*, + united.
einmal, +once, 39, 41.
ei'nnehmen, take possession of, see nehmen. In 85 genommen ein for eingenommen by poetic license.
Einöde, *f., w.*, solitude, desert, 511, *a.*
eins, + one, 531, 2; for cognate Acc., 204.

einst, +once, 531, 2; 555, 2.
ei'nstubie'ren, to study well, commit to memory.
einzeln, *adv.*, singly, 555, 3.
eitel, vain; uninflected "nothing but," 212, 1.
-el, noun-suffix, 46, 428, 5; 499; gender of such nouns, 161, 1; 161, 3; adj.-suffix, 71, 523, 1; verb-suffix, 106.
elend, wretched; *etym.*, 401, among Examples.
elf, +eleven, 77; 529.
elk, +Elch, Elentier, 490, 3.
-eln, in verbs, 536; connecting vowel in –, 118, 3.
Eltern, parents, + elders, 174, 404.
-em in nouns, 501, 523, 2.
emp–< ent–, 541.
empfehlen, empfahl, empfohlen, recommend. IV., 127; 464, 3; (empföhle, du empfiehlst, empfiehl).
-en, noun-suffix, 46; 428, 5; 501; 502; indicates masc. gend., 160, 1; in the n-declension, 61, 62; in the pl. of foreign nouns, 64, 2, 3; in D. and A. of proper nouns, 66; in G sg. of adj. for es, 72; 91, 3; 216, 1; in pronouns, 244, 2; 440, 2; in mixed declension, 63; in comp. nouns, 518, 1, 2.
Adj.-suffix, 71; 211; 524. In the past part., 107; 453; 502; 524. In the inf., 106; 451. In adverbs, 551.
-end (nt), in the pres. part., 107; in nouns, 505; in the gerund, 107.
Ende, *n., -s, -n*, + end.
enge, narrow, 408, 4.
Engel, *m., –*, +angel.
-ens, adv.-suffix, 555, 2
ent–, 541.
Ente, duck, 430, 1.
entgegen, + against, "to meet," 303, 6; 557, 1; see gegen.
entsagen, to renounce.
entweder (— oder), +either — or, 343, *d*, 2; 558.
er, he, 81.
er für Herr, gentleman, Mr., 230, 3.
-er, noun-suffix, 428, 5; 65, 507; indicates masc. gend., 161, 1; 163, 3; as sign of plural, 56, 431.
Adj.-suffix, 71, 523, 3; 507, 2; in adverbs, 551; 556; compar. suffix, 79; 438; in the G. of pronouns, 82, 88, 244, 2; 440, 2; in verbs, see -ern.
er–, 542.
Erbe, double gender, 162, 3; neut. pl. Erbe is rare.
Erde, *f., w.*, + earth, 62, R.
-erei, noun-suffix, 497, 8, R
erhaben, lofty, 129, R.; 524, 4.
erkalten, to grow cold } 535, 2.
erkälten, refl., to catch cold
-erlich, adj.-suffix, 526, 3, *c.*
erlöschen, erlosch, erloschen, to go out (candle, fire), VIII., 133; (erlischest, du and er erlischt, erlisch).
-ern, adj.-suffix, 524, 3; adj. in —, uninflected, 211.

-er(n), verb-suffix, 537, 2; connecting vowel in, 118, 8.
erreichen, +reach, attain.
erschallen, erscholl, erschollen, resound, VIII., 133; (es erschallt).
erschrecken, erschrak, erschrocken, to be frightened, IV., 127; (erschrickst, erschrickt); when trans. generally weak.
erst, first, +erst, 76, 2, b; 439, 2.
erwägen, erwog, erwogen, consider, VIII., 133; (erwägst).
erwähnen, to mention; etym., 457, 2.
(Erz- + arch-, 516, 6.
es, + it, N. and A. sg neut., 81; peculiar uses of, 236; gender, 168; replacing cognate A., 204; 236, 6; G. of masc. and neuter, 82; 183; A. supplanted by prepos., 234, 1; indefinite subject, 236, 1, 2, 4, 5; grammatical subject and expletive = there, 236, 3; 313; position of es (A.), 352, e; es (N.) and inversion, 236, 3, a.
es sei benn, baß, unless, 339; 340, 2.
essen, aß, gegessen +eat, V., 128, 1; (bu issest or ißt, er ißt, iß); pres. part., 294, 1; etym., 400, 1; 466.
Essig, vinegar, +acid, 509.
etlich-, some, 96.
etwas, something, anything, somewhat, 96; 199, 1; 260.
eu, pronunc. of, 32; analys. of, 372, 3; origin of, 488, 5; eu — ie, 400.
euch+you, D. and A. of ihr, q. v., 81; refl., 83; reciprocal, 84; 238.
euer+your, possessive pron., 85.
eurer for euer (G.), 82.
Ew. +your, 86; 311, 2.

F.

f, pronunc. of, 9; description of, 380; Eng. correspondents of, 410, 2; 414, 2; 415, 1; 493, 4; f — b, 416.
-fach, -fold, 531, 1.
Fach, n., "-er (and -e); compartment, pigeonhole;
Faben, m., pl. and meanings, see 48, 1.
fahen, archaic for fangen, q. v.; 417, 1; 458, 2.
fahren, fuhr, gefahren, drive, + fare, VI., 129; 400; 467; + spazieren, 290, 2; (fährst).
Fahrt, f., w., journey, ride, 430, 1, a.
fallen, fiel, gefallen, + fall, VII., 130, 1; 458, 2; (fällst).
falls, adverbial G. in comp., = case, 91, 3; conj., 340.
falsch + false, 74, 5.
fangen, fing, gefangen, to catch, VII., 130, 1; (fängst).
far + fern, 76, 2.
fassen, to seize, (bu fassest or faßt), 118, 4.
fast, almost, 300, 1; 554, 1.
faulenzen, to be lazy, 539, 3, a.
Fährte, f., w., trude, 430, 1, a.
fällen, to fell, 535, 1, a.
-fältig + -fold, 531, 1.

fechten, focht, gefochten + fight, VIII., 133; (bu fichtst, ficht, also weak).
Feder, f., w., +feather, pen.
fehlen +fail, lack, 494.
Feind, m., -e, enemy, +fiend, 505; partial adj., 219.
Feld, n., -er, field.
Fels, m., w., } rock, 46, 4.
Felsen, m., - ,
fest, firm, 554, 1.
Feuer, n., +fire; pl. of, 173.
Fichtelgebirge, n., a mountain range in N. E. Bavaria, < bie Fichte, fir.
finden, fand, gefunden + find, III., 125, 1; 464; (findest).
Fint, m., w., +finch.
fischen+fish (bu fischest or fischt, er fischt), 118.
Finsternis, f., -nisse, darkness.
flach, shallow, level, 74, 5.
flechten, flocht, geflochten, to braid, VIII., 133; (bu flichtst or flichst, er flicht, flicht or flechte).
Flexionslehre, f., w., accidence.
fliegen, flog, geflogen, + fly, II., 124, 2; (fleugst, fleug are archaic).
fliehen, floh, geflohen, + flee, II., 124, 2; 490, 3, b; (fleuchst, fleuch are archaic).
fließen, floß, geflossen, II., 124, 1 535, 1, a; (bu, er fleußt, archaic).
Floß, n., "-e, +raft, 54; 429, 1.
flößen+to float, trans., 535, 1, a.
folgend(es) +the following, 146, 1.
forlorn, 416, 1.
fort+forth, on, 76, 1.
fr-, 545; see ver-.
fragen, frug, to ask, 129; 457, 2; construction after, 199.
Frau, f., w., woman, wife, Mrs.
Frauenzimmer, n., -, lady; 166.
Fräulein, n., -, young lady, Miss, 166.
frei+free.
freilich, to be sure, 300, 1; 339; 554, 2, b.
fressen, fraß, gefressen, + eat, V., see essen; 108, 3; 128, 1.
Freund, m., -e, +friend, 505.
ber Friebe(n), m., no pl., peace, 46, 4; 47, 2.
frieren, fror, gefroren, to freeze, II., 124, 2.
froh, cheerful, 74, 5.
fromm, pious; harmless.
frug, pret. of fragen, 129, 461.
früh, early. 300, 1; 554, 1.
Frühstück, n., -e, } breakfast, 137, 1; 421, 1.
frühstücken,
funden, past part. of finden, 453, 2.
Funke(n), m., spark; see 46, 4.
Furche, f., w., +furrow, 430, 1.
further, 76, 2.
Fuß, m., -es, "-e, +foot, 430, 1.
Füchsin, f., pl. -innen, +vixen, 504.
führen, to guide, 535, 1, a.
füllen, colt, +foal, 502, 2.
für + for, 76, 2, b; 304, 3; 306, 9; 516, 5.
fürbaß, onward, 76, 1.
fürchten, to fear; (fürchtete); 454, 3.
fürlieb nehmen, to put up with, 528, 7.
Fürst, m., w., prince, 76, 2, b; 439, 2.

G.

g, pronunc. of, 10; 375, 3, 4; 391, 2; in foreign words, 378, 4; 383, 1, Rem.; after u in N. G., 383, 1, a; Eng. correspondents of, 408, 3, 4; gg, 493, 4; description of, 383, 2; see ge-.
gan — gunnen > gönnen, 471, 5.
ganʒ, whole.
gar, *adj.*, done; *adv.*, even, very; + nicht, not at all.
Garderobe, *f., w.,* + wardrobe.
gären, gor, gegoren, to ferment, VIII., 133; (gärst, rarely gierst, often weak throughout).
ge-, g-, 516, 7; 543; in the past part., 107, 108; 453, 2; 528; in nouns of neuter gend., 161, 3; in p. p. of compound verbs, 546, 2.
gebären, gebar, geboren, to bring forth, + bear; IV., 127, 398; (pret. subj. gebäre, du gebierst, gebier).
geben, gab, gegeben, + give, V., 128, 1; (giebst, gieb); 466; impersonal, 205; 236, 4; 399.
Geck, *m., w.,* coxcomb.
Gedacht(er), the above mentioned, 146, 1; < gedenken, *q. v.*
Gedante(n), *m.,* + thought, see 46, 4; 47, 2.
gedenken, gedachte, gedacht, + think of, mention; see denken.
gedeihen, gedieh, gediehen, thrive, I., 122, 2.
Gedicht, *n., -e,* poem.
gediegen, *adj.,* solid, pure, past part. of gedeihen, according to Verner's Law, 411; 524, 4.
Gefalle(n), *m.,* pleasure (in), favor, see 46, 4; 47, 2.
gegen + against, 304, 4; see entgegen, zu, nach, um.
gegenüber, opposite, 303, 7
gehen, ging, gegangen, + go, VII., 130, 1; 136, 1; 457, 2; 474; + inf., 290, 2; past part., 296; (du gehst, geht).
Geisel
Geißel } for meaning, etc., see 162, 3.
Geist, *m., -er,* + ghost; wit.
geizen, to be stingy, *etym.,* 539.
Gelb und Gut, lit. money and property = all one's possessions.
gelegen, convenient, 524, 4.
gelingen, gelang, gelungen, to be successful (in), III., 125, 1.
gelten, galt, gegolten, to be worth, valid, III., 121, 125, 3; impersonal, 205; (göltegälte, du giltst, er gilt, imper. gelte as a rule).
Gemach, *n., "er,* apartment.
gemäß, according to, 303 8.
Gemüt, *n., -er,* soul, disposition.
gen, towards, 304, 4.
Genera'l, *m., -e* or *"e,* + general.
genesen, genas, genesen, to recover, V., 128, 1; (du genesest, er genest, genese).
genießen, genoß, genossen, to enjoy, II., 124, 1; (du genießest or genießt).
gering, small, compar. of, 76, 1.

geschäftig, busy.
geschehen, geschah, geschehen, to happen, V., 128, 1; (es geschieht).
Geschlecht, *n., -er,* race, generation.
Geschmeide, *n., -,* set of jewelry.
geschweige, *conj.,* = say nothing of, 230.
Geselle, *m., w.,* journeyman, fellow, companion.
Gesellschaft, *f., w.,* company, party.
Gesicht, *n.,* see 57, 58.
Gespenst, *n., -er,* spook, ghost.
gessen, past part. of essen, 128, R.
gestalt, shaped, past part. < stellen, 455, 3.
gesund + sound, wholesome, 74, 5.
Getreide, *n., -,* grain, *etym.,* 511.
getrost, confident, 419; past part. < trösten, 455, 3.
Gevatter, *m., -,* + god-father.
Gewand, *n., -e, "er,* garment, 58.
gewandt, active, clever, 74, 5; past part. of wenden, 455, 3.
Gewerbe, *n., -,* trade.
Gewimmel, *n., -,* swarming.
gewinnen, gewann, gewonnen, win, III., 125, 2; (gewönne — gewänne).
gh, G. correspondents of, 415, 1.
gewiß, certain, *etym.,* 412, 2; past part., 453, 1.
gießen, goß, gegossen, + to pour, II., 124, 1; (geußt, geuß rare, gießest or gießt).
Gift, *n., -e,* poison, + gift; *etym.,* 399; 403, 1; gender of, 162, 3.
Glas, *n., -es, -er,* + glass, 492, 3.
glauben + to believe.
Glaube(n), *m.,* + belief, see 46, 4.
gleich + like; for sogleich = immediately; + inverted order, 339.
-gleichen, in comp. with pron., + the like of, 87.
gleichen, glich, geglichen, to be like, I., 122, 1.
gleißen, *w. v.,* deceive, 122, 1.
gleißen, gliß, geglissen, + glitter, I., 122, 1; du gleißest or gleißt, er gleißt).
gleiten, glitt, geglitten, + glide, I., 122, 1; (er gleitet).
glimmen, glomm, geglommen, + to glimmer, VIII., 133.
Gnade, *f., w.,* grace.
Gold, *n., no pl.,* gold.
gönnen, not to grudge; *etym.,* 471, 5.
Gott, *m., -es, "er,* + God, 408, 3.
graben, grub, gegraben, to dig, VI., 129; (du gräbst).
greifen, griff, gegriffen, to seize, I., 122, 1.
greinen, grien, gegrienen; + grin (generally weak, rare), I., 122, 1.
Graf, *m., w.,* count.
Griffel, *m., -,* style (slate-pencil).
grinsen, + grin < greinen, 122, 1.
groß + great; compar. of, 73.
Großmutter, *f., "-,* + grandmother.
grüßen + greet; (du grüßest).
gut + good; compar. of, 76, 1; compared with wohl, 299, 2, *a*; 439.
gülden + golden, 524, 2.

WORD-INDEX AND GERMAN-ENGLISH VOCABULARY.

H.

h, pronunc. of, 11; description of, 374; Eng. correspondents of, 410, 3; 415, 1; silence of, 33; 363, 2; 491, 2; loss of, 415, 3; sign of length, 33, 363, 2, 3; h — ch, 73; 490, 3, b; h — g, 124, Rem.; 416.
haben + have, infl. of, 110; contracted forms, 111, 1; impersonal, 205; in comp. tenses, 265; 283, 1, 2; + inf., 290, 1.
-haft, adj.-suffix, 546, 2.
Hagestolz, m., w., bachelor; pl. also -e.
halb, before cardinals, 226, 2; after ordinals, 229, 1.
-halben, for . . . sake (of), comp. with pronouns, 87, 89; prep., 302, 4.
halber + half, prep., 302, 4.
halten, hielt, gehalten, + hold, VII., 130, 1; (du hältst, er hält).
Hand, f. -̈e, + hand, 53; 429, 1.
-handen, in comp., 429, 1.
handeln, to act, trade.
handgemein (werden), to come to blows, 219.
Handschuh, m., -e, glove.
hangen, hing, gehangen, + hang (intr.), VII., 130, 1; (du hängst).
hassen + to hate, 414, 1 Ex.; du hassest or haßt.
hast + hast, see haben.
Haß, + hate, 414, 1 Ex.
hat + has, see haben.
hauen, hieb, gehauen, + hew, strike, VII., 131; (du haust).
Haufe(n), m., + heap, crowd, troop, 46, 4.
Haus, n., -es, -̈er, + house; — unb Hof, house and farm, — and home.
hauß + out here < hie + aus, 41, 1.
Häupten, D. pl., see 59.
Hebel, m., -, lever.
heben, hob (hub), gehoben, VI., 129; VIII., 132; 457, 1; 467; (höbe — hübe, du hebst).
Hehl, n. and m., no pl., concealment; in 82 he makes no secret of it . . .
Heide, m., w., + heathen, 162, 3; 435, 3.
Heimsuchung, f., w., visitation.
heint + this night, 443, 2.
Heirat, f., w., marriage, 511, a.
heiser + hoarse.
heißen, hieß, geheißen, command, be called, + hight, VII., 108, 1; 131, 458, 2; intrans., 179, 1; trans. 201; + inf., 290, 2, 4; + past part., 296, 2; (du heißest or heißt, er heißt).
-heit + -head, 515, 1; indicates fem. gender, 161, 2; 431, 2.
heiter, serene, 71.
Held, m., w., hero.
helfen, half, geholfen, + help, III., 125, 3; past part. of, 108, 1; 464; + inf., 290, 2; (du hilfst, hilf).
Hemd, n., -es, -en, shirt.
her + hither, + here, 443, 2.
Herr, m., w., lord, master, Mr.; reduced to er, 230, 3; short e, 488, 3.
herrlich, splendid.
hervo'rthun, refl., to distinguish one's self; see thun.
Herz, n., + heart, infl. of, 63, 1; 435, 1.
Herzog, m., -̈e, + duke, 416, 1.
Herzogtum, n., -̈er, + dukedom.
hetzen, incite, hunt, 535, 1, b, R. 2.
heuer + this year, 443, 2.
heute + to-day, 443, 2.
hier + here, after pron., 245, 2; etym., 443, 2.
Himmel, m., -, heaven.
hin, thither, away, 443, 2.
hinter + behind, prep., 306, 4; in comp. verbs, 549, 2; adj., 76, 2.
Hirte, m., w., + herdsman.
his — its, 243, 2.
hoch + high, 73; 490, 3, b. Infl. hoher, hohe, hohes.
Hoffart, f., no. pl., pride, 528, 2, b.
hoffen + hope.
hohl + hollow, compar. 74.
hold, gracious, compar. 74, 405.
holen, fetch, + hale, haul.
Hopfen, m., -, + hops.
Hose, f., w., trousers, + hose.
hören + hear, instead of gehört, 108, 1; 113; + inf., 290, 3.
Huld, f., no pl., favor, grace, 405
Hund, m., -e, dog, + hound.
hundert, n., -e, + hundred, 226; 529, 2.
Hüfte, f., w., + hip, 430, 1; 512, 2.
Hündchen, n., -, little dog,

J.

i, pronunc. of, 12; description of, 369, 1, 2; < ie. 488, 4; < u, 489, 2; < e, 489, 5.
ich + I, 81.
-ich, 509; indicates masc. gend., 161, 1; 489, 5.
-icht, 509, 1; 525, 3.
ie, pronunc. of, 33, 3; see i; in reduplicating verbs, Cl. VII., 458, 2; 488, 3, a.
ie — eu, 124, 406.
-ie, noun-suffix, 489, 4; 493, 2; indicates fem. gender, 161, 2.
-ieren, verbs in, 108, 4; 493, 2; 538.
-ig, + -y, adj.-suffix, 525, 1-3; 489, 5; for -ich, 509; 526, 3, a.
-igen, verb-suf., 539, 4.
-igkeit, 515, 2.
-iglich, adj.-suf., 525, 2.
ihm, ihn, ihnen, see er, sie, es, pers. pron.
ihr, poss. pron., her, their, with cap. your, 85; origin of, 243, 2.
ihrer, G. of pers. and poss. pron., see sie, ihr.
Jhro, your, 86; 441, 2.
in + in, 306, 5; for in den, 40.
-in, noun-suffix, 504; fem. gender, 161, 2; 167; 430, 3.
indem, conj., while, 330, 1; 332; because, 337.
-ing, noun-suffix, 506.
inner + inner, 76, 2.
innerhalb, within, prep., 302.

in jofern, in wiefern, +in so far as, 336.
irbifch +earthly.
irgenb, any, with pron. and adv., 260.
Srrtum, m., ≞er, +error, 56.
-ifch + -ish, adj.-suffix, 211; 514; 525,4.
its, 243, 2.

J.

j, pronunc. of, 13; 378, 4; description of, 375, 4; disappeared, 491, 2.
jagen, hunt, chase; strong pret., VI., 129.
Jahr, n., -e, +year; after numerals, 175.
Jäger, m., -, hunter.
je +ever; conj. 334; before cardinals with distributive force = "at a time"; je nachbem = "that depends"; +aye.
jeb(er), every, each, infl. of, 97; 216, 1; 445, 1; in comp., 97; pl. of, 261, 3; +either.
jebes, each, 168.
jebweber, every one, each, 97; 261, 8; 445, 2.
jeglich, every, +each, 97, 445, 1.
jemand, some one, 97; 260; 445, 1.
jen(er), that, + yon, 90; 443, 1; G. sing. of, 216, 1; use of, 245, 246.
jug, see jagen.
jung +young.
Junge, m., w., boy; n., w., + young of animals.
Jungfer, f., w., maiden; etym., 516, 12, a.
Junfer, young nobleman, +younker, 516, 12, a.
Juwel, n., -s, -en, +jewel.
jüngft, lately; etym., 555, 2.

K.

k, pronunc. of, 14, 383,-1; Eng. correspondents of, 409, 3; description of, 383, 1.
kahl, bald, +callow; compar. of, 74.
Kaifer, m., -, emperor, +Cesar, Czar.
kalt +cold, etym., 409, 3.
kann, see können.
kannte, see kennen.
Kar-, in comp., 422, 8.
Katzenkönigin, f., pl. -innen, +queen of cats.
kaum, hardly; word-order, 330, 2.
Käfe +cheese, 46, 3; etym., 428, 5.
keck, bold, +quick, 403, Ex.
keifen, kiff, gekiffen, + scold (like an old woman), I., 122, 1.
kein, no, none, 72; 95; 445, 2.
-keit, noun-suffix, 515, 2; fem. gend., 161, 2; 430, 2.
kennen, kannte, gekannt, to be acquainted with, 119, 1; 267, 1; (kennte).
Kette, f., w., +chain. 435, 4.
kiefen, see küren; bu kiefeft or kieft.
Kind, n., -es, -er, child, 60.
Kindlein, n., -, little child.
Kirfche, f., w., +cherry.
klar +clear, 74.

Kleinod, n., -e, also -ien as if a foreign word; jewel, 511, a.
klieben, klob, gekloben, split, + cleave, II., 124, 2.
klimmen, klomm, geklommen, + climb, VIII., 133.
klingen, klang, geklungen, to sound, ring, III., 125, 1.
Knabe, m., w., boy, +knave, 413, 3.
knarren, creak.
kneifen, kniff, gekniffen, pinch, I., 122, 1.
kommen, kam, gekommen, + come, IV., 127; 465; 489, 1; umlaut in pres., 127, R.; +past part., 296; 409, 3.
konnte, see können.
Kopf, m., -es, ≞e, head.
koften + cost; constr. with, 207, 1, R.; (kofteft, koftet).
König, m., -e, +king.
können, konnte, gekonnt, +can, 135, 8; 108. 2; 267, 1.
Kraft, f., ≞e, strength, +craft; prep., 302, 5, 6.
Krebs, m., -e, +crayfish, 512.
kreifchen, krifch, gekrifchen, scream, I., 122, 1.
kreifen, see kreifchen.
triechen, kroch, gekrochen, + creep, crawl, II., 122, 2; (kreuchft, kreuch are archaic).
Kuh, f., ≞e, +cow, kine.
kund + known, + (un)couth; constr. with 219.
kunnt for konnte, q. v.; in 347.
küren, kor, gekoren, +choose, II., 124, 2; 132; 411; 416. 1; 463; (bu kürft).
Küffen, n., no pl., +kissing.

L.

l, pronunc. of, 15; description of, 381; 385, 4.
-l, see -el.
laben, lub, gelaben, + load, summon, VI., 129; also weak; (bu läbft, er läbt).
lahm +lame, 74.
Land, n., -, ≞nd, pl. see 58.
Landsmann, m., pl. -leute, fellow countryman, 172.
lang +long.
Langeweile, f., ennui; accent 422, 1.
laffen, ließ, gelaffen, +let, VII, 130, 1; past part. without ge-, 108, 1; constr. after, 199, 202, 1; 267, 7; +reflexive, 272; in the imper., 287, 4; + inf., 290, 2, 3, b; 266, 4; (bu läffeft or läßt, er läßt).
laß, weary, 74; 76, 2; 439, 2; + late.
lau, tepid, +luke, +low, 74.
laufen, lief, gelaufen, run, VII., 131; 212; 1; 458, 2; (bu läufft).
laut + loud; etym., 396; 415; prep., 302, 6.
lauter, nothing but, 100.
lächeln, smile.
längft, long ago, 555, 3.
leben + live.
lebe'nbig + living; accent 420, 1.
legen + lay, 535, 1. a.
lehren, teach; instead of gelehrt, 108, 1;

constr. after, 199; in passive, 202, 2; + inf., 290, 2; 395.
-lei, 533.
Leib, m., -es, -er, body.
leiben, litt, gelitten, suffer, I., 122, 1; 411; 416, 1; (du leibest).
Leiben, n., -, suffering.
leiber, unfortunately, 225, 2.
leiben, lieh, geliehen, + lend, I., 122, 2.
-lein, noun-suffix, 46, 1; 500, 2; neut. gend., 161, 3; 493, 4.
Leitstern + lode-star, 520, 4, a.
-ler, noun-suffix, 500, 4; indicates masc. gender, 161, 1.
lernen + learn; instead of gelernt, 108, 1; for lehren, 199, 2; +inf., 290, 2; 395.
lesen, las, gelesen, read, V., 128, 1; 395; (du liesest or liest, er liest, ltes).
leserlich, legible, 526, 3, c.
let, in imperative, 287, 4.
letzt + last, 439, 2; 76, 2; after ordinals, 532, 2.
Leumund, m., no pl., repute; etym., 396; 494, 3.
-leute, in comp., 172.
-lich + -like, + -ly, 211; 525, 4; 526, 3; adverbial suffix, 544, 2.
Licht, n., + light, pl. see 58.
lieben + love, 496.
Liebesbrief, m., -e, + love-letter, 518, 3.
liegen, lag, gelegen, + to lie, V., 128, 2; 457, 1; II., 132; +inf., 290, 3.
-lig, 526, 3, c.
-ling + -ling, noun-suffix, 500, 3; indicates masc. gender, 161, 1.
-lingen, in names of places, 500, 3, a.
-lings, 553.
link, left (hand), only used attributively like adjectives in 211.
loben, praise, 496.
Lorber, m., -s, -(e)n, + laurel.
lore + Lehre, 395.
Los, n., -es, -e, + lot.
los + loose. + -less in adj., 526, F.
löschen, trans. and weak, to extinguish, unload; intrans., to be extinguished, see erlöschen.
Ludwig + Louis + Chlodwic, 396.
Luther + Luther, 396.
Lust, f., -̈e, pleasure, + lusts.
lügen, log, gelogen, + lie, II., 124, 2; 132.
Lügen strafen, to give the lie, 199, 2.

M.

m, pronunc. of, 16; description of, 388; Eng. correspondents of, 490, 4, 5.
-m, see em.
machen + make, + inf., 290, 2; 266, 4; das (Acc.) macht = the reason is . . .
mag, see mögen.
Magd, f., -̈e, + maid-servant, 512, 3.
mager + meager, 71; no umlaut in compar., 74.
Magister, m., -, + master (of arts).
mahlen + grind, originally of VI., see 400; past part. gemahlen still common.

Maid + maid, 512, 3; (poetic form).
Majestät, f., w., + majesty.
mal, once, probably = einmal, 41, 1; in comp., 531, 2.
man, one, 98.
manch + many a, 100; 262; 525, 1; + ein, 144.
Mann, m., + man; pl, 58, 59; in comp., 172.
März, m., -̈e, + march; f., w., + marsh, 162, 4.
marschieren + march, 103, 4.
Mast, m., -es, -en, + mast; f., w., fattening, stall-feeding.
maßen, because, 337, 1.
matt, faint, + mate in check-mate; compar., 74.
Maulwurf, m., -̈e, + mole, etym., 400; 494, 3.
Mäuslein, n., -, little + mouse.
Meer, n., -e, ocean, + mere.
mehr + more, compar. of, 76, 1; 100; 439; used in comparative, 224.
mehrer-, several, 76, 1; 100.
mehrst-, + most, 100.
meiden, mied, gemieden, avoid, L, 122, 2; (meidest).
mein, G. of ich, see meiner; mein-, possess. pron., 85; in mein Tag, Lebtag, 243, 1.
meiner, comparat., + more mine, 225, 2; G. of ich, 86.
meinig-, poss. pron., + mine, 85.
meist + most, compar. of, 76, 1; 100.
Meißel, m., -, chisel.
melden, announce, (meldete).
melken, molk, gemolken, + milk, VIII., 133; (du melkst and milkst, melke and milk).
Melodei, f., w., + melody, 189, 2.
Mensch, m., w., + man; n., see 59, 514.
messen, maß, gemessen, + measure, V., 128, 1; (du missest or mißt, er mißt).
Messer, n., -, knife; m., -, measures; see 162, 3.
Mette, f., w., + matins, 435, 4.
mich + me, Acc. of ich, 81.
minder, less, comparison of, 76, 1; 439; used in compar., 224.
mines, in comp., 87.
mir + me, to me, D. of ich, 81.
Miß- + mis-, 453, 1; 516, 8; 544.
Misse-, see Miß-.
mit, with, 303, 9.
Mittagsstunde, f., w., hour of noon.
mittel- + middle, 76, 2, b.
mittelst, see mittel-, prep., 302, 7.
Mitternacht, f., -̈e, + midnight, 519, 2.
Mittwoch, m., also f., w., Wednesday, 164, d.
mm < mb, + Eng. mb, 490, 4.
Mohr, m., w., + Moor.
Mord, m., -es, pl. see 51.
morsch, rotten, 74.
mouse — mice, 429, 1.
mögen, mochte, gemocht + may, 135, 4; 108, 2; 267, 3; 412, 2; (er mag, pret. subj. möchte).
Mund, m., -es, -e, older -̈e, + mouth.
Muskel, m., -n, also f., w., + muscle.

-mut, in comp., 164, a; +mood.
Mutter, f., ⸚, +mother; see Verner's Law, 411.
Mücke, f., w., +midge, 413, 4.
müde, tired.
müssen, mußte, gemußt, +must, 135, 6; 108, 2; 207, 3; 471, 3; (du mußt, er muß, müßte).

N.

n, pronunc. of, 17; nature of, 386, 387, final n in foreign words, 386, 1, Rem.; short before sonant stops, 385, 4; n = g., i. e., "guttural" nasal, 386, and see nt, ng; before labial, 388, 1; lost in Eng., 417, 1; entered the N. of nouns of the n-decl., 435, 2; loss of, 435, 3, 4; 502; 506, 1; Eng. correspondents of, 490, 5. See -en.
nach, after, 303, 10; see zu and gegen.
Nachbar, m., -s, -n, +neighbor. 63, 1.
nachdem, conj., after, 330, 2; according as, 334.
Nacht, f., ⸚e, +night, 53, 2; 429, 1.
nahe+near, +nigh, 73.
Narr, m., w., +fool.
Natu'r, f., w., +nature.
nächst+next, 73; 303, 11.
-nd, part.-suffix, 505.
'ne for eine+a, 41, 1.
neben, by the side of, 306, 6; 557.
nebst, besides, together with, 303, 12; 555, 2.
needs, 552, 1.
nehmen, nahm, genommen, take, IV., 127; Wunder —, 199, 1, 2; (du nimmst, nimm).
-ne(n), verb-suf., 537, 1; 118, 1, 2.
'nen for einen+, 41, 1
nennen, 119, 1; 455; constr. with, 201; 290, 2; 296, 2; 303, 4.
-ner, noun-suf., 502, 1; masc. gend., 161, 1.
neu+new.
ng, pronunc. of, 17, 383, 1, a; 386, 1.
nicht, nichts, +not, +naught, 99; 199, 1, 2; 309, 1; position of, 354; in compar. clauses, 333, 2; 490, 3; after verbs of hindering, 309, 2.
Nichte, f., w., +niece.
nichts weniger als, anything but..., 333, 2, a.
nid+beneath, 551, 3.
nieder-, adj., +nether, 76, 2.
niemals, never.
niemand, no one, 97, 445, 1.
-nis+-ness, 50; indicates neuter and fem. nouns, 161, 2, 3; 428, 6; origin of, 503.
nt, pronunc. of, 17; 386, 1.
nobel+noble, 74.
noch, still; = nor with correlative weder; noch nicht, not yet, 354.
Norden, m., +North.
Nöten, old D. pl., 429, 1.
nun+now; = because, 337, 1.
nur, only; +daß, 336; 336, 1.

O.

o, pronunc. of, 18; description of, 370, 1, 2; in ablauts, VI., 459, 4; < u, 405, 489, 4; < â, 489, 3.
ob, prep., +above, 302, 8; conj., whether, 325, 2; although, 339.
ober- in comp., chief, + upper; accent, 422, 7.
ober-, adj., +upper, 76, 2.
obgleich, obschon, obwohl, although, 339.
Obiges+the above, 146, 1.
Ochse, m., w., +ox, 62, 2.
Odem, m., no pl., breath, see Atem.
oe as sign of umlaut, 362, 2.
Ohnmacht, fainting, 489, 3; 516, 10.
ohne, without, 291, 1, R.; 304, 5; in comp., 489, 3; +516, 10; +daß = without+part. clause, 332.
ohnedem, without that, 304, 5.
Ohr, m., -es, -en, +ear.
on+an, 306, 2.
once+einst, 555, 2, a.
-or, noun-end., 63, 2.
Ort, m., pl. see 57, 58.
Osten, m., -s, no pl., +east.
ou, Eng. — G. au, 488, 5.
o-umlaut, see ö.
ö, pronunc. of, 31; description of, 370, 3, 4; ö — e 489, 1; < û, 489, 4.

P.

p, pronunc. of, 19; description of, 385, 1; Eng. correspondents of, 413, 3; 414, 2, a; 493, 3.
Pala'st, m., pl. Paläste, 163, 1; 493, 1; 494.
Pantoffel, m., -s, -n, slipper.
pf, pronunc. of, 19; description of, 389, 1; Eng. correspondents of, 409. 2; 414, 2.
Pfalz, f., w., castle, +Palatinate.
Pfau, m., w., +peacock, 414, 2.
pfeifen, pfiff, gepfiffen, whistle, I., 122, 1.
Pferd, n., -es, -e, horse, +palfrey.
pflegen, pflog, gepflogen, carry on, VIII., 133; 469; (du pflegst, pflege); always weak = to cherish.
Pfund, n., -es, -e, +pound; after numerals, 175.
ph, pronunc. of, 19.
platt, flat, 74.
plump, awkward, +plump. 74.
preisen, pries, gepriesen, +praise, I., 122, 2; (du preisest, er preist).
Prinz, m., w., +prince (of a royal family).
probieren, try, 108, 4.
putzen, dress up, burnish, (du putzest), 118, 4.

Q.

q, pronunc. of, 20; 409, 3; as symbol, see n and 386.
quellen, quoll, gequollen, to gush forth, well

WORD-INDEX AND GERMAN-ENGLISH VOCABULARY. 281

up, (quillſt, quillt, quill; also weak quelleſt, quelle).
quëman, see kommen.

R.

r, pronunc. of, 21; 391, 3; description of, 374, 2; 377; < s, 411, 416.
Rabe, crow, +raven, 413, 3; 435, 3; 502.
Rab, n., -es, "er, wheel, 56.
Ranc, m., -es, "er, edge, brim.
raſch, quick, +rash, 74.
raſen, rage, 118, 4; (du, er raſt).
Rat, m., -es, pl. see 173.
raten, riet, geraten, advise, VII., 130, 1; (du rätſt, er rät).
Ratſchlag, ratſchlagen, advice, to advise, 137, 1.
rauch-, rauh, +rough, 490, 3, b.
rächen, rächte, gerächt or gerochen, +wreak vengeance, VIII., 133; generally weak; (du rächſt).
Rätſel, n., -, +riddle.
recht, +right.
Recht, n., -e, +right, pl. jurisprudence; 221, 4, a.
rechnen, +reckon, 118, 2; 537, 1; (rechnete).
reben, to speak (rebete), 118; 537, 1.
regnen+rain, 118, 2; 537, 1; (regnete).
reiben, rieb, gerieben, rub, +rive, I., 122, 2.
reich+rich.
Reich, n., -e, empire.
-reich + -rich, + ric, 515, 3, a.
Reichsfreiheit, f., w., +freedom of the empire, immediate dependence upon the empire.
Reichtum, m., "er, wealth.
reißen, riß, geriſſen, tear, I., 122, 1; (du reißeſt or reißt, +write).
reiſen, travel, 118 (du reiſeſt or reiſt).
reiten, ritt, geritten, +ride, I., 122, 1; +ſpazieren, ride for pleasure, 290; (du reiteſt, er reitet).
rennen, rannte, gerannt, rush, +run, 119, 1.
retten, save (rettete).
-rich, + -ric, 515, 3.
riechen, roch, gerochen, smell, II., 124, 1.
ringen, rang, gerungen, wrestle, +wring, III., 125, 1; ringen, umringen, etc., are of different origin and weak, though umrungen, surrounded, is not uncommon.
rinnen, rann, geronnen, drip, III, 125, 2; 457, 2; ronn, rönne also occur.
Ritter, m., -, knight.
Rock, m., "e, coat.
roh+raw, 74; 415, 3.
Rohr, n., -e, reed, 55.
rot+red.
Röhre, f., w., pipe.
Röslein, n., -, little rose.
rufen, rief, gerufen, call, VII., 131; constr. after, 196; (du rufſt, in classics sometimes ruſte).
rund+round.
Rüden, m., -, +ridge, 413, 4.

S.

ſ, s, pronunc. of, 22-24; 391, 4; description of, 378, 1, 2, 3; in G. sg. of m. and n. nouns, 42; of f. nouns, 66, 518, 3; in G. s. of Eng. adverbs (needs), 552, 1; in the pl., 66; 67; in composition with poss. pron., 87; in compound nouns, 518, 2, 3.
ſſ < ſt, 412, 2; ſ in Verner's Law, 411, 416; Eng. correspondents of, 414, 1; 417, 5; 490, 2.
-s, noun-suffix, 513; in adverbs, 552.
's for das, 41; for es, q. v.
Sachſe, m., w., +Saxon.
ſacht, gently, + softly, 417, 1; mostly adverb.
Sack, m., "-e, +sack.
ſagen+say.
-ſal, noun-suffix, 50, 51; 500, 1; nouns of doubtful gender, 161, 2, 3.
-ſam + -some, 526, 4.
ſamt, with, 303, 13.
Same(n), m., +seed; infl., 46, 4.
ſanft+soft, gentle, 74; 417, 1.
ſatt+satisfied (+sad), 74.
Satz, m., -es, "-e, sentence.
ſaufen, ſoff, geſoffen, drink (of animals), II., 124, 1; 463; (du ſäufſt, +sup and +sip).
ſaugen, ſog, geſogen, +suck, II., 124, 2; (du ſaugſt, not ſäugſt < ſäugen).
Saus und Braus (uninflec.), revel and riot.
Säbel, m., -, +sabre.
Sänger, m., -, +singer.
Säule, f., w., column, 430, 1.
ſch, pronunc. of, 23; description of, 378, 3; 389, 4; Eng. correspondents of, 412, 1; 490, 1; origin of, 490, 1; 514.
-ſch, 514; see -iſch.
Schabe(n), m., harm, damage, 46, 4; 48, 1.
ſchaffen, ſchuf, geſchaffen, to create, +shape, VI., 129; (du ſchaffſt, weak = work, procure).
-ſchaft + -ship, 515, 4; fem. gender, 161, 2; 430, 2.
ſchallen, ſcholl, geſchollen, to sound, generally weak, 133; (du ſchallſt).
Schar, f., w., troop, host.
ſchauen, to look.
-ſche, suffix of surnames, 514, a.
ſcheiden, ſchied, geſchieden, to separate, depart, I., 122, 2; VII., 131; (du ſcheideſt, er ſcheidet).
ſcheinen, ſchien, geſchienen, +shine, seem, I., 122, 2.
ſcheißen, ſchiß, geſchiſſen, cacare, I., 122, 1.
ſchellen, ſcholl, geſchollen, to ring (the bell), VIII., 133; (du ſchillſt, ſchill are very rare, also weak).
ſchelten, ſchalt, geſcholten, +scold, III., 125, 3; 401, 2; (du ſchiltſt, er ſchilt, ſchilt or ſchelte, ſchölte).
-ſchen, suf. in verbs, 539, 2.
ſcheren, ſchor, geſchoren, +shear, VIII., 133; (du ſcherſt, ſchier, also weak.
ſcheuen, avoid; refl., to fear.
ſchieben, ſchob, geſchoben, push, +shove, II., 124, 2.

schier, *adj.*, brilliant, pure; *adv.*, almost, (quick, comp. bold + bald).
schießen, schoß, geschossen, + shoot, II., 124, 1; (du schießest or schießt).
Schild, *n.* and *m.*, + shield, sec 58; 162, 4.
schinden, schund (schand), geschunden, to skin, III., 125, 1; (du schindest).
schlafen, schlief, geschlafen, + sleep, VII., 130, 1; pres. part., 294, 1; (du schläfst).
schlaff, slack, 74.
schlagen, schlug, geschlagen, strike, + slay, VI., 129; *recipr.*, = to fight; (du schlägst).
schlant, slender, 74.
schleichen, schlich, geschlichen, to sneak, I., 122, 1.
schleifen, schliff, geschliffen, to sharpen by grinding, I., 122, 1; weak = to raze.
schleißen, schliß, geschlissen, wear off, + slit, I., 122, 1; (du schleißest or schleißt).
schließen, schloß, geschlossen, to slip, II., 124, 2; (du schleußt, schleuf very rare).
schließen, schloß, geschlossen, close, conclude, II., 124, 2; (du schließest or schließt, schleußt etc., rare).
schlinden, see schlingen.
schlingen, schlang, geschlungen, to twine, + sling, devour, III., 125, 1.
Schluck, *m.*, -e, swallow; *pl.*, 51.
schlüpfen + slip < schliefen according to 535, 1, R. 2.
Schmach, *f.*, *no pl.*, disgrace, 490, 3, *b*.
schmachten, to pine (schmachtete).
schmeicheln, flatter, 536, 2, Ex.
schmeißen, schmiß, geschmissen, throw, + smite, I., 122, 1; (du schmeißest or schmeißt).
schmelzen, schmolz, geschmolzen, + melt, VIII., 133; (du schmilzest or schmilzt, er schmilzt, trans. is weak).
Schmerz, *m.*, -es, -en, pain, + smart, 63.
schnauben, schnob, geschnoben, snort, puff, + snuff, II., 124, 2, also weak; (du schnaubst).
Schneewittchen, + Snow-white (witt is L. G. for weiß).
schneiden, schnitt, geschnitten, + cut, I., 122, 1; 416, 462; (du schneidest).
schnieben, see schnauben.
schnitzen, carve, 535, 1, R. 2.
schon, already, 339; position of, 354; form of, 554.
schön, beautiful, 522.
schrauben, schrob, geschroben, + screw, II., 124, 2; (du schraubst); also weak.
schrecken, schrat, geschrocken, to be frightened, see erschrecken.
Schreck(en), *m.*, fright; infl., 46, 4.
schreiben, schrieb, geschrieben, write, I., 122, 2.
schreien, schrie, geschrieen, cry, + scream, I., 122, 2.
schreiten, schritt, geschritten, to stride, walk, I., 122, 1; (du schreitest, er schreitet).
Schritt, *m.*, -es, -e, stride, step; after numerals, 175.
schroff, rugged, uncouth, 74.
schweigen, schwieg, geschwiegen, to be silent, I., 122, 2.
Schwein, *n.*, -e, pig, + sow, + swine, 502, 2.
schwellen, schwoll, geschwollen, + swell, VIII., 133; (du schwillst, schwill).

schwinden, schwand, geschwunden, disappear, III., 125, 1; (du schwindest, schwände — schwünde).
schwingen, schwang, geschwungen, + swing, III., 125, 1; (schwänge and schwünge).
schwimmen, schwamm, geschwommen, + swim, III., 125, 2; 464; (schwömme and schwämme).
schwören, schwur and schwor, geschworen, + swear, VI., 129; VIII., 132; 457, 1; (du schwörst).
Se. < Seine, His, 311, 2.
sehen, sah, gesehen, + see, V., 128, 1; instead of geichen, 108, 1; + inf., 290, 3; 410, 3; 411, Ex.; (du siehst, sieh).
sein, G. s. of er, es; see seiner.
sein, his, its, 85; not referring to subject, 242, 1; 243, 2; referring to indefinite subj., 98; seemingly for ihr in „seiner Zeit," 343, 2.
sein, to be, 110; 473, 1; in comp. tenses, 266, 283, 1-3; in passive, 273; + inf., 290, 3, *a*; + past part., 296, 2; + pres. part., 274, 6.
seiner, G. s. of er, es, of him, of it, 81.
seit + since, *prep.*, 303, 14; + since, *conj.*, 330, 2.
seitdem, see seit.
seitens, on the part of, *prep.*, 302.
-seits, in comp. with poss. pron., 87, 552.
-sel, noun-suf., 46, 1; 500, 1; mostly neut. gend., 16, 13.
selb-, selber, + self, 91, 2; before numerals, 229, 1; 530; strengthens refl. pron., 237, 2; use of, 249.
selbander, two of them, of us (according to the person of the verb), 229, 1.
selbig-, same, 248, 2.
selbst, see selb-.
-selig, adj.-suf., 528, 2, *a*.
-sen + -se, verb-suf., 539, 1.
senden, sandte, gesandt, + send, 119, 1; 455, 1; pret. subj., sendete.
senken, senkte, gesenkt, *trans.*, + sink, 535, 1, *a*.
Sessel, *m.*, -, (easy, large) chair.
Seuche, *f.*, *w.*, epidemic disease, 396.
sh — sch, 490, 1, *d*.
shall + sollen, 266, 5; in fut., 266, 6; 279, 3; 283, 4.
sich, A. and D., sing. and pl. of refl. pron., him- and herself, themselves, 83; reciprocal pron., 84, each, one another; supplants pers. pron., 237, 1; 243, 3, R.; position of, 353, *e*.
sie, N. and A., fem. sing., and pl. of all genders, + she, her, they, them, 81.
Sie, you in address, 230, 2; 233.
siech, infirm, + sickly, 396.
sieden, sott, gesotten, boil, + seethe, II., 124, 1; 416, 1; 463; (du siedest); figur. weak.
sin-, in comp., 494, 8.
singen, sang, gesungen, + sing, III., 125, 1.
sinken, sank, gesunken, + sink, III., 125, 1.
Sinn und Verstand = all reason, lit. sense and reason.

finnen, fann, gefonnen, meditate, III., 125, 2; (fänne and fönne).
fint+since, *prep.*, 303, 14.
fintemal, because, 337, 1.
fiben, faß, gefeffen, +sit, V., 128, 2; 457, 1; [du fißeft, er fißt, fiß(e)].
fo+so; in main clauses preceded by depend. claus., 329; 333; 330, 3, *a*; 348, 2; in consecutive clauses, 335; in compar. clauses, 333, 3; in concessive cl., 339; relative adv., 257; =wenn, 340; +ein, 250, 2.
Sohn, *m.*, ⸚e, +son, 405.
folch+such, 91, 3; 443, 1; force of, 250; +ein, 91, 3; 144; 157; 333, 3.
fofern, *conj.*, +in so far as, 340.
Solba't, *m.*, *w.*, +soldier.
follen, follte, gefollt, + shall, ought, 135, 5; 108, 2; 471, 2, 4; force of, 267, 5; 279, 3; 283, 2, 5.
fonder, without, 304, 6; 489, 4.
fondern, but, 320, 2, R.; word-order after, 343, *c*.
fonft, at other times, 320; 551, 3.
fp, pronunc. of, 24; 378, 3; 389, 4; 391, 1; Eng. correspondents of, 412, 1.
Spaß, *m.*, -es, ⸚e, joke, fun.
fpaßen, to joke, 118, 2; (fpaßeft, fpaßte).
fpät, *adv.*, late, 300, 1; 554. 1.
Spaten, *m.*, -, +spade.
Spat, *m.*, *w.*, also -es, -e, +sparrow.
fpazieren, walk about, with verbs of motion, 290, 2.
fpähen+spy, 494, 1.
fpät, late, see also fpat.
fpeien, fpie, gefpieen, + spit, + spew, I., 122, 2.
Speife, *f.*, *w.*, food.
fpinnen, fpann, gefponnen, +spin, III., 125, 2; (fpänne and fpönne).
Spion, *m.*, -e, +spy, 494, 1.
fpleißen, fplih, gefplißen, + split, I, 122, 1; (du fpleißeft or fpleißt, er fpleißt).
Sporn, *m.*, +spur, for infl. see 63, 1.
fprechen, fprach, gefprochen, + speak, IV., 127; (du fprichft, fprich; with A., to see, in § 66.
fprießen, fproß, gefproffen, +sprout, II., 124, 1; (du fprießeft or fprießt, er fprießt; old, fpreußt, fpreuß).
fpringen, fprang, gefprungen, + spring, run, III., 125, 1; (fpränge).
Sproß, *m.*, -ffes, -ffe, +sprout, scion.
st, pronunc. of, 24; 378, 3; 389, 4; 391, 1; Eng. correspondents of, 412.
-ft, superl. suffix, 73; 438, 1; in ordinals, 80; 530; in nouns, 512, 3.
Staat, *m.*, -es, -en, +state, government.
Stachel, *m.*, -, sting.
Stadt, *f.*, ⸚, city, 430, 1, *a*; 490, 1, *b*.
Stamm, *m.*, ⸚, +stem.
starr, stiff, +staring, 74.
statt+instead of, 302, 1; 490, 1, *b*.
Statt, *f.*, no *pl.*, place, +stead, see Stadt.
Stätte, *f.*, *w.*, spot, see above.
stechen, stach, gestochen, sting, puncture, +stick, IV., 127; 457, 2; 465, 1; (du stichst, stich).

stecken+to stick (not stab, but weak).
stehen, stand (stund), gestanden, +stand, 129; 136, 2; 457, 2; 475; (du stehst, stehe, ich stünde or stände).
stehlen, stahl, gestohlen, + steal, IV., 127; 398; 465; (du stiehlst, stiehl or stehle, stöhle or stähle).
steigen, stieg, gestiegen, to ascend, mount, I., 122, 2.
Stein, *m.*, -e, +stone.
Steinmeß, *m.*, *w.*, also strong, stone-cutter.
steinreich+stony, very rich, 422, 4.
sterben, starb, gestorben, +to die, IV., 125, 3; (+starve, stirbst, stürbe, rarely stärbe).
stieben, stob, gestoben, fly, scatter like dust, I., 124, 2; (du stiebst, older steubst).
Stift, gender and meaning see 58.
stinken, stank, gestunken, +stink, III., 125, 1; (stänke, rarely stünke).
stolz, proud, 74.
stoßen, stieß, gestoßen, push, thrust, VII., 131; 458, 2; (du stößt, er stößt).
straff, stretched, tight, 74.
Strauch, *m.*, ⸚e and ⸚er, shrub.
strecken+stretch, in § 79 to die.
streichen, strich, gestrichen, + strike out, +stroke, I., 122, 1.
streiten, stritt, gestritten, contend, I., 122, 2; (du streitest); "strong," 428, 8.
Stube, *f.*, sitting-room (+stove).
Stuhl, *m.*, ⸚e. chair, + stool, throne.
stund, pret. of stehen, *q. v.*
-stund in comp., 531, 2.
Stute, mare, +stud, 430, 1.
stutzen, be startled, clip, < same root as stoßen; see 535; du stutzest, 118, 2.
suchen + seek, 454, 3.
Sucht, *f.*, *w.*, passion, mania, 396; *orig.*, lingering disease; +sick.
-süchtig in comp., 528, 2, *b*.
Süden, *m.*, -s, +south.
Sündflut, *f.*, *w.*, Deluge, 494, 3.
süß+sweet.
ß, pronunc. of, 22, 35-

T.

t, pronunc. of, 25; see th; Eng. correspondents of, 408. 1; 412; 413, 1; 414, 1; description of, 384, 1; in ⸚, 389, 3, 4; excrescent, 87; 89; 91, 2; 491, 2; 512, 2, 3; stops into spirants before, 412; tr, 414, 1.
-t, noun-suffix, 512; fem. gend., 161, 2; 163, 5.
-t, in the participle of weak verbs, 453.
-t, 2. pers. sg. in pret.-pres. verbs, 470, 2.
Tafel, *f.*, *w.*, formal meal; bei —, at+table.
Tag, *m.*, -e, +day.
taugen, to be fit, +do, 471, 5.
Tausend, *n.*, -e, +thousand, 226.
tch, G. correspondents of, 414, 3.
-te, suf. in ordinals, 80, 530.
-te, in pret., 117; 454, 1.
teils, in part; in comp. with poss. pron., 87.

-tel, in comp., 532, 2.
-ter, noun-suf., 508.
têta, see thât.
Teutones, 492, 3.
th, pronunc. of, 25 ; origin of, 363, 3 ; 384, 1.
thât + did, 274, 6 ; 290 ; 476, 2.
Thor, gend. and meaning, 162, 4 ; 408, 1.
Thräne, tear, 430, 1.
Thron, m., -e and -en, + throne, 63, 1.
thun, that, gethan, + do, 136, 3 ; 454, 1 ; 476 ; as an auxil., 294, 6 ; 294, 1 ; (thâte).
Thür, f., w., + door, 408, 1 ; 430, 1.
Thürchen, n., -, little door.
Tier, n., -e, animal (deer).
Tisch, m., -e, table (+ disk, + dish).
Tochter, f., ⸚, + daughter, 46, 48, 408, 1.
Tod, m., -es, pl. of, 173.
toll, mad, + dull, 74.
tragen, trug, getragen, carry, VI., 129 ; (du trägst).
Trant, m., ⸚e, + drink.
trauen (with D.), to trust.
treffen, traf, getroffen, hit, IV., 127 ; (du triffst, trifft).
treiben, trieb, getrieben, + drive, I., 122, 2.
treten, trat, getreten, + tread, step, V., 128, 1 ; (du trittst, er tritt, tritt or trete).
triefen, troff, getroffen, + to drip, drop, II., 124, 1 ; 463 ; (du triefst, rarely treufft).
triegen, see trügen.
trinken, trank, getrunken, + drink, III., 125, 1 ; (tränke, older trünke).
troden + dry, 524, 4.
Tropf(en) m., -, + drop, 46, 4.
Tropf, m., ⸚e, fool, orig. "struck with paralysis."
trotz, in defiance, in spite of, 302, 9.
trösten, to comfort, 535, 1, a ; (tröstete).
-trunken, intoxicated, 528.
Trübsal, f., -e, sorrow.
Trümmer, a pl., ruins, 59.
trügen, trog, getrogen, to cheat, II., 124, 2 ; 132 ; (du trügst, older treugst).
Tuch, n., -es, ⸚er, cloth, shawl, 58, 85.
-tum, + -dom, 57, 4 ; mostly neut. gend., 161, 3 ; origin of, 501 ; 515, 5.
tz, pronunc. of, 389, 3 ; 414, 1 ; tz — z, f, 535, 1, R. 2 ; see z.

U.

u, pronunc. of, 26 ; description of, 368, 1, 2 ; < uo, 488, 4 ; u — o, 405 ; + nasalis and liquida sonans, 459, 3, a.
ue, as sign of umlaut, 362, 2.
um + zu, in order to, 291, 1, 4, R. ; 335, 1 ; 338, 1 ; 304, 7 ; in comp. verbs, 549, 4 ; + so, 324.
umringen, surrounded, see ringen.
un- + -un, accent, 422, 6 ; 516, 10.
und + and, 319 ; + inversion, 339, 1.
-ung + -ing, 506, 2 ; gend., 161, 2.
uns, D. and A. of wir, + us, to us, 81 ; also refl., 83 ; and reciprocal pron., 84.
unser, G. of wir, 81.

unser, poss. pron., + our, 85.
unsrer, for unser, 82.
unter-, adj., lower, + under, 76, 2.
unter, prep., + under, 306, 8, 10 ; in comp. verbs, 549, 5.
Unterschied, m., -es, -e, difference, 458, 3.
Unterthan, m., w., subject (of a ruler), 63, 1.
Ur- + or-, 516, 9.
Urahne, great grandmother in § 143.
urbar, arable, 526, 1.
ü, pronunc. of, 31 ; sign of umlaut, 362, 2 ; 368, 4 ; description of, 367 ; 368, 3, 4 ; < üe, 488, 4 ; ü — i, 489, 2.
über + over, 306, 7: in comp. verbs, 549, 3.
ü'berfahren, to cross.
überhau'pt, in general, 423 ; 552, 3.

V.

v, pronunc. of, 27 ; 380, 1, 2 ; see f ; 415, 1.
Vater, m., ⸚, + father, 46, 48, 2 ; 411 ; 478. 4.
Vaterland, n., -es, -e, + fatherland.
ver- + for-, 516, 11 ; 545 ; in certain participles, 295, 2 ; 545, E.
verderben, verdarb, verdorben, to spoil (intr.), III., 125, 3 ; (du verbirbst, verbirb, verdürbe, rarely verdarbe).
Verdienst, gend. and meaning, 162, 3.
verdient, deserving, meritorious, 295, 2.
verdrießen, verdroß, verdrossen, to vex, II., 124, 1 ; (du verdrießest or verdrießt, old verdreußt).
vergessen, vergaß, vergessen, + to forget, V., 128, 1 ; past part. in comp., 295, 2, a ; (du vergissest or vergißt, er vergißt, vergiß).
verhältnißmäßig, comparatively.
verkaufen, to sell.
verlassen, to forsake, see lassen.
verlegen, embarrassed, past part., 295, 2, a ; 524, 4.
verlernen, to forget how to . . ., + unlearn.
verlieren, verlor, verloren, + lose, II., 124, 2 ; 416.
vermöge, by virtue of, 302, 11.
verwirren, to confuse, strong past part., verworren = complicated, VIII., 133.
Vetter, m. or mixed decl., cousin, 63, 1.
Vieh, n., -es, -e, cattle (+ fee), 410, 3.
viel, much, compar. of, 76, 1 ; 100 ; 199, 1, 2 ; 263.
vixen + Füchsin, 504.
voll- + full, 74, 540, 6.
voller + full, 219, 1.
vollkommen, perfect, 421, 1.
Volk, n., ⸚er, people, + folk.
Vo'lksetymologie' + folk-etymology, 494, 2.
vom < von dem, from the, 40.
von, from, by, 303, 15 ; compar. with durch, 269 ; 304, 2 ; 306, 7, R. ; + selbst, of . . . self, 249, 2.
vor + before, in point of, 306, 9 ; 516, 5 ; compar. with für, 304, 3.
vorau'sverkündigen, announce beforehand, 546, 2.
vorder-, the front one, 76, 2 (short o).

WORD-INDEX AND GERMAN-ENGLISH VOCABULARY. 285

Vorfahr, m., w., ancestor.
vor'habend, intended, 294, 1.
Vormund, m., -es, ¨-er, guardian.

W.

w, pronunc. of, 28; description of, 379; 380, 2; loss of, 417, 2; Eng. correspondents of, 410, 3; 415, 2; 490, 6.
wachsen, wuchs, gewachsen, grow, + wax, VI., 129; 417, 5, a; (du, er wächst).
Wagen, m., + wagon, + wain, 494, 1; 48, 2.
Waggo'n, m., pl. in -s, car, 494, 1.
wain + Wagen, 494, 1.
wahr, true, 74.
Wahrheit, f., w., truth.
Wald, m., -es, ¨-er, forest, + wold.
walten, rule (waltete).
wandeln, walk, change, 118, 3.
wandern + wander, 118, 3.
wann + when; for relat. pron., 258; conj., 330, 1; etym., 551, 2.
war, pret. of sein, q. v.; also wësan.
warb, pret. sing. of werben, 111, 2; 460.
warum + why, + wherefore, 251, 4; 551, 2.
was, interrog. pron., 92; 444; use of, 251; + G., 251, 1; preceded by zu, mit, 251, 3; with für and ein, 144, 253; force of warum, 251, 4; relat. pron., 93; 256; 256, 2; indef. pron., 96; 204; 260.
was, archaic of wësan, 466, 1.
waschen, wusch, gewaschen, + wash, VI., 129; 412; (du wäschest or wäschst).
Wasser, n., -, + water, 414, 1, Ex.
wägen, see wiegen.
während, during, 302, 11; conj., 330, 1.
-wärts, + -ward, 553, 2.
"weak," 428, 3.
weben, wob, gewoben, + weave, VIII., 133; (du webst); weak = to move.
weder — noch + neither — nor; + whether, 444, 3; in compar. clauses, 333, Ex.
-wegen, on account of, in comp. with pron., 87, 89; prepos., 302, 13.
weh thun + D., to pain, see thun.
Weib, n., -es, -er, + woman, + wife, 166.
weich, soft (+ weak).
weichen, wich, gewichen, to yield, I., 122, 1; weak = to soften.
Weihnachten, Christmas, 429, 1.
weil, because, 337; + while, 330, 1.
-weise, -wise, 552, 3.
weisen, wies, gewiesen, show, I., 122, 2.
weissagen, prophecy, 547, 3; (p. p. geweissagt).
weiss, see wissen.
welch, interrog. pron., 92, 2; 444, 2; with ein, 144; 252; relat. pron., 93, 2; 255, 256; indef. pron., 96, 260; etym., 415, 2.
wem, D. of wer, q. v.; 92, 1.
wenden, wandte, gewandt, turn (+ wend), 119, 1; 307; 453; (du wendest, pret. subj. wendete).
wenig, little, few; comparison regular or as in 76, 1.

wenn, conj., + when, = if in temporal cl., 330, 1; = if in concessive cl., 339; = if in condit. cl., 340; etym., 551, 2.
wer + who, interrog. pron., 92; 251; 410, 3; 444; relat. pron., 93, 3; 254; 256; indef. pron., 96; 254; 260; 339.
werben, warb, geworben, recruit, sue for, III., 125, 3; (du wirbst, wirb, würbe or wärbe).
werden, ward or wurde, geworden, become (+ worth), III., 125, 3; infl. of, 110; 111, 2; 460, 1; in passive, 273; in comp. tenses, 283, 2-5; + zu, 303, 16; (du wirst, er wird, werde, würde).
werfen, warf, geworfen, throw, III., 125, 3; (du wirfst, wirf, würfe or wärfe).
Werk, n., -es, -e, + work, 60.
wes, wessen, weß, 92, 1; 256, 4.
wesen, wësan, V., 128, 5; 411; 466.
weshalb, wherefore, 92, 1.
wessent-, in comp., 92, 1.
Wicht, m., -e, + wight, + whit.
wider, against, 304, 8; in comp. verbs, 549, 7.
widmen, dedicate (widmete), 118, 2.
wie, + how, as, 444, 1; in tempor. clauses, 330, 1, 2; in compar. cl., 333; after comparative, 333, 2.
wieder, adv., again, in comp. verbs, 549, 8.
wiegen, wog, gewogen, + weigh, VIII., 133; (also wägen, du wiegst).
wild + wild.
will, see wollen; 267, 6.
willen, for the sake of, in comp. with pron., 87, 89; prepos., 302, 14.
winden, wand, gewunden, + wind, III., 125, 1; (du windest).
wissen, wußte, gewußt, for infl. see 135, 1; 412, 2; 471, 1; 472, 1; compar. with kennen, können, 267, 1.
with + wider, 306, 8.
Wittum, n., -e, jointure, allowance, 501.
wo(r) + where, supplants cases of interrog. and relat. pron., 251, 2; 258; in local clauses, 331; in tempor. cl., 330, 1; in condit. cl., 340, 340, 4; origin of, 551, 2.
wofern, conj., in so far as, 336; 340; 340, 2.
wohl + well, pronunc. of, 381; 339; 489, 1; position of, 354; 299, 2, a.
wohlgeboren, (Your) Honor, lit. + well born.
wollen, wollte, gewollt, + will, be willing, for infl. see 135, 7, and 108, 2; 472, 2; special force of, 267, 6; 279, 3; 283, 5.
womöglich, if possible, 340, 4.
worden, past part. of werden, 108, 5.
Wort, n., -e and ¨-er, + word, 58.
Wunder, n., -, + wonder, see nehmen.
wurde, pret. of werden, 111, 2.
Wurm, m., ¨-er, and ¨-e, + worm.
wußte, see wissen.
Würde, f., w., dignity, + worth.

X.

x, pronunc. of, 29; 389, 2; 417, 5, a; Engl. x as symbol, 395.

Y.

y, pronunc. of, 31.

Z.

z, pronunc. of, 30; 389, 3, 4; Eng. correspondents of, 409, 1; 414, 1; 490, 2; 535, 1, R. 2.
zahm + tame, 74, 398.
Zahn, m., ⸚e, + tooth, 409, 1; 417, 1.
zart, tender, 74.
zähmen + to tame, 535, 1, a.
Zähre, f., w., + tear, 430, 1.
zehn + ten, 77, 529.
Zeichen, n., -, + token.
zeichnen, draw, delineate, 118, 1.
zeihen, zieh, geziehen, accuse, I., 122, 2; 395; 462.
-zen, verb-suf., 539, 3.
zer- + dis-, verb-pref., 546.
zerreißen, to tear to pieces, see reißen.
Zeuge, m., w., witness.

ziehen, zog, gezogen, draw, II., 124, 2; 416; (du zeuchst, zeuch are archaic).
-zig + -ty in numerals, 529, 1.
zittern, tremble, etym., 457, 3.
zu + to, 303, 16; before inf., 291; before adj., 291, 4; 333, 3; see gegen and nach.
Zuber, tub, etym., 398.
Zucker, m., no pl., + sugar.
zufolge, in accordance with, 302, 15.
zum < zu dem + to the, 40.
Zunft, f., ⸚e, guild, 398.
Zunge, f., w., + tongue, 414, 1, Ex.
zur < zu der + to the, fem., 40.
zurückbringen + bring back, see bringen.
zusammen, together.
zwar, to be sure, 339; 555, 3; position of, 354.
zween + twain, + two, 79; 529.
zwei + two; infl. of, 78; form and gend. of, 79; 529.
zwelf + twelve, 77; 529; 489, 1.
zwie- + two-, 520, 1.
zwier + twice, 531, 2.
zwingen, zwang, gezwungen, to force, III., 125, 1.
zwischen + between, 306, 10; compar. with unter, 306, 8; 305, 1, 2.
zwo + two, fem., 79; 529.
ʒ, Grimm's sign for the sound between z and s, 414; > s, 490, 2.

THE STUDENT'S
MANUAL OF EXERCISES

FOR TRANSLATING INTO GERMAN

WITH FULL VOCABULARY, NOTES, REFERENCES, AND GENERAL SUGGESTIONS

PREPARED AND ARRANGED TO ACCOMPANY

BRANDT'S GERMAN GRAMMAR

BY

A. LODEMAN, A.M.

PROFESSOR OF GERMAN AND FRENCH IN THE MICHIGAN STATE NORMAL SCHOOL

Boston
ALLYN AND BACON
1888

Copyright, 1885, *by G. P. Putnam's Sons.*

REMARKS AND EXPLANATIONS.

The following EXERCISES have been prepared with the twofold purpose of furnishing to the student material for translating into German, and of assisting him in the analysis and translation of the more difficult illustrations in *Brandt's German Grammar*.

That examples from the *German classics* are the proper kind of illustrations for a text-book of such high order and merit as Professor Brandt's, cannot be doubted. Had the author illustrated his rules by means of sentences especially adapted to the understanding of the young student, the latter, upon completing the course in grammar, would not be well prepared to read and enjoy the works of the great German authors. If the examples found in Brandt's Grammar, in some instances, force the student to greater application, he will feel amply repaid for his extra labor when he takes up the study of the masterpieces of German literature.

At all events, the present Exercises will, it is hoped, enable even the beginner to derive the full benefit from the large number of excellent illustrations drawn from the acknowledged masters of German style and embodied in Brandt's Grammar. Should he find any difficulty in translating any one of them, he has only to refer, by means of the table given below, to the corresponding English Exercise, and he will find that one or more of the English sentences will greatly aid him in the understanding of the German example.

The Grammar referred to throughout the book (including the Vocabulary) is *Brandt's Grammar of the German Language.* Paragraphs to be read over merely are put in ( ).

In the Exercises, words in [ ] should not be translated, while those in ( ) are required by the German idiom.

The cognate mark (+) is put, as a rule, only where even the beginner can recognize the common origin of English and German words after having had his attention called to it. When the German word is preceded by the article, the + is placed before the latter.

Figures at the end of sentences refer to those sections in the Grammar in which more or less of the material required for the German sentence may be found.

The VOCABULARY contains all words not explained in the notes, except such grammatical words (pronouns, prepositions, etc.) as are easily found in the very paragraphs to which the student is referred for each exercise. The notes under the first twenty exercises are so full as to do away with the use of the Vocabulary.

TABLE

SHOWING IN WHICH EXERCISES ILLUSTRATIONS OF THE VARIOUS PARAGRAPHS OF THE GRAMMAR MAY BE FOUND.

Para.	Ex.	Page	Para.	Ex.	Page	Para.	Ex.	Page
38	1	7	110	5	9	226-29	17	33
39	1	60	"	31	45	230	18	34
40	2	61	111	5	63	"	7	11
41	1	60	112	3	8	231-32	7	65
42	1	7	113	6	64	233-34	18	34
43	2	7	114	4	9	235-36	19	35
44-5	1	7	"	5	10	237-41	20	36
46	2	7	115	2	22	242-43	7	65
48	1	9	116	4	9	244-48	21	36
49-50	3	8	"	6	11	"	8	65
51	1	60	117	2	7	249-54	22	37
52-3	4	9	118	7	65	"	8	65
56-8	5	10	119	6	11	255-63	23	38
59-60	1	60	120-3	18	19	"	8	65
61-2	6	11	124-8	19	20	264-66	24	39
63-4	7	11	129-33	20	20	267	25	39
65	8	12	134	11	15	"	26	40
66	1	60	135	11	15	268-73	27	41
67	8	12	"	12	15	274-75	28	42
68	1	60	"	13	16	276-79	29	43
69-72	9	13	"	14	16	280-83	30	44
73-5	10	14	136	15	17	284-85	31	45
76	11	15	137	16	18	286-90	32	46
77-8	12	15	"	3	61	291-93	33	47
79	17	33	138	14	16	294-300	34	47
80-2	13	16	139-46	1	21	301-3	35	48
83-5	14	16	147-50	2	7	304	36	49
86-7	7	65	151-58	3	23	305-7	37	50
88	15	17	159-63	4	24	308-17	1	51
89	7	65	164-69	5	24	318-22	2	52
90-1	15	17	170-77	6	25	323-28	3	52
92-3	16	18	178-79	7	26	329-32	4	53
94-100	17	18	180-83	8	27	333-35	5	54
101-2	2	7	184-88	9	27	336-40	6	55
"	3	8	189	10	28	341	16	18
"	5	10	190	10	28	"	16	32
103	1	7	"	3	61	"	7	56
"	2	7	191-97	11	29	342-43	16	32
"	5	10	198	11	29	"	7	56
"	31	45	"	3	61	344	16	32
104-5	7	11	199-202	11	29	"	8	57
106-7	8	12	203-9	12	29	345-49	8	57
108	8	12	210-12	13	30	350	3	8
"	10	14	213-17	14	31	"	5	10
109	3	8	218-21	15	32	"	9	57
110	1	7	222	16	33	"	3	61
"	2	7	"	10	14	351-53	9	57
"	4	9	223-25	16	32	354-59	10	58

ABBREVIATIONS.

acc.	= accusative.		part.	= participle.
adj.	= adjective.		perf.	= perfect tense.
aux.	= auxiliary verb.		pers.	= personal.
B. T.	= Bayard Taylor.		plup.	= pluperfect tense.
conj.	= conjunction.		plur.	= plural.
dat.	= dative.		poet.	= poetical.
def. art.	= definite article.		p. p.	= past participle.
Ex.	= Exercise.		prep.	= preposition.
F.	= Faust, Hart's Edition.		pret.	= preterite.
f. and ff.	= following.		pron.	= pronoun.
gen.	= genitive.		pr. pts.	= principal parts.
Ha.	= James Morgan Hart.		sep.	= separable.
imp.	= impersonal.		str.	= strong verb or noun.
indef. art.	= indefinite article.		subj.	= subjunctive.
inf.	= infinitive.		subord.	= subordinating.
insep.	= inseparable.		trans.	= transitive.
intrans.	= intransitive.		v. tr.	= transitive verb.
irr.	= irregular.		w.	= with.
lit.	= literally.		wk. v.	= weak verb.
n.	= noun.		+	= of common origin with, or *cognate*.
nom.	= nominative.			

I., II. . . . denote classes of strong nouns or verbs.

In the VOCABULARY *separable* and *strong* verbs are marked *sep.* and *str.* respectively; inseparable and weak verbs are not marked.

FIRST SERIES.

Exercise I.

38, 42, 44, 45—103, 110, *Present Indicative of* loben, haben, sein—(*The first sentence of each of the following paragraphs:* **178, 180, 189, 198**).

1. The father praises the son. 2. The brother has a house. 3. The bath is in the house. 4. The strength of the sons is great. 5. Have you a trade? 6. The angels perform miracles. 7. The days are short. 8. Is the thread long or short? 9. Where is the gardener's spade? 10. The gardener has the spade.

REMARK.—Most of the nouns in these Exercises will be easily found in the §§ above referred to.

1. *Father* + der Vater. *To praise,* loben. *Son* + der Sohn; acc. den Sohn. 2. *Brother* + der Bruder. *To have* + haben. *House* + das Haus; gen. —es, dat. —e, acc. = nom. 3. *Bath* + das Bad. *To be,* sein. *In,* in (prep. here w. dat.). 4. *Strength,* die Kraft. *Of the sons,* der Söhne. *Great* + groß. 5. *Trade,* das Gewerbe. 6. *Angel* + der Engel. *To perform* = do + thun (3d pers. plur. the same). *Miracle,* das Wunder. 7. *Day* + der Tag. *Short,* kurz. 8. *Thread,* der Faden. *Long* + lang. *Or* + oder. 9. *Where?* wo? *Gardener* + der Gärtner. *Spade* + der Spaten. 10. Sentences 9 and 10 suggest an easy method of introducing *conversation* in connection with these Exercises.

Exercise II.

43, 46—103, 110, *Preterite Indicative of* loben, haben, sein—
(**117—275, 2, 101, 102**).

1. The grain was on the floor. 2. The daughter loved the father more than the mother. 3. The little child was

playing with the little dog. 4. The knight presented a set of jewelry to the daughter. 5. On the rock [there] was a well. 6. I had a thought. 7. The floor rests on the beams. 8. The father and the brother-in-law rested in peace.

1. *Grain*, das Getreibe. *On*, auf (prep. here w. dat.). *Floor*, der Boden. 2. *Daughter* + die Tochter. *To love* + lieben (inflected like loben). *More* + mehr. *Than*, als. *Mother* + die Mutter. 3. *Little child*, das Kindchen. *To play*, spielen (inflected like loben). The German has but one form for the English simple, emphatic, and progressive forms; hence, *was playing* = spielte. *Little dog*, das Hündchen. *With*, mit (prep. w. dat.). 4. *Knight*, der Ritter. *To present*, schenken (inflected like loben). *Set of jewelry*, das Geschmeibe. 5. *Rock*, der Felsen. *Well*, n., der Brunnen. 6. *Thought*, n., + der Gedanke. 7. *To rest*, ruhen (inflected like loben). *Beam*, der Balke. 8. *Brother-in-law*, der Schwager. *Peace*, der Friede.

Exercise III.
49, 50—101, 102—109, 112—265, 1—350.

REMARK.—It is not intended that the rules on the Declension of Nouns, as presented in the Grammar, should be committed to memory. The student, by carefully perusing them, in connection with the written exercises, will learn to observe closely the various forms; and, in the future, he should learn, as far as possible, the *Nom. Sing.*, *Gen. Sing.*, and *Nom. Plur.* of each noun, as all the other cases can be given when these are known.

1. The dog has caught a badger. 2. My friend has seen two hawks. 3. The youth has been in (the) prison. 4. We have made many attempts. 5. A year has twelve months, a month has thirty days. 6. What have you heard? 7. I have not heard a sound. 8. The kings on the thrones are not free from tribulations. 9. (The) salmons are larger than (the) herrings. 10. The smith can carry the anvil with one hand.

1. *Dog*, der Hund. *To catch*, fangen, str. v. (pr. pts., fangen, fieng, gefangen). *Badger*, der Dachs. 2. *My* + mein (declined like the indefinite article ein, see **38**) *Friend* + der Freund. *To see* + sehen, str. v. (pr. pts., sehen,

ſah, geſehen). *Two* + zwei. *Hawk* + der Habicht. 3. *Youth* (young man) + der Jüngling. *To be*, ſein, war, geweſen. The compound tenses of ſein are formed with ſein, not with haben ; hence, I have been = ich bin geweſen (see **266**, 3). *Prison*, das Gefängniß—in dem may be contracted into im (see **40**). 4. *To make* + machen, machte, gemacht. *Many*, viele. *Attempt*, der Verſuch. 5. *Year* + das Jahr. *Twelve* + zwölf. *Month* + der Monat. *Thirty* + dreißig. *Day* + der Tag. 6. *What?* + Was? *To hear* + hören, hörte, gehört. 7. Render : *I have heard no sound.* *No*, kein (declined like ein). *Sound*, der Laut. 8. *King* + der König. *On*, auf (here w. dat.). *Throne* + der Thron. *Free from* + frei von (w. dat.). *Tribulation*, die Trübſal. 9. *Salmon*, der Lachs. *Large, larger, largest*, groß, größer, größt. *Than*, als. *Herring* + der Hering. 10. *Smith* + der Schmied, str. II. *Can* + kann. *To carry*, tragen, str. v. (pr. pts., tragen, trug, getragen). *Anvil*, der Amboß. *With*, mit (w. dat.). *One* + ein (declined like the indefinite article). *Hand* + die Hand, str. III.

Exercise IV.

52, 53—110, *Present and Preterite Indicative of* werden— **(114, 116).**

1. The maid will kill the goose. 2. The cow is [being] killed. 3. Rafts are made out of the trunks of (the) trees. 4. You will hear the mice in the night. 5. The guests were at the ball in the city. 6. The son's betrothed will come tomorrow. 7. The song of the choir was heard in the garden. 8. They will seek excuses. 9. Do you see the eagle in the air ? 10. The fruit of the tree will soon be ripe.

1. *Maid* + die Magd. *To kill* (of animals), ſchlachten, wk. v. *Goose* + die Gans. 2. *Cow* + die Kuh. Note that *is killed* is the passive voice. 3. *Raft*, das Floß. *To make* + machen, wk. v. *Out of*, von (prep. w. dat.). *Trunk*, der Stamm. *Tree*, der Baum. 4. *To hear* (see Ex. III., 6). *Mouse* + die Maus. *Night* + die Nacht. *In*, here with the dat. 5. *Guest* + der Gaſt. *At*, here auf (w. dat.). *Ball* + der Ball. *City*, die Stadt *In*, here w. dat. 6. *Betrothed*, n., die Braut (bride). *To come* + kommen, str. v. (pr. pts., kommen, kam, gekommen). *To-morrow* + morgen. 7. *Song* + der Geſang. *Choir* + der Chor. *Garden* + der Garten, str. I. *In*, here w. dat. 8. *To seek* +

suchen, wk. v. *Excuse* (subterfuge), bie Ausflucht. 9. *Do you see?* Sehen Sie? *Eagle*, ber Aar, str. II. *Air*, bie Luft. *In*, here w. dat. 10. *Fruit* + bie Frucht. *Soon*, balb. *Ripe* + reif.

Exercise V.

56 to 58—*Review* **101 to 103, 110, 114, 116, 350.**—**103,** *Present and Preterite Indicative of* singen.

1. The men turn the wheels. 2. Do you believe in ghosts and spectres? 3. Our mind is not free from errors. 4. He read all [the] words on this leaf. 5. The villain did not listen to the words of his friend. 6. The girls wear shawls and ribbons. 7. The ties of (the) blood are strong. 8. The foxes live in the forest. 9. The scholars write with pencils. 10. I have forgotten the word. 11. We found the leaves under the shrubs. 12. His friends are under shelter.

1. *Man* + ber Mann. *To turn*, brehen, brehte, gebreht. *Wheel*, bas Rab. 2. *To believe*, glauben, glaubte, geglaubt. *In*, here an (w. acc.). *Ghost* + ber Geist. *Spectre*, bas Gespenst. 3. *Our*+unser. *Mind*, ber Geist. *Free from*, see Ex. III., 8. *Error* + ber Irrtum. 4. *To read*, lesen, las, gelesen. *All*, plur., + alle. *Word* + bas Wort. *On*, auf, here w. dat. *Leaf*, bas Blatt. 5. *Villain*, ber Bösewicht. *To listen to*, hören auf (w. acc.); *did not listen* (see Ex. II., 3). *His*, sein (declined like ein). *Friend*, see Ex. III., 2. 6. *Girl*, bas Mädchen (**46**, 1); notice that in German *all diminutives are of the neuter gender*, no matter what they signify (**161**, 3). *To wear*, tragen, trug, getragen. *Shawl*, bas Tuch. *Ribbon*, bas Banb. 7. *Tie*, bas Banb. *Blood* + bas Blut, gen. –es. *Strong*, stark. 8. *Fox* + ber Fuchs, gen. –es, plur. Füchse. *To live* + leben, lebte, gelebt. *Forest*, ber Wald. 9. *Scholar* + ber Schüler (**46**, 1). *To write*, schreiben, schrieb, geschrieben. *Pencil*, ber Bleistift (bas Blei, lead; ber Stift, "small pointed object"; see **164**). *With*, mit (w. dat.). 10. *To forget* + vergessen, vergaß, vergessen. 11. *To find* + finden, fanb, gefunben (inflected like singen, sang, gesungen; see, however, **104, 118, 121** first sentence). *Shrub*, ber Strauch. *Under* + unter, here w. dat. 12. *Under shelter* = unter Dach unb Fach (bas Dach, roof; bas Fach, compartment).

Exercise VI.

61, 62—119—*Review* 116, 350.

1. The messengers were sent to the prince. 2. The students sent a present to the poet. 3. The finches sing beautifully. 4. The democrats hate monarchs, kings, princes, counts; they honor the peasants. 5. The architects have built a house for the Hungarian. 6. The lights were burning. 7. The astronomer thinks of the stars. 8. The fellow brought a bear out of the woods. 9. Not all kings are heroes. 10. (The) Men believe in God.

1. *Messenger,* ber Bote. *To send* + fenben, fanbte, gefanbt. *To,* when denoting motion toward a person, is usually translated by zu, w. dat. *Prince,* ber Fürst, + ber Prinz. 2. *Student* + ber Stube'nt. *Present,* n., das Geschenk (**50**, 4). *Poet* + ber Poe't (**62**, 8), or ber Dichter (**46**, 1). 3. *Finch* + ber Fink. *To sing* + singen, sang, gesungen. *Beautifully,* schön. 4. *Democrat* + ber Demokra't. *To hate* + hassen, haßte, gehaßt. *monarch* + ber Mona'rch. *King* (see Ex. III., 8). *Count,* ber Graf. *To honor,* ehren, ehrte, geehrt. *Peasant,* ber Bauer. 5. *Architect* + ber Archite'ct. *To build,* bauen, baute, gebaut. *For* + für (w. acc.). *Hungarian* + ber Ungar. 6. *Light* + das Licht (**58**). *To burn* + brennen, brannte, gebrannt (see Ex. II., 8). 7. *Astronomer* + ber Astrono'm. *To think of* + benken an (w. acc.); benken, bachte, gebacht. *Star* + ber Stern, str. II. 8. *Fellow,* ber Bursche. *To bring* + bringen, brachte, gebracht. *Bear* + ber Bär. *Out of* + aus (w. dat.). *Woods* = forest, ber Wald. 9. *Not* + nicht. *Hero,* ber Held. 10, *Man* = human being, + ber Mensch. *To believe in* (see Ex. V., 2). *God* + Gott.

Exercise VII.

63, 64—104, 105—230, 1, 2.

1. Thou hast eyes and seest not; and thou hast ears and hearest not. 2. You are losing your slippers. 3. Do you know the doctors and professors of the university? 4. Mary was the mother of Jesus Christ. 5. I feel a pain in my heart.

6. Go, and take this atlas to the director of the seminary. 7. My cousin's neighbor has written dramas. 8. Canst thou find the minerals? 9. Tell me the cases of the singular and plural. 10. The insect has lost its sting.

1. *Eye* + das Auge. *Seest* + siehst (128, 1). *Ear* + das Ohr. *To hear* (see Ex. III., 6). 2. *To lose* + verlieren, verlor, verloren. *Slipper*, der Panto'ffel. 3. *Do you know?* Kennen Sie? *Doctor*, der Doktor. *Professor*, der Professor. *University*, die Universitä't (43, 1). 4. *Mary*, Mari'a. *Jesus Christ*, Jesus Christus. 5. *To feel* + fühlen, fühlte, gefühlt. *Pain*, der Schmerz. *My*, see 154. *Heart* + das Herz. 6. *To go* + gehen, gieng, gegangen. *Take*, here to be rendered by bringen. *Atlas* + der Atlas. *Director*, der Director. *Seminary* + das Semina'r. 7. *Cousin*, der Vetter. *Neighbor* + der Nachbar. *To write* (see Ex. V., 9). *Drama* + das Drama. 8. *Can* (see 135, 3). *Find* (see Ex. V., 11). *Mineral* + das Minera'l. 9. *To tell*, sagen, sagte, gesagt. *Me* + mir (dat. of ich). *Case* + der Casus. *Singular* + der Singular (gen. -s). *Plural* + der Plural (gen. -s). 10. *Insect* + das Inse'ct. *Its*, here seinen. *Sting*, der Stachel.

Exercise VIII.

65, 67—106, 107, 108, 3.

1. The Prussians have a king, the Americans a president. 2. Many Englishmen wander through Switzerland. 3. The students have sung a song on the Rhine. 4. Alsace used to belong to France. 5. The palace of (the) emperor Charles stood in Aix-la-Chapelle. 6. The generals of the great Frederic were heroes. 7. Anna's sister has left England. 8. The Fichtel-mountains are covered with snow. 9. The pupils have read of the two Marys. 10. Goethe's works are instructive.

1. *Prussian* + der Preuße. *American* + der Amerika'ner. *President* + der Präside'nt (62, 3). 2. *Many* (see Ex. III., 4). *Englishman* + der Engländer. *To wander* + wandern, wanderte, gewandert. *Through* + durch (w. acc.). *Switzerland* + die Schweiz (see 147, 2). 3. *Student* (see Ex. VI., 2). *Sing* (see Ex. VI., 3). *Song*, das Lied. *On*, auf (here w. dat.). *Rhine* +

ber Rhein—(An bem Rhein would mean *on the bank of the Rh.*). 4. *Alsace* + bas Elſaß. *To belong to*, gehören zu (w. dat.); *used to belong*, here to be rendered by the (present) perfect of gehören. *France* + Frankreich. 5. *Palace* + ber Pala'ſt. *Emperor*, ber Kaiſer. *Charles* + Karl. *To stand* + ſtehen, ſtand, geſtanden. *Aix-la-Chapelle* + Aachen. 6. *General* + ber Genera'l. *Of the great Frederic* (see **65**, 3, last example). *Hero* (see Ex. VI., 9). 7. *Anna* + Anna. *Sister* + die Schweſter. *To leave*, verlaſſen, verließ, verlaſſen. *England* + England. 8. *Fichtel-mountains*, das Fichtelgebirge. *To cover*, bebecken, bebeckte, bebeckt. *With*, mit (w. dat.). *Snow* + ber Schnee. 9. *Pupil*, ber Schüler (**46**, 1). *To read* (see Ex. V., 4). *Of*, von (w. dat.). *Two* + zwei. *Mary* + Mari'e. 10. *Work* + das Werk, str. II. *Instructive*, belehrend (originally the pres. part. of belehren, to instruct, see **274**, 6).

REMARK.—In the following pages, any new nouns that are given will be followed by the terminations of the *genitive singular* and of the *nominative plural*, if there is any; if the vowel is modified it will be indicated thus, ¨.
The other cases may then be found as follows:
1. SINGULAR: *Dative* = nominative, but 1) when the genitive ends in es, the e is usually retained in the dat.; 2) when the gen. ends in en, the same ending is found in the dative.
Accusative = nominative, but when the genitive ends in en, the same ending is found in the accusative. The words under **46**, 4, end in en in the dative and accusative.
Rule: Feminine nouns do not vary in the singular.
2. PLURAL: Genitive and accusative = nominative; the dative always ends in n.

Exercise IX.

69, 70, (71), 72.

1. Good men are loved. 2. Dear friend! write me often. 3. Cold water is wholesome. 4. The young poet has made a very fine poem. 5. I shall never forget the wise words of my dear mother. 6. William has written his little letter with a poor pencil. 7. A red cherry is a nice fruit. 8. In the cities on the Rhine [there] live many pretty girls. 9. The good old man has lost his only son. 10. The late president Lincoln was a noble man.

1. *Man* (see Ex. VI., 10). *To love* + lieben (see **116**). 2. *Dear* + teuer, lieb. *Friend* + ber Freund, es, e. *Write*, ſchreiben, str. v. (**122**, 2). *Me* + mir

(dat. of id)). *Often* + oft. 3. *Cold* + kalt. *Water* + das Waſſer, s, –. *Wholesome*, geſund. 4. *Young* + jung. *Poet* (see Ex. VI., 2). *To make* + machen, wk. v. *Very fine*, herrlich. *Poem*, das Gedicht, es, e. 5. *Never* + nie. *Forget* + vergeſſen, vergaß, vergeſſen. *Wise* + weiſe. *Word* + das Wort, es, ⸚e. 6. *William* + Wilhelm. *His*, ſein (declined like ein). *Little*, klein. *Letter*, der Brief, es, e. *With*, mit (w. dat.). *Poor* = bad, ſchlecht. *Pencil* (see Ex. V., 9). **Bear in mind 350.** 7. *Red* + rot. *Cherry* + die Kirſche. *nice*, hübſch. *Fruit* + die Frucht, –, ⸚e. 8. *City*, die Stadt, –, ⸚e. *On* + an, here w. dat. *To live* + leben, wk. v. *Pretty*, hübſch, ſchön. *Girl*, das Mädchen, s, –. 9. *Old* + alt. Note that two or more adjectives, limiting one noun, follow the same declension. *To lose* + verlieren, str. v. (**124**, 2). *His*, ſein (declined like ein). *Only*, adj., + einzig. *Son* + der Sohn, es, ⸚e. 10. *Late* = deceased, verſtorben. *President* (see Ex. VIII., 1). *Noble*, edel.

Exercise X.

73, (74), 75—108, 1.—222 (*five lines*).

1. Henry is younger than Edward. 2. I have bidden the elder brother go. 3. The well has the clearest water. 4. He has sent for the finest dress. 5. We have never had (a) greater fun. 6. The flower is lovely. 7. This tree is the highest. 8. Is the doctor richer than the merchant? 9. I have heard it said. 10. The straight way is the shortest. 11. Mary has the sweetest voice of the three sisters. 12. We shall come next week.

1. *Henry* + Heinrich. *Young* + jung. *Than*, als. *Edward* + Eduard. 2. *To bid*, heißen, hieß, geheißen. *Go* + gehen, gieng, gegangen. *Old* + alt. 3. *Well*, n. (see Ex. II., 5). *Clear* + klar. *Water* + das Waſſer, s, –. 4. *To send for* = let (*or* cause to) come, kommen laſſen. *Fine*, ſchön. *Dress*, n., das Kleid, es, er. 5. *Never* + nie. *Had* (p. p.), gehabt. *Great* + groß. *Fun*, der Spaß, es, Späſſe. 6. *Flower*, die Blume, –, n. *Lovely*, allerliebſt. 7. *Tree* (see Ex. IV., 3). *High* + hoch. 8. *Doctor* (see Ex. VII., 3). *Rich* + reich. *Merchant*, der Kaufmann. 9. See **290**, 3, *b*, and **108**, 1. 10. *Straight*, gerade. *Way* + der Weg, es, e. *Short* + (?) kurz. 11. *Sweet* + ſüß. *Voice*, die Stimme, –, en. *Of*, von (w. dat.). *Three* + drei (see **226**, first line). *Sister* + die Schweſter, –, n. 12. *Next* + nächſt. *Week* + die Woche, –, n.

Exercise XI.

76, 1, 2—(134)—135, 1.

1. Thou knowest more than I. 2. To-day is better than to-morrow. 3. (The) most people are poor. 4. Nobody knew it. 5. The man at the left provoked him. 6. To-morrow [I will write] more. 7. The inner circle is smaller than the outer [one]. 8. The middle position is the safest. 9. The poor [man] has fewer cares than the rich [man]. 10. He was seen no more.

1. *To know*, wiſſen (**135**, 1). 2. *To-day* + heute. *To-morrow* + morgen. 3. *People* = men + Menſchen, Leute. *Poor*, arm. 4. *Nobody*, niemand. *It* + es. 5. Render: *The left man; left*, link. *To provoke*, here hetzen. wk. v. *Him*, ihn. 7. *Inner* + inner. *Circle*, der Kreis, es, e. *Small*, klein. *Outer* + äußer. 8. *Middle* + mittler. *Position*, die Stellung, -, en. *Safe*, ſicher. 9. See **220**, first two lines. *Fewer*, weniger (see **263**, first four lines). *Care*, die Sorge, -, n. 10. *No more*, nicht mehr. *To see* + ſehen, ſah, geſehen.

Exercise XII.

77, 78—135, 2, 3.

1. Canst thou count in German? 2. I can count from one to one hundred. 3. You may take three apples. 4. How many millions has Rothschild? 5. I do not know (it). 6. We write now eighteen hundred eighty-four. 7. There (=it) was one who took it to heart. 8. You can choose one of two things. 9. The boy knows the multiplication-table. 10. Thirty times twenty is six hundred.

1. *To count*, zählen, wk. v. *In German*, auf Deutſch. 2. *From — to*, von — bis. 3. Render *may* by dürfen or können. *To take*, nehmen, nahm, genommen. *Apple* + der Apfel, s, ̈. 4. *How many*, wie viel, viele (see **263**, first four lines). *Million* + die Millio'n, -, n. 5. *To know*, wiſſen (**135**, 1). *It*, es (see Ex. III., 3). 6. *To write*, ſchreiben, ſchrieb, geſchrieben.

Now, jeṯt. 7. Render: *who took it to heart*, by *to whom it went to the heart* (see **78**). 'S war = es war. 8. *To choose*, wählen, wk. v. *One of two things* (see **78**). 9. *Boy*, der Knabe, n, n. *To know*, in the sense of *to have mastered* = können. *Multiplication-table*, das Einmaleins. 10. *Times* (denoting repetition), mal (**175**).

Exercise XIII.

80, 81, 82 (*first two lines*)—135, 4, 5.

1. He may be the fourth. 2. You shall have the twentieth part of the whole sum. 3. They shall not tease you. 4. The banker sent us one thousand dollars. 5. She cannot see thee. 6. Thou canst not see her. 7. Charles may be in his twenty-fifth year. 8. We are not permitted to speak with them. 9. Give him the pencil. 10. You can give me the first piece.

1. *May* + mag, 3d sing. of mögen. 2. *Part*, der Teil, es, e. *Whole*, ganz. *Sum* + die Summe, -, n. 3. *To tease*, quälen. *You*, Sie, euch. 4. *Banker* + der Bankier (pronounce ier = Eng. iā). *To send* + senden (**119**, 1). *Dollar* + der Dolla'r, plur. -s (silent). 5. *To see* + sehen, sah, gesehen. 6. In this sentence, and the preceding one, place nicht after the pronouns. 7. *Charles* + Karl. *In his*, render *in the* by in dem, or im (**154**). 8. *To be permitted*, dürfen. *To speak* + sprechen, sprach, gesprochen. *With*, mit (w. dat.). 9. *To give* + geben; imperative, gieb, geben Sie, gebt. *Pencil* (see Ex. V., 9). 10. *Piece*, das Stück, es, e.

Exercise XIV.

83 to 85—135, 6, 7—138.

1. I am glad to see you. 2. He is afraid of ghosts. 3. The brothers and sisters love one another. 4. We will not quarrel. 5. You must not be surprised. 6. The student must not be afraid of work. 7. Give me my shawl. 8. I have given it to thy niece. 9. Your house is new; mine is old. 10. His

father and mine are cousins. 11. I have seen it with my own eyes. 12. She has lost her money.

1. *To be glad* = rejoice, ſich freuen. 2. *To be afraid of*, ſich fürchten vor (w. dat.). *Ghost* (see Ex. V., 2). 3. *Brothers and sisters*, die Geſchwiſter. *One another* + einander (preceded by the reciprocal pronoun; here ſich). 4. *To quarrel*, ſich zanken (wk. v.). The reflexive pronoun, in this case, is, of course, uns. 5. *To be surprised*, ſich wundern (wk. v.). Bear in mind that the reflexive pronoun must correspond with the subject; thus, we may use in this sentence : Du — dich, or Sie — ſich, or ihr — euch. 6. *Student* (see Ex. VI., 2). *To be afraid of*, ſich ſcheuen vor (w. dat.), ſich fürchten vor (w. dat.). *Work*, die Arbeit, -, en. 7. *Shawl*, das Tuch, es, ⸚er. 8. *It*, here, of course, es, since Tuch is neuter. *Niece* + die Nichte, -, n. 9. *New* + neu. *Mine*, here + das meinige, since Haus is neuter. *Old* + alt. 10. *Cousin* (see Ex. VII., 7). 11. *Own*, adj., + eigen (dat. plur. eigenem). *Eye* (Ex. VII., 1). 12. *To lose* (see Ex. VII., 2). *Money*, das Geld, es, er.

Exercise XV.

88, 90, 91—136, 1, 2, 3.

1. This astronomer is very famous. 2. I cannot walk in these shoes. 3. Are you going this way or that way? 4. The roof of this house is steeper than that of the church. 5. My uncle lives in that city. 6. Those trees stand before his door. 7. What is your friend doing? 8. Such beautiful flowers are rare. 9. I cannot forget such an insult. 10. My sister and I are using the same inkstand.

1. *Astronomer* (see Ex. VI., 7). *Very*, ſehr. *Famous*, berühmt. 2. *To walk*, go, gehen. *In*, here w. dat. *Shoe* + der Schuh, es, e. 3. *Way* + der Weg, es, e. *This* (that) *way*, acc. 4. *Roof*, das Dach, es, ⸚er. *Steep*, ſteil. *Church* + die Kirche, -, n. 5. *Uncle* + der Onkel, s, -. *To live* = reside, wohnen (wk. v.). *City*, die Stadt, -, ⸚e. 6. *Tree*, der Baum, es, ⸚e. *Before*, vor, here w. dat. *Door* + die Thür, -, en. 7. *What?* + Was? 8. *Flower*, die Blume, -, n. *Rare*, ſelten. 9. *Insult*, die Beleidigung, -, en. 10. *Sister* + die Schweſter, -, n. *To use*, gebrauchen (wk. v.). *Inkstand*, das Tintenfaß, -faſſes, -fäſſer.

Exercise XVI.

92, 93—137—341, 344 (*first four lines*).

1. Who is this boy? 2. Whose pen is this? 3. To whom shall I give the flowers? 4. What a tumult along the streets! 5. What mountains, what deserts do still separate us? 6. The letter which I have copied is very short. 7. Whoever does not understand a language cannot speak it. 8. Nobody has ever conquered without fighting. 9. We will write down all the words which you have learned. 10. Send him to prison, no matter what he says.

1. *Boy*, der Knabe, n, n. 2. *Pen*, die Feder, –, n. 3. *Shall* + soll. *To give* + geben, str. v. 4. *Tumult* + das Getümmel, s, –. *Along the streets*, Straßen auf (poet.); die — hinauf or entlang (prose). 5. *Mountain*, der Berg, es, e. *Desert*, die Wüste, –, n. *To separate*, trennen, wk. v. *Still*, noch. 6. *Letter*, der Brief, es, e. *To copy*, abschreiben (see Ex. XII., 6). *Very*, sehr. *Short* + kurz. 7. *Whoever*, wer. *To understand*, verstehen (**137, 136**, 2). *It*, here sie, since Sprache is feminine. *To speak* + sprechen, sprach, gesprochen. 8. *Nobody*, keiner. *Ever*, je, noch. *To conquer*, siegen, wk. v. *Without fighting*, render: that has not fought. *To fight*, streiten, stritt, gestritten (see **93**, 1). 9. *To write down*, aufschreiben (see **137**). *Word* + das Wort, es, ⸚er (see **58**). *To learn* + lernen, wk. v. 10. *To send* (see **119**, 1). *Prison*, das Gefängniß, sses, sse. *To*, here in's (contracted from in das). *No matter*, etc. (see **93**, 4).

Exercise XVII.

94 to 100.

1. The one is going, the other is coming. 2. Some ladies are dancing in the other room. 3. Nobody is born (as) a master. 4. Everybody ought to know what is best for him. 5. Have you seen anybody in the garden? 6. People say that you are studying too much. 7. They do not believe him. 8. It is better to do something than nothing at all. 9. Thou

must have a little patience. 10. There were many stones and little bread. 11. All Germany lay in shame and woe. 12. The whole of Germany shall be our fatherland.

1. See Ex. II., 3. 2. *Lady*, bie Dame, -, n. *To dance* + tanzen, wk. v. *Room*, das Zimmer, s, -. 3. *To be born* + geboren werden (see **95**). 4. *Ought to know*, sollte wissen. *For* + für (w. acc.). *Best* + am besten. 5. *Anybody*, jemand. *Garden* + der Garten, s, ". 6. *People say* = one says, man sagt. *That*, conj., daß (bear in mind **344**). *To study* + studi'eren, wk. v. (see **108**, 4). 7. *They* = one, man (see **98**). 8. *Something*, etwas. *Nothing at all*, gar nichts. 9. *Patience*, die Geduld. 10. *There were*, es gab, or, in the inverted order, gab es, and with elision, gab's (see **100**). *Stone* + der Stein, es, e. *Bread* + das Brot, es, e or "e. 11. *To lie, lay, lain*, + liegen, lag, gelegen. *Germany*, Deutschland. *Shame*, die Schmach. *Woe*, der Schmerz (see **100** and **63**, 1). 12. *The whole of G.* = all Germany (see **100**). *Fatherland* + das Vaterland.

Exercise XVIII.

REMARK.—The following three Exercises are intended to make the student acquainted with the various changes of the *strong verbs*, as presented in paragraphs 120-133 of the Grammar. The mastery of these verbs will be most easily and conveniently obtained in connection with the reading and future grammar lessons.

The figures accompanying the verbs refer to the classes and divisions in the Grammar, pp. 38-43.

120 to **123**—*The nouns occurring in this exercise will be found by turning back to Ex. 1-5.*

1. The dog has bitten (I., 1) my brother. 2. We suffered (I., 1) much while we were not under shelter. 3. The king rode (I., 1) through the city. 4. (The) Night will yield (I., 1) to (the) day. 5. The villain stole into the daughter's room. 6. The eagle has torn the mouse. 7. Our guests have fought bravely. 8. The maid is cutting (I., 1) the fruit. 9. The youth threw (I., 1) the salmon into the water. 10. The man screamed (I., 2) like a child.

2. *While*, während (conj., requires the verb to stand at the end of the sentence [**344**]). 3. *Through* + durch (w. acc.). 5. *To steal* = sneak,

ſchleichen (I., 1). 6. *To tear* (to pieces), zerreißen, zerriß, zerriſſen (I., 1). 7. *To fight* = strive, ſtreiten (I., 1). 9. *Into*, in (here w. acc.). 10. *Child*, das Kind, es, er.

Exercise XIX.

124 to 128—*For the nouns in this exercise see Ex.* 1–10.

1. The leaves are sprouting (II., 1) on the trees. 2. The Rhine was flowing (II., 1) gently. 3. Charles has jumped (III., 1) into the cold water. 4. The scholars found (III., 1) this mineral in the Fichtel-mountains. 5. Your general has won (III., 2) the battle. 6. Who will help (III., 3) me? 7. Recommend (IV.) me to the doctor. 8. Do not speak (IV.) so loud. 9. The cows have eaten (V., 1) the flowers. 10. The king was sitting (V., 2) on the throne.

1. *On*, auf (w. dat.). 2. *Gently*, ruhig. 3. Springen, *to jump*, takes ſein for its auxiliary (**266**, 1). 5. *Battle*, die Schlacht, -, en. 6. Helfen + *to help*, governs the dative. 8. *Loud* + laut. *So* + ſo.

Exercise XX.

129 to 133—*For the nouns in this exercise see Ex.* 1–15.

1. My niece has driven (VI.) home. 2. They have not invited (VI.) us. 3. The student caught (VII., 1) a fish. 4. Will you hold (VII., 1) my shawl? 5. Why did the people run (VII., 2) out of the church? 6. Your teacher has called (VII., 2) you. 7. The smith lifted (VIII.) the anvil with one hand. 8. The snow melts (§ 133) in the sun. 9. Has the maid milked (§ 133) the cows? 10. The peasants have thrashed (VIII.) the grain.

1. *To drive* = ride in a carriage, fahren (VI.). *Home*, nach Hauſe, + heim. 2. *To invite*, einladen, lud ein, eingeladen (VI.). 3. *Fish*, n., + der Fiſch, es, e. 5. *People*, die Menſchen. *Out of*, aus, w. dat. 6. *Teacher*, der Lehrer, s, -. 8. *Snow*, der Schnee, s. *Sun* + die Sonne.

SECOND SERIES.

Exercise I.

REMARK.—In the Exercises of the Second Series frequent reference is made to German illustrations in the Grammar, which may serve the student as an aid in translating the English sentences into German. In such cases the paragraph containing such German illustrations is given in ( ), at the end of the sentence, or referred to in the foot-notes.

Words not explained in the foot-notes will be found in the Vocabulary, at the end of the volume.

Syntax of the Article—**139, 141 to 146.**

1. Humboldt and Goethe lived to an advanced age, but Schiller died comparatively young (**141**). 2. Gold is more precious than silver (**141**). 3. Will you give me a pound of tea? 4. The thread of thought is broken (**142**). 5. The mixed throng of the ancient gods has vanished (**142**). 6. Students often lead a jolly life. 7. I am already losing reason and sense (**143**). 8. No earthly meat or drink suffices the fool (**143**). 9. You may write with a style, chisel, or quill (**143**). 10. We saw the great-grandmother, grandmother, mother, and child together in the close room (**143**). 11. What is that for? (**267, 5**). 12. Of what use is all joy and sorrow! (**144**). 13. What a busy company you are! (**144**). 14. Of what nationality is he? (**144**). 15. Philoktetes, who is all nature, leads Neoptolemus also back to nature (**145**). 16. Faust was called Magister, yea, Doctor (**145**).

1. Render *lived to* by erreichen, fol. by acc., to attain, + reach. *Advanced*, here hoch; see **71.** last line. 3 and 4. For the construction, see

350. 5. *Mixed*, here bunt. 6. *To lead a jolly life*, in Saus und Braus leben. 7. See Series I., Ex. II., 3. 8. Translate: Not earthly is the fool's meat or drink. 9. *May*, use können, **135**, 3. 10. *In*, in, here w. dat. 11. Use the verb sollen; see **267**, 5. 12. Translate: *of what use is*, by was soll, etc. 13. *What a*, welch ein. 14. Render: *of what nationality*, by was für ein Landsmann. 15. For the word-order, see **344**. *Lead*, here bringen (**119**, 2). 16. *To be called*, heißen, str. VII., 2. Magi'ster, Do'ctor, the same as in English.

Exercise II.

Syntax of the Article continued—147 to 150—110, 115.

1. The Guelfs lost the throne of Hanover. 2. The bust of Schiller is more beautiful than the bust of Socrates. 3. If you had been to Henry, what Henry was to you, you would now be the best [of] friends (**147, 1**). 4. He allows himself to be called Wallenstein (**147, 1; 201**). 5. This evening they play Minna von Barnhelm; Mr. S. plays [the part of] Tellheim. 6. The [statue of] Hercules is damaged (**147, 1**). 7. Moldavia and Wallachia are the Danubian Principalities. 8. The source of the Danube is in the Black-Forest. 9. "Winter is a man of honor" (**147, 4**). 10. In January we move into Kaiser-street (**147, 4**). 11. "My tears gush forth; the earth takes back her child" (**148**). 12. Even the Mameluke exhibits courage; but obedience is the ornament of the Christian (**149**). 13. The message I hear, but faith is wanting (me) (**149**). 14. Blood has been shed. 15. Let [them] reach me a cup of the best wine in [a vessel of] pure gold (**150**).

1. *Guelf*, pl. Guelfs (a princely family), der Welf, en, en. *Hanover*, Hanno'ver. 2. The gen. of Schiller is Schillers, used without the article; while Socrates, which has the gen. like the nom., should be preceded by the article (see **147**, 1, fourth line). 3. *To Henry* is here best translated by dem Heinrich, as Heinrich, without the article, would be ambiguous (**147. 1**).

4. *Allows*, translate by laſſen, str. VII., 1. *To be called*, see **290**, 3, b.
5. *This evening*, use the acc. *They*, here man; see **341**, 2, and **343**, d. *M. v. B.*, title of a comedy by Lessing. 8. *To be*, here ſich befinden, str. III., 1. 10. *Move*, when meaning *to change one's residence*, is ziehen, str. II., 2; see **341**, 2, and **343**, d. 11. From B. Taylor's translation of Faust. Say: *The tear gushes forth, the earth has me again.* 13. *To be wanting*, fehlen, with dat. of person. 14. *Has been shed* = has flowed.

Exercise III.

Syntax of the Article continued—151 to 158.

1. Why are the people running through the streets? **(151)**. 2. The cavalry had reached the river, but the infantry was far behind **(151)**. 3. "The little god o' the world sticks to the same old way" **(152)**. 4. The God who made the iron grow created no slaves **(152)**. 5. Their language was full of noble sentiments. 6. There were better times. 7. Old Barbarossa keeps himself concealed in the mountain. 8. The cheeks of the marble [statue] are cold **(153)**. 9. His head aches **(154)**. 10. They have taken my coat. 11. She gently touched his shoulder **(154)**. 12. Eggs cost one mark a dozen **(156)**. 13. We see each other four times a year **(156)**. 14. You have been the teacher and friend of my son. 15. The uncle and the god-father of the child were [present] at the baptism **(158)**.

2. *Far behind*, weit bahinten. 3. *Sticks*, etc.. = remains ever of the same kind. *Same*, gleich. 4. Render *made* by ließ (from laſſen). For the order, see **341**, 3, and **344**. 5. *Full of* + voll, followed by gen. **(182)**. 6. *There was, there were*, es gab, followed by acc. **(236**, 4). 7. *Barbarossa* + Rotbart, surname of Emperor Frederic I. (1152–1190). *Himself*, ſich. *Concealed*, verborgen. *In*, here w. dat. 9. Render: *the head aches to him*. 11. Similar to the preceding sentence. 15. *At*, bei, w. dat.

Exercise IV.

Syntax of the Gender — **159** to **163**.

REMARK.—The *gender of nouns* has to be learned mainly by practice, and the student should therefore endeavor to learn with each German noun the article (ber, bie, or baš) belonging to it. The rules in the Grammar (159, ff.), however, will be of great service; some in a practical way (*e. g.*, 159, 161, 3, 164), and others, because they will help the student in getting an insight into the "genius of the language."

Wherever a large number of examples are given, as in these paragraphs, it will hardly repay the beginner to learn the *meanings* of all of them; the nouns under 160 might be mentioned, with their meanings, by the teacher, letting the pupil state the gender; while the gender of those under 161 may be determined by their form alone, without reference to their meaning.

1. (The) Queen Louisa was a noble woman. 2. The Danube, the Oder, the Elbe, the Weser, and the Rhine are the largest rivers of Germany. 3. Many prefer beautiful Spain to colder France. 4. The little boy lies in the cradle. 5. Thou art a heathen. 6. The witches were dancing on the heath. 7. The workman has placed his earnings in the bank. 8. The merit of the minister is great. 9. The boy has again lost his knife. 10. Bring me the third volume of Bancroft's history. 11. Is not this blue ribbon too dark? 12. The knight has a shield, the merchant a sign-board. 13. What a fool you are! 14. In the gate [there] is a small door. 15. The marble of Carrara is white. 16. "Bands of robbers move about."

3. *Prefer*, ziehen — vor (see **137**; **350**). 4. *Little boy*, baš Knäblein (**161**, 3). 5. *Heathen*, see **162**, 3 (**435**, 3), where also some of the nouns in the following sentences are to be found. 7. *Placed*, here gebracht. *Earnings*, p. 59. *In*, here auf, w. acc. 13. *What a*, see **92**, 2, 3. For word-order, see 3. sentence.

Exercise V.

Syntax of the Gender continued — **164** to **169**.

1. Humility and gentleness are Christian virtues; yet pride is also found even among Christians. 2. On Wednesday the city was illuminated. 3. What is your answer? 4. The girl

has taken leave; all trace of her is lost. 5. Hermann has chosen the exiled maiden (**166**). 6. The angel said to Mary: Blessed [art] thou among women (**166**). 7. The young lady, as a guest, was treated with especial esteem. 8. Mary Stuart said to Elizabeth: I am your *king;* and the Hungarian nobility exclaimed: We will die for our *king*, Maria Theresa! 9. They step forward, a lady here, a gentleman there; they wish to dance. 10. All are running, saving, rescuing (**168**). 11. "Then may delight and distress, and worry and success, alternately follow, as best they can." 12. He spoke while leaving the room. 13. The bishop was preaching; all listened in silence, each returning to his own thoughts. 14. The fair one descended from her stately castle. 15. Bismarck has accomplished great things for Germany.

1. *Is also found,* translate: *one finds also,* using the inverted order (after bennoch). *Among,* here bei. 2. *On Wednesday,* am Mittwoch. The adverbial phrase introducing the sentence, the inverted order is required (**343**, *d*) 4. *All trace of her,* translate: *her trace.* 6. *Blessed,* gebenedeiet; the be-, in the obsolete verb benedeien, *to bless,* is of course no prefix, but the first syllable of the Latin *bene (benedicere);* hence the prefix ge- in the p. p. (see **166**). 7. *Young lady,* das junge Mädchen (see **167**). 8. *Mary,* as a historical name, Mari'a; in other cases usually Mari'e. 9. *Step forward* may be rendered by hervorkommen (see **168**; **137**). 11. B. T.'s version of F., 1756–8 (see **168**). *To follow alternately,* mit einander wechseln (lit. to exchange with each other). 12. *While leaving*=while (indem) he left. Bear in mind that indem introduces a dependent clause (**341**, **3**, and **344**). 12 and 13. See **168**, last sentence. *In silence,* stillschweigend. *Each returning* = while each returned. *To his own thoughts* = into himself. 14. The words holde Schöne (gracious fair one) in **169** are perhaps best rendered by *fair one* alone. 15. *Great things,* Großes (**169**).

Exercise VI.

Syntax of Singular and Plural—**170** to **177**.

1. We are reading the history of Germany under the Henrys and Ottos. 2. Will your grace be present at the

representation of "Wallenstein"? 3. Most of the gentry were in the country. 4. Here is a list of the conflagrations and deaths during the week. 5. We have our vacation about Easter. 6. Nearly three hundred thousand men were besieging the city (175). 7. His father is bent with old age; he is over ninety years old. 8. Germany lies between the forty-seventh and fifty-fifth degrees, north latitude. 9. The third and fourth verses are usually omitted. 10. Why do these pupils hold their hands before their mouths? 11. Three hundred miners have lost their lives. 12. All raised their hands.

1. *Under* + unter, here w. dat. Die Heinriche, bie Ottonen. 2. *Your grace,* Euer Gnaben, usually abbreviated into Ew. Gnaben. *To be present at,* beiwohnen (sep. comp.), w. dat. In regard to the number of the verb, see **311,** 2. 3. *In the country,* auf bem Lanbe (as opposed to *in the city*). 7. *Bent with old age,* vor Alter gebückt (**175, 353**). 8. *Between,* zwischen, here w. dat. (see **177**). 9. See **177**. *Are omitted,* translate *are not sung* (werben, etc.). 10. *Do — hold =* hold (see I. Series, Ex. II., 3). See **177, 343,** *a*.

Exercise VII.
Syntax of the Cases, Nominative—**178, 179, 270.**

1. The ages of the past are to us a book [closed] with seven seals. 2. To stroll with you, (Sir) Doctor, is honor and profit [unto me]. 3. The decrees of Heaven are the best for man. 4. Henry will become [a] soldier. 5. Everybody imagines himself to be a wise man; but this fancy does not make one wise. 6. I come as [a] messenger of the court. 7. Which prince is called the "silent"? And which the "conqueror"? 8. He is looked upon as a good-for-nothing fellow. 9. I dare not call myself a favorite of Fortune. 10. It is better to be called a thief than to be one.

1 and 2. See **178.** 3–6. See **179,** 1. 3. *For man,* für ben Menschen. 4. *I shall become,* ich werbe werben. *I will become,* ich will werben. 5. *Wise*

man, to be rendered by the adjective used substantively. Translate: *does not make one wise* = makes not the wise [man] (**162, 3**). 7. *The "silent,"* der Schweiger (see **179, 2**). 9 and 10. *To call*, in a bad sense, may be rendered by schelten, str. III., 3. *To be one*, einer zu sein.

Exercise VIII.

Syntax of the Cases continued, Genitive—**180 to 183.**

1. The love of God surpasses all understanding. 2. The poets speak frequently of the invisible hand of Fate. 3. Lessing admired the taste of the ancient artists. 4. You are a dead man! 5. Humboldt found that a certain height of the water was of the same age as certain rude monuments of human industry. 6. The maiden offered them the best of all gifts, the most beautiful of all flowers. 7. Five [members] of the order had fallen the victims of their temerity. 8. Three Prussians fought their way through a hundred of the enemy. 9. I will show you something beautiful. 10. Does not this forged paper show that they wish to pledge us to no good [purpose]? 11. Are you not tired of the long quarrel? 12. The dead are freed from their bodies. 13. Our horses are impatient for the stable.

1. *Surpasses*, ist höher als (or denn). 2. *Of*, von, w. dat. *Fate* + das Fatum (**180, 4**). 3. The use of the possessive pronoun, as in the last sentence, **180, 4**, is not to be imitated. 4. *A dead man*, in this phrase, des Todes (**180, 5**). 5. *Height of the water*, der Wasserstand (see **180, 5**). *The same*, here ein. 6. *Offer*, here darbieten, str. II., 2 (see **180, 7**). 8. *Fight one's way through*, sich durchschlagen, sep., str. VI. *Enemy*, use the plural. 9. *Something beautiful*, see **181, (230)**. 10. See p. 66, second line. *No good* (purpose), nichts Gutes. 11–13. See **181 and 183**.

Exercise IX.

Syntax of the Cases; Genitive continued—**184 to 188.**

1. Not all those who scoff at their chains are free. 2. Release me from a proof of my nobility. 3. In 1848 many

Germans were exiled. 4. One cannot always banish gloomy thoughts. 5. The shepherd pitied the old nobleman. 6. "A righteous man regardeth the life of his beast." 7. Early in the morning the birds sing the most sweetly. 8. In the afternoon we usually go out for a walk. 9. "Oh the Frenchman," exclaims Lessing, "who had no understanding to consider this, and no heart to feel this!" 10. Oh the unfortunate prisoner, to whom it is not granted to breathe the fresh air!

2. *Release from*, entlaffen, w. gen. (str. VII., 1). *Proof of nobility*, bie Ahnenprobe. 3. *In 1848* (see **226**, 1). 4. *Banish*, here fich entfchlagen, w. gen. (str. VI.; see **185**). 5. *Nobleman*, ber Edelmann, or (poetically) ber hohe Herr (see **186**). 6. "*Regardeth the life of*" = pities, fich erbarmen, w. gen. 7. *Early in the morning*, see **187** (under *Time*). *The most sweetly*, see **300**, 2. *Sweet*, here fchön. 8. *Go out for a walk*, fpazieren gehen; ich gehe fpazieren, etc. (**290**, 2). 9 and 10. See **188**.

Exercise X.

Syntax of the Cases; Dative—189, 190.

1. Life's unmixed joy has fallen to the share of no mortal. 2. License, exempt from punishment, mocks at morals. 3. He defends them, instead of accusing them. 4. One can wrench nothing from Nature with levers and screws. 5. Faust cursed everything that ensnares the soul with enticing visions. 6. The governor bore Tell a grudge. 7. Shall we yield to this impulse? 8. The images of the night receded before the dawning day. 9. Do not defy the king's commands. 10. Take care whom you trust! 11. The minister gives place to the prince. 12. The mother watched the play of her children.

1. Compare with these sentences the German examples under **190**, p. 69 (see also **350**). *Exempt from punishment*, ftraflos. 5. *Enticing visions* (B. T.), Lock- und Gaukelwerk. 6 *To bear a grudge*, grollen, w. dat.

10. Proverb: Traue, schaue wem. (The verbs are in the imperative: Trust, (but) look whom (you trust). 11. *Give place to*, nachstehen, str. VI., w. dat.

Exercise XI.

Syntax of the Cases; Dative continued—191 to 197—Accusative—198 to 202.

1. Hide from me the surging crowd. 2. Nobody should forfeit the right which Nature has given him. 3. The Turks have their swords set with diamonds. 4. It was hard for the emperor in hot and in cold weather. 5. Fortune favored their wishes in the beginning. 6. The black suit is not becoming to him. 7. Will you pay me now? 8. I have paid the money to your father. 9. How often do we imagine life [to be] other than it is! 10. "You see a man, as others be" (198). 11. Teach me to do what is right. 12. You must send for the physician. 13. He will give you the lie. 14. I feel as though I were born an avenger of my kinsman. 15. The ridicule of the foreigners grieves me to the very heart.

2. *Should*, pret. of sollen, 135, 5. *Given*, here vergönnt. 3. *Sword*, der Säbel, s, -; the plural Säbels, which occurs in Lessing, is colloquial and incorrect (60). The ethical dative, dir, in this example (192), has very much the force of the English *I tell you*. 4. *It is hard for*, es wird sauer, w. dat. *In*, here bei. 5. *In the beginning*, anfangs. 6. *Becoming*, passend (see 195). 7 and 8. See 196. 9. *Imagine*, denken (see 197). *Other*, translate by the adv. anders. 13. *To give the lie*, Lügen strafen. 14. *Born* + geboren (see 127). Translate: I feel myself born as the a. of my k. 15. *To the very heart*, in tiefster Seele.

Exercise XII.

Syntax of the Cases; Accusative continued—203 to 209.

1. Her jealousy proved stronger than her sympathy. 2. The Saxons sided with the French. 3. The boy told you a

lie on his own account. 4. Your honor and his happiness are at stake (**207**). 5. I shall not retreat one step. 6. We saw a few wanderers travel along this road; but the main body marched down the upper valley. 7. The messenger may be here at any moment. 8. Alexander von Humboldt travelled for years. 9. The general made [the soldiers] attend prayers early in the morning. 10. You must leave town this very night. 11. Mœros, with a dagger concealed under his garment, stole up to Dionysius, the tyrant. 12. The culprit knelt upon his cloak, his neck already bared.

1. *To prove stronger than*, es gewinnen über (w. acc.). 2. *To side with*, es halten mit (see **236**, 6). 3. *To tell one a lie*, Einem etwas vorlügen. *On one's own account*, auf eigene Rechnung. 5. *Not — one*, kein. 6. *Travel*, when speaking of a number of persons, may be rendered by ziehen (str. II., 2). *Along this road* (see **207**, 2. *Main body*, der Hause. 7. *At any moment* = every moment (acc.). 8. *Travel*, here reisen; not, as in 6, ziehen. *For years*, Jahre lang. 9. *Made*, here to be translated by lassen. *To attend prayers*, Betstunde halten. *Early*, here gleich (immediately). 10. *This very night*, noch diese Nacht. 11. *Mœros* = Möros, a proper name. *With a dagger*, etc., use the absolute acc. (see **209**). *Stole up to*, pret. of schleichen (str. I., 1), followed by zu.

Exercise XIII.

Syntax of the Adjective—**210** to **212**.

1. The delivery at the post-office of this city takes place every hour. 2. He has fed us on dainties and cooling froth. 3. Doctor Faust's dog was a very droll animal. 4. The marksman fired at random. 5. Three Rhenish feet are somewhat more than three English feet; and ten Flemish pounds are equal to ten kilograms. 6. The Dutch were a good-natured, orderly, commercial people; they enjoyed the luxurious fruits of their blessed industry and were watchful over the laws, which were their benefactors. 7. The government of the

grand-duchy of Baden is very liberal. 8. Woe to you, if you touch his worthy ancestral lumber. 9. They talk nothing but nonsense.

1. *Of this city*, to be rendered by the adj. hiesig. *Takes place every hour* = is an hourly one (see **211**, 1). 2. *On*, here mit (after nähren). 3. *Very droll*, pudelnärrisch; "pudel is occasionally used as an intensive" (Ha.). 5. *Rhenish feet*, etc. (see p. 75, second line). *Somewhat more*, etwas mehr (see **175**). 7. *The government of the g.-d. of B.* (see **212**, 3). 8. *Ancestral lumber*; this is B. T.'s translation of Hausrat, in the sense of *old* furniture. 9. *Nothing but*, lauter (indeclinable).

Exercise XIV.
Syntax of the Adjective continued—213 to 217.

1. One fine day the cage was empty. 2. The Egyptian pyramids have been called [the] silent keepers of lifeless treasures. 3. Such an excellent monarch, as (the) Emperor William, is dear to his people. 4. In the army, there is many an officer of great courage and bloody fame. 5. He who never ate his bread in sorrow does not know you, ye heavenly powers. 6. I salute you, noble lords, and you, fair ladies! 7. You lazy fellows are now kept on short allowance. 8. Since the acquisition of the two large houses we have room for one hundred guests. 9. The count treated us to good white wine. 10. [The] following pretty song is by Heine.

1. *One fine day*, may be expressed by the adverbial genitive (followed, of course, by the inverted order). 2. *Have been called* = one has called, etc. 3. *Such*, see **91**, 3. *Dear to his people*, bei dem Volke beliebt. 4. *There is*, giebt es (followed by the acc.; see **205**, Rem.). *Many a* + manch ein. *Great* = high. 5. *He who* = whoever, **93**, 3. *In sorrow* = with tears. *To know*, kennen (**119**). 6. *I salute you* = be saluted [by] me (dat.). *Lord*, der Herr, n, en. *And you, fair ladies*, repeat the p. p. gegrüßt (= saluted, you, fair ladies!). 7. *To keep on s. a.*, Einem den Brotkorb höher hängen (see **216**, 2, last sentence), lit. *to hang the bread-basket higher for any one*. 9. *To treat to* + traktieren mit (w. dat.). 10. *By*, von. *Heine*, the German lyric poet.

Exercise XV.

Syntax of the Adjective continued—**218** to **221**.

1. My desire is great, but my power is weak. 2. Your faith will save you. 3. Who could hate this kind old man? 4. If I am fortunate enough to get possession of them, I shall send them to you. 5. The soldiers fought hand to hand. 6. Her life was full of sorrows and sickness. 7. People begin with little things and end with great ones. 8. Körner's Sword-song begins with the words: "Thou sword at my left [side]." 9. Birds of a feather flock together. 10. She has spoken English from her childhood. 11. How is this in French? 12. High officials have been discharged. 13. The new servant has an agreeable appearance. 14. He translated the verse into his beloved German (**220**).

3. *Who could . . .* , wer könnte . . . *Hate* = be enemy to, feind sein (w. dat.). 4. See **219**. *To get possession of*, habhaft werden (w. gen.). 5. *To fight hand to hand*, handgemein werden. 6. *Full of*, see **219**, 1. 7. *People*, man (one). *Little things, great ones*, to be rendered by the adjective-substantive in the singular (see **220**). 9. *Birds*, etc. = like loves like = like and like associate gladly (see **220**). 10. *From childhood*, von klein an, von Jugend auf, von Kind auf. 11. *In*, auf. 12. *High* = in a high position, hochgestellt (see **221**, 4).

Exercise XVI.

Syntax of Comparative and Superlative—**222** to **225**—(**341** to **345**, *the largest type*).

1. When was the theatre the most crowded?—When Booth played Richelieu. 2. This fact points to a highly interesting natural phenomenon. 3. The German word "Fürst" is originally a superlative, and, like the English "first," signifies the foremost. 4. The noun "Eltern" is a comparative.

5. We study the modern languages. 6. I am more to blame than he. 7. The peasant was more stupid than malicious. 8. The larger of these two houses belongs to my parents. 9. The mill is running. 10. If the wind is blowing, the mill runs. 11. Yesterday the mill was not running, because the wind did not blow the whole day. 12. If I were not Alexander, I should like to be Diogenes.

1. *When?* (interrogative adv.) + wann? *When* (subord. conj.) = als. 2. *To point to*, beuten auf (w. acc.). *Natural phenomenon*, das Naturereignis, -sses, -sse. 3. Order: *and signifies, like the E. "first," the foremost. Like*, wie. 6. *To be to blame*, schuld sein. 8. Use the superlative (225). *Two*, use beibe. 9. *To run*, here gehen. 11. *The whole day*, ben ganzen Tag. 12. *I should like to be*, ich möchte sein (but in what order?).

Exercise XVII.

Syntax of the Numerals—**226** to **228**—**79**—(**229**, *three lines*).

1. The testimony of two witnesses always establishes the truth. 2. Goethe was born on August 28, 1749. 3. What time is it? It is a quarter past five. 4. We will meet at a quarter of six, ten minutes before the train leaves. 5. There were twelve of them, when they arrived **(227)**. 6. One says jokingly: Eleven means (the) sin, because it transgresses the ten commandments. 7. It belongs to [the character of] a great man, both to treat trifles as trifles, and important matters as important matters. 8. Give me eight yards and a half of this cloth. 9. This package weighs two pounds and a half. 10. The transatlantic cable was laid between 1860 and 1870. 11. My friend is a man about fifty years old. 12. Bring me a bottle of the wine of the year 1852.

1. Testimony, der Mund, es. (This term occurs in the proverb under **236**.) Translate *always* by the adjective *all*, with the German equivalent of *truth*. *To establish*, here sund thun (or machen). 3. *What time is it?* Wie viel ist die Uhr? 4. *Before* (subord. conj.), ehe. *To leave* (of a train, etc.),

abfahren, str. VI., sep. 6. *Means* = is, ift. 7. *Both — and*, beides, see **228**, 1. 8. *Eight and a half*, see **229** and **175**. 9. *Two and a half*, see **229** and **175**. 10. *Between 1860 and 1870*, in ben sechziger Jahren. 11. *A man about fifty years old*, ein Fünfziger. 12. *Wine of the year 1852*, Achtzehnhundertzweiunbfünfziger.

Exercise XVIII.

REMARK.—The following Exercises on the pronouns involve mainly what is printed in the largest type in the Grammar; whenever other topics are involved, special attention is called to it in the foot-notes.

Exercises to be written in connection with the paragraphs in smaller type will be found in the Fourth Series.

Syntax of the Pronouns—**230, 1, 2, 233, 234, (231).**

1. "Spirit sublime, thou gav'st me, gav'st me all for which I prayed." 2. How old are you, if I may ask? 3. Please, tell me where you are living at present. 4. I have heard nothing of him. 5. No greeting to my sweetheart! I won't consent to it. 6. When you go to school, be well prepared. 7. What do you think of the matter? 8. I do not think much of it. 9. This pen is poor; I cannot write with it. 10. Do not open the cage; there is a bird in it. 11. This is a useful book; you can learn a great deal from it. 12. Yonder is his house; an oak-tree stands near it.

1. *For which*, warum (lit. wherefore). 2. *May*, barf; use Sie for the subject. 3. Translate *please* by the adverb gefälligst (after the indirect object mir); use Sie for the subject. 4. While *of him* is to be translated literally, by the prep. with the pers. pron., *to it*, in the following sentence, *of it, with it*, etc., in 8, 9, and ff. examples, should be rendered by bavon, bamit, etc. (**234**). 5. *No greeting* is in the acc., a transitive verb (such as bringen) being understood. *I won't consent to it* = I won't listen to it, ich will bavon nichts hören. B. T. has: *I'll resent it.* 6. *When* = whenever + wenn (subord. conj.). *To*, in, w. acc. *Be well prepared* = have yourself well prepared; use ihr for the subject. 7. *To think of*, halten von; use bu for the subject. 8. *Of it* = thereof. 9. *Poor*, here

ſchlecht. *With it* = therewith (of course to be placed before the infinitive; 350). 10. *Do not open* = open not. *In it* = therein. 11. *This* + bieß, or baß. *A great deal* = much. *From it* = there — out. 12. *Near*, bei.

Exercise XIX.

Syntax of the Pronouns continued—235, 236, *including the small type under* 4.

1. It had been raining and freezing, so that the roads were [very] slippery; but now it is thawing. 2. We had company yesterday; there was dancing, singing, and playing. 3. "Now, whither shall we go?" 4. Three students went across the Rhine. 5. His youthful companion walked briskly at his side. 6. There are wheels that are made of paper. 7. There were many ladies who did not dance. 8. "Hey, there we (they) had Westphalian ham." 9. He is afraid, and he repents having been so wicked. 10. In this sense, you may venture it. 11. She thinks you are gone; and half and half you are so. 12. He wished to be a senator, and now he is one.

1. *It had been raining* = it had rained. *So that*, ſo baß. *The roads are slippery* may be rendered by the imp. verb eß glatteiſt (see 547, 1, 2). Notice that the second clause is *dependent*, and that the order in the third clause should be *inverted*, on account of *now*. 2. *There was*, etc., to be rendered by the passive voice with the imp. subject eß (236, 2). 3. In place of *we* use the imp. eß. 4. *Students*, here Burſche. *Went*, translated by ziehen (str. II., 2). *Across*, über, here w. acc. 5. *Youthful*, here blühend. *At his side*, ihm zur Seite. 6. *There are*, 236, 4. In the relative clause the verb stands, of course, at the end. 7. *Did not dance*, see 274, 6. (What is said of the Present applies to the Preterite as well.) 8. *We (they) had* = there was. 9. *I am afraid*, eß iſt mir bange. *I repent*, eß reut mich. *Having been* ... = that he has been ... 11. *You are*, use the subjunctive. *Gone* may be rendered by the p. p. of entfliehen, str. II., 2, to escape. *So*, see 236, 6. 12, Translate *one* by eß.

Exercise XX.

Syntax of the Pronouns continued—**237, 238, 239** (*including* 1 and 2), **240, 241.**

1. The humble [person] conquers himself. 2. Humility does not boast. 3. He is taking liberties. 4. Hermann and Dorothea nodded to each other and greeted each other in the mirror of the water. 5. The king and the emperor made war upon each other. 6. *Mine* and *thine* are the causes of all contention. 7. Did you see your father? 8. Whither will your presumption lead you? 9. Behold the arrogance of the man whom you have led through your bridal room to the throne! 10. You have done your duty; I shall do mine (**240**).

3. *To take liberties* = to permit one's self liberties. 5. *To make war upon,* befehben, befriegen, w. acc. 6. Put the verb in the singular (**239**). 7. *Your father,* Ihr Herr Vater (polite). *Especial attention is called to the caution in* **239,** 2. Sentences 8–10 may each be given in three different ways, with bu, Sie, ihr.

Exercise XXI.

Syntax of the Pronouns continued—**244, 245** (*including* 1), **246–248.**

1. [Much] as I yearn to see you, I have a secret horror of that man. 2. Voltaire's works are written in a skeptical spirit; woe to him who does not read them with a skeptical spirit! 3. The voice of this young woman is much admired. 4. William and Charles do not agree about the weather; the latter desires it dry, the former damp. 5. He urges the validity of this paper. 6. Is that your neighbor? 7. Mephistopheles said to Faust: That is the way to deal with witches. 8. Who else, but you in Vienna, is to blame for that? 9. The

minstrel is silent with regard to that; politeness compels him to be so. 10. According to this you are right; but I have an entirely different reading. 11. Those who have got their lessons may go to the theatre. 12. She spent the alms with the same fidelity as before; the poor enjoyed them.

1. *Of,* vor. (For the attributive adjective, see **212,** 1.) 2. Notice that *are written* denotes a state or condition, not action; hence, sein (and not werden) should be used (**273,** 1 and 2). 3. *Young woman,* das junge Frauenzimmer (see **159,** 1). *Is admired;* in this case an action is expressed (= people admire), and not a state or condition; hence, the passive voice (werden, not sein) is required. 4. *Do not agree about,* sind nicht derselben Ansicht über (w. acc.). 5. *To urge the validity of,* geltend machen (**245**). 8. *But,* als. *For that,* see **246**. 9. *With regard to that* = of that. *To be so* = to be that. 10. *To be right* + recht haben. 11. *Those who,* see **247**. *Got,* gemacht. *May,* use können. *To,* in (w. acc.).

Exercise XXII.

Syntax of the Pronouns continued—**249** (*including* 1 and 2), **250** to **253**.

1. Nathan was generosity itself. 2. He who digs a pit for others falls into [it] himself. 3. Even the friends did not approve of the union, because the young people were too unequal. 4. Reflection tells me that I am not able to pursue this course; benevolent powers! show me the right way! 5. What do I care in whose forest we are? 6. Who has robbed the lioness of her young? 7. What is the meaning of your speech? 8. What monstrous deed do you demand from me? 9. What kind of paper is that? 10. What a beautiful painting! 11. See, what beautiful cloth I have bought for you.

1. Use the article before *generosity* (**149,** page 54). 4. *Reflection,* use the article. *To be able,* vermögen (compound of mögen, **135,** 4). *To pursue a course,* einen Weg verfolgen. 5. *What do I care,* was kümmert es mich.

6. *To rob one of something,* Einem etwas rauben, or Einen einer Sache berauben. 8. *Monstrous deed,* das Ungeheure. 11. *Cloth,* here der Stoff (es, e). *For you,* either für dich, or the dat. without preposition.

Exercise XXIII.

*Syntax of the Pronouns continued—***255, 256** (*including* 3), **257** to **263.**

1. A person who puts on rouge is disgusting to me (**255**). 2. He who will not listen [to advice] must suffer. 3. A splendid word is at [your] command for what enters, or does not enter, the human brain. 4. You must earn [anew] what you have inherited from your ancestors, in order [really] to possess it. 5. Pitch defileth. 6. Whoever wants to become a master must practise while young. 7. A thing, whose design is so obvious, cannot be called accidental. 8. Wallenstein speaks of moments when man is nearer the soul of the world than usual. 9. There was a time when the land of the Swiss was not free. 10. Tell me something else. 11. He earns at least something. 12. I have bought a pound of cherries. Do you want some? 13. Did he say anything? 14. Many are called, but few are chosen. 15. I have much to tell you.

1. *To put on rouge,* sich schminken. 2. *He who* = whoever (**93, 3**). Translate *suffer* by fühlen. 3. *To be at — command,* zu Diensten stehen (**256**). Notice that dreingehen (= dareingehen) means *to enter it;* hence, if a prepositional phrase is used, drein must be omitted. 5. Render: *He who touches pitch soils himself.* *To touch,* angreifen, str. L, 1. 6. See **256, 3.** *Must practise* = practises. *While young* = early. 7. *A thing* = that + das (**257**). *To be obvious,* in die Augen leuchten. 8. *When,* see **258**. *Man,* man. *Soul of the world* (God), der Weltgeist. *Usual* = at other times, sonst. 9. *There is,* es giebt (**205**). *When,* see **258**. 10. *Something else,* etwas (was) ander(e)s (**260**). 11. *At least something,* wenigstens etwas, or doch immer was. 12. *Some,* referring to a noun mentioned, welcher, e, es (**260**). 15. Use haben with the infinitive preceded by zu.

Exercise XXIV.

Syntax of the Verb—**264** to **266**.   Haben and Sein.

1. The groom rode up and down [for] an hour. 2. The pedestrian has been in the city; he went there and back in one hour. 3. The watch went once, but now it stops. 4. The children have gone to school; school has commenced. 5. That has pleased him very much. 6. The carpenter fell from the roof; his assistant probably fell too. 7. The horse has drawn the wagon into the barn. 8. The cranes have gone south. 9. We moved yesterday (**266**). 10. The travellers have not yet arrived. 11. The rope broke, and the light went out. 12. The apprentice fell asleep and slept [for] three hours. 13. If the fellow had not drunk so much, he would not have fallen into the lake and been drowned. 14. All this has happened before. 15. No consolation has been left me.

1. The compound tenses (perf. or pluperf.) should be used in this and the following sentences. *Up and down,* hin und her, lit. auf und nieder. 2. *There and back,* hin und her, or hin und zurück. 4. *To school,* in, w. acc. and def. art. 5. *Very much,* sehr. 6. *Probably fell too,* to be expressed by the future perfect (**279**; **266**). 8. *Have gone,* perf. tense of ziehen (str. II., 2). *South* + nach Süden (**266**). 13. *If,* etc., wenn, w. plup. subj. *To be drowned,* ertrinken (**266**, 2). 14. *Has happened before* = has already been there (**266**, 3). 15. *To be left* = to remain (**266**, 3).

Exercise XXV.

Syntax of the Verb—**267**, 1, 2, 3, **135**.   Können—Dürfen— Mögen.

1. He could not [do] otherwise. 2. They might draw you into their toils. 3. Do you know Italian? 4. Do you know this gentleman? 5. Do you know who this gentleman is?

6. Then, too, you may show yourself without restraint. 7. Nobody is allowed to hunt without [a] license. 8. Posterity very likely will hesitate to subscribe to this judgment. 9. The sight of the works of God gives strength to the angels, though nobody can comprehend them (**267**, 3). 10. You may keep the goblet. 11. Who may that fellow in a green coat be? 12. I like to grant her whatever is consistent with my duty. 13. I should not like to have him hear of it. 14. The child is not fond of soup.

2. *Might*, pret. subj. of können. *To draw into one's toils*, in fein Garn ziehen. 3, 4, 5. *To know*, when practical ability is implied (such as to *speak* a language) = können ; *to know*, in the sense of *be acquainted with* = kennen ; *to know*, meaning *to have learned by heart* = wissen. Ex.: Ich kenne das Gedicht, I am acquainted with the poem ; ich weiß das G., I have memorized the poem ; ich kann das G., I can recite the poem (the latter two being, in this case, equivalent). Wissen usually takes a clause or its equivalent for its object: Ich weiß, wo er wohnt ; ich weiß sein Haus (know where it is); ich kenne sein Haus (am acquainted with it, can tell it). 6. This is a free version of the example under **267**, 2, 1. *Without restraint*, frei. 7. *License* (to hunt), der Jagdschein, e, e. 8. See **267**, 2, 4. 11. *Fellow in a green coat*, der Grünrock, s, ⸚e. 13. *To hear of* (what has been said), wieder erfahren (str. VI.). *To have him hear of it* = that he should hear of it (**267**, 3). 14. *To be fond of* = to like, mögen.

Exercise XXVI.

Syntax of the Verb continued — **267**, 4, 5, 6, 7. Müssen— Sollen—Wollen—Lassen.

Special attention is called to the important idiomatic phrases under **267**, 6 (*small type*).

1. You must not let the dog run into the street without a muzzle. 2. No sound shall strike upon my ear a second time, unless it should convey a special meaning. 3. A miller, who never thought of wandering, must be a poor miller. 4. A metre of this velvet is to cost eight *thaler*. 5. The treasure

of the Nibelungen is said to lie [buried] in the Rhine. 6. Should you see him, tell him we could not wait any longer. 7. What are you going to do with the dagger? 8. The prince was about to die when the news arrived. 9. The witness claims to have seen the defendant. 10. The witness is said to have seen the defendant. 11. He claims to have deceived me for a good purpose. 12. The poor woman did not utter a complaint.

1. *Remark.*—Of two infinitives the one dependent upon the other stands first, hence: laufen laſſen. 2. *Strike upon my ear* = resound, erſchallen (w. dat. of pers. pron.). *Meaning*, here Sinn. *Convey*, here begründen. 3. *Who never thought of* = to whom . . . never occurred, einfallen (w. dat.). See **267, 4**. According to the regular order fiel would stand last. 5. *Nibelungen*, the people, or family, in possession of the Nibelungen hoard. 6. *We could not wait any longer* = we had (*subj.*) not been able to wait [any] longer; see the remark under 1, in this exercise. 7. *Are you going to do*, to be rendered by the present tense of wollen. 8. *Was about to*, see **267, 6**. *When*, als. 9, 10. (See **267, 5, 6**.) 11. *For a good purpose*, zu einem guten Zwecke. 12. *Did not utter* = let resound no, etc.

Exercise XXVII.

Syntax of the Verb continued—**268** to **273**.   *The Passive.*

Special attention is called to the use of the reflexive in **272**, *and to the examples under* **273**, 2.

1. If assistance is rendered them, they can carry on the business. 2. All were happy; there was much laughing and singing. 3. Yesterday they did not play. 4. The letter was delivered through a porter; it was read by the whole family **(269)**. 5. We were early taught to respect old age. 6. The girls were taught dancing. 7. Of what was he accused, of theft or of high-treason? 8. The poor should always be remembered **(271)**. 9. That is easily said, but not so easily done. 10. "Released from ice are brook and river." 11. The

basin is bordered by mountains. 12. A contrast of perfections and imperfections is required to [produce] the ridiculous. 13. This point has been much contested. 14. Homer was without doubt diligently read in olden times. 15. The spy was without ceremony fastened to a branch and hanged.

1. *To render assistance* = to help + helfen, str. III., 3 (w. dat.). 2. *There was*, etc., to be expressed by the passive. 3. Use the passive with the subject es, or, placing the adverb first, without subject. 5. *To teach*, lehren ; use the passive with es for subject and the dat. of person. (The construction in the example under **270**, 1, is not to be imitated.) 6. *To teach something*, unterrichten in einer Sache. 7. *Of what*, gen. of was. 9. Use lassen. See **272**. 10. See **273**, 2. *Released*, befreit. In 10 and 11 no action, but a state or condition, is expressed. 14. In this sentence sein or werden may be used, with scarcely any difference of meaning, but present usage would favor ward. *Without doubt*, unstreitig ; but *no doubt*, ohne Zweifel. *In olden times*, vor Alters. (In other instances, the substitution of sein for werden may essentially change the meaning of the sentence, *e. g.*, die Stadt w u r b e verbrannt = people were burning it, it was on fire; die Stadt w a r verbrannt = lay in ashes.) 15. *Without ceremony*, ohne weiteres. *To*, an, w. acc.

Exercise XXVIII.

Syntax of the Verb continued—274, 275. Tenses.

1. How bright is the sun, how smiling the field! 2. He that goes borrowing, goes sorrowing. 3. They imitate the example set at Linz ; the armies desert him ; they curse the memory of the traitor. 4. I have (already) been here seven days. 5. I have only been here seven days. 6. Who knows who will command us to-morrow ? **(274, 5.)** 7. He does no longer rummage in empty words. 8. Our friends were formerly living in the country, but at present they are working in the city. 9. The doctor went out to the steward's and found the young man on the floor among Charlotte's children;

some of them were crawling over him, others were teasing him. 10. That was a bold word!

2. Say: To borrow makes sorrows (**274**, 2; **288**). 3. *Set*, gegeben. *Linz*, a city in Austria. *The example set at Linz;* gegeben, being used attributively, must precede the noun and be declined; ʒu Linʒ depends upon gegeben, and therefore must precede it (**353**). Hence, we have to render the phrase: "The at Linz given example." 4 and 5. See **274, 4**. This use of the present tense is one to which most students find it difficult to accustom themselves. The adverb ſchon, in such cases, implies that the time mentioned seems *long*, while the adverb erſt conveys the opposite idea. Analogous to this use of the present tense is the use of the preterite (in German) for the pluperfect (in English); *e. g.*, We *had already been* there three days, wir waren ſchon brei Tage ba. 7. Exceptionally, the English emphatic form (with *do*) may be retained in German (see **274, 6**). 8. *Were living, are working*, see **274, 6**. *In the country*, auf bem Lanbe. 9. *Doctor*, physician, ber Arʒt, ber Doktor (ber Medicus). *To crawl over*, herumkrabbeln auf, here with dat.

Exercise XXIX.

*Syntax of the Verb continued—***276** *to* **279**. *Tenses.*

1. I have enjoyed the happiness of this earth. 2. Schiller has written a history of the Revolt of the United Netherlands. 3. The king raised his camp at Schwedt and marched toward Frankfurt on the Oder, when Tilly had scarcely commenced his retreat. 4. What will become of you? 5. Who is knocking? It is probably the servant. 6. You shall not go to-day (**278, 3**). 7. The soldiers will in vain have sacrificed themselves for their general. 8. I shall make use of this paper when a deed shall have been done that bears incontestable evidence of high-treason. 9. What are they going to elicit by their questions, if the man is innocent? 10. It is to be hoped that the imperial diet at Augsburg will mature our projects.

1. *Of this earth* = earthly. 2. *Revolt of the U. N.*, ber Abfall ber vereinigten Niederlande. 3. *To commence*, antreten (str. V., 1), sep., lit. *to enter*

on. 4. *Of,* aus (w. dat.). 5. *Probably,* see **278, 2.** 8. *To make use of,* brauchen. *Shall have been done* may be expressed by the perfect (see **279, 2**). *To bear evidence of,* bezeugen. *Incontestable,* use the adverb. 9. See **279, 8.** *To elicit by questions,* herausverhören. 10. For a free translation of this sentence, see **279, 3.** The German adverb hoffentlich has to be rendered by the phrase *it is to be hoped. Imperial diet,* der Reichstag, es, e.

Exercise XXX.
Syntax of the Verb—**280, 281, 282.** *Tenses continued.*

Explanation.—In the sentences of this Exercise, the figures at the end of the clauses indicate whether one or two forms of the verb are possible; the reason, in each case, should be assigned by reference to §§ **280, 281** (for sentences 1–5) and to § **282** (for the remaining sentences).

Aside from these variations, the conditional clauses (with *if*) may be rendered in two ways, either with wenn expressed, or by indicating its omission by the inverted order (see **343,** *c*).

1. If you had not advised me so (1), I should not have done it (2). 2. What would you do in my place (2)? 3. If you had been here (1), my brother would not have died (2). 4. The fever would from now on gradually disappear (1), if the patient would take his medicine regularly (1). 5. Nobody would believe him upon oath (1). 6. The herdsman says the trees are charmed (1). 7. People believe that the hand of him who injures trees will grow out of the grave (1). 8. The herdsman said the trees were charmed (2). 9. Egmont affirmed that the whole matter was nothing but a jest made at the dinner-table (2). 10. The boy says he has not done it (1). 11. The boy said he would not have done it (2), if he had not been misled by his comrades. 12. If they forgave him (2), he said, he would not do it again (2). 13. The witness swore that he had seen the defendant (2). 14. The guide told us, those were the planets (2) which control destiny (2). 15. We thought you would explain the mystery (1).

1. Translate *so* by the pronoun es. 2. *In my place,* an meiner Stelle. 4. *From now on,* von dieser Stunde an. 5. *Upon oath,* auf einen Eid.

6. *Charmed,* gebannt. 7. *People,* bie Leute. *That the hand,* etc., = that whoever (wer) injures ... his (= to him the) hand, etc. *Will grow,* pres. subj. 8. The herdsman, in making the statement, used the present tense ; hence, in this indirect speech, the present subj. is correct (**282**); but also the preterit subj. (**282**, 1). 9. *The whole matter,* das Ganze. *Nothing but,* nichts als. *Jest ... table,* der Tafelscherz, es, e. 14. *Those were,* das, etc. (**245,** 1). If the pret. subj. "controlled" is used, the relative clause expresses the guide's opinion only; "control" pres. ind. denotes a general statement or fact.

Exercise XXXI.

Syntax of the Verb continued—**284, 285**—**103, 110.** *Moods.*

1. Let all be silent, let each incline his ear to solemn tones. 2. Let each one take care how he acts and how he fares. 3. Will the gentleman please enter. 4. May a gracious fate lead you through this stormy life! 5. "O full [and splendid] Moon ... would thy glow for the last time beheld my woe!" 6. O harmless staff, would that I never had exchanged thee for the sword! 7. I make rhyme tolerably well, I should think, what belongs together. 8. How is it possible to write everything? 9. Whether you are a good or a bad fellow, go to bed. 10. Everything might be excellently settled, if things could be done over again. 11. You would be a dead man. 12. Yes, said the lantern to the moon, what would men do if we were not [there]? Thereupon it went out.

1. *All* + Alles (see **168**). 2. *To take care,* sehen, str. V., 1. Translate: "Let each one see how he manages it, let each one see what become of him." What become of him = where he remain. 3. Third person plur. pres. subj. of eintreten, str. V., 1. *Please,* gefälligst, adv. 5. *Full* [and splendid] *moon,* voller Mondenschein. *Thy glow* = thou. *To behold,* sehen auf (w. acc.). *Would* is to be expressed by the pret. subj. of the principal verb. 7. *To make rhyme,* zusammenreimen, sep. *I should think,* pret. subj. of *to think.* 8. Use the pret. subj. of lassen, with the reflexive pronoun (see Examples under **284**, 3). 9. *Whether,* to be omitted (**284**, 4). *To*

go to bed, here colloquially, ſich auf's Ohr legen, for the classical : ju Bett(e) gehen. 10. *Might be,* use the pret. subj. of laſſen, with the reflexive pronoun. *To do over again,* zweimal verrichten. 11. *A dead man,* des Todes.

Exercise XXXII.

Syntax of the Verb continued—286 to 290.   *Moods—Imperative.*

1. Beat the drum, and take the field! 2. George, you stay with me. 3. No man ought to be obliged [to do a thing]. 4. He wanted to see the pedlar. 5. He must have seen the pedlar. 6. He claims to have seen the pedlar. 7. He was forced to call the police. 8. One must not count the chickens before they are hatched. 9. Then they separated. 10. You do nothing but complain. 11. Shall we walk out, or drive? 12. Bid him be silent, and teach him to do what is pleasing to God. 13. They saw him first suspended over the abyss, and afterwards the guide found his dead body lying at the foot of the rock. 14. What has the Tyrolese sticking on his hat? 15. "I've often heard it said, a preacher might learn, with a comedian for a teacher." 16. That would be tempting God.

1. Use the past participle. *To take the field,* in's Feld ziehen, str. II., 2. 2. *With,* bei (w. dat.) or um (w. acc.). 3. Use müſſen twice in this sentence. 4–7. See **288**, 1. 7. *To be forced,* müſſen. 8. The German proverb is : "One must (ſoll or muß) not praise the day before the evening," which may be substituted for this sentence. 9. One version of this sentence is found in **290**, third example. 11. *Walk out* (for exercise), ſpazieren gehen ; in the same way, ſpazieren fahren, reiten (**290**, 2). 12. *What is pleasing to God* = according to the pleasure (das Wohlgefallen) of God. 13. *To be suspended,* ſchweben. 15. Say : A comedian could teach a preacher. For *said* here = boasted. 16. *Would be,* pret. subj. of heißen, VII., 1.

Exercise XXXIII.

Syntax of the Verb continued—**291** to **293**. *Moods—Infinitive.*

1. That cannot be helped. 2. That remains still to be considered. 3. The youth felt impelled to win the prize. 4. We have dug a new bed in order to turn aside the current of the river. 5. Instead of coming nearer he ran away. 6. They did not delay, but began to hoe and dig. 7. Nobody thinks of granting him the favor. 8. It is dangerous to play with the lion. 9. Lessing was too proud to reap without having sown. 10. My brother is ready to keep you company. 11. If he has done nothing all his life, one can hardly say that he is resting from his work. 12. The countess has diamonds which are known to be diamonds. 13. No smoking here. 14. The student began translating the poem; but it was almost untranslatable **(291, 2)**. 15. The heirs were weeping; but their weeping was a secret laughing.

1. Bear in mind that *possibility* may be expressed by the infinitive **(291)**. 2. *Remains*, in this connection, may be rendered by fein, bleiben, or ſtehen. 3. *Felt impelled* = it (some power) impelled the youth. 7. *Thinks of granting* = thinks of it, to grant ; *of it* to be rendered by an adverb. 10. *To keep one company*, Geſellſchaft leiſten (w. dat.) ; Einem zur Geſellſchaft hier (da) bleiben. 11. *All his life*, ſeinen Lebtag. A clause with daß is preferable to the acc. w. the inf. **(292)**. 12. *Which are known* = which one knows, or, of (von) which one knows that . . . 13. Smoking is forbidden here.

Exercise XXXIV.

Syntax of the Verb continued—**294** to **300**. *Participles.*

1. From the gable of the house, which commanded an extensive view, we could see the steeples of the city. 2. The matter is important, but if you are in ill-health we will wait

(294, 2). 3. The air is glowing as though [it came] from the mouth of a furnace. 4. Give me some boiling water. 5. The ships under sail, with their masts encircled with wreaths, vanished in the distance. 6. A handsome squire came riding along the way. 7. I call that lying (296, 2). 8. Well begun is half done (296, 2). 9. Was the whole family present? All, except the youngest daughter. 10. You have read Lessing's Laocoon; if you now apply those principles to works of art you will become a better critic. 11. She spoke of her child, her eyes dim with tears. 12. Faust had powerfully attracted the spirit. 13. "The lofty works, uncomprehended, are bright as on the earliest day." 14. "To Him above bow down." 15. "The Woman-soul leadeth us upward and on."

1. Translate the relative clause by the pres. part. of weitschauen (**294**, 1). 3. *Air*, the German equivalent is sometimes used in the plural. *As though*, wie. 5. *Under sail* = p. p. of absegeln + to sail off (**295**, 1). *Encircled with wreaths*, laubumkränzt. 10. *If you now apply*, to be rendered by the p. p. absolute (**297**). 11. *Dim*, etc., = dimmed from weeping. 13–15. See **299**; **299**, 1 and 3. *Uncomprehended* = incomprehensibly. *Bow down* = stand bowed; use stehen. 15. *Woman-soul*, B. T.'s version of das Ewig-Weibliche. *To lead on and upward*, hinanziehen.

Exercise XXXV.

Syntax of the Preposition—(**301**), **302**, **303**.

1. Instead of songs, a stream of blood rose from his breast. 2. The son became head of the family by virtue of the ring [in his possession]. 3. The grenadiers wept on account of the doleful intelligence. 4. We shall start in spite of the bad weather. 5. For his sake I will explain myself more clearly (**302**, 14). 6. In company with you 1 defy our whole generation (**303**, 9). 7. Next to life we implore the blessing of God. 8. The count, together with all his men, offered himself to the duke. 9. Since that unhappy day every mouth is silent

(to me). 10. From Easter to Pentecost is fifty days. 11. The general saw that he was deceived by his officers. 12. A German song begins with the words: At Strassburg, on the bulwark, etc. 13. They said they would make him president; but they made only a fool of him. 14. The prisoner had no coffee with his rye bread and sausage. 15. We shall go either at Easter or on Trinity-Sunday.

1. *To rise*, here hoch aufspringen, str. III., 1, sep. 2. (**302**, 5.) 3. (**302**, 8.) 6. *To defy*, in die Schranken fordern (lit. to challenge, or summon, into the lists). *Generation*, das Geschlecht, here das Jahrhundert (in this sense a poetical and hyperbolic expression). 8. *To offer one's self* = to bring one's self. 12. See **303**, 16. *Etc.*, u. s. w. = und so weiter. 13. *To make a fool of one*, Einen zum besten haben.

Exercise XXXVI.

Syntax of the Preposition continued—**304**.

1. The Indian was wounded by an arrow. 2. Scissors are no playthings for children. 3. Truth does not exist for him. 4. In the war no substitute will take the soldier's place. 5. He did not wish to bind himself (toward me). 6. Against stupidity even the gods struggle in vain. 7. In comparison with Rothschild you are a poor man. 8. The lords of the empire were sitting around the emperor. 9. Several portraits of kings surrounded the throne in a semicircle. 10. [According] to you everything is to be had for money. 11. You have made a mistake of six-pence. 12. We never play for money. 13. Do not weep for the fallen heroes. 14. The loss of her fine hair would be a pity. 15. I feel sorry for your aunt.

4. Translate *substitute* by anderer, and *take the place of* by eintreten für (str. V., 1). 5. *To bind one's self*, sich verpflichten. 8. *Lords of the empire*, die Großen der Krone. 9. *Portraits of kings*, Königsbilder. *To surround*, um . . . her stehen (**136**). 10. *To be had* = to be for sale, feil sein. 11. *To*

make a mistake (in accounts), ſich verrechnen. 14. Say : It would be a pity about her fine pair. *To be a pity,* ſchade ſein. 15. *I feel sorry*, es thut mir leid.

Exercise XXXVII.

*Syntax of the Preposition continued—*305, 306, (307).

1. The university [of] Strassburg was re-opened in 1872. 2. Is your father out of town? Yes, he has gone to a watering-place for a fortnight. 3. Medicine is needed for the emigrant who is suffering from the intermittent fever. 4. The bear is led by a chain. 5. Can you recall the circumstances? 6. The defendant was proud of his innocence, and angry with his accuser. 7. One hundred pence make one *mark* (306, 3). 8. The hero's name is living, although his body has crumbled into dust. 9. I was going to put on the belt, when it tore into two pieces. 10. The heirs were astonished at the large property of which the will disposed. 11. He is vexed with me. 12. Sometimes a whole life is spent over a fine illusion. 13. Cambrai will, amid rejoicing, open her gates to the archbishop. 14. None among the imperial officers came up to Friedland. 15. She would like to guard against certain remembrances. 16. The boy was not able to see the woods for all the trees.

1. *In* = in the year. 2. *Out of town*, verreiſt. *Gone*, use reiſen (see 266). 3. *Is needed*, es fehlt an (306, 1). 6. *To be proud of*, trotzen auf, ſtolz ſein auf. 9. *Was going to*, use wollen. 12. *To be spent* = pass away. 13. *Cambrai*, the name of a place. 14. *To come up to* = to be equal to, reichen an. *Friedland* = Wallenstein, duke of F. 15. *Would like to*, use mögen. 16. See 306, 9. *All the*, lauter (see Ex. XIII., 10). Compare: Not to see the city for all the houses.

THIRD SERIES.

Exercise I.

*The Simple Sentence—***308** *to* **317.**

1. Life is not the highest of goods. 2. "One sees that in nothing no interest he has." 3. You have advanced the work more in these three days, than it has formerly thriven in many weeks. 4. Child, take care that you don't spill anything. 5. Happiness is so near; why will you wander farther and farther? 6. Such is the fate of the Beautiful on earth. 7. "Great cry and little wool." 8. Ill-humor and desire for combat were gnawing his mind. 9. Rather let his contemporaries and posterity judge him. 10. His majesty has been pleased to pension the privy counselor. 11. The master and mistress are gone out. 12. The young band of reapers go into the field. 13. Three huntsmen went a-shooting deer. 14. The world's history is the world's judgment. 15. Necessity is the mother of invention. 16. Mars, the star of ill-fortune, has often severed what Venus, the bringer of good-fortune, had united.

1. Use the def. art. 2. *To have interest in,* Anteil nehmen an. 3. *To take care,* sich in Acht nehmen. 4. *Not . . . anything* = nothing. 6. Translate *such* by that. 7. *Great* = much. 9. *Let,* use the pres. subj. of the principal verb. 10. *To be pleased* (in this connection), geruhen. *Privy counselor,* der geheime (Hof) Rat. 11. *Master and mistress,* die Herrschaft. 13. *To go a-shooting deer,* auf die Birsch ziehen. 16. *Bringer,* see 317.

Exercise II.

The Compound Sentence—Co-ordinate Sentences—318 to 322.

1. In part they drew him, in part he sank down. 2. We will neither deny nor palliate the deed. 3. In the first place, they wish it; and secondly, it is the custom. 4. I will either act with absolute freedom, or not command at all. 5. The fleet did not dare to attack the enemy, but returned without having effected its purpose. 6. Lessing would like to call Corneille "the gigantic" or "the prodigious," but not "the great" (**320, 2**). 7. He is not a millionaire, but he is rich. 8. He is not rich, but poor. 9. The matter seems so plain, and yet it is a mystery. 10. It was difficult to enlist more soldiers; for fortune had forsaken the army. 11. Wallenstein had assumed the title of "Highness"; therefore it was necessary for him to keep soldiers. 12. Goetz von Berlichingen had one iron hand; thus it was insensible to a kind pressure.

3. *In the first place*, erſtens. 4. *Absolute*, here vollkommen (complete). 5. *Without having effected its purpose*, unverrichteter Sache (adverbial gen.). 6. *Would like*, use pret. subj. of mögen. 11. *Had assumed the title of* = had himself called (**321**). *It was necesary for him* = he must. *To keep*, here halten, str. VII., 1. 12. *Kind pressure*, Druck der Liebe (**322**). *To*, gegen, w. acc.

Exercise III.

The Compound Sentence continued—Subordinate Sentences— Substantive and Adjective Clauses—323 to 328.

1. The curse of an evil deed is that it brings forth evil (**324**). 2. The student cheerfully carries home what he has in black and white in his note-book. 3. "Out of the abundance of the heart the mouth speaketh" (**324**). 4. Can you not understand that it is far more difficult to do right than

to indulge in pious dreams? (**325, 2**). 5. Have you [received] information [of] what has happened in Schwyz? (**325, 2**). 6. The day is almost spent, and you must explain yourself, whether you will do without me or without your friend. 7. Has the ship sunk? Yes, but they still hope to raise it again (**325, 3**). 8. Sweet peace, that art from heaven, come into my heart! 9. The church we visited last week has not yet been dedicated (**326, 327**). 10. "See that you most profoundly gain what does not suit (in) the human brain" (**327, 2**). 11. (The) European governments have sometimes sent to the United States people unable to support themselves. 12. The government, a year or two ago, complained of the landing of paupers who were sent over.

2. *In black and white*, ſchwarz auf weiß. 3. Say: Of what the heart is full, of that the mouth flows over. *To flow over*, here übergehen (sep.). 4. *To do right*, gut handeln. *To indulge in pious dreams*, andächtig ſchwärmen. 6. *Is . . . spent*, use ſich neigen. 10. Translate *most profoundly* by tiefſinnig, and *gain* by faſſen. 12. *Ago*, see **306, 9**.

Exercise IV.

The Compound Sentence continued—Adverbial Clauses — **329 to 332**.

1. When the weak [man] succumbs to his fate, the strong conquers it. 2. "Man, while he striveth, is prone to err" (**330**). 3. As the king gave a sign with his hand, the [gate of the] prison opened. 4. After the king had left the city, it was found that he had taken the precaution of providing it with a sufficient garrison (**330, 2**). 5. The bell-founder, before letting the metal flow, spoke a short prayer; then the workmen rested from their hard work till the bell was cooled. 6. Often, where ideas fail, (there) words [will] offer themselves [as substitutes] (**331**). 7. The lawyer, casting a furious glance

at his opponent, left the room **(332)**. 8. We never go to town without visiting our old aunt **(332, 1)**. 9. Henry studied German for two years without ever understanding the principles of the language. 10. Instead of paying what he owed, he contracted more debts.

1. *Conquer*, here zwingen, str. III., 1. 2. *Is prone to err* = errs. 3. *To give a sign with one's hand*, mit bem Finger winken. 4. *It was found*, see **272**. *Taken* = had. *Of providing*, see **291**, 4. 5. Say : Before the b. let the metal flow, he . . . *Short prayer*, ber fromme Spruch. *Rested from* . . . = let the . . . work rest. 6. *To offer one's self*, here sich einstellen. 7. *Casting* = while (indem) he cast. *At*, auf (w. acc.). 10. *To contract debts*, Schulden machen.

Exercise V.

The Compound Sentence — Adverbial Clauses continued —
333 to 335.

1. The slow progress of the war had been as advantageous to the rebels as it had been injurious to the king **(333)**. 2. He had grown as fleshy as Doctor Luther. 3. Goliath was by one head taller than all the rest. 4. His hair stood on end as if the hand of Death had seized him. 5. The scholar seeks knowledge as if he were for ever to live on this earth. 6. There was a hissing as when water comes in contact with fire **(333, 1)**. 7. We lived a more retired life than we had lived in Philadelphia. 8. You are too good to expect such things of us **(333, 3)**. 9. The peace was concluded too hurriedly to be of long duration. 10. Our provisions diminished more and more ; and, of course, the less we had to eat, the more terrible grew our hunger **(334)**. 11. The tyrant was so detested by the Swiss people, that he could no longer find any tool. 12. I would gladly bear the trouble, so important is the matter to me **(335, 1)**. 13. Do you consider him so unprincipled that he should cheat a poor widow?

1. *To be advantageous* = to bring advantage. *To be injurious* = to do harm. 2. Translate literally; a version of this sentence, in students' slang, is found in F. 2129-30 (see **333**). 3. *All the rest* = all people. 4 and 5. The subordinate clauses may be given in two ways (see **343**,*c*; **333**, 1). *For ever*, ewig. *On this earth* = here. 6. *To come in contact with*, sich mengen mit. 8. *To expect*, use als daß with subj. (**333**, 3). 9. *Of long duration* + dauerhaft, adj., or von + dat., or genit. of characteristic.

Exercise VI.

The Compound Sentence — Adverbial Clauses continued —
336 to 340.

1. Poetry describes beings, and, in as far as these beings are corporeal, it describes bodies. 2. I shall not go away, unless you pay me what you owe me **(336)**. 3. With the best intention I cannot accomplish much, because a thousand obstacles stand in my way. 4. The minister will only be able to save himself by speedily concluding peace. 5. (The) Man has been endowed with understanding (for this), that he may reflect upon that which he does. 6. Though the night is dark, our right is as clear as the light of day **(339)**. 7. However [much] the human will may waver, the will of God is immutable. 8. Whatever position you may take, you will get talked about **(339)**. 9. Be ever so good, there will be somebody to slander you **(339, 1)**. 10. If (the) nations rebel against rightful authority, prosperity will not be theirs **(340)**. 11. Why should I not avoid the utmost if I can escape it ? **(340)**. 12. Bring me a few lilies if you find them on your way. 13. If the judge had been there, matters would never have come so far. 14. As long as the deed is merely planned, it is a crime; if [once] carried out, it will be a grand enterprise.

1. *Are corporeal* = are bodies. 3. *In any way*, see **154**. 4. *Save* = help. 5. *Has been endowed with*, use the verb werden with the dat. of the person (**338**). 6. Use no conjunction in the first clause. *Is ... day*, to be expressed simply by the verb leuchten. 8. Say: However you may

place (ſtellen) yourself. *To get talked about*, in'ß Gerede kommen. 9. *There will . . . be*, see **236**, 4. 10. *Rebel . . . authority* = free themselves. *Will not be theirs* = cannot thrive. 12, 13. Use no conjunction (**340**, 1). *Your*, see **154**. 13. *Matters* = it. *To come so far*, dahinkommen (str. IV., sep.), impersonal. 14. *As long as; if*, see **340**, 4.

Exercise VII.

Word-Order—**341** to **343**.

1. Once, warlike hordes were raging through this valley; may that day never return! 2. "If you would know exactly what is proper, you have only to inquire of noble women." 3. He pocketed the bracelets and rings as if they were toadstools. 4. Stand still, and the dog will leap up on you. 5. Where I feel a breath of thy spirit, there I am happy. 6. That Caylus should have read this passage, is impossible. 7. "Whatever brings [us] nearer to heaven," he said, "is no delay." 8. "You are all very intelligent," he began full [of] cunning. 9. It is true, the limits of art are now incomparably wider than they formerly were, but they do not comprise such works. 10. The ward of the key is deftly wrought, but it does not open the lock. 11. If it were not a universal superstition, nobody would admire the beauty of these paintings. 12. I cannot help you any more; have I not given you my last dollar! 13. The queen, indeed! is no better than a woman of the middle class. 14. Why are you so modest, since he has no advantage over you?

2. *Know* = learn, find out, erfahren, str. VI. *If*, not to be translated. *You have . . . to inquire*, use the imperative. 4. *Stand still*, use the pres. ind. (**343**, 3, small type). 6. *Caylus*, the name of a French critic. The sentence should be translated by a single clause, beginning with the perf. inf. (**343**, *d*). 8. *To begin*, here anheben, str. VI., VIII. 9. *It is true*, zwar (**343**, *d*, 2). 10. *Deftly wrought*, here kraus, lit. curly, complicated. 11. For the order in the principal clause, see **343**, *d*, 3. 12. *Have I not*,

etc., use bod), and no negation (**343**, *e*). 13. Translate *indeed* by bod).
A woman . . . class, baš Bürgerweib. 14. The force of *since* may be rendered by bod).

Exercise VIII.

Word-Order continued—**344** to **349**.

1. Proud as she is, she had to confess never having seen the like (**344**). 2. How deeply the picture is imprinted on my mind! and yet I was not conscious of it, until the sound of your voice called it up (**344**). 3. The teacher greatly confused the girl; [it is strange] that a well-meaning person should be able to make one so confused! (**345**). 4. The president declared he had been obliged to make the appointment at once (**345**, 2, 1). 5. Everybody knows [that] you are to blame for it. 6. We have learned from your letter how strangely you have been misunderstood and misjudged (**346**). 7. [It is] impossible that he was present. 8. Perhaps (that) he did not wish to suffer the tyranny. 9. Were I rich, how glad would I be to assist the poor woman! 10. How fortunate that they remained in the country!

1. *As*, fo (at the beginning of the sentence). *Having seen*, to be rendered by a clause; see **325**, 1 and 4. 2. *To call up*, here weden. 3. *One*, see **98**. 5. *For it*, see **234**, lines 5 and 6. 6. In this and some of the following sentences, the auxiliary may be dropped. 7, 8. Use the (pres.) perf. *Wish*, wollen.

Exercise IX.

Word-Order continued—**350** to **353**.

1. No shield intercepted the murderous blow dealt by his adversary (**350**, **353**). 2. The Wagner-concert, [which was] announced yesterday, did not take place. 3. The cholera [which was] spreading drove us from the village (**351**, **353**).

4. Finally, the emperor ceased to delude the estates by a promise of a long-wished-for peace (**352, 353**). 5. The two prisoners were fixed upon to be the victims of the general discontent. 6. The count has at all times devoted his services to the imperial house. 7. We have told him so, but he has not taken it to heart (**352**, *e*). 8. How can one imagine such a thing? 9. The armies occupied all [the] passes, in order to close to them (viz., the enemy) the way to the Bohemian capital. 10. The increased power of the government left them (viz., the estates) no independence (**352**, *e*). 11. The compulsion is disgraceful to him, but we cannot release him from it. 12. Shakspere's works are no maxims of virtue, arranged in chapters and explained by speaking examples.

1. Bear in mind that participles, used attributively, are declined like adjectives (**294, 295**). 2, 3. The modifiers of the subject should precede the latter. 4. *To delude by a promise of peace,* ben Frieden zeigen (w. dat.). *Long-wished-for,* lang erwünscht. 5. Transl.: to the general discontent for (zu) the sacrifice. 6. *At all times,* stets. 7. *So,* see **236**, 6. Use the reflexive pronoun in the second clause. 9. *In order to,* see **291**. 11. *Release him from it* = remit it to him. 12. See **353**. Place the predicative nominative last, so that all its modifiers precede it. *To arrange,* here bringen (**119**).

Exercise X.

*Word-Order continued—Position of Clauses—***354** to **359**.

1. My brother is still coughing a little; his sickness has exhausted him very much. 2. We listened to her in silence [for] many minutes, but we do not yet know what she really wants. 3. To-day it is not pleasant to dance on this floor; it is too slippery. 4. The policeman left on the train yesterday afternoon at five o'clock; at seven, he was found drunk in the mud on the road. 5. We shall soon celebrate in a splendid

manner the day of the Declaration of Independence. 6. What you have in writing, and confirmed by a seal, is certainly secure. 7. I shall never refuse him the honor which is due to him. 8. When Antony had killed himself, Cleopatra, who saw that Octavianus only spared her to make her appear at Rome in his triumphal procession, took poison, or, according to other reports, placed an asp on her bosom. 9. After casting away his whole previous life, he put himself in harmony with fate.

3. Use the reflexive form with es. *Pleasant,* here gut. 6. *In writing . . . seal,* verbrieft und verſiegelt. 8. For the order, see **343**, *d*; put the relative clause immediately after its antecedent. *According to other reports* = as others report, should follow the verb. *To make appear* = to show. *Her,* see **154**. 9. *Fate,* see **149** (page 54, line 4).

FOURTH SERIES.

ADDITIONAL EXERCISES, INVOLVING TOPICS OF ESPECIAL DIFFICULTY, AND FORMS AND CONSTRUCTIONS OF RARE OCCURRENCE.

Exercise I.

Use of the Cases—**178** to **209**—(*also:* **39, 41, 48, 51, 59, 60, 66, 68**).

1. On Saturdays I have to give but one lesson, but next Saturday I shall give two (**39**). 2. He has broken his leg, and has to stay in bed the whole month (**41**). 3. Our gardens and fields are situated an hour's walk from the city (**48**). 4. So many murders have been committed this year, that one feels no longer secure (**51**). 5. The erection of these buildings cannot reasonably be approved (**51**). 6. A company of one hundred men was sent in pursuit of the ruffians (**59**). 7. His children and children's children will remember this noble deed (**60**). 8. Tell Mary that I am sorry not to be able to agree with her (**66**). 9. I am vexed that we ever called on the Millers (**68**). 10. If anybody inquires after me, tell him that I went down the avenue, and am coming back the same way. 11. We will ask father for (**191, 1**) the knife he uses for pruning trees. 12. Banish all gloomy thoughts.

4. *Secure* = sure of one's life (**98**). 8. See **353**; which of the two infinitives in this sentence depends upon the other? 11. *For ;* the German prep. ¡u, after certain verbs and adjectives, denotes *purpose, use,* etc.

Exercise II.

Use of the Prepositions—**301** to **306**—(*also* **40**).

REMARK.—The correct use of the prepositions, in any language, can only be acquired by long observation and practice. The student, to perfect his knowledge of this difficult portion of the German language, should observe and learn many prepositional phrases which he finds in his reading-lessons. *The same is true of the topic treated in the following Exercises* (III. and IV.). *No grammar can exhaust these subjects.*

1. The lawyer has robbed the widow of her entire property. 2. When we play cards, we never play for money (**304**, 7). 3. We are going to Paris; come with [us]. 4. A year from to-day you will meet again (**306**, 7). 5. The colonel ranks above the captain. 6. The count took him from pity into his house (**303**, 2). 7. Not far from the river a church has been standing for many years (**303** ; **274**, 4). 8. This wine has a taste of metal. 9. We knew you by the feather upon your hat. 10. Mark well what I have told you (**306**, 4). 11. This young man wants to become a soldier (**306**, 8). 12. In the reign of Louis XIV. the French court was a model for all other European courts.

3. The object of the prep. mit is frequently dropped when easily understood from the context.

Exercise III.

Separable and Inseparable Compound Verbs—**137, 350, 547, 548, (190, 198).**

1. The conference took place as soon as the ambassadors had breakfasted. 2. The king consulted with his minister [for] two hours. 3. If we kept house, we should welcome our friends in our own home. 4. It has been lightening all night (**274**, 6). 5. I do not like to expose you to the laughter of the company. 6. William has beaten the dog to death.

7. Show me how to do it, and I will do it after you. 8. Many prophecies were given to the Jews. 9. We always take a great interest in your welfare. 10. The estates will assemble next month (**274**, 5). 11. If you stay here, I will bring the chest here; if you go home, I will send it there. 12. The cashier was a man forgetful of his duty.

5. Use the adv. gern (*e. g.*, I like to read, id̄ lefe gern). 7. Use vo'rmad̄en and na'd̄mad̄en, both w. dat. 8. Say: Among the Jews there was much prophesying (Passive; see **236**, 2). 9. Whenever the idea expressed in English by a *substantive* is implied in the German *verb*, the modifying *adj.* is, of course, changed into an *adv.* (here *greatly*).

Exercise IV.

Separable and Inseparable Compound Verbs continued—**549**.

REMARK.—As the verbs occurring in this Exercise are all translated in the Grammar (549), they are not given in the Vocabulary. The figures, at the end of the sentences, refer to the sections of § **549**.

1. I have looked the book through, but I must have overlooked that passage (1, 3). 2. After the teacher had repeated the verse several times, without skipping a word, he found that the child had not heard a considerable portion of it (3, 8). 3. If you dare (= make bold) to go out without putting on your cloak, your father will tell you to turn back immediately (4, 5). 4. As we had taken a roundabout course, it was so late that we had to spend the night in the village (3, 4). 5. The ferry-man took the priest over [the river]; he will bring (= fetch) him back to-morrow (3, 8). 6. Fifty miners perished last week (4). 7. The boy has deceived his mother, but he is now penetrated with the feeling of his guilt (1, 2). 8. It was so easy to see through his designs, that we could frustrate (= prevent) them before he undertook to execute them (1, 2, 5, 6). 9. The two sisters were seen in the water, as they embraced each other, and went

down together (4, 5). 10. The soldier contradicted and resisted the officer, without considering that it was entirely useless.

2. Notice that überhö'ren does *not* have the meaning of the Eng. *overhear*. *Without*, see **291** (p. 115). 3. *Dare to go out*, ſich hinau'swagen = to venture out. 7. *With*, von.

Exercise V.

Use of Sein *and* Werden *(Passive Voice), and certain German equivalents for the English Passive—***268** *to* **273** *(also* **111, 531, 532, 533**).

1. The city was built upon a rock; nevertheless, it was taken by the enemy **(273)**. 2. Yesterday our whole family drove into the country; you were mentioned in our conversation more than once. 3. The poor fellow was made to believe that he was the heir. 4. No stopping here! 5. The animals will be fed at noon. 6. An answer is requested. 7. These difficulties are easily overcome **(291, 1)**. 8. It is to be hoped that at least one-fourth of the company will remain **(291, 1)**. 9. The paper is wound up by means of a spring **(272, 302, 7)**. 10. Authors are often praised by those who have not read their works **(269, 88)**. 11. An author once said: We wish to be less praised and more read. 12. To him who hath shall be given. 13. You shall be helped if you will follow us **(271)**. 14. The forefathers of the French were conquered twice; first by the Romans, and afterwards by the Germans. 15. When nearly all Europe was conquered by Napoleon, the emperor was almost idolized by his nation.

2. Subject in the second clause: Es. 3. Subject: Man. 4. Passive. Begin the sentence with *here* (see **236**, 3, *a*, fourth line). 5. Subject: Man (see **304**, 7). 6. Subject: Es. 11. Did the author wish for a changed *condition* of things, or was the object of his wish an *action?* Or may either be maintained?

Exercise VI.

Various Ways of rendering the English Participle (see **113**).

1. Giving is better than receiving (**291, 3**). 2. Having made the necessary arrangements for the journey, he counted upon leaving the next morning (**330, 2; 291, 2; 234**). 3. This boy likes fishing, and dislikes studying (**291, 2**). 4. The Dutch are living in Holland (**274, 6**). 5. The children came running to the spot where the knight lay bleeding (**296; 294, 3**). 6. The senator kept us waiting a long time (**290, 2**). 7. The royal palace is now building (**274, 6**). 8. The policeman saw the thief climbing through the window (**330, 1; 290, 3**). 9. The danger of the merchant losing his way was great (**325, 1**). 10. The judge being ill, the session did not take place (**337**). 11. This said, they left the room (**330, 2**). 12. The living and the dead will be judged (**107**). 13. You will gain nothing by waiting. 14. The pupil went out, without saying a word. 15. The boy went out, without the teacher noticing it. 16. They spoke of his owing them a large sum. 17. Many a man is proud of having defeated his opponent. 18. In spite of your boasting [so] much, people do not respect you.

1. *Receiving* = taking. 2. REMARK.—The Eng. pres. part., preceded by a prep., must always be rendered by an infinitive or conjunctive clause, preceded by such adverbs, as: davon, daran, damit, etc. (according to the prep. required by the principal verb). A conjunctive clause must be used whenever the subject of the participle is not the same as that of the principal verb. 6. *Kept* = made. 8. To be translated in two ways. 11. Use the passive, or the active with man. 13. See note, under 2. Mit with the infin. may also be used here. 18. Whenever the Eng. participle is translated by a verbal noun (infinitive, **288**), the accompanying adverb is, of course, changed into the corresponding adjective.

Exercise VII.

Additional Sentences on the Pronouns— **230** to **243**, *small type* —(*also* **86, 87, 89, 118**).

1. You will excuse my importunity, sir! 2. It was amusing to see how his Excellency was catechised by her Majesty. 3. I pray you, interest yourself for the poor orphan (**232**). 4. Show me the city of Paris upon this map; put your finger upon it (**234**). 5. Call yourself godlike, for aught I care; but I am afraid it will not last long. 6. My friend is willing; so am I (**236**). 7. On a sudden, he resolved to live no longer for himself. 8. They loved themselves, and hated each other (**238**). 9. The teacher spoke with his pupil of his (viz., the pupil's) future (**242**). 10. The teacher's words were so impressive, that the boy will think of them all his life (**243**). 11. Clara Schumann was once a great pianist. 12. My poor head is crazed, my poor mind disturbed.

4. *City of Paris.* REMARK.—Proper names of countries, places, and months, modifying a common noun, are in apposition with the latter. Ex.: The kingdom of Prussia, das Königreich Preußen. 7. *For himself,* dat. without prep. 12. For the translation, see **243**, 3.

Exercise VIII.

Pronouns continued— **244** to **263**, *small type.*

1. The fate of those who fell before Troy was sad; but still more sad was the end of those who returned (**244**, 1, *c*). 2. We took a walk, and talked of this thing and that thing (**245**, 2). 3. The artist is painting on these two pictures; he will soon have this [one] done, but that [one] takes more time. 4. It is difficult to comprehend how all this can be worked into a novel. 5. This emigrant has been cheated by

the porter; the same porter has cheated me (**248, 1**). 6. Such a braggadocio, who is constantly talking of virtue, gets warm over his own thoughts (**250, 2**). 7. Would you not like to live in such a hut overgrown with moss? How gaily we might adorn it! 8. What a hero! No wonder that everybody honors him! (**252**). 9. One could not determine the child of which mother it was (**255, 1**). 10. The old gentleman gave his son and daughter instruction in dancing, which cannot have been very becoming to him (**256, 2**). 11. "I stand up for the party in whose service I am." 12. Mephistopheles gave the student various precepts; the latter felt quite stupid from all he said.

3. *To have done,* fertig werben mit. 4. *Work into* = knead into. 6. *Who . . . virtue* = Tugendschwäßer. 7. *Would you not like,* **267, 3**. *Might,* **267, 1**. 8. *No wonder,* was Wunders (**251, 1**). 10. *In dancing,* see **288**; **293**. 11. Meaning of the German proverb, in **256, 4**. 12. *Felt,* use werben, with the dat. of the person, and es as subject. See **263, 1**; **261, 1**. *All he said.* REMARK.—The relative pronoun can never be omitted in German (**256**).

VOCABULARY.

A, an, ein, *indef. art.* (38).
about, um.
abyss, der Abgrund, –es, ̈-e.
accidental, zufällig.
accomplish, vollbringen, *irr.* (119, 2); leisten.
according to, nach, *w. dat.*
accuse, anklagen, *sep.*
accuser, der Ankläger, –s, –.
ache, *v.*, weh thun (136, 3).
acquisition (by purchase), der Ankauf, –s, ̈-e.
admire, bewundern.
adorn, ausschmücken, *sep.*
advance, *v. trans.*, fördern.
advantage, der Vorteil, –s, –e; to have an — over one, etwas vor einem voraus haben.
adversary, der Gegner, –s, –.
advise, raten, *str. VII.*, 1.
affirm, beteuern.
afraid, I am —, mir ist bange.
afternoon, der Nachmittag, –s, –e.
afterwards, nachher; später.
again, wieder.
age, das Alter, –s, –; die Zeit, *pl.* –en; old —, das Alter, –s.
agree, beistimmen, *sep., w. dat.*
agreeable, angenehm.
air, die Luft, *pl.* ̈-e.
all + all (100); = the whole of, ganz.
almost, fast, schier.

alms, die Gaben, *n. pl.*
already, schon.
also, auch.
although, obgleich.
always, immer.
ambassador, der Gesandte, –n, –n.
among, unter, bei.
amusing + amüsa'nt.
ancestors, die Väter.
ancient, alt.
and + und.
angel + der Engel, –s, –.
angry (with), erbost (auf, *w. acc.*).
animal, das Tier, –es, –e.
announce, ankündigen, *sep.*
answer + die Antwort, *pl.* –en.
Antony + Anto'nius.
anybody, jemand.
anything, etwas; was; irgend etwas, irgend was.
appearance (=exterior), das Äußere.
apply, anwenden, *irr.* (119, 1), *sep.*
appointment, die Ernennung, *pl.* –en.
apprentice, der Lehrling, –s, –e.
approve (of), billigen, *w. acc.*
archbishop + der Erzbischof, –s, ̈-e.
army + die Arme'e, *pl.* –n; das Heer, –es, –e.
arrangement, to make —s, Anstalten treffen, *str. IV.*
arrive, ankommen, *str. IV., sep.;* eintreffen, *str. IV., sep.*
arrogance, der Übermut, –s.

arrow, der Pfeil, -s, -e.
art, die Kunst, *pl.* ⸚e.
artist, der Künstler, -s, -; (der Arti'st, -en, -en).
as + als; indem; wie; as — as, so—als; so — wie; as if, als ob; als wenn; as when, als wenn; wie wenn.
ask, fragen; — for, bitten (um, *w. acc.*), *str. V.*, 2.
asp, die Natter, *pl.* -n.
assemble, zusammenkommen, *str. IV., sep.*
assist, helfen, *str. III.*, 3, *w. dat.*
assistant, der Gehülfe, -n, -n.
associate, *v.*, sich gesellen.
astonish, to be —ed, stutzen (**306**, 7).
attack, *v.*, angreifen, *str. I.*, 1; *sep.*
attract, anziehen, *str. II.*, 2; *sep.*
aught, for — I care, meinetwegen.
August + der Augu'st.
aunt + die Tante, *pl.* -n.
author, der Schriftsteller, -s, -.
avenue, die Alle'e, *pl.* -n.
avoid, meiden, *str. I.*, 2.

back, *adv.*, zurück.
bad, schlimm.
band (= troop), die Schaar, *pl.* -en; *poetical:* das Volk, -es; — of robbers + die Räuberbande, *pl.* -n.
banish (= cast away), sich entschlagen, *str. VII., w. gen.*
bank + die Bank, *pl.* -en.
baptism, die Taufe, *pl.* -n.
bare, *v.*, entblößen.
barn, die Scheune, *pl.* -n.
basin, *topograph.*, der Kessel, -s, -.
bear, *n.*, + der Bär, -en, -en.
bear, *v.*, tragen, *str. VI.*; überneh'men, *str. IV.*
beast (= cattle), das Vieh, -es.
beat to death, totschlagen, *str. VI., sep.*

beautiful, schön.
beauty, die Schönheit, *pl.* -en.
because, weil (*subord. conj.*).
become, werden (**110**).
bed, *n.*, + das Bett(e), -(e)s, -en.
before, *adv.*, zuvor; *conj.*, bevor, ehe; *prepos.* + vor.
begin, anfangen, *str. VII., sep.*
behold! siehe!
being, *n.*, das Wesen, -s, -.
believe, glauben (*w. dat. of person*), to make one —, einen glauben machen.
bell, die Glocke, *pl.* -n.
bell-founder, der Glockengießer, -s, -.
belong, gehören, *w. dat.*
beloved, geliebt.
belt, *n.*, der Gürtel, -s, -.
benefactor, der Wohlthäter, -s, -.
benevolent, hilfreich.
besiege, belagern.
better, best + besser, best.
between + zwischen (**306**, 10).
bid, *v.*, heißen, *str. VII.*, 2.
bind + binden, *str. III.*, 1; *refl.*, sich verpflichten gegen, *w. acc.*
bird, der Vogel, -s, ⸚.
bishop + der Bischof, -s, ⸚e.
black, schwarz.
Black-Forest, der Schwarzwald, -es.
blame, to be to —for, schuld sein an (*w. dat.*).
bleed + bluten.
bless, segnen.
blessing, der Segen, -s.
blood + das Blut, -es.
bloody + blutig.
blow, *n.*, der Streich, -es, -e; murderous —, der Mordstreich.
blow, *v.*, wehen.
blue + blau.
boast, *v.*, (sich) rühmen; prahlen.

body, der Körper, -s, -; (the human), der Leib, -es, -er; dead —, der Leichnam, -s, -e.
Bohemian, adj., + böhmisch.
boil, v., kochen.
bold, kühn.
book + das Buch, -es, ⸚er.
border, v., begrenzen.
born + geboren, p. p. of gebären, str. IV.
bosom + der Busen, -s, -.
bottle, n., die Flasche, pl. -n.
bow, to — down, bücken.
boy, der Knabe, -n, -n.
bracelet, die Spange, pl. -n.
braggadocio, der Worthelb, -en, -en.
brain, das Gehirn, -s, -e.
branch, n., der Ast, -es, ⸚e; der Zweig, -es, -e.
bread + das Brot, -es, -e.
break, v., + brechen, str. IV., (= tear), zerreißen, str. I., 1.
breakfast, v., frühstücken.
breast + die Brust, pl. ⸚e.
breath, der Hauch, -es.
breathe, atmen.
bridal, — room, das Brautgemach, -es, ⸚er.
bright, herrlich; to be —, glänzen.
bring + bringen, irr. (119, 2); — forth, gebären, str. IV.; — here, herholen, sep.
brook, der Bach, -es, ⸚e.
brother + der Bruder, -s, ⸚.
build, bauen.
building, der Bau (51).
bulwark, die Schanz(e), pl. -(e)n.
business, das Geschäft, -es, -e.
bust + die Büste, pl. -n.
busy, geschäftig.
but, conj., aber; allein; sondern (320, 2, Remark); (= only), nur.
buy, kaufen.

cable, n., + das Kabel, -s, -.
cage + der Käfig, -s, -e.
call, v., rufen; berufen, str. VII., 2; nennen, irr. (119): to — upon (= pay a visit), besuchen.
camp, das Lager, -s, -.
can, v. (= am able), + können (135, 3).
capital, die Hauptstadt, pl. ⸚e.
captain, der Hauptmann, -s (172).
card + die Karte, pl. -n.
carpenter, der Zimmermann, -s (172).
cashier + der Kassi'rer, -s, -.
carry on, fo'rtführen, sep.; — out, vollfü'hren.
cast, v., werfen, str. III., 3; — away, wegwerfen, sep.
castle, das Schloß, Schlosses, Schlösser.
catechise + katechisieren.
cause, n., die Ursache, pl. -n; der Ursprung, -s, ⸚e (origin).
cavalry, die Reiterei'.
cease, aufhören, sep.
celebrate, feiern.
certain, —ly, gewiß.
chain, n., + die Kette, pl. -n.
chapter + das Kapi'tel -s, -.
Charles + Karl.
Charlotte + Charlo'tte, -ns; Lotte, -ns.
charm, v., bannen in II. S., Ex. XXX.
cheat, v., betrügen, str. II., 2.
cheek, die Wange, pl. -n; die Backe, pl. -n.
cheerfully, getrost, 455, 3.
cherry + die Kirsche, pl. -n.
chest + die Kiste, pl. -n.

child + das Kind, —es, —er.
chisel, n., der Meißel, —s, —.
cholera + die Cholera.
choose, wählen, erwählen.
Christian, n., + der Christ, —en, —en; adj. christlich.
church + die Kirche, pl. —n.
circumstance, der Umstand, —es, ̈—e.
city, die Stadt, pl. ̈—e.
Cleopatra + Kleo'patra.
clear, —ly, + klar; deutlich.
climb, steigen, str. I., 2.
cloak, der Mantel, —s, ̈—.
close, adj., dumpf.
close, v., schließen, str. II., 1; verschließen.
cloth, das Tuch, —es, e.
coat, der Rock, —es, ̈—e.
coffee + der Kaffee, —s.
cold + kalt, comp. kälter; — weather, die Kälte.
colonel, der Oberst, —en, —en.
come + kommen, str. IV.
comedian, der Kommödia'nt, —en, —en.
command, n., der Befehl, —s, —e.
command, v., befehlen, str. IV., w. dat.
commandment, das Gebot, —es, —e.
commence, anfangen, str. VII., 1, sep.
commercial, — people, das Handelsvolk, —es, ̈—er.
commit, begehen (136); to be committed (= to happen), geschehen, str. V., 1.
companion, der Genoß, Genossen, Genossen.
company, die Gesellschaft, pl. —en; (of soldiers) + die Kompanie', pl. —en.
comparative, der Compara'tiv, —s, —e.
comparatively, verhältnißmäßig.
compel, zwingen, str. III., 1.

complain, klagen ; to — of, sich beschweren über (w. acc.).
complaint, die Klage, pl. —n.
comprehend, fassen; = fathom, ergründen.
comprise, einschließen, str. II., 1, sep.
compulsion, der Zwang, —es.
comrade, der Gefährte, —n, —n.
concert + das Conce'rt, —es, —e.
conclude, schließen, str. II., 1.
conference + die Konfere'nz, pl. —en.
confess, gestehen, str. VI.
conflagration, die Feuersbrunst (173).
confuse, make confused, verlegen machen.
conquer, bezwingen, str. III., 1 ; (a land), erobern; (a people), besiegen.
conqueror, der Eroberer, —s, —.
conscious, bewußt (w. gen.).
consider, überlegen ; (= estimate), halten für (w. acc.), str. VII., 1; verneinen (rare).
considerable, bedeutend.
consistent, to be — with, sich vertragen mit, str. VI.
consolation, der Trost, —es.
consult, bera'tschlagen (547, 2).
contemporaries, die (Mit) Welt.
contention, der Zank, —es.
contest, v., bestreiten, str. I., 1.
contrast, n., + der Contra'st, —es, —e.
control, v., regieren.
cool, v. intr., + sich abkühlen, sep. ; sich verkühlen.
cooling, adj. part., + kühlend; frisch.
cost, v., + kosten.
cough, v., husten.
count, n., der Graf, —en, —en.
count, v., (upon), rechnen (auf, w. acc.).
countess, die Gräfin, pl. —nen.

country, das Laub, -es, -̈er; in the —, auf dem L.; into the —, auf das L.
courage, der Mut, -(e)s.
course, of —, natürlich.
court (of justice), das Gericht, -es, -e; (of a prince), der Hof, -es, -e.
cradle, n., die Wiege, pl. -n.
crane + der Kranich, -s, -e.
create, (er)schaffen, str. VI.
crime, das Verbrechen, -s, -.
critic + der Kritiker, -s, -; der Beurtheiler, -s, -.
crowd (in motion), das Gedränge, -s.
crowded, voll.
crumble, zerfallen, str. VII. (w. sein).
cry, n., das Geschrei, -es.
culprit, der Schuldige, -n, -n.
cunning, n., die Arglist.
cup, n., der Becher, -s, -.
current (of a river), die Strömung, pl. -en.
curse, n., der Fluch, -es, -̈e.
curse, v., fluchen, w. dat. of person; verfluchen, w. acc.
custom, der Brauch, -es, -̈e.

dagger, der Dolch, -es, -e.
dainties, süße Kost.
damage, v., beschädigen.
damp, adj., feucht.
dance, v., + tanzen.
danger, die Gefahr, pl. -en.
Danube + die Donau.
Danubian Principalities, die Donau-Fürstentümer.
dare + dürfen (135, 2).
dark, dunkel.
daughter + die Tochter, pl. -̈.
dawn, v., + tagen.
day + der Tag, -es, -e; to-day, heute.
dead, n., + der Tote, -n, -n.
dead, adj., + tot.

deal, v., (a blow), führen; — with, umgehen mit, sep.
dear + teuer.
death + der Tod, -es (173).
deceive, betrügen, str. II., 2; hintergehen, str. VII., in II. S. Ex. 85.
Declaration of Independence, die Unabhängigkeitserklärung.
declare + erklären.
decree, n., die Fügung, pl. -en (dispensation).
deed + die That, pl. -en.
deep, —ly, + tief.
dedicate, einweihen, sep.
defeat, v., besiegen.
defend, das Wort reden (w. dat.).
defendant, der Angeklagte, -n, -n.
defy, trotzen.
delay, n., der Aufenthalt, -es.
delay, v. säumen.
delight, n., der Genuß, Genusses, Genüsse.
deliver (a letter, etc.), besorgen.
delivery + die Lieferung, pl. -en; die Auslieferung.
demand, v., to — something of (from) one, Einem etwas ansinnen, str. III., 2; sep.
deny, leugnen.
descend, herabkommen, str. IV., sep.
describe, schildern.
desert, v., abfallen (von), str. VII., 1.
design, n., die Absicht, pl. -en; der Plan, -es, -̈e.
desire, n., der Wunsch, -es, -̈e; die Lust; — for combat, die Kampfbegier.
desire, v., begehren.
destiny, das Geschick, -es, -e.
determine, bestimmen.
detest, verabscheuen.
devote, widmen.

diamond + der Diama'nt, -en, -en.
die, v., sterben, str. III., 3.
different, verschieden; ander.
difficult, schwer.
difficulty, die Schwierigkeit, pl. -en.
dig, graben, str. VI.
diligently, fleißig.
dim, v., trüben.
diminish, schmelzen, str. VIII.
disappear, verschwinden, str. III., 1.
discharge, v., entlassen, str. VII, 1.
discontent, der Unwille, -ns.
disgraceful (to), schimpflich (w. dat.).
disgusting, eklig; ekel.
dislike (*strongly*), hassen.
dispose (of), verfügen (über).
distance, n., die Ferne.
distress, n., der Schmerz, -es, -en.
do + thun; — without, entbehren.
dog, der Hund, -es, -e.
doleful, kläglich.
dollar + der Dolla'r, -s, -s (*silent*).
door + die Thür, pl. -en.
down, *prep.*, entlang.
dozen + das Dutzend, -es, -e.
draw, ziehen, str. II., 2.
drink, n., + der Trank, -es, ⸚e.
drink, v., + trinken, str. III., 1.
drive, v., + treiben, str. I., 2 ; (=ride), fahren, str. VI.
drunk + betrunken.
dry, *adj.*, + trocken.
due, to be —, gebühren, w. dat.
duke + der Herzog, -s, ⸚e.
duration + die Dauer.
during, während (302, 12).
dust, der Staub, -es.
Dutch, n., der Niederländer, -s.

each other, einander.
early, früh.
earn, erwerben, str. III., 3 ; verdienen.

earnings, der Verdienst, -es, -e.
earth + die Erde, pl. -n.
earthly + irdisch.
easily, leicht.
Easter + Ostern (174, b).
easy, leicht.
eat + essen, str. V., 1.
egg + das Ei, -s, -er.
Egyptian, adj., + ägyptisch.
eight + acht.
either — or, entweder — oder.
Elbe + die Elbe.
else, sonst.
emigrant, der Auswanderer, -s, -.
emperor, der Kaiser, -s, -.
empty, adj., leer.
end, n.. + das Ende, pl. -n.
end, v., aufhören, sep.
enemy, der Feind, -es, -e.
English, adj., + englisch.
enjoy, genießen, str. II., 1 ; sich erfreuen, w. gen.; schwelgen in, w. dat.
enlist, werben, str. III., 3.
ensnare, umspannen.
enterprise, das Unterneh'men, -s, -.
entire, —ly, ganz.
equal (to), gleich, w. dat.
erection + die Errichtung, -en.
err + irren.
escape, umge'hen (136).
especial, besonder (*only used attributively* [211]).
estates, die Stände (*pl.*).
esteem, n., die Achtung.
Europe + Euro'pa.
European + europä'isch.
even, selbst (249, 1); soga'r.
evening + der Abend, -es, -e.
ever, je ; — so, noch so.
everybody, jeder, jedermann.
everything, alles.
evil, n., Böses, das Böse.

VOCABULARY.

evil, *adj.*, böſe.
exactly, genau.
example, das Beiſpiel, -s, -e.
Excellency, die Excelle'nz, *pl.* -en.
excellent, —ly, trefflich.
except, *v.*, ausnehmen, *str. IV.*, *sep.*
exchange, *v.*, vertauſchen; to — for, vertauſchen mit.
exclaim, rufen; ausrufen, *str. VII.*, 2; *sep.*
excuse, *v.*, entſchuldigen.
exhaust, angreifen, *str. I.*, 1; *sep.*
exhibit, *v.*, zeigen.
exile, *v.*, verbannen; des Landes verweiſen, *str. I.*, 2; vertreiben, *str. I.*, 2.
exist, vorhanden ſein.
expect, erwarten.
explain, erklären, erläutern.
expose, preisgeben, *str. V.*, 1; *sep.*

fact, die Thatſache, *pl.* -n.
fail + fehlen.
fair, ſchön; the — one, die Schöne.
faith, der Glaube(n); *see* **46**, 4.
fall, *v.*, + fallen, *str. VII.*, 1; — to the share of, zu teil werden (**190**); — into, hineinfallen, *sep.*
fall asleep, einſchlafen, *str. VII.*, 1, *sep.*
fame, der Ruhm, -es.
family + die Fami'lie, *pl.* -n.
fancy, der Dünkel, -s.
farther and farther, immer weiter.
far, not — from, unweit (**302**, 10).
fasten, knüpfen.
fate, das Geſchick, -es, -e; das Schickſal, -s, -e; + das Fatum, -s.
favor, *n.*, die Gunſt.
favor, *v.*, hold ſein, *w. dat.*
favorite, der Günſtling, -s, -e.
feather + die Feder, *pl.* -n.
feed, *v.*, nähren; + füttern.

feel + fühlen; ſpüren; verſpüren.
feeling + das Gefühl, -s, -e.
fellow, der Burſche, -n, -n, also *str. II.*; der Geſelle, -n, -n.
ferry-man + der Fährmann, -s, *pl.* Fährleute.
fever + das Fieber, -s, -.
few, a —, einige, wenige.
fidelity, die Treue.
field, die Flur, *pl.* -en (*poetical*); der Acker, -s, "; + das Feld, -es, -er.
fight, *v.*, + fechten, *str. VIII.*
finally, endlich.
fine, *adj.*, + fein, ſchön in II. S. Ex. 36.
find + finden, *str. III.*, 1.
finger + der Finger, -s, -.
fire, *n.*, + das Feuer, -s, -.
fire, *v.* (= *shoot*), ſchießen, *str. II.*, 1, first, *see* **532**, 1.
fix upon, beſtimmen.
fish, *v.*, + fiſchen.
fleet, + die Flotte, *pl.* -n.
Flemish + flämiſch.
fleshy, dick.
floor, der Boden, -s, "; der Fußboden; (die Erde).
flow, *v.*, fließen, *str. II.*, 1; (*takes aux.* ſein).
flower, die Blume, *pl.* -n.
following + folgend.
fool, der Thor, -en, -en; der Narr, -en, -en.
foot + der Fuß, -es, "e.
for, *conj.* denn; *prep.* + für (**304**, 3).
forbid + verbieten, *str. II.*, 2.
forefathers, die Vorfahren.
foreigner, der Fremdling, -s, -e.
foremost, der erſte.
forfeit, *v.*, verſcherzen.
forge, *v.*, fälſchen; verfälſchen.
forgetful of one's duty, pflichtvergeſſen (**548**, 2, *a*).

forgive + vergeben, *str. V.*, 1.
former, the — the latter, dieser — jener.
formerly, früher.
forsake, verlassen, *str. VII.*
fortnight, vierzehn Tage.
fortunate, glücklich.
fortune, das Glück, –es.
four + vier; — times, viermal.
fourth, *n.*, + das Viertel, –s, – (532).
France + Frankreich, –s.
free, *adj.*, + frei.
free, *v.*, + befreien.
freed (from), ledig (*w. gen.*).
freeze + frieren, *str. II.*, 2.
French, *n.*, see Frenchman.
French, *adj.*, + französisch.
Frenchman + der Franzose, –n, –n.
frequently, oft.
fresh + frisch.
friend + der Freund, –es, –e.
from, von (303, 15).
froth, der Schaum, –es.
fruit + die Frucht, *pl.* ¨-e.
full + voll.
furious, wütend.
furnace, der Ofen, –s, ¨.
future, die Zukunft.

gable + der Giebel, –s, –.
gaily, lustig.
gain, *v.*, gewinnen, *str. III.*, 2.
garment, das Gewand, –es, ¨-er.
garrison, die Besatzung, *pl.* –en.
gate, das Thor, –es, –e.
general, *n.*, der General, –s, ¨-e; der Feldherr, –n, –en.
general, *adj.*, allgemein.
generosity, die Großmut.
gentleman, der Herr, –n, –en.
gentleness, die Sanftmut.

gently, leise.
gentry, die Edelleute (172).
George + Georg.
German, *n.*, der Deutsche, –n, –n.
German, *adj.*, deutsch.
Germany, Deutschland, –s.
gift + die Gabe, *pl.* –n.
gigantic + gigantisch.
give + geben, *str. V.*, 1.
glad, froh.
gladly, gern.
glance, *n.*, der Blick, –es, –e.
gloomy, schwarz.
glow, *v.*, + glühen.
gnaw + nagen; to — one's mind. Einem am Herzen nagen.
go + gehen (136); to — out, ausgehen, *sep.*; (out of the room, etc.) hinausgehen, *sep.*; (of light, fire, etc.) erlöschen, *str. VIII.* (133).
goblet, der Becher, –s, –.
godfather, der Pat(h)e, –n, –n.
godlike, gottähnlich.
gold + das Gold, –es.
Goliath + Go'liath.
good, *n.*, + das Gut, –es, ¨-er.
good, *adj.*, + gut.
good-for-nothing (fellow), der Taugenichts, –, –e.
good-natured, gutartig.
government, die Regierung, *pl.* –en.
governor, der Landvogt, –es, ¨-e.
gracious, gnädig.
gradually, allmählig.
grand, groß, großartig.
grandmother, die Großmutter, *pl.* ¨.
grant, *v.*, gewähren; vergönnen.
grave, *n.*, + das Grab, –es, ¨-er.
great-grandmother, die Urgroßmutter, *pl.* ¨.
greatly, sehr.
greet + grüßen.

greeting + der Gruß, -es, ⸗e.
grenadier + der Grenadier, -s, -e.
grieve, schmerzen.
groom, n., der Stallknecht, -es, -e.
grow, wachsen, str. VI.; (= become), werden.
guard, v. (against), sich hüten vor, w. dat.
guest + der Gast, -es, ⸗e.
guide, n., der Führer, -s, -.
guilt, die Schuld, pl. -en = debts.
gush forth, quellen, str. VIII. (133).

hair + das Haar, -es, -e.
half + halb; see 229.
ham, der Schinken, -s, -.
hand + die Hand, pl. ⸗e.
handsome, schmuck.
hang + erhängen (of persons).
happen, geschehen, str. V., 1.
happiness, das Glück, -es.
hard + hart; streng (of work).
hardly, kaum.
harm, der Schaden, -s, ⸗.
harmless, unschuldig; fromm.
harmony, die Einigkeit.
hat + der Hut, -es, ⸗.
hate + hassen.
head, der Kopf, -es, ⸗e; (= chief) das Haupt, -es, ⸗er.
hear + hören.
heart + das Herz, -ens, en; die Brust.
heath + die Heide, pl. -n.
heathen + der Heide, -n, -n.
heaven, der Himmel, -s, -.
heavenly, himmlisch.
heir, der Erbe, -n, -n (162, 3d group).
help + helfen, str. III., 3.
Henry + Heinrich.
herdsman + der Hirte, -n, -n.
here + hier; here — there, hier — da (dort).

hero, der Held, -en, -en.
hesitate, Bedenken tragen, str. VI.
hey! + ei!
hide, v. verhüllen.
high-treason, der Hochverrat, -s.
Highness, die Durchlaucht; die Durchlauchtigkeit.
himself, selbst (249), preceded by a case of er.
hiss, v., zischen; there was a hissing, es zischte.
history, die Geschichte, pl. -en.
hoe, hacken.
hold + halten, str. VII., 1.
Holland + Holland, -s.
home, n., + das Heim, -es, -e; das Haus, -es, ⸗er.
home, adv., nach Hause.
Homer + Home'r.
honor, n., die Ehre.
honor, v., ehren.
honorable, ehrenvoll.
hope + hoffen.
horde + die Horde, pl., -n.
horror, das Grauen, -s.
horse, das Pferd, -es, -e.
hot + heiß; — weather, die Hitze.
hour, die Stunde, pl. -n; an —'s walk, eine Stunde Weges.
house + das Haus, -es, ⸗er.
how? + wie?
however, wie auch; wie immer; — much, wie auch.
human, menschlich.
humble, demütig.
humility, die Demut.
humor, ill —, der Unmut, -s.
hundred + hundert.
Hungarian, adj., + ungarisch.
hunger + der Hunger, -s.
hunt, v., jagen; auf die Jagd gehen.
huntsman, der Jäger, -s, -.

hurriedly, schnell; eilig.
hut +, die Hütte, pl., -n.

ice +, das Eis, -es.
idea, der Begriff, -es, -e.
idolize, vergöttern.
if, wenn.
ill (= sick), krank.
ill-fortune, das Unglück, -s.
ill-humor, der Unmut, -s.
illuminate, erleuchten.
illusion, der Wahn, -es.
image, das Gebilde, -s, -.
imagine, sich denken (119), w. dat.; to — one's self, sich dünken.
imitate, nachahmen, sep.
immediately, sofo'rt, sogleich.
immutable, unwandelbar.
impatient (for), begierig (nach).
impel, treiben, str. I., 2.
imperfection, die Unvollkommenheit, pl. -en.
imperial, kaiserlich.
implore, erflehen.
important, wichtig.
importunity, die Zudringlichkeit.
impossible, unmöglich.
impressive, eindrucksvoll.
imprint (on), einprägen (w. dat.), sep.
impulse, der Drang, -es.
in +, in (305, 1, 5).
incline, neigen.
incomparably, ungleich.
incomprehensibly, unbegreiflich.
incontestably, unwidersprechlich.
increase, vergrößern.
independence, die Unabhängigkeit.
Indian +, der India'ner, -s, -.
industry, der Fleiß, -es; der Kunstfleiß, -es.
infantry, das Fußvolk, -es.
information, die Kunde.

inherit, erben; ererben.
innocence, die Unschuld.
innocent, unschuldig.
inquire (of), anfragen (bei); — after, fragen nach.
insensible, unempfindlich.
in spite of, see 302, 9.
instead +, anstatt.
instruction, der Unterricht, -s.
intelligence (= news), die Kunde.
intelligent, klug, intellige'nt.
intention, die Absicht, pl. -n; der Wille, -ns, -n.
intercept, auffangen, str. VII., 1; sep.
interest, to take an — in, teilnehmen an, str. IV., sep.
interest, to — one's self for one, sich jemandes annehmen, str. IV., sep.
interesting, interessa'nt.
intermittent, — fever, das Wechselfieber, -s, -.
into, in, w. acc.
invention, die Erfindung, pl. -en.
invisible, unsichtbar.
iron, n., +, das Eisen, -s, -.
iron, adj., +, eisern.
itself, selbst (249).

January +, der Januar, -s.
jealousy, die Eifersucht.
Jew +, der Jude, -n, -n.
jokingly, im Scherz.
journey, die Reise, pl. -n.
joy, die Lust; die Freude, pl. -n.
judge, n., der Richter, -s, -.
judge, v., richten.
judgment, das Urteil, -es, -e; das Gericht, -es, -e.

keep, halten, str. VII., 1; to — house +, haushalten, sep.
keeper, der Hüter, -s, -.

key, ber Schlüssel, -s, -.
kill, töten.
kilogram + das Kilogramm, -s, -e.
kind, *n.*, die Art, *pl.* -en; ber Schlag, -es, ⸚e.
kind, *adj.*, gut; freundlich.
king + ber König, -s, -e.
knead + kneten.
kneel + knieen.
knife, das Messer, -s, -.
knight, ber Ritter, -s, -.
knock, klopfen.
know, wissen (135); (= to recognize by), erkennen (an).
knowledge, bie Wissenschaft.

landing + bie Landung.
language, bie Sprache, *pl.* -n.
lantern + bie Laterne, *pl.* -n.
large, groß.
last, *adj.*, + letzt.
last, *v.*, bauern.
late, spät.
latter + ber letztere; the former — the latter, dieser — jener.
laugh + lachen.
laughter + das Gelächter, -s, -.
law, das Gesetz, -es, -e.
lawyer, ber Advoca't, -en, -en.
lay + legen.
lazy, faul.
lead, *v.*, führen.
leap up, hinaufspringen (an), *str. III.*, 1; *sep.*
learn + lernen; erfahren, *str. VI.*
least, at —, wenigstens.
leave, *n.*, ber Abschied, -s; to take —, Abschied nehmen.
leave, *v.*, lassen, *str. VII.*, 1; to — over, übrig lassen; (a place), verlassen, *trans.*; abfahren, *str. VI., sep., intrans.*

less, weniger.
lesson, die Aufgabe, *pl.* -n; to give a —, eine Stunde geben.
let + lassen, *str. VII.*, 1.
lever, ber Hebel, -s, -.
liberal, *adj.*, libera'l.
liberty, die Freiheit, *pl.* -en.
license, *n.*, die Freiheit, *pl.* -en; die Erlaubnis.
lie (lay, lain) + liegen, *str. V.*, 2.
life + das Leben, -s.
lifeless + leblos; tot.
light, *n.*, + das Licht, -es, -er.
lighten, wetterleuchten.
like, the —, bergleichen.
like, *v.*, lieben, mögen.
lily + die Lilie, *pl.* -n.
limit, *n.*, die Grenze, *pl.* -n.
lion + ber Löwe, -n, -n; ber Leu (*poetical*).
list + die Liste, *pl.* -n.
listen, hören; zuhören, *sep., w. dat.*; anhören, *sep., w. acc.*
little, klein; a —, ein wenig.
lock, *n.*, das Schloß, Schlosses, Schlösser.
lofty, hoch.
long + lang; no longer, nicht mehr; no longer any (*w. substantive*), kein ... mehr; a — time, lange.
look, to — upon, betrachten.
lose, *v.*, + verlieren, *str. II.*, 2.
Louis + Ludwig, -s.
luxurious, üppig.
maiden + das Mädchen, -s, -.
Majesty + die Majestä't, *pl.* -en.
make + machen.
malicious, heimtückisch.
man + ber Mann, -es, ⸚er; *abstract:* ber Mensch, -en, -en.
manage, treiben, *str. I.*, 2.
many a, *see* 262.

map, die Karte, pl. –n.
marble + der Marmor, –s.
march, v., + marschie′ren, rücken in II. S. Ex. 29.
mark (coin = 24 cents) + die Mark.
mark well, see 306, 4.
marksman, der Schütze, –n, –n.
mast + der Mast, –es, –en (for –e).
master + der Meister, –s, –.
matter (= thing), n., die Sache, pl. –n; das Ding, –es, –e.
mature, v., zur Reife bringen (119, 2).
maxim of virtue, die Tugendlehre, pl. –n.
may + mag (inf. mögen, 135. 4).
me + mir, mich (81).
meaning, der Sinn, –es.
meat (food), die Speise, pl. –n.
meet, v. (of persons), sich treffen, str. IV.; to — again, sich wiedersehen, str. IV., 1; sep.
medicine + die Medizi′n, pl. –en.
memory, das Andenken, –s, –.
mention in one's conversation, sprechen (str. IV.) von; erwähnen (w. gen.).
merchant, der Kaufmann, –s, pl. (172).
merely, bloß; nur.
merit, n., das Verdienst, –es, –e.
message, die Botschaft, pl. –en.
messenger, der Gesandte, ein Gesandter (see 220): der Bote, –n, –n.
metal + das Meta′ll, –es, –e.
metre + das Meter, –s, –.
mill + die Mühle, pl. –n.
miller + der Müller, –s, –.
millionaire + der Millionär, –s, –e.
mind, das Gemüt(h), –es, –er.
miner, der Bergmann, –s, pl. (172).
minister + der Mini′ster, –s, –.
minstrel, der Sänger, –s, –.

minute + die Minu′te, pl. –n.
mirror, n., der Spiegel, –s, –.
mislead, verleiten.
misjudge, verkennen (119).
misunderstand, mißverstehen, str. VI., 546, 2, insep.
mock at, Hohn sprechen, w. dat.
model, n., das Vorbild, –es, –er.
modest, bescheiden.
modern + mode′rn; the — languages, die neueren Sprachen.
Moldavia + die Moldau.
moment, der Augenblick, –s, –e.
monarch + der Mona′rch, –en, –en.
money, das Geld, –es, –er.
month + der Monat, –es, –e.
monument, das Denkmal, –s, ⸚er.
moon + der Mond, –es, –e.
morals, die Sitten (pl.).
more + mehr; — and —, immer mehr.
morning, + der Morgen, –s, –.
mortal, sterblich.
moss + das Moos, –es, –e.
most + die meisten (pl.).
mother + die Mutter, pl. ⸚.
mountain, der Berg, –es, –e.
mouth, der Mund, –es, pl. Munde, Münde, Münder; der Rachen, –s, –.
move (change one's residence), umziehen, str. II., sep.; — about, umhe′rziehen, sep.
much, many, viel, viele.
mud, der Dreck, –es.
murder, n., + der Mord, –es (51).
murderous + mörderisch; — blow, der Mordstreich, –es, –e.
muzzle, n., der Maulkorb, –es, ⸚e.
my + mein (85).
mystery, das Rätsel, –s, –.

nation + die Natio′n, pl. –en.
nature + die Natu′r, pl. –en.

VOCABULARY. 79

near, nahe (*comp.* näher, *sup.* nächst). *w. dat.*
nearly, fast; beinahe.
necessary, nötig.
necessity, die Not, *pl.* ⸗e (rare).
neck, der Hals, -es, ⸗e.
neighbor — der Nachbar, -s, -n.
neither — nor, weder — noch.
never, nie.
nevertheless, dennoch.
new + neu, frisch.
news, die Nachricht, *pl.* -en.
next + nächst.
night + die Nacht, *pl.* ⸗e.
nine + neun.
no, *indef. numeral*, kein (**95**).
nobility, der Adel, -s.
noble, edel (**71**).
nobody, niemand (**97**).
nod, to — to one, zuwinken, *w. dat.*, *sep.*; zunicken, *w. dat., sep.* (Ex. XX., II. Series).
none, keiner (**95**).
nonsense, der Unsinn, -s.
noon, der Mittag, -s, -e.
not, nicht; not at all, gar nicht.
note-book, das Heft, -es, -e.
nothing, nichts.
nothing but, lauter.
notice, *v.*, bemerken.
noun, das Hauptwort, -es, ⸗er.
novel, *n.*, der Roma'n, -s, -e.
now, jetzt; + nun.

oak-tree + die Eiche, *pl.* -n.
obedience, der Gehorsam, -s.
obliged, to be —, müssen (**135**, 6).
obstacle, das Hindernis, -nisses, -nisse.
occupy, besetzen.
o'clock, at ... —, um ... Uhr.
Oder + die Oder.
of, von (**303**, 15).

officer + der Offizi'er, -s, -e.
official, *n.*, der Beamte, -n, -n; ein Beamter, *pl.* Beamte.
often + oft.
old + alt.
once, einmal; + einst (formerly); seiner Zeit (**443**, 2); at —, sogleich; sofo'rt.
one, *indef. pron.*, man.
only, nur.
open, *v.*, + öffnen; sich öffnen.
opponent, der Gegner, -s, -.
order (= fraternity) + der Orden, -s, -; in — to, um zu, *w. inf.*
orderly, gesittet.
originally, ursprünglich.
ornament, der Schmuck, -es.
orphan, der (die) Waise, -n, -n.
other + ander; + anders (*adv.*).
otherwise + anders.
over + über (**306**, 7).
overcome, überwinden, *str. III.*, 1.
overgrown with moss, moosbewachsen.
owe, schulden; schuldig sein.
own, *adj.*, + eigen.

package + das Packe't, -es, -e.
paint, *v.*, malen.
painting, das Gemälde, -s, -.
palace + der Pala'st, -es, ⸗e.
palliate, beschönigen.
paper + das Papi'er, -s, -e; sheet of —, das Blatt, -es, ⸗er.
parents, die Eltern.
Paris + Pari's.
part, in —, teils, halb.
patient, *n.*, der Kranke (**220**).
pass, *n.*, + der Paß, Passes, Pässe.
pass away, *v.*, dahin gehen.
passage (in a book), die Stelle, *pl.* -n.
pauper, der Arme (**220**).
pay, *v.*, bezahlen.

peace, der Friede (46, 4).
peasant, der Bauer, -n or -s, -n.
pedestrian, der Fußgänger, -s, -; der Schnelläufer, -s, -.
pedlar, der Hausi'rer, -s, -.
pen, die Feder, *pl.* -n.
pence, *see* penny.
penny + der Pfennig, -s, -e.
pension, *v.*, + pensionieren.
Pentecost + Pfingsten.
people, das Volk, -es, ̈-er; die Leute; the young —, die jungen Leute.
perfection, die Vollkommenheit, *pl.* -en.
perhaps, vielleicht.
permit, *v.*, erlauben.
person + die Perso'n, *pl.* -en; der Mensch, -en, -en.
physician, der Arzt, -es, ̈-e.
pianist, der Klavi'erspieler, -s, -; die Klavierspielerin, *pl.* -nen.
picture, das Bild, -es, -er.
piece, *n.*, das Stück, -es, -e.
pit, *n.*, die Grube, *pl.*, -n.
pity, *n.*, das Mitleid, -s.
pity, *v.*, erbarmen; sich erbarmen.
place, to take —, stattfinden, *str. III.*, 1; *sep.*
place, *v.*, setzen (upright); legen.
plain (= clear), klar.
plan, *v.*, entwerfen, *str. III.*, 3.
planet, der Plane't, -en, -en.
play, *n.*, das Spiel, -es, -e.
play, *v.*, spielen.
plaything, das Spielzeug, -es, -e.
please, gefallen, *str. VII.*, 1; *w. dat.*
pledge, *v.*, verbinden. *str. III.*, 1.
pocket, *v.*, einstreichen, *str. I.*, 1; *sep.*
poet, der Dichter, -s, -.
poetry, die Poesie', *pl.* -n.
point, *n.*, der Punkt, -es, -e.
poison, das Gift, -es, -e.

police, *n.*, die Polizei'.
policeman, der Polizi'st, -en, -en.
politeness, die Höflichkeit, *pl.* -en.
poor, arm; dürftig.
porter, der Dienstmann, -s, ̈-er.
portion, der Teil, -es, -e.
possess, besitzen, *str. V.*, 2.
posterity, die Nachwelt.
post-office + die Post, *pl.* -en.
pound + das Pfund, -es, e (175).
power, die Kraft, *pl.* ̈-e; die Macht, *pl.* ̈-e.
powerful, —ly, mächtig.
practise, sich üben.
praise, loben.
pray, bitten, *str. V.*, 2.
preach + predigen.
preacher + der Prediger, -s; Pfarrer, -s.
precaution, die Fürsorge.
precept, die Lehre, *pl.* -n.
precious, kostbar.
prepare + präparieren.
present, at —, jetzt; to be—, dabeisein, *sep.*
president + der Präside'nt, -en, -en.
presumption, die Vermessenheit.
pretty, hübsch; niedlich.
previous, vorhe'rgehend.
pride, der Hochmut, -s.
priest + der Priester, -s, -.
principle + das Prinzi'p, -s, -ien; der Grundsatz, -es, ̈-e.
prison, der Zwinger, -s, -.
prisoner, der Gefangene, -n, -n.
prize, *n.*, der Preis, -es, -e.
prodigious, ungeheuer.
profit, der Gewinn, -es, -e.
progress, *n.*, der Fortschritt, -es, -e; der Gang, -es, ̈-e.
project, *n.*, + das Proje'ct, -es, -e.
proper, to be —, sich ziemen.

VOCABULARY. 81

property, das Vermögen, -s, -.
prophesy, weissagen.
prosperity, die Wohlfahrt.
proud, stolz.
provide, versehen, *str. V.*, 1.
provisions, der Vorrat, -s, "-e.
prune, *v.*, beschneiden, *str. I.*, 1.
Prussian + der Preuße, -n, -n.
pupil, der Schüler, -s, -.
pure, rein, + pur.
put, setzen (upright); legen; — on, anthun, *sep.* (**136**, 3).
pursuit, to send in — of, nachsenden (**119**), *w. dat.*
pyramid + die Pyrami'de, *pl.* -n.

quarrel, der Hader, -s; das Hadern, -s.
queen, die Königin, *pl.* -nen.
quill, die Feder, *pl.* -n.
quite, ganz.

rage, toben.
rain, *v.*, + regnen.
raise, heben; aufheben, *str. VIII.*, *sep.*
random, at —, auf gut Glück.
rank, to — above, stehen (**136**) über.
rather, eher.
reach, *v.*, + reichen, erreichen.
read, lesen, *str. V.*, 1.
reading (*e. g.*, various readings in several editions), die Lesart, *pl.* -en.
ready + bereit.
really, eigentlich.
reap, ernten; einernten, *sep.*
reaper, der Schnitter, -s, -.
reason, *n.*, der Verstand, -es.
reasonably, *see* **187**.
recall, *v.*, sich besinnen (auf), *str. III.*, 2.
rebel, *n.*, der Rebe'll, -en, -en.
recede (before), weichen, *str. I.*, 1; *w. dat.*

reflect, nachdenken (**119**, *sep.*) über, *w. acc.*
reflection, die Ueberle'gung.
refuse, verweigern.
regularly, regelmäßig.
reign, *n.*, die Regierung, *pl.* -en; in the —, *see* **306**, 8.
rejoicing, der Jubel, -s; der freudige Zuruf.
remain, bleiben, *str. I.*, 2.
remember, gedenken (**119**, 2), *w. gen.*; sich erinnern, *w. gen.*
remembrance, die Erinnerung, *pl.* -en.
remit, erlassen, *str. VII.*
re-open, wieder eröffnen.
repent, reuen.
report, *v.*, berichten.
representation, die Vorstellung, *pl.* -en.
request, to — something, um etwas bitten, *str. V.*, 2.
require, erfordern.
resolve, sich entschließen, *str. II.*, 1.
resound, schallen; erschallen, *wk.*, also *str. VIII.*
respect, *v.*, achten.
rest, *v.*, ruhen.
retired, to live a — life, zurückgezogen leben.
retreat, *n.*, der Rückmarsch, -es, "-e.
retreat, *v.*, zurücktreten, *str. V.*, 1; *sep.*
return, *v.*, zurückkehren, *sep.*; wiederkehren, *sep.*; lehren (*poetical*).
Rhenish + rheinisch.
Rhine + der Rhein, -es.
ribbon, das Band, -es, "-er.
ride, *v.*, + reiten, *str. I.*, 1.
ridicule, *n.*, der Spott, -es.
ridiculous, lächerlich.
right, *n.*, + das Recht, -es, -e.
right, *adj.*, + recht.

righteous + gerecht; the — (man), der Gerechte (220).
ring + der Ring, -es, -e.
river, der Fluß, Flusses, Flüsse.
road, die Straße, *pl.* -n.
rob, to — one of something, Einen um etwas bringen (119).
rock, der Felsen, -s, -.
Roman + der Römer, -s, -.
Rome + Rom.
room (= space) + der Raum, -es, -̈e; der Platz, -es, -̈e; (= dwelling-room), die Stube, *pl.* -n; das Zimmer, -s, -.
royal, königlich.
rude, roh.
ruffian, der Bösewicht, -es, -e (-er).
rummage, kramen.
run, *v.*, laufen, *str. VII.*, 2; to — away, weglaufen, *str. VII.*, 2.; *sep.*
rye-bread, das Schwarzbrot, -es, *lit.* black-bread.

sacrifice, *v.*, opfern.
sacrifice, *n.*, das Opfer, -s, -.
sad, traurig.
salute, *v.*, grüßen.
same, the —, derselbe (91).
Saturday, der Sonnabend, -s, -e; der Samstag, -s, -e.
sausage, die Wurst, *pl.* -̈.
save, selig machen.
Saxon + der Sachse, -n, -n.
say + sagen.
scholar, der Gelehrte, -n, -n.
school + die Schule, *pl.* -n.
Schwyz + Schwyz (one of the cantons of Switzerland).
scissors + die Scheere, *pl.* -n.
scoff at, spotten, *w. gen.*
screw + die Schraube, *pl.* -n.

seal + das Siegel, -s, -.
secondly, zweitens.
secret, geheim; heimlich.
secure + sicher.
see + sehen, *str. V.*, 1; schauen, in II. S., Ex. 21.
seek + suchen.
seize, halten, *str. VII.*, 1; fassen.
semicircle, der Halbkreis, -es, -e.
senator + der Senator, -s, -en (*see* 63, 2).
send + senden (119); schicken; to — there, hinschicken, *sep.*; to — over, herüberschicken, *sep.*; to — for, kommen lassen.
sense, der Sinn, -es, -e.
sentiment, das Gefühl, -s, -e.
separate, trennen.
servant, der Diener, -s, -; der Bediente, -n, -n.
service, der Dienst, -es, -e.
session, die Sitzung, *pl.* -en.
set (to — with gems, etc.), besetzen.
settle, schlichten.
sever, zerreißen, *str. I.*, 1.
several, mehrere; — times, mehrmals.
shepherd, der Hirte, -n, -n.
shield + der Schild, -es, -e.
shoulder + die Schulter, *pl.* -n.
show, *v.*, zeigen.
sickness, die Krankheit, *pl.* -en.
sight, der Anblick, -s, -e.
sign-board, das Schild, -es, -er.
signify, bedeuten.
silence, in —, schweigend.
silent, stumm; to be —, schweigen, *str. I.*, 2.
silver + das Silber, -s.
since + seit (303, 14).
sink + sinken, *str. III.*, 1; untergehen (136, 1), *sep.*; hinsinken (sink down), *sep.*

Sir! Mein Herr; der Herr (230, 3); Ew. Wohlgeboren (86).
sister + die Schwester, *pl.* –n.
sit + sitzen, *str. V.*, 2.
situated, to be —, liegen, *str. V.*, 2.
skeptical + skeptisch.
slander, *v.*, verleumden.
slave + der Sklave, –n, –n.
sleep + schlafen, *str. VII.*, 1 (266, 2).
slippery, glatt.
slow, langsam; träge.
smiling, to be — (= lovely), lachen.
smoke, *v.*, rauchen, + schmauchen.
soil, *v.*, besudeln.
soldier + der Soldat, –en, –en; der Knecht, –es, –e (rare).
solemn, ernst.
somebody, jemand.
something, etwas.
sometimes, zuweilen; bisweilen.
son + der Sohn, –es, ⁻e.
song, das Lied, –es, –er.
soon, bald; as — as, sobald als.
sorrow, *n.*, der Schmerz, –es, –en.
sorry, to be —, bedauern; leid thun (*imp.*), *w. dat.*
soul + die Seele, *pl.* –n.
sound, *n.*, der Klang, –es, ⁻e.
soup + die Suppe, *pl.* –n.
source, die Quelle, *pl.* –n.
sow, *v.*, + säen.
spare, *v.*, schonen.
speak + sprechen, *str. IV.*; reden.
special, besonder.
speech, die Rede, *pl.* –n.
speedily, schleunigst.
spend, verwenden (119).
spill, vergießen, *str. II.*, 1.
spirit, der Geist, –es, –er.
splendid, prächtig; in a — manner, großartig.
spot, *n.*, die Stelle, *pl.* –n.

spread, *v.* (of epidemics, etc.), überhand nehmen, *str. IV.*
spring, *n.*, die Feder, *pl.* –n.
spy + der Spion, –s, –e.
squire, der Edelknecht, –es, –e.
stable, der Stall, –es, ⁻e.
staff + der Stab, –es, ⁻e.
stake, to be at —, es gilt.
stand + stehen, *str. VI.*; to — on end (of the hair), sich sträuben.
star + der Stern, –es, –e.
start, *v.*, abfahren, *str. VI.*
stately + stattlich; stolz.
stay, *v.*, bleiben, *str. I.*, 2.
steeple, der Kirchturm, –es, ⁻e.
step, *n.*, der Schritt, –es, –e.
steward, der Amtmann, –s, ⁻er.
stick, *v.*, + stecken.
still, *adv.*, noch.
stop (*intrans.*), still stehen (136, 2).
stormy + stürmisch; wild bewegt (of life).
strangely, seltsam, sonderbar.
stream of blood, der Blutstrahl, –s.
street + die Straße, *pl.* –n.
strength, die Stärke.
strive + streben.
stroll, *v.*, spazieren.
strong, stark.
struggle, *v.*, kämpfen.
student + der Student, –en, –en.
study + studieren.
stupid, dumm.
stupidity, die Dummheit, *pl.* –en.
style (writing-instrument), der Griffel, –s, –.
sublime, erhaben.
subscribe to, unterschreiben, *str. I.*, 2 (*w. acc.*).
success, der Erfolg, –es, –e; das Gelingen, –s.
succumb, unterliegen, *str. V.*, 2.

such + solch; such things, so etwas.
sudden, on a —, Knall und Fall.
suffer, leiden, *str. I.*, 1; dulden.
sufficient, hinlänglich.
suit (of clothes), der Anzug, –es, ⸚e.
suit, *v.*, passen.
sum, die Summe, *pl.* -n.
superlative + der Su′perlativ, –s, –e.
superstition, der Aberglaube, –ns.
support, *v.*, ernähren.
sure + sicher, *w. gen.*
surge, *v.*, wogen.
swear + schwören.
sweet + süß.
sweetheart, das Liebchen, –s, –.
Swiss, *n.*, + der Schweizer, –s, –; the — people, das Volk der Schweizer.
sword + das Schwert, –es, –er.
sword-song, das Schwertlied.
sympathy + die Sympathie, *pl.* –en.

take, nehmen, *str. IV.*; to — a city, etc., einnehmen, *sep.*; to — place, stattfinden, *str. III.*, 1; *sep.*; to — to heart, zu Herzen nehmen.
talk, *v.*, reden; sprechen, *str. IV.*; schwatzen.
tall, groß; lang.
taste, *n.*, der Geschmack, –s, ⸚e; to have a — of, schmecken nach.
tea + der Thee, –s, –s.
teach, lehren.
teacher, der Lehrer, –s, –.
tear, *v.*, zerreißen, *str. I.*, 1.
tear, *n.*, die Thräne, *pl.* –n.
tease, *v.*, necken.
tell, sagen; (= relate), erzählen.
temerity, kühner Mut(h).
tempt, versuchen.
terrible, fürchterlich; schrecklich.

testimony, das Zeugnis, –sses, –sse.
thaw, *v.*, + tauen.
the — the, je — desto.
theatre + das Thea′ter, –s, –.
theft, der Diebstahl, –s, ⸚e.
their, ihr (85).
then + dann.
there + da; *expletive :* es.
therefore, darum; drum.
Theresa + Theresia.
thereupon + darauf; da; dann.
thief + der Dieb, –es, –e.
think + denken (119, 2); meinen.
this + dieser (90).
thought, *n.*, der Gedanke, –ns, –n.
thread, *n.*, der Faden, –s, ⸚; (without umlaut) = fathoms.
three + drei.
thrive, gedeihen, *str. I.*, 2.
throne + der Thron, –es, –e.
through + durch (304, 2).
thus, so, daher.
till, *adv.*, bis.
time, die Zeit, *pl.* -en; several times, mehrmals.
tired, müde.
to + zu, *w. dat.*
toadstool, der Pfifferling, –s, –e.
together, beisammen.
to-morrow + morgen.
tone + der Ton, –es, ⸚e.
too + zu.
tool, das Werkzeug, –es, e.
touch, *v.*, berühren (*w. acc.*); rühren an (*w. acc.*).
toward, gegen (304, 4).
town, die Stadt, *pl.* ⸚e.
trace, *n.*, die Spur, *pl.* -en.
train (railway —), der Zug, –es, ⸚e; on the —, *per* Eisenbahn.
traitor, der Verräter, –s, –.
transatlantic + transatlantisch.

transgress, überschreiten, *str. I.*, 1.
translate, übersetzen.
traveller, der Reisende (220).
treason, high —, der Hochverrat, -s.
treasure, *n.*, der Schatz, -es, ⸚e.
treat, *v.*, behandeln.
trifle, *n.*, die Kleinigkeit, *pl.* –en.
Trinity-Sunday, das Trinita'tsfest (*in a popular song:* Trinitat).
triumphal procession, der Triumphzug, -es, ⸚e.
trouble, *n.*, die Mühe, *pl.* -n; die Plage, *pl.* -n.
Troy + Troja, -s.
truth, die Wahrheit, *pl.* –en.
Turk + der Türke, -n, -n.
turn aside, *trans. v.*, ableiten, *sep.*
twice, *see* 531, 2.
tyranny + die Tyrannei'.
tyrant + der Tyra'nn, -en, -en.
Tyrolese + der Tyro'ler, -s, -.

unable, unfähig.
uncle + der Onkel, -s, -; der Oheim, -s, -e.
under + unter (306, 8).
understand, verstehen (136, 2); begreifen, *str. I.*, 1.
understanding, der Verstand, -es; die Vernunft (reason).
unequal, ungleich.
unfortunate, unglücklich.
union, die Verbindung, *pl.* –en.
unite, verbinden, *str. III.*, 1; binden, in III. S., Ex. 1.
United States, die Vereinigten Staaten.
universal, allgemein.
university + die Universitä't, *pl.* –en.
unmixed + ungemischt.
unprincipled (ohne Grundsätze); schlecht.
until, bis.

untranslatable, unübersetzbar (422, 6).
upper + ober.
use, *v.*, sich bedienen, *w. gen.*
useful, nützlich.
useless, unnütz.
usually, gewöhnlich.
utmost, äußerst.

vacation, die Ferien (*pl.; see* 174, 6).
vain, in —, vergebens.
valley, das Thal, -es, ⸚er.
vanish, verschwinden, *str. III.*, 1 (*aux.* sein).
velvet, der Sammt, -es, -e.
venture, *v.*, wagen.
verse + der Vers, -es, -e.
very, sehr; — much, *adv.*, sehr.
vexed, to be —, verdrießen (*imp.*, *w. acc.*); sich ärgern über, *w. acc.*
victim, das Opfer, -s, -.
Vienna + Wien.
village, das Dorf, -es, ⸚er.
virtue, die Tugend, *pl.* –en.
visit, *v.*, besuchen.
voice, *n.*, die Stimme, *pl.* -n.
volume, der Band, -es, ⸚e.

wagon + der Wagen, -s, -.
wait, warten.
walk, to take a —, spazieren gehen (136).
walk, *v.*, gehen (136); schreiten, *str. I.*, 1.
Wallachia + die Wallachei'.
wander + wandern; schweifen.
wanderer + der Wanderer, -s, -.
want, *v.* (= wish), wollen (135, 7); wünschen.
war, der Krieg, -es, -e.
warlike, kriegerisch.
ward (of a key), ' er Bart, -es, ⸚e.

warm, to get — over, sich wärmen an (*w. dat.*).
watch, *n.* (time-piece), die Uhr, *pl.* -en.
watch, *v.* (= look on), zusehen, *str. V.*, 1; *sep.* (*w. dat.*).
watchful, wachsam (auf, *w. acc.*).
water + das Wasser, -s, -.
watering-place, das Bad, -es, ⁻er.
waver, wanken.
way + der Weg, -es, -e; die Art, -en.
weak + schwach; — man, der Schwächling, -s, -e.
weather + das Wetter, -s.
week + die Woche, *pl.* -n.
weep, weinen.
weigh + wiegen, *str. II.*, 2 (*see* 133 and 124).
welcome, *v.*, + bewillkommen.
welfare, das Wohlergehen, -s.
well-meaning + wohlmeinend.
Weser + die Weser.
Westphalian + westfälisch.
what? + was?
whatever, was.
when? + wann? (*conj.*), als.
wheel, *n.*, das Rad, -es, ⁻er.
where + wo.
which + welch (92, 2).
while, *conj.*, während; so lange als.
white + weiß.
whither? wohin?
who (*rel. pron.*), der; welcher (93).
whole, ganz.
why? warum? was?
wicked, böse.
wide + weit.
widow + die Wittwe, *pl.* -n.
will, the last —, das Testame'nt, -es, -e.
will, *v.*, + wollen (135, 7).

William + Wilhelm.
willing + willig.
win, erwerben, *str. III.*, 3.
wind + der Wind, -es, -e.
wind up, aufwinden, *str. III.*, 1; *sep.*
window, das Fenster, -s, -.
wine + der Wein, -es, -e.
winter + der Winter, -s, -.
wise + weise; — man, der Weise (220).
wish, *n.*, + der Wunsch, -es, ⁻e; die Lust.
wish, *v.*, wollen (135, 7); + wünschen.
witch, die Hexe, *pl.* -n.
without, ohne (304, 5).
witness, *n.*, der Zeuge, -n, -n.
woe, *n.*, + das Weh, -es; die Pein.
woe! + wehe! (*w. dat.*).
woman, das Weib, -es, -er; die Frau, *pl.* -en.
wool + die Wolle.
work, *n.*, + das Werk, -es, -e; — of art, das Kunstwerk.
work, *v.*, arbeiten.
workman, der Arbeiter, -s, -.
works (the — of an author), + die Werke; die Schriften.
world + die Welt, *pl.* -en; the —'s history, die Weltgeschichte; the —'s judgment, das Weltgericht.
worry, *n.*, der Verdruß, Verdrusses.
worthy + würdig.
wound, *v.*, + verwunden.
wrench (from), abzwingen, *str. III.*, *w. dat.*
write, schreiben, *str. I.*, 2.

yard, die Elle, *pl.* -n.
ye + ihr.

yea, gar.
year + das Jahr, –es, –e.
yearn, sich sehnen.
yesterday + gestern.
yet, doch, dennoch; *of time:* noch; not yet, noch nicht.
yield (= obey), gehorchen, *w. dat.*

yonder, dort.
you, Sie, + ihr.
young + jung; the — people, die jungen Leute; — of an animal, das Junge, ein Junges, *see* **220**.
youth (= young man), + der Jüngling, –s, –e.

www.ingramcontent.com/pod-product-compliance
Lightning Source LLC
Chambersburg PA
CBHW031954230426
43672CB00010B/2144